TRANSFORMING
FLORIDA YARDS

TRANSFORMING
FLORIDA YARDS
A Regional Food Forest Guide

AMANDA ALDERS PIKE, PHD, ATR-BC

Pineapple Press

Palm Beach Florida

Pineapple Press

An imprint of Globe Pequot, the trade division of
The Rowman & Littlefield Publishing Group, Inc.
4501 Forbes Blvd., Ste. 200
Lanham, MD 20706
www.rowman.com

Distributed by NATIONAL BOOK NETWORK

British Library Cataloguing in Publication Information available

Library of Congress Cataloging-in-Publication Data

Names: Pike, Amanda Alders, author.
Title: Transforming Florida yards : a permaculture garden and food forest guide / Amanda Pike.
Identifiers: LCCN 2022042079 (print) | LCCN 2022042080 (ebook) | ISBN 9781683343295 (paperback) | ISBN 9781683343301 (ebook)
Subjects: LCSH: Gardening—Florida. | Permaculture—Florida. | Handbooks and manuals.
Classification: LCC SB453.2.F6 P55 2023 (print) | LCC SB453.2.F6 (ebook) | DDC 635.09759—dc23/eng/20220928
LC record available at https://lccn.loc.gov/2022042079
LC ebook record available at https://lccn.loc.gov/2022042080

∞™ The paper used in this publication meets the minimum requirements of American National Standard for Information Sciences—Permanence of Paper for Printed Library Materials, ANSI/NISO Z39.48-1992

To my husband:
for all our home-grown meals together.

To my son:
for opening my eyes to the wonders of nature.

To my friends and grandparents:
for sharing in the joys of gardening.

To my parents:
for valuing creativity, which has found a place in my food forest.

CONTENTS

LIST OF FIGURES

PREFACE

My goal with this book is to empower home gardeners, landscapers, land developers, parents, and educators alike to enhance food security and to create a beautiful landscape through permaculture. In a time when climate change news reports can feel overwhelming, creating a food forest has helped me be optimistic about environmental betterment. I created the one-page plant profiles as the foundation of this book so the information is accessible and easy for quick reference. My dream is for permaculture gardens to become the new normal—a revolution of improved health, nature, and quality of life.

As I write this, the COVID pandemic has created ripple effects throughout our communities. Nutrition affects immune system health, including vaccine effectiveness, so a diet rich in fresh produce is more important than ever.[1] Our food forest has helped my family have fresh produce year-round and has made us feel more alive and healthier than ever! I wish the same for you and your family. Being in the garden has given us feelings of liberation and security, especially during COVID shutdowns and social distancing. While the war in Ukraine is leading some to worry about future food shortages, we are content and confident in being able to provide for our son—regardless of inflation, political instability, or worldwide breaks in food-supply chains. I want to share this feeling of confidence and security with you through practical strategies, simple steps, and straightforward plant lists. Whether worst-case scenarios come to pass or not, a permaculture garden offers beauty, shade, and joy far beyond peace of mind.

Creating a food forest is fun and rewarding! You don't need a degree or special training to create an edible landscape. Gardening is primarily intuitive; it's a lifestyle and source of pride and pleasure. In fact, most food foresters simply use gardening as their escape—their therapy. Anyone can create a Garden of Eden. *You* can do this! And as you do, you will inspire others. I'm here if you need moral support or just want a cheerleader; just visit www.pike-wellness.com. Bon appétit!

1

CREATE YOUR OWN GARDEN OF EDEN!

WHY CREATE FOOD FOREST GARDENS?

With climate change, political instability, desertification, and more, what will be left for our children in the years to come? For those cultivating food forests and permaculture gardens, the answer is simple: *beautiful abundance*. The skill and chance involved with gardening is a shared, multigenerational experience that creates bonds and opportunities for people to nurture one another.[1] Children are nearly always fascinated with the natural world, and older generations often have wisdom of how to sow seeds for success. As a result, a food forest is a lifelong family culture grounded in creating joy, promoting health, and restoring ecosystems.

Florida provides a nearly ideal backdrop for enhancing food security through permaculture gardens and food forests.[2] Our abundant rainfall and warm climate, averaging around 70°F year-round, allows for the rapid growth of plants, resulting in a sustainable food source that can be passed from one generation to the next.[3] Given this advantage, food foresters in Florida are posed to be societal leaders in changing and uncertain environments and climates (see Figure 1.1). With a few hand tools and a few hours a week, Floridian food foresters debunk the myth that growing your own food is time-consuming, expensive, labor-intensive, or hard. There isn't a wealth barrier to developing a food forest or food security. Cuttings, seeds, and seedlings can be obtained for very low cost—if not free—and seeing a space become lush and alive with plants is gratifying for a wholesome lifestyle.

Although this gardening opportunity is simply waiting for Floridians to seize it, Florida has higher rates of food insecurity than the national average;

Figure 1.1. Sara Henick Montage, 2021, Pine Flatwoods Ecotype, Zone 10b

nearly one-third of children in Florida are food insecure.[4] There is an obvious need to adopt more resilient food systems, reduce food waste, and strengthen local food production. However, many don't know where to start or how to begin. Now is the time to learn. The world's population is expected to increase, so the demand on food will also increase in Florida and beyond.[5] Some researchers fear Earth will soon have more people than food-supply chains to support them unless more sustainable approaches are quickly adopted.[6]

Food insecurity and climate change are growing concerns across the world, but school leaders, and homeowners alike have the essential resource needed to address these issues: yards. In the United States, yards are typically dedicated to lawns. In fact, there are more acres of lawns than farms devoted to corn, wheat, and fruit trees combined.[7] With expensive irrigation, ongoing fertilization, herbicides, and pesticides, some researchers joke that lawns are the United States' primary crop. This leaves many asking,

Why spend money on toxic landscapes that are essentially worthless?[8]

Replacing lawns with food forests sustainably enhances food security; all that is required to get started is a shift in mind-set. Sustainability isn't a remote ideal. It is a system of values on which to build a life and routine. Most Americans carry insurance for their businesses, houses, cars, health, and lives. A food forest is also insurance—one related to food security, nutrition, and wellness.

Seventy-eight percent of land in the United States is privately owned.[9] This means that landowners have an enormous opportunity to make a positive environmental impact. Personal actions can be powerful especially when they inspire collective action. As one Harvard scholar points out, if just one-third of schools in a single state converted a quarter-acre lawn to a food forest, the result would be staggering. The school could produce hundreds of millions of pounds of fresh, healthy food for children while saving more than $4 million in pollution-management costs over 30 years.[10] Food forests could transform schools, communities, and homes into more sustainable and ecologically rich environments.

WHAT ARE FOOD FORESTS AND PERMACULTURE GARDENS?

Food forests are an approach to edible landscaping designed to be both beautiful and prolific.[11] In other words, a food forest is an elaborate garden with seven to nine layers of edible crops that can grow in as little as 3,000 square feet. That's less than one-tenth acre—just a portion of many backyards! These food forest layers include

1. Tall trees,
2. Short trees,
3. Shrubs,
4. Herbaceous plants,
5. Ground covers,
6. Tubers, and
7. Vines.

They may also include

8. Aquatic/wetland crops and
9. Mushrooms.

The result is a resilient, biodiverse ecosystem. This resilience lies in employing a historically rich approach to farming called "permaculture," as the plants are "permanent." The entire ecosystem does not die or get plowed down after a few months or a single year as with modern-day agriculture. This leads to desertification! In contrast, food forests offer a chance to guarantee a food supply for generations to come while allowing us to better adapt to climate change.[12]

Permaculture is growing in popularity, but it dates back to the Garden of Eden, which is thought to have existed in modern-day Turkey, Syria, and Iraq.[13] The increasing interest in returning to food forestry is in part because the impacts of climate change are expected to slow economic growth, increase poverty, and erode food security.[14] In the United States, interest in permaculture began around the Dust Bowl period of the Great Depression. During this time, a combination of drought, plowing, and shallow-rooted annuals turned farms into deserts. Many starved as the soil blew away, and people realized the importance of permanent crops.

Modern-day food forests provide life-sustaining foods, but they also add beauty and sanctuary, reducing the toil and energy needed to take care of oneself and one's family.[15] Harvesting and eating is not the only pleasure that awaits those who create a food forest, though! Seeing the comings and goings of birds and butterflies and the changing of seasons through colorful flowering and fruiting cycles enhances quality of life.[16] A beautiful setting is a natural stress relief.

PERENNIAL PLANTS: CARBON SEQUESTRATION AND WATER CONSERVATION

One in three US households now grow fruits and vegetables. Reasons include food-safety concerns, finances, interest in environmental sustainability and healthy eating, and a simple desire to get back to life's basics.[17] Likewise, many school leaders are already investing in gardens; however, current efforts are often based on annual crops in raised beds, which require extensive maintenance and input while adding little to the ecosystem over the long haul.[18]

Annual crops die back after just one season, so the work of maintaining a traditional garden is never-ending. Although annuals may produce a crop faster than a perennial in the first year, over consecutive years, perennials become self-sustaining and regenerative, eliminating the need for extensive effort.[19] Instead of repeating the same intensive work of establishing a garden each year, food foresters simply prune, add mulch, and propagate—a much-less work-intensive process. While annuals require fertilizer and constant irrigation, perennials are hardier and can thrive on neglect. For example, the ensete tree—similar to a banana—can survive for up to eight years in a drought by going dormant and then suddenly revive when the rain returns. Additionally, many perennials in a food forest flourish even in poor soils.

Overall, perennials require fewer external inputs like fertilizer and fewer maintenance hours than a raised bed planted with annuals.[20] There are also ecological benefits of perennials. Their slow and steady decomposition of roots and leaves improves the soil's organic matter, structure, and porosity, resulting in better water-holding capacity.[21]

What sets a food forest apart is this reliance on perennial instead of annual plants. Perennials have a lifespan of multiple years, so more nutrients remain in the soil and less carbon is released into the atmosphere.[22] Perennials, especially trees, help moderate climate change by capturing atmospheric carbon and sequestering it in long-term storage as soil humus and plant parts.[23] Trees are among the most effective ways to produce food because they require less fuel, fertilizer, and pesticides, if any at all, and there is no tillage after planting. They are also more resilient to extreme climate changes.[24] In fact, trees can help regulate climate by providing cooling shade in summer or sustaining warmth in winter by blocking cold winds.

Even more interesting, not only are perennials better for the Earth, but they also are better for our health. Many perennial crops are more nutritious in both macro- and micro-nutrients than annuals, so a transition to perennial staple crops can provide win–win solutions for both food production and ecosystems.[25] Creating a permaculture garden is a safeguard for the future. Those growing food forests explain that "healthy soil is a legacy that can be left for future generations . . . a much-improved condition for the next citizens to work with."[26] I want to leave my own son an improved, healthy environment, not a degraded one. More and more people are expressing the same desire but don't know where to get started. The general population in the United States suffers from a lack of knowledge of sustainability and nutrition.

EVIDENCE BASIS FOR FOOD FORESTS

Ironically, in the US "land of plenty," 74% of Americans are overweight, primarily due to being undernourished.[27] Lacking access to nutritious food is associated with obesity in the United States and is called the "hunger-obesity paradox."[28] Just consider fast-food diets—high in calories but low in nutrients. Many of those who are overweight are deficient in vitamins and minerals due to modern food-production and -processing methods. Micronutrient deficiency is considered a hidden hunger because it can and often does occur even if the diet contains adequate calories.[29] These micronutrient deficiencies underlie many illnesses, and as a result, nearly half of American adults have at least one preventable chronic illness related to diet.[30] Even mild deficiencies can impair immunity, stunt growth, and impede cognitive development resulting in poor school performance, work productivity, and increased infant and maternal mortality.[31]

The COVID-19 pandemic created even greater disparities in access to nutrition.[32] This was devastating for those living in food deserts—areas where little, if any, fresh produce is sold.[33] The average food prices in food deserts are 36% higher than non-food-deserts, and much of what is eaten in food deserts comes from convenience stores or fast-food restaurants, increasing the likelihood of diet-related illness.[34] Even if fruits and vegetables are available in food deserts, they are unlikely organic.

Organic food has been found to have substantially more minerals—as much as 90% more compared with commercial foods.[35] While organic produce may not be affordable for everyone, those cultivating a food forest can simply create their own affordable, organic foods. Additionally, the process of creating a food forest provides substantial health benefits. Simply being outdoors provides pleasing visual stimuli along with fresh air and sunshine. This alone can lead to a more cheerful, energetic disposition; lower blood pressure; decreased stress hormones; and improved immunity.[36]

Specifically, researchers associate gardening with a decrease in "lifestyle diseases," including obesity.[37] Working in the garden restores dexterity and strength, and the aerobic exercise involved can easily use the same number of calories as being in a gym.[38] Digging, raking, and mowing are particularly calorie-intense, and the social interaction during community gardening can counteract isolation.[39] Additionally, natural environments like food forests reduce mental fatigue and can enhance work productivity.[40]

A FOOD SECURITY AND WELLNESS MODEL

With food security concerns affecting so many in Florida, staple crops are often the most productive first choices for a food forest. Staple foods are those that people consume almost daily because they provide a bulk of nutrients.[41] By initially prioritizing a mere 20 staple crops, you can more easily cook from your garden daily. To decide which plants should be your top 20, consider what you already eat. In the United States, only three crops (rice, wheat, and maize/corn) account for 60% of calories consumed.[42]

Before starting my food forest, wheat made up the bulk of my diet (bread, pasta, crackers), but wheat is too labor-intensive to grow and process myself—it's an annual! I would need my entire two acres dedicated exclusively to wheat, and even then, my soil health would nosedive. Also, the machinery I would need to harvest and process the grain would be costly. That said, to continue eating the comfort foods I'm used to, I found less-labor-intensive perennial alternatives to wheat, like coconut, cassava, jackfruit seeds, green banana, and more. These staples provide me with my comfort foods (green banana makes an excellent pasta!), while other plants provide me with a wider range of nutrients.

When creating a permaculture garden to promote food security, the process goes beyond just growing enough staple crops for the daily 2,000 calories recommended by the US Department of Agriculture (USDA). Just consider the hunger-obesity paradox: Calories do not necessarily mean nutrition. For those growing a food forest, there is a natural increase in food variety. Seasonal foods pour into the home. Food is fresh—not packaged. Yet to combat micronutrient deficiencies, a food forester may want to plant the following percentages to boost nutritional health:

- 60% macronutrient sources: staples and dense calories
  - pure starch (starch with under 5% oil or protein), like achira, cassava, or unripe banana
  - balanced carbohydrates (starch or sugar with 5–15% protein and/or oil, similar to maize, rice, wheat), like jackfruit, maya nut, or lotus nuts
  - protein (more than 16% protein and less than 15% oil), like pigeon pea or winged bean
  - protein oil (more than 16% protein and more than 16% fat, equivalent to soybean), like cocoplum seeds or tropical almond

- oil (more than 16% oil and under 15% protein, similar to olive oil), like coconut, moringa, or avocado oil
  - 30% micronutrient sources: vitamins and minerals
    - dark leafy green vegetables, like aibika or moringa leaves
    - cruciferous vegetables, like perennial collards or broccoli
    - B_{12} sources, like fermented food/tea; certain algae; mushrooms; and livestock, like chickens and eggs
    - colorful fruits, vegetables, and tubers, like pink papaya, yellow mango, and purple sweet potato
  - 10% phytochemical sources: medicinal flavor enhancers
    - spices, herbs, teas, and unrefined sweets, like sage, mushrooms, raw sugarcane, and longevity spinach.[43]

The father of medicine, Hippocrates, said famously, "Let thy food be thy medicine and medicine be thy food." But with so many diverse cultures and foods in the United States, what are you supposed to eat? For me, the answer comes from those living the longest, healthiest lives. Research shows that the oldest, healthiest people in the world eat simple meals made with only 6 or so ingredients harvested from just 20 or so different backyard plants.[44] Clusters of these healthy people are called "blue zones," and in these areas, people regularly live to over 100. Most care for a permaculture garden in their backyard. Typical ingredients in blue zones, which easily grow in Florida, include

- beans, nuts, and starchy tubers, like sweet potatoes or cassava;
- herbs, like rosemary, oregano, and sage;
- healthy fat sources, like olives, coconut, and avocado;
- cruciferous vegetables, like collards and broccoli;
- colorful, vitamin-rich fruits, like papaya, mango, and citrus;
- "wild" greens, like chicory and Chaya;
- medicinal roots, like garlic, turmeric, and ginger;
- mushrooms;
- flavor enhancers, like peppers and green onions;
- staple crop vegetables, like pumpkin; and
- above-ground starches, like bananas.[45]

PREPARING TO PLANT: PRIORITIZING NATIVES

Floridians can grow nearly everything that those in the blue zone use to feed themselves and their families. However, before you pick 20 staple crops to plant, you may want to consider your ideal food forest layout. If you're like many of us, you've inherited a property covered in sod, and most, if not all, the native trees have been removed. The heat on these properties is severe, and the UV rays are intense. The soil fertility is likely low. As a result, the process of creating a food forest and ecologically restoring the area can seem daunting.

Don't worry! Strategically, the first three goals are to restore soil fertility, retain rainwater, and filter the sunlight to make it gentler for you and your crops. Otherwise, you will need to spend money on irrigation and ongoing disease and pest control. The plants that can help you achieve these three goals best are "pioneer" species, especially natives. Oaks are the all-stars in this category. Pioneer species are covered in the plant profiles in Chapter 4.

Native trees are protective and make gardening much less work! For example, oaks host beneficial insects that will keep pests and even diseases down to a minimum. I grow my pumpkins under oaks and have huge harvests. A friend visited and said, "Everything I know about gardening is wrong!" She was growing exotic pumpkins in raised annual beds in full Florida sun, and her pumpkins never produced. They were stressed by the heat and preyed on by pests. In contrast, my native Seminole pumpkins were producing dozens of gourds in the shade and were growing in native soil without irrigation or fertilizers. Additionally, you can purchase insects to stock your food forest. Just make sure the host plants are in the ground before you release them. For instance, you can purchase ladybugs or praying mantises from your local nursery or online (e.g., Amazon, www.naturesgoodguys.com) to rid yourself of aphids or whiteflies.

To explore native plants right for your yard, use the "native plant finder" on the National Wildlife Federation website. Many natives are listed in the Chapter 4 profiles, but you will want to find the specific variety according to your zip code. Also, consider reviewing Doug Tallamy's work for more information on "keystone" natives and "pollinator-friendly yards" to host beneficial insects. Organizations like the Native Plant Society, Plant Real Florida, and the Institute for Regional Conservation can also help.

When deciding which natives to plant, focus on edible natives whenever possible because they serve a dual purpose. Consider local food forester Brook Wood, who prioritizes natives in her food forest and eats daily from her garden. She grows 50% of her food! She is quick to remind new gardeners that many Florida natives are edible. Just consider the following (listed in order of power to host the most native insects):

- oak
- cherry
- peach
- plum
- pine
- blueberry
- maple
- hickory/pecan
- elm
- blackberry
- chestnut
- grape[46]

IT'S EASY: JUST KNOW YOUR FLORIDA HARDINESS ZONES AND ECOTYPES

Creating a food forest is a natural process. Plants will grow without any human intervention! Yet we may need to unlearn some lessons from traditional agriculture to be successful. In Greek mythology, Sisyphus was punished by being forced to roll an immense boulder uphill only for it to roll down every time it neared the top, for eternity. If you try to impose an unnatural system in your garden, then you will work harder than necessary. The goal is to work with nature rather than against it; planting into an existing hardwood oak forest is easier than starting with a bare field.[47]

When beginning to plan a food forest, it is important for gardeners to know their USDA hardiness zone and Florida ecotype category. To find your hardiness zone, visit the National Gardening Association website. They have a zip-code search that will pull up your hardiness zone along with gardening tips. Also, Plant Real Florida's website can help you identify some ecosystems within your hardiness zone and provide a list of matching native plants. This information is useful because Florida has distinct ecosystems that fall into broad categories like

- beaches/dunes and maritime forests,
- pine flatwoods,
- rocklands,
- hardwood forests,
- scrub forests,
- sandhills,
- swamp/hydric hammock forests,
- saltwater and freshwater marshes,
- cabbage palm forests, and
- prairies.

Knowing these ecosystems will help you determine which 20 staples will work best for your yard. However, more than one ecosystem may be present on your property. For instance, I am in zone 10a, and I mostly have a hydric hammock ecotype, but I also have pockets of pine flatwoods and old-wood oaks. Each ecotype and the associated plants present opportunities for "companion planting" and "guilds." For example, in hydric hammocks, plants like banana, achira, sugarcane, ginger, cardamom, and katuk grow well once the land is heavily mulched. In pine rocklands and rockland hammocks, shallow-rooted plants like agave, aloe, rosemary, and thyme grow easily. In upland forests with oaks, fruit trees and even ginger and turmeric do well. Pine flatwoods are great locations for plants like pineapple, tomato, potato, and pumpkin.

Regardless of hardiness zone and ecotype, Florida permaculture gardens should be designed to withstand hurricane winds and flooding. One way to do this is to plant windbreaks—multilevel rows of trees and shrubs that protect the home, structures, and landscapes from prevailing winds.[48] Similarly, riparian plants protect floodplains and shorelines from erosion during floods and include plants like bananas, achira, raspberries, chufa, cattails, and more.[49] In the Chapter 4 profiles, I list if a plant is a windbreak or if it prevents erosion by stabilizing the soil.

If you're lucky enough to have mature native trees on the property, then leave them—even if they aren't traditionally considered edible! Mature trees create a greenhouse effect, acting as a blanket to protect understory plants from temperature extremes and wind.[50] Interplant your edibles between your mature trees or even at the base. Not only will the shade make the gardening experience cooler and more pleasant for you in the summer, but it will also protect you and the plants from cold winds. The measurement of your food forest success is your enjoyment, health, and pleasure. Planting in direct sun in Florida is not fun. I plant trees along all my pathways to prevent direct sun exposure and create dappled light. All my plants seem to like that light the best. I certainly do!

One important point to remember when starting out is you don't actually need a lot of space to create a food forest. Even small spaces can provide an abundance of food because food forests use nine layers of a permaculture system:

1. tall canopy trees, like oaks or maya nuts
2. short trees, like pruned mango or jackfruit
3. shrubs, like Barbados cherries
4. herbaceous plants, like chia; edible flowers; and herbs, including basil and rosemary
5. groundcovers, like longevity or Okinawa spinach
6. tubers, like sweet potato, turmeric, and ginger
7. vines, like loofah or passionfruit
8. aquatic/wetland plants, like cattails, pickerelweed, and arrowroot
9. mycelial/fungal, layers like oyster mushrooms[51]

The profiles in Chapter 4 include plants from all nine of these layers. Appendix A sorts plants by their permaculture layer for easy reference during your design phase.

By maximizing the use of these nine layers, a permaculture garden can provide ongoing food security and a relaxing botanical setting for the whole family—even in small yards! Just

Figure 1.2. Mama Snow from MamaSnowCooks.com, Residential Area With an HOA, Zone 9b

consider that on one-tenth of an acre (3,900 square feet), one family consistently produces 6,000–7,000 pounds of food annually, enough for 90% of their household nutrition while generating a sustainable income.[52] Additionally, researchers with the Biosphere II project found that it takes only 2,691 square feet (.06 acres) to grow a nutritionally complete diet for one person in tropical conditions.[53]

On one-tenth of an acre, Mama Snow, a food forester and blogger, is able to produce so much that she sells homemade food (see Figure 1.2). Her kids help her harvest and cook and learn about sustainability in the process. As she explains, "With a little yard and limited space, I plant edibles I use in my recipes on a daily basis. . . . So far, scallions are the most frequently used edibles from my garden." Mama Snow has the added challenge of creating a food forest in an HOA community. Any landscaping done to the front yard has to have a committee's okay first, but she has found clever ways around this: "I wanted a flower bed and I take it literally. . . . [A]ll my edibles, trees, or shrubs have some kind of flowers."[54]

2

CREATING BOTH BEAUTY AND BOUNTY

LOGISTICS AND PRACTICAL ISSUES

In a food forest, trees, shrubs, flowers, and vines can work double duty, creating an attractive, unique yard bursting with edible plants. Crops can perform many of the same functions as ornamental species, offering surprising beauty, form, and fragrance to the landscape. Consider blushing-pink cherry blossoms; ruffled collards with shades of purple; rainbow hues of edible flowers; distinguished stalks of cassava; scented pathways of oregano and rosemary; or spiky, bold pineapple. Even roses are edible yet are mostly noted for only their beauty. In considering the overall design, the following elements apply to both traditional and edible landscapes:

- **Focal Points:** accent plants, paths, water features, and sculptures as eye-catchers
- **Clustering:** similar plants grouped together to show purpose and intent
- **Variety:** diverse color and texture to create interest[1]

The goal with a residential or even a commercial food forest is an edible landscape with less or equal maintenance as with a conventional landscape. However, food forests offer what traditional landscapes don't: cost savings through an ongoing food supply, leisure, and recreation.[2] Beyond aesthetics, recreation, and nutritional benefits, food forests also reduce noise and air pollution.[3] These plants can even enhance home security, such as planting prickly pear cactus under windows.[4]

As with ornamentals, though, quality landscape takes time and requires multiple years to mature. In fact, food forest experts suggest planning for a design that will mature in five years.[5] As such, a food forest is designed around long-term commitments, goals, and rewards. Just consider the fact that a tree is expected to live and produce crops for decades or even centuries—five years is worth the investment![6]

Although it may take five years for the landscaping to mature, it will not take that long to begin harvesting if all nine layers are planned out. Take, for instance, Floridian food forester Katie Haley, who lives on a quarter-acre. Within a year of developing her permaculture garden, she can eat daily from her yard: greens, berries, herbs, and veggies. Right now, at Year 1, 15% percent of her food is from her food forest. She anticipates that she will get that number up to 50% by the second year and 90% by the fifth year.[7]

RIGHT PLANT, RIGHT LOCATION

A successful edible landscape results from good planning, thoughtful design, and regular maintenance. To save money and time in the long run, a veteran food forester in Zone 10b, Christina Nicodemou, offers these words of advice:

> [L]ook at the natural systems at play through seasonal observation. How does the sun move through your space with the changing of the seasons? How does the water flow through the landscape? Water is life and we want to slow it down, spread it, and sink it into the system. How are the winds moving through the system? Winds bring heat or cooler temps so this can have an impact on how plants grow. We can use trees and shrubs to funnel or block winds from moving through the system at different times of the year. Focusing on these elements and planting to create guilds [gives] the space a diverse ecosystem.[8]

To create a cohesive design, I grow plants from seed, cuttings, or grafts to afford duplicates (I discuss this more in later chapters). Although this requires planning, I am able to plant the same crop in multiple locations. It's a low-stress approach, and the results are often excellent. It's often hard to know which spot is perfect for each plant. Having a "shotgun" approach keeps it fun for me, and when plants succeed in a given location, I add more of those same types to create clusters. The design unfolds organically, and I learn a lot about the microecosystems on my property throughout the seasons.

As fun as this process is, there are some delicate aspects of home and landownership. For instance, plants with invasive roots may disturb the house foundation. Also, it is important to consider septic and well areas, the house perimeter and driveway areas, and the property edges.

1. Septic and Well Areas

Septic and well areas may need regular maintenance and can malfunction if the wrong plants are growing on top of them. Right after buying our property, we had to remove several trees with roots affecting the septic area and replace the entire drain field, which cost us thousands. We never want to have to do this again, so we avoid planting water-loving and salt-sensitive plants in this area. Instead, we choose shallow-rooted plants, which ensure coverage and prevent erosion while allowing evaporation (e.g., wildflowers).

In addition to a septic system, we have a well. Luckily, we haven't had any issues with the well so far. To prevent future issues, we avoid planting anything within four feet of the wellhead because roots are a private well's worst enemy; they can destroy the casing. Also, we don't add plant fertilizers or pesticides to the soil around the well or septic tank, and we don't plant any tree closer than 10 feet to a well, septic tank, sewer line, or underground utility. Larger trees and those with more aggressive roots get planted much farther away—20 to 30 feet.

2. House Perimeter and Driveway Areas

House perimeter and driveway areas are prone to contamination, so planting tubers and delicate leafy greens or edible flowers can pose a health risk if there is air, water, or soil pollution. Our house had a suspicious tilt in the floor in one room when we first bought it. We relocated some plants and had a foundation company come and level out the incline. Also, we discovered that the rock fascia on the outside of our house had become a nesting area for wildlife. With these surprises, we quickly learned that we want to be sure whatever we plant around the house doesn't attract pests or have invasive roots that can compromise the foundation. Slow-growing plants that do not accumulate toxins as readily or that have a thick rind protecting edible content have been good choices. Some of our favorites for bordering our home are agave, aloe, and pineapple.

Some of my neighbors who moved to Florida from the North are really set on raised beds because culturally that is what they are used to seeing. Because digging in native soil for tubers, like sweet potatoes, can damage tree roots and vital mycorrhizal relationships, I find that tubers are a perfect use of raised beds. In the blue zone of Okinawa, Japan, those living healthily to more than 100 years historically have had a simple diet that is nearly 70% sweet potato.[9]

> *If you are going to spend money on building a raised bed and filling it with soil, then wouldn't it be great if it provided 70% of your food supply with minimal effort? Sweet potatoes are garden bed all-stars.*

For raised beds, I recommend first lining them with a nontoxic, geotextile bottom layer and filling with soil from a certified source. Tubers are more likely to accumulate soil toxins, so clean soil is worth the investment. Growing tubers in beds has the added benefit of blocking weeds, freeing you from ongoing, back-breaking labor. They grow well even in poor soil, so they will not create ongoing soil expenses each year, as long as you mulch to prevent run-off.

Property Edges

Property edges are ideal locations for an edible privacy hedge. Neighbors may not have the same sustainability vision or understand what a food forest is, but a hedge can help avoid misunderstandings. However, my husband and I chose to go the opposite direction and established a four-foot mow zone all around our fence to send a clear message to neighbors that we were maintaining our property and allow for collaboration. Our relationship with our neighbors is great! They help us by bringing cardboard, compost, and even pineapple tops to plant!

That said, property boundary areas may be prone to water extremes, like drought and flooding, as well as road and traffic contaminants. Choosing evergreen trees and shrubs with thick-skinned fruit (e.g., mango, avocado, tropical almond, papaya, banana) or shelled nuts (e.g., tropical almond, pecan, cashew, macadamia) protect the edible content. However, we are always careful to wash the fruit and nuts prior to peeling or shelling to reduce the likelihood of contaminating the edible portion. Also, we researched setback rules and right-of-way clauses before planting near the road because we wouldn't want anything cut down later!

When we bought the property, we knew we wanted a food forest and immediately started planting. At one point, I encountered a PVC pipe with cables running through it and was a little worried there was a safety issue or that I damaged something important.

Thankfully, there was no issue, but I recommend avoiding this anxiety all together. Sunshine 811 (1-800-632-4949) can help you locate underground pipes and wires *before* planting to prevent damage, outages, or injury. This is a public service in Florida, and utilities send out locators to mark where underground lines are free of charge.

DO IT YOURSELF OR HIRE OUT?

Many food foresters use rules of thumb, like those discussed here, to create their own Gardens of Eden from scratch. Others opt to hire a professional. In either case, you'll want to know what is planted and how to prepare it to eat safely. New Florida food forester Bree Goldstein, who hired a landscaping company to create her two-thirds-acre permaculture garden, offers a word of caution:

> I've learned a lot from fixing and redoing the mistakes left from the food forest installation company I hired. . . . I learned that more oversight from the homeowner is needed. I should have kept a record of plants or requested to see them prior to install. Itemized invoices may have resolved this. They quoted us around $15,000–$20,000 for the entire project. . . . I could've done it myself for a lot less, but I'm sure there are plenty of other companies that would've charged a lot more. Months later, the irrigation still isn't done. . . . I look at it now as a work in progress . . . and a labor of love.[10]

Many food foresters install irrigation. However, this can be costly. Other food foresters opt for free mulch from arborists, landscapers, and tree trimmers (e.g., from chipdrop.com) to retain moisture from rainfall and limit evaporation. As Muaaz Hassan, a Zone 9b food forester without irrigation in a pine flatland (susceptible to drier seasons), explains, "Mulch, Mulch, Mulch . . . the deeper the better."[11] He suggests using wood chips preferably from native oak or pine trees. In Florida, this mulch breaks down quickly, leaving the food forest with a moisture-retentive, rich, organic, dark soil. Three inches or more of mulch suppresses weeds, moderates the ground temperature, creates biomass for soil creation, provides habitat for the soil food web and mycorrhizal fungi, and—most importantly—retains moisture.[12] His method is paying off: 50% of his daily food comes from his 1.49 acre garden. Similarly, Christina Nicodemou, with a Florida scrub pine food forest, explains,

> A healthy soil biome with as much organic matter as possible is the foundation of a thriving food forest. Using free material like mulch from local arborists and landscape companies to build up the soil helps bring in that organic material. A technique called *Hügelkultur* involves burying and backfilling clippings and yard waste then planting into the mound. This keeps materials on the land while slowly breaking down over time, producing a rich soil (ask those neighbors for their yard waste!). Inoculation of beneficial bacteria and microbes into your soil system through compost teas or a system called JADAM helps build up these microbe and fungal systems. Lastly, cover crops, especially in the early stages, help build soil (plants like Cow Peas are great for southern Florida).[13]

Healthy soil can suppress and prevent plant diseases and make crops resilient to pests. In fact, good soil renders insect and pest problems few and far between. This is because compost primes plants to better defend themselves, saving you work, so it pays to always put soil care first and plant care second.[14] To build fertility, some food foresters even make their own biochar after enjoying a campfire. Biochar is a biologically active charcoal that is extremely porous and therefore has a high capacity to store water and nutrients and is an excellent habitat for soil microorganisms.[15] The process to make it is simple: Burn brush and extinguish it while still red hot by soaking it in nutrient-rich liquid, like compost tea or horse-manure water.[16]

Although you can create and build a food forest largely on your own, many aspects of food forestry are more collaborative. Most food foresters will attest: Those bags of oak leaves and pine needles neighbors rake up and bag weekly make excellent leaf mold and can serve as mulch for your perennials, as well.[17] As this implies, building relationships with neighbors can be an essential part of creating a food forest. If you're lucky enough to have food-forester friends, then you likely experience what Sue-Ann Pinney Cowan has: "Sharing is caring. . . . [S]hare and trade ideas, clippings, seeds and plants with others. Help others with the love of gardening while learning new ideas and exploring new techniques!"[18] Food is the greatest community builder. Creating a food forest is not about doing everything yourself. Share, trade, and co-create. We need each other. Together we can address food justice and food sovereignty while trying to limit our own carbon footprint.[19] Along these lines, Jungle Jay, an avid Zone 9b pine flatwood food forester, has had an "11-year success . . . [of] pure gift economy with *no* money exchanged"; instead, he brought his community a "vision [to] . . . benefit the future for everyone."[20]

For more formal sharing, some communities establish community-supported kitchens (CSK) and community-supported-agriculture (CSA) programs. Additionally, Earth Day and multicultural holidays based on agriculture can provide an opportunity for "moveable feasts," where different community members host potlucks. For example:

- In spring, Tu Bishvat is historically considered a "tree birthday party." On this day, food foresters could share a list of their planted trees, trade cuttings, and teach grafting and air-layering.
- In summer, the solstice is historically celebrated and is an excellent time to acknowledge the role of wind and rain. Swaying leaves can help to make wind direction visible, and gardeners could share wind- and flood-tolerant plants and designs in preparation for hurricane season.
- In fall, Oktoberfest is celebrated. Started in 1811 to promote agriculture and the economy, the holiday now is associated with fermentation processes. Food foresters could gather to share culinary methods for foods and beverages, like sourdough, kimchi, vinegar, beer, and wine.
- In winter, the solstice celebrations have historically related to oaks in many cultures. Among food foresters, oak seedlings and other native host plants can be gifted to promote healthy ecosystems. Additionally, bonfires were traditional in winter, so creating biochar for improving soil conditions could enrich the community. Making meals together for holiday feasts and touring one another's yards could also inspire. These tours can provide an opportunity to discuss keys to success, like composting (discussed more in later chapters).

In my family, our Christmas tree is a potted fruit or nut evergreen, which we plant in our food forest after the holidays. No more throwaway Christmas trees! Last year was a beautiful cinnamon tree. Also, for birthdays, Mother's Day, and Valentine's Day, my husband and our relatives all know what to gift me: food forest plants! It keeps holidays simple, and our home doesn't get cluttered with stuff we don't really need—or want. Our garden is thriving, and I consider that the best gift ever!

HOME RESALE VALUE: PRINCIPLES OF DESIGN

For those concerned about aesthetics and resale value, fear not. The design of good landscape can lead to the highest and best return, far exceeding the costs to install.[21] Most buyers look for shade, privacy, and aesthetics in yards.[22] For the food forest to contribute to the home's resale value, it must have utility, abundance, and satisfaction (see Figure 2.1).[23]

Utility

In terms of design, an open space for children or animals to play is often important to families. We created navigable paths by mowing walkways and designed shade for outdoor gathering areas and parking spaces. One thing I wish we had done is limit beds and zones to four-foot diameters or widths so they can be pruned from the paths easily. This helps to prevent soil compaction, keeping plants healthy. We are working on adding new mow paths to limit the widths of the planted zones.

Utility	Abundance	Satisfaction
a. Meadows	e. Water feature	i. Aromatics
b. Paths	f. Signposts	j. Color
c. Shade	g. Night lighting	k. Butterfly hosts
d. Parking	h. Art features	l. Picnic tables

Figure 2.1. A Food Forest Yard Offering Utility, Abundance, and Satisfaction

When it comes to the actual crops, many food foresters who have sold their properties will tell you to be sure to include recognizably edible plants, such as fruit trees. However, across all cultures, complex carbohydrates are the axis around which all other elements of a diet revolve.[24] So if you are planning for utility related to food security, then design the food forest around staple starches and carbohydrates first.[25] These are your macronutrients, and bananas and pigeon peas are an easy and low-maintenance option for this category. Second, add as many greens as possible to have your micronutrients. Many choose chaya, among others, for this category because it is attractive and grows like a weed. Third, layer in diverse herbs and sweet fruits for flavors and textures. These will provide your phytonutrients. Papaya and rosemary are easy to grow and produce prolifically, easily fulfilling this category. But rare and exotic fruit trees are also useful for adding variety to your diet. Sue-Ann has a mature red mombin that is prolific (see Figure 2.2). I had never even heard of this plant before meeting her, and the fruits are so delicious!

Figure 2.2. Sue-Ann Cowan, Forest of Abundant Cabbage Palms/Pineland, Zone 10b

Abundance

When the United States was colonized, many people came here in hopes of freedom from oppressive landlords and hunger. Creating a food forest means you have something most people never achieve: self-sufficiency, the American dream. Large trees, especially fruit trees, are becoming rare on home properties, yet they are desirable. They reduce smog, dust, heat, and noise and are associated with increased property values.[26] Additionally, many food forests feature valuable, rare, and endangered plants, like those listed on United Plant Savers' website (https://unitedplantsavers.org/). Imagine being in your backyard, harvesting fresh fruits and vegetables year-round—just like in fairy tales (see Figure 2.3).[27] Wealth at one time implied the ability to sit inside with nothing to do. In today's world of chronic illness and obesity, a food forest implies new luxuries: health, fitness, access to free organic produce, rare fruits, and stress-relieving time outdoors in the cool shade of dappled light.

Figure 2.3. Anna Hackel, Pine Flatwoods Food Forest, Zone 9b

Satisfaction

As author and popular food forester David the Good explains, strolling through a food forest is like taking a botanical tour.[28] When this is your backyard, the pleasure is free and available daily. What a luxury! A food forest offers the opportunity to experience an enhanced quality of life. It can be a romantic spot to dine al fresco! By incorporating plants that stimulate all five senses (sight, sound, taste, touch, and smell), the food forest can maximize pleasure while decreasing stress and improving overall well-being.[29] Colorful aromatics like herbs and flowers are valued in a food forest for their medicinal and culinary value but also serve as nectar and host plants, attracting bees, endangered butterflies, and other beneficial insects. Research which edible plants are butterfly hosts for your area on the National WildLife Federation website (https://www.nwf.org/NativePlantFinder).

Incorporating a food forest in the landscape is not an all-or-nothing proposition. Some gardeners aim to replace up to 90% of their groceries with food-forest staple crops, thereby creating food security. Others are simply interested in supplementing their diet with food-forest harvests.[30] In either case, those with a food forest have an opportunity to save on food costs and decrease waste from food packaging. Beyond grocery savings, there is also the economic potential of selling excess crops, seeds, cuttings, and propagated plants for a supplemental income.[31] Some food foresters even host permaculture workshops, survivalist trainings, homesteading, and foraging lessons. Additionally, once your food forest is established, you may be able to receive agricultural exemption, which offers significant tax savings.

Mike Elson, in Zone 9b on a wetland swamp and hydric hammocks food forest, has operated for decades as a Florida nursery, complete with a nursery license, hemp licenses, and fruit crop operation.[32] Close to 90% of his food comes from his garden, and with his chicken and egg production ramping up, he anticipates that the overall percentage of his diet coming from his food forest will increase beyond 90%.[33] This is an example of maximizing your own backyard. Rather than sinking thousands a year into managing a lawn, food foresters use the same budget to create a financial return!

POLICY, LAWS, ETHICS, CODES, AND ZONES

Creating a garden is freeing and empowering. That said, some plants may not be permitted in your area. For instance, if you have an area designated as wetland, then you may need to develop it according to specific guidelines. City planning and zoning ordinances, homeowners' association rules, and other local codes may influence what is allowed on the property.[34] Planting edible Florida natives will help establish a healthy ecosystem within your food forest and requires less caution because regulations often favor natives.

When adding exotic species to your food forest, you'll want to know if its growth habit warrants the label "invasive." This label means the plant displays rapid growth without natural controls (e.g., something to eat it). If you are eating it, then there are natural controls, and the label may not apply on your land. Even inedible invasives can be an ongoing source of nectar for pollinators, green manure, and mulch, eliminating the need for costly and potentially environmentally harmful chemical herbicides and fertilizers (e.g., tithonia). However, edible invasives provide ongoing food supplies! Pineapples and coconut trees are just two examples of many edible plants often called "invasive." In contrast, the terms *noxious* and *prohibited* are legal designations used for specific plants subject by law to restrictions.

Creating a food forest is a natural means of ecological restoration, but ethically, food foresters will want to be careful with planting exotics.[35] As described in the classic book *The Secret Garden*, "Where you tend a rose bush, a thistle cannot grow."[36] Creating a food forest involves planting and maintaining many different plant species while removing noxious ones. If you are cultivating edibles, then you will naturally remove pests to make room for desirables. Just take it from Carl Andren in Zone 9b on a scrub food forest. Before he started developing his three acres, the location was covered with the noxious, prohibited Brazilian pepper (which can cause dermatitis and asthmatic allergies). Now, this invasive is gone, and his garden is so diverse that he eats from it daily![37]

UNDERSTANDING CULTURAL AND HISTORICAL USES OF PLANTS

On larger properties, an edible invasive may find its way into the food forest. In this case, research the plant. Find out the cultural and historical uses of the plant. You may be able to harvest the material for food, building, or fodder, which is a good way to remove it without waste. If safe, then consuming the plant will help to introduce a natural control that is otherwise lacking. If a plant valued in one culture is brought into another culture where the mainstream population does not use it, then the unchecked growth cannot be contained by consumerism.

Take, for instance, kudzu (*Pueraria montana*), introduced into the United States at the Philadelphia Centennial Exposition in 1876. By 1900, kudzu was available through mail order as an inexpensive livestock forage. The plant was later sold by the US Department of Agriculture (USDA) and planted for erosion control. This plant may show up in your food forest spontaneously, but do *not* plant it, as it is now a prohibited plant. Kudzu can grow into impenetrable patches sprawling 100 acres in some cases, covering and killing trees and growing up to 1 foot per day reaching 60 feet.[38]

Interestingly, though, kudzu is a staple food in Japan. The peeled root contains 27.1% carbohydrates and is a good source of calcium and iron.[39] The flowers can be cooked or made into pickles; the stems and young leaves can be eaten raw or cooked; and overall, kudzu is considered a very nutritious food. Some report that the fresh, young shoots taste like a cross between a bean and a pea.[40] Considering this plant's edibility and the widespread food insecurity in Florida, one may conclude that the problem is not the plant itself but the lack of education that could result in commercialization and marketing of the plant as a food source. Where there is profit, there is a solution. Kudzu may be a missed economic opportunity for someone, but it leads to other important questions:

- Should growing food be easier?
- Why do we spend state and local tax revenues to destroy food rather than harvest it?
- How can edible invasives like kudzu be better commercialized to feed an increasing population?

As philosopher and ecologist Aldo Leopold proclaimed, "The oldest task in human history [is to] live on a piece of land without spoiling it."[41] Cultural knowledge and revival is necessary for sustainability; we must strive to use what is abundant.[42] Food is more than something to eat; it is a reflection of a culture, a way of life. Seeking inspiration from cultures that eat well, stay healthy, and get the most out of life can be helpful.[43]

LIVESTOCK AND WILDLIFE

Livestock can enhance the productivity in a food forest. For instance, bees are considered a livestock in Florida, and I lease my food forest to a beekeeper in exchange for honey (see

Figure 2.4. James Pike With Son, 26 Beehives in Their Food Forest, Zone 10a

Figure 2.4). She sells queen bees, and I get plants pollinated as well as an unrefined sweetener. The relationship is a win-win. Additionally, having this livestock helped me obtain yearly agricultural-exemption-tax savings. As any gardener knows, bees pollinate flowers as well as many edible plants: fruits, vegetables, and even nuts. Beeswax is also useful for everything from traditional medicine to candles. I make my own facial cream from the wax, and it is far better than any commercial product I've ever used. It's so luxurious!

In some cultures, livestock is ranked by the space required, maintenance costs, and potential for the animal to be destructive to crops. For instance, edible insects and their products (which includes bees and their honey) quickly reproduce and can promote ecosystem health by serving as pollinators. Other livestock, like goats, may readily escape confines and eat crops. The following ranks livestock according space, maintenance, and destruction:

- **Level 1:** microorganisms, like yeasts for sourdough and wine and bacteria for vinegar
- **Level 2:** insects, like bees for honey and crickets for wheat substitute or flour, and snails for escargot
- **Level 3:** shellfish, like crayfish and prawns; reptiles, like iguanas; and fish, like tilapia
- **Level 4:** chickens, like cream legbar breeds for eggs; rabbits, like the Cinnamon breed for meat; and goats, like the dwarf Nigerian breed for milk

Figure 2.5. Muaaz Hassan, 2021, Florida Food Forester With Livestock

Livestock may or may not become a part of your food forest. However, many food foresters like me and Muaaz Hassan, choose to keep chickens as part of the permaculture garden because eggs supplement our diet (B_{12}, D_3, iodine; see Figure 2.5). Also, the chickens offer weed- and pest-management solutions, while their manure is a nitrogen-rich fertilizer. In general, chickens are considered an easier Level 4 livestock because of their lower cost to keep, fast reproduction, and high yield (e.g., eggs).

If you want to add livestock, then be sure to research your jurisdiction's zoning regulations and municipal codes, including health codes, noise ordinances, and roaming-animal laws.[44] Look for a "permissive use" reference, such as for chickens. Building officials and land-record clerks may be able to help you determine your property zone and the applicable regulations. Call them directly. If livestock like chickens are permitted on your property, then additional limitations may pertain to the number of chickens, whether roosters are allowed, if you can process them for meat onsite, and waste management regulations.[45] Some counties will require you to apply for a "backyard chicken" permit. Also, note that keeping livestock requires enhanced precautions. Chickens can transmit salmonella and may attract predators, including bobcats, and pests, like rodents. Another consideration is that some chicken feeds are contaminated with arsenic, so review and buy wisely because the feed may end up in the soil.[46]

When creating a food forest, you will also be creating a wildlife habitat. In fact, many food foresters take advantage of the Audubon Society's Certified Backyard Habitat Program and proudly display their plaques. We do! Rabbit, wild turkey, quail, deer, and other game may very well find their way onto your property. Their presence speaks to the role of food forests in today's rapidly deforested world.

Wildlife onsite may pique your hunting interests, yet recreational hunting licenses and permits may be required in most areas, even if you are hunting on your own property. There may be required online safety courses. Research hunting seasons and bag limits for your area. Those with ponds may find alligators swimming in there seasonally, but shooting them is illegal without a permit. Florida food forester Sue-Ann Pinney Cowan explains,

> My sons and a few friends were awarded permits. . . . The Statewide Alligator Hunt is one of FWC's most popular limited entry hunts, and more than ten thousand applicants will apply for about six thousand permits on alligator management units that are established with sustainable harvest quotas. Each alligator hunting permit includes two CITES tags, authorizing the holder to harvest two alligators. The harvest areas and hunt dates are specific for each permit, and the permits specify the boundaries or limitations of the harvest area. The statewide alligator hunting season begins on August 15 and ends on the morning of November 1.[47]

With this permit, her son hunted a gator, harvested one of her cabbage palms, and made her gator and cabbage palm stew—a one-of-a-kind food-forest dish for sure!

FAST-GROWING, SHADE-BEARING EDIBLES

When just getting started, there are ways to speed up progress. For instance, if you choose fast-growing crops to enhance your soil, then your food forest will transform quickly. I live in South Florida, so my top three plants are pigeon pea (dry areas), banana (wet areas), and papaya (well-draining areas). These plants grow to a shade-bearing height in a matter of months and are also among the most space-efficient, abundantly producing edibles with the lowest start-up cost. Neighbors gifted me banana pups for free, I bought pigeon pea as a dried bean at a local grocer, and I grew a self-fertile/hermaphrodite papaya variety from seed (i.e., solo sunset). Knowing where to plant your top plants will also save time and money. For instance, if banana, papaya, and pigeon pea grow in your hardiness zone, then take advice from Florida food forester Jay Reynolds in Zone 11:

1. **Wait until a heavy rain. Go outside, and observe where puddles have formed.** Mulch heavily, and plant bananas there. "Bananas are essential components of a Florida food forest. They are among the fastest growing fruits and can bear within one year. Also a high biomass producing herb, not a tree!"[48]
2. **Don't water for one month. Go outside, and observe where the sod has died.** Plant pigeon pea there. "Pigeon Pea is a fast-growing, drought-tolerant legume shrub/sub-tree. Overall, it is a very tolerant pioneer species which can grow anywhere with little care. It fixes nitrogen, provides shade, has an excellent edible pea, and lives several years."[49]
3. **Don't mow for three weeks. Go outside, and observe where wildflowers, like Bidens alba, are blooming.** Plant papaya there. "Papayas are one of the best and fastest fruiting pioneer trees. They make fruit within one year and are both a fruit when ripe and a vegetable when eaten green; they are capable of making 150 lbs. of fruit per season!"[50]

With these three crops, you have fruit (ripe banana and papaya), vegetables (unripe papaya and banana, their flowers and stalk, green pigeon pea), protein (green pigeon pea), flour for baking bread (unripe banana, mature pigeon pea), vinegar (fermented banana peels), and more. By mulching these areas and mowing between these plants, you will create natural swales—the lowest contour on the property where water can flow. This is a great start to a food forest.

Even if these plants don't grow in your hardiness zone, the same general concept and principles can help you choose your top three plants. To start your food forest in a hurry, pick a nitrogen-fixing protein plant (beans/peas), a high-yielding fruit tree, and a starchy vegetable—this combination will offer all three nutrient areas: macronutrients, micronutrients, and phytochemicals.

The easiest way to garden in Florida is to create mulched mounds. These planting "zones" should be a maximum of four feet wide so you can reach in without walking on top and compressing the soil. Compacted soil causes water to run off instead of sinking down, choking off the roots' air and nutrient supply.[51] However, the zones can be as long as you'd like. Create paths between these zones at least two feet wide so you can mow or push a wheelbarrow through.[52]

Whichever plants you choose to start with as your first few plants, the key is to observe first and plant second. Veteran Florida food forester Judith Gulko explains,

> Observe and be slow: Slow is fast. Take the time to observe. It can be hard to be slow, but it saves you time and energy in the end. Visit a lot with the land you want to create a food forest on. . . . Sit and watch. Learn the sun, shade, and wind patterns, . . . how and where water flows through the landscape, . . . the people and other creature patterns. Really be present with how it feels to be there. Go at different times of day.[53]

After figuring out where to plant initial crops, you'll want to mulch and fertilize to prepare areas for planting. The two ways to achieve this for free include (1) calling local tree trimmers and asking for their chips (e.g., chipdrop.com) and (2) contacting horse farmers. Horse farmers may use a service that removes their aged manure and can drop it on your property free of charge. Just make sure the horses were not grazing on land contaminated with pesticides, which can pass through their digestive tract and into your plants. To secure manure, post on Freecycle (https://freecycle.org) or Buy Nothing forums on Facebook, reach out to local 4-H groups, go to farmers markets, or visit county fairs. Other free resources for your food forest include discarded pavers from pool and driveway-resurfacing companies and old hot tubs, which are useful as raised ponds.

ENSURING DIVERSITY

After your initial 20 plants are in and you have enough of your top three plants to feed you daily, aim to increase plant diversity in your food forest to 100 to 200 species. Chapter 4 includes 200 plant species and provides a solid reference point. Having diversity ensures a hierarchy of natural predators, like insects and hawks, which can limit pests, like insects and rodents.[54] Christina Nicodemou elaborates, "A healthy ecosystem needs biodiversity. The more diverse an ecosystem, the more resilient the system will be to pest pressures."[55] In other words, as Florida food forester Anni Ellis explains, "Let the insects work for you. Plant natives and watch the predatory insects show up."[56] When planting for diversity, think about the different levels of plants—"rhizome plants, vines, shrubs, trees, and more."[57]

If you follow the 30–20–10 biodiversity rule, then you'll maximize protection against pest and disease outbreaks. To do this, plant only

- 30% from the same family,
- 20% of the same genus, and
- 10% from the same species.[58]

Chapter 4's profiles list plant families to help you promote diversity. I also include the botanical name so you know the genus and species. Much like your first and last name, the botanical name aids positive identification with two references: the genus (like a last name) and the species name (similar to a first name). In plant names, the last name comes first.

POSITIVE IDENTIFICATION

When selecting plants or figuring out what is on your property, positive identification will help you address numerous safety concerns at once. To positively identify a plant, match characteristics (e.g., plant size, form, leaf shape, flower color, odor) with a Latin scientific botanical name. Common names may refer to many different plants, so the botanical name is important. Empowered with a plant's Latin name, research its attributes. This is especially important for understanding plant toxicity. For example, the common name *elephant ear* is a generic reference to many plants, including caladiums, water elephant ear, and more, but most of these plants are inedible. Positive identification can help you differentiate toxic species from the edible elephant ears, like malanga, eddo, and taro, three staples valued across the world.[59]

Planting a food forest can be a bit like foraging for food because plants will self-seed, or you may forget what you planted. As a result, correctly identifying plants is important. Additionally, many of the plants listed in the profiles are akin to wild edibles. If you are doing independent research and trying to determine the edibility and safety of a new plant, then it's safer to use more than one reference source. Some ways to learn about plants include apps like PlantSnap, PlantNet, iNaturalist, and

- PLANTS Database: the most comprehensive plant database in the country developed by the USDA Natural Resource Conservation Service
- Local cooperative extension offices and associated master gardeners (e.g., University of Florida Institute of Food and Agricultural Sciences)

Plants for a Future (https://pfaf.org) can also provide insight into safety and edibility. Florida Foraging (www.floridaforaging.com) and Eat the Weeds (https://www.eattheweeds .com) are also noteworthy sites. If using Google, prioritize research on .org, .edu, and other credible sites by typing "site:.org" or "site:.edu" after your keywords. For example, before eating an unripe banana, type into a search bar "green banana unripe edibility safety site:. edu." If you want to do deeper research then use Google Scholar (https://scholar.google. com) to look up published research articles.

SCHEDULING AND TOOLS

Quality gardening tools will save you time and effort. Garage sales, flea markets, freecycling groups like Buy Nothing, and more can provide high-quality tools. Some examples of essential tools and equipment to get include

- pitchfork,
- shovel,
- gloves,
- goggles,
- waterproof boots,
- shears,
- machete,
- weed whacker,
- wheelbarrow,
- Gorilla Cart,
- five-gallon bucket,
- hose,
- mower,
- hand trimmer,
- watering can,
- hardware cloth,
- staple gun, and
- cement or putty.

Another time- and money-saving trick is to plan gardening, harvesting, and food preparation by each season. Even if a perennial can be planted any time of year, planting by season will allow you to chunk your time while also budgeting. Purchasing seeds and cuttings seasonally means you will have plenty of time to pot and plant the seedlings before the next season. The benefit here is that you can limit being overwhelmed or overextended financially.

SPRING IDEAS FOR THE FOOD FOREST

Spring is a great time to grow plants that germinate at an average temperature range of 77°F–84°F. Examples include chufa; gingers/galangal; red roselle; African potato mint; edible flowers; herbs (fennel, cilantro); passion fruit; pigeon pea; Seminole pumpkin; amaranth; yams; tomatoes; arrowroot; water chestnuts; malanga; cranberry hibiscus; chayote; okra; cassava; loofah; sunchokes; turmeric; quinoa; aibika; and coconut.

During this season, you can maximize your harvests by eating sprouts as you thin out your seedlings. Another fun option is to harvest honey and tree sap, which are more abundant in spring. You may also notice that some plants need to be pruned to grow fuller. Spring is an ideal time to eat your pungent herbs, like rosemary, fennel, and basil, which benefit from being cut back. Spring can also be a delightfully social time with barbecuing—ideal for preparing prickly pear, which requires heat over an open flame to singe off the spines.

If you feel ready for a decent workout, then spring is a great time to spread manure and fertilize around fruit trees after a heavy rain.[60] Your primary gardening tools will likely be a shovel and wheelbarrow or Gorilla Cart as you fertilize, mulch, and plant. When planting, remember that it is far better to place a tree in a hole too shallow than too deep as most trees settle. By planting high, you ensure proper drainage, stimulate development, and prevent diseases.[61] Newly planted trees should receive a deep watering once a week until the rains pick up. Also, take advantage of new growth and collect many softwood cuttings to propagate plants, which are perfect Mother's Day gifts.

Spring is also a time for extra precautions with livestock like chickens because mating season brings predators. We have lost quite a few chickens to hawks and bobcats in spring. One bobcat took to sleeping under our fruit tree, just waiting for us to let the chickens out of the coop in the morning. We had to chase her off and even go after her to retrieve a traumatized chicken! Having a few feisty roosters solved that problem entirely the following season.

SUMMER IDEAS FOR THE FOOD FOREST

Summer is a great time to grow plants that germinate at an average temperature range of over 81°F. Examples include cowpea; sunflower; sweet potatoes; banana; oregano; fruit trees, like starfruit, mango, and avocado; tropical spinaches, like longevity, Malabar, and Egyptian; flood-tolerant natives, like cocoplum and Simpson's stopper.

As you very likely know, summer is *hot* in Florida. The upside in a food forest is that you get to prioritize eating the abundant raw, fresh delights to cool and hydrate you, like mango, pineapple, and longan fruit salads. Yum! If you don't mind spending a bit of time in the kitchen, then summer is the perfect opportunity to practice the art of salad-making, arranging colors and shapes with leaf fans; scooped balls of cooked veggies and fruits; and edible flowers, including butterfly pea. The options are endless. Harvest leaves for salads in the early afternoon when chlorophyll is at its peak.[62] Make brothy, egg-drop soups with aibika and chives. Enjoy flower and leaf herbal teas, like mint, because they will be growing in abundance. Design a floral arrangement for the table!

As long as you don't mind a bit of cleansing sweat, summer gardening can be effortless and dreamlike. The rain and sun help everything flourish. Your primary tools will likely be a weed whacker, mower, hand trimmer, shears, machete, Gorilla Cart, and pitchfork. These will all help you guide the abundant growth in your food forest.

The afternoon rains are delightfully refreshing and can be managed with swales (mow paths) to direct excess water. If you elevate plant zones with mulch or biomass through chop-and-drop and Hügelkultur (i.e., mounds of sticks and logs), then the swales will simply become short-lived creeks in torrential rainstorms. We bought skim boards to take advantage. Now we just have to learn to use them!

FALL IDEAS FOR THE FOOD FOREST

Fall is my favorite time of year because everything is blooming, and it is cool enough to spend even more time outdoors. To increase abundance in your food forest, fall is a great time to grow plants that germinate at an average temp range of 75°F–85°F. Examples include Seminole pumpkin; papaya; okra; peppers; tomato; lemongrass; chives; leeks; collards; and drought-tolerant natives, like beautyberry. Also, fall is the time to sow wildflowers!

If you like to cook, then autumn is also root-harvesting time, so "potato" dishes (e.g., cassava, sweet potato, African potato mint) are the center of many classic holiday spreads. Additionally, many food foresters prepare for winter by making vinegars, infusions, and oxymels for flu home remedies in fall. Such wonderful and thoughtful gifts! Being in the kitchen with friends and learning to ferment can be a special time. Sour flavors may take center stage with foods like sourdough, sauerkraut, olives, pickles, rose-hip tea, wine, tofu, and tempeh. For many, including my family, fall is the time for slow-cooked foods over low heat. Stovetop-simmered stews help warm the house and body. I freeze portions for aging family members and stock their coolers whenever they visit. It helps me feel like I am nourishing them. Maybe they will live to 100!

As fun as it can be to be creative in the kitchen, fall is such a productive time in the garden. To maximize this time, consider harvesting seeds and take hardwood cuttings midmorning in fall to propagate plants. Plants make excellent holiday gifts! Also, early fall is the best time to design and begin site preparation. Lay down cardboard and mulch. Dig that pond. Draw out your plans. If you've considered starting a business from your food forest, then fall is a great time to test out your skills. So much anticipation can build in fall. It's an exciting time, and in my family, we dream up new plans and make resolutions early!

Offsetting the excitement in our first year in our house, we learned a sobering lesson. We woke up several nights in a row to an alarming pitter-patter in the attic. Fall is when animals also start to prepare for winter. Take it from me: Seal up and clean out all entry points or safe havens to ensure wildlife cannot enter attics, garages, or chimneys. For this purpose, primary tools are likely hardware cloth and a staple gun, along with cement or putty. In fall, we also mow down brush 18 or more inches from the house to prevent animals from nesting too close, and we haven't had an issue since. I ended up planting a pineapple guild all around the house because it doesn't provide nesting, is easy to maintain, produces a clean look, supplies a slow-growing food, and creates a buffer.

WINTER IDEAS FOR THE FOOD FOREST

Winter is a wonderful time of year when everyone flocks to Florida. Our Airbnb gets lots of demand, and giving tours is such a pleasure. Winter is a great time to grow plants that germinate at an average temperature range of 50°F–82°F. Because tropical plants may not enjoy the cold, we end up prioritizing herbs, which can be sprouted from seed, and take cuttings indoors or in sheltered locations. Also, drought-tolerant natives, evergreens, perennial shrubs, and trees are perfect plants to focus on during the cold months.

With all the festivities, the kitchen becomes a focal point in our family. Salty and savory flavors dominate with warming cereal coffees, like chicory. Dehydrated fruits, like mulberries, and roasted nuts keep recipes interesting, along with winter-producing crops, like purple collard trees and red roselle. Nothing beats red roselle "cranberry sauce"! Beans baked with warming spices, like cinnamon, garlic, chives, and ginger, keep everyone cozy, and honey, royal jelly, and pollen provide a seasonal health boost. Also, sprouts tossed onto rich, creamy avocado soups can be delectable!

With some plants going dormant and weeds growing more slowly, I like to focus on mulching to regain a semblance of control in the food forest. For this reason, primary winter tools are often a pitchfork, Gorilla Cart, wheelbarrow, and shears. Winter drought is a real danger to plants, so mulch thoroughly to make plants more resilient.[63] As a bonus, many subtropical and tropical trees can thrive even when planted in the dry season if provided with a thick layer of mulch.[64] After the mulch is down, I like to broadcast seeds, leaving some stands for birds.

As a shortcut, use winter to plant under deciduous trees because their dropped leaves will fertilize understory transplants that are at least a foot tall. That way, the leaf litter doesn't bury them! Once all the leaves have dropped, provide those deciduous plants a hard pruning, and many will fruit vigorously on the new growth. Proper pruning (cutting a stem back to a bud) helps crops produce better. There are four pruning strategies:

- **Coppicing:** cutting a plant almost to the ground to stimulate new growth (e.g., moringa)
- **Pollarding:** cutting off the top of a plant to promote ideal growth patterns (e.g., mango)
- **Shaping:** edible hedges
- **Cutting to the ground:** herbs, like African basil[65]

If you're nervous about pruning, then perhaps you can be inspired by advice from Florida food forester Sue-Ann Pinney Cowan in Zone 10b: "Pruning is your friend! It encourages new growth and shapes your tree with strong limbs to support heavy fruits. It also allows light through to the understory plants. I find the best time to prune is right after you harvest. Remove the crossing and dead branches and keep to desired height to be able to harvest fruits easier."[66]

PROPAGATE YEAR-ROUND

If you eat from your food forest regularly, then you will naturally propagate; when you harvest, replanting cuttings and seeds is a natural process. However, if you are just starting and buying new seeds, please don't make the same mistake I did (planting all male trees). Interestingly, plant sex falls into three categories: monoecious (male and female flowers on the same plant), hermaphrodite (self-fertile flowers), and dioecious (male and female flowers on separate plants). You may need more than one plant or gender to have a crop. The Chapter 4 profiles note if a plant is dioecious (i.e., male or female trees); these plants require special attention to fruit, and you may not want to grow them from seed. Instead, these plants are best grown from cuttings or grafting.

When I first started buying seeds, most didn't germinate. If they did, then they died shortly after, and I blamed myself. I was really discouraged. However, after a while, I realized that these seeds were not adapted to my area. Ideally, buy from someone within a few miles of you so that the plant is adapted to your ecotype. Etsy and eBay allow you to sort and shop by distance or zip code, which can be very useful. Although, I have had a few experiences with scammers on these sites, most people are honest backyard gardeners. That said, the best option is to find other food foresters in your area. A community that supports each other will flourish faster. I am so thankful for my neighbors and their generosity. When visitors tour my elaborate garden and I tell them that most of my plants were grown from cuttings or seeds gifted by friends, they often struggle to imagine how that can be possible. Gardening friends are one of the most important parts of creating a food forest.

Once you have seed in hand, soak them for a few days in a shot glass of water mixed with a cap of hydrogen peroxide to help them germinate faster and give them a strong start. This is chemical scarification. Other options are filing the seeds with sandpaper, but I have damaged seeds this way. Some seed instructions suggest cold stratification, where you put seeds in the fridge. If you live in South Florida and have mild winters, don't do this. Seeds that require it will not do well. Instead, soak seeds, plant 20 or more in a single one- or three-gallon pot, and then divide any that sprout. This is lower stress and helps prioritize plants that are better adapted to your ecotype.

When growing from seed, remember that some plants do not grow true to type, meaning they may not resemble the parent plant in flavor or growth. Consider human siblings and parent appearances: A child may have blond hair and blue eyes, while their parents have brown hair and brown eyes. To propagate cultivars and maintain parent characteristics, like fruit flavor, more advanced methods of propagating are needed. Some of those methods include the following:

- **Tip layering:** placing the tip of a current season's growth in soil. The tip grows roots and resprouts upward. This tip can then be separated from the parent plant and transplanted.
- **Grafting or budding:** splicing one plant into another so new growth takes on specific taste or growth characteristics. This is usually done while both scion and rootstock are dormant.
- **Air layering:** removing leaves, twigs, and bark on a stem; wrapping it with moss or soil; and securing it with aluminum foil or plastic until roots form.[67]

While tip layering is great for herbaceous plants, like blackberries, grafting or budding and air layering are ideal for propagating fruit and nut trees. Grafting or budding merges a branch (scion) and plant (rootstock) together, while air layering creates roots on a branch so it becomes an independent plant. All these methods can be learned within an afternoon of watching YouTube tutorials and require very few, if any, specialized tools. When growing a food forest, permaculture YouTube videos are very helpful!

3

HEALTH AND SAFETY CONSIDERATIONS

REAPING HEALTH BENEFITS: FRESH FOODS

Who doesn't crave food bursting with flavor and aroma? Consider a perfectly ripe mango. Nothing smells better, and what is more gratifying than a warm, juicy bite that leaves sweet nectar dripping down your chin?

Deliciously fresh food offers many health benefits, yet many gardeners will tell you that store-bought produce isn't bursting with flavor. That's part of the reason many kids (and adults!) don't like vegetables or even fruit. Most Americans never eat the recommended five to seven daily servings of fresh produce a day due to taste complaints.[1] Grocery produce, picked underripe for shipment, can taste overly acidic. Flavor helps to reveal nutrients. Most produce stays fresh and is therefore nutritious for only a few days. Consider the average head of broccoli, which travels more than 1,800 miles before it gets to the store—let alone to your table![2] The most flavorful and healthy fruits and vegetables are those grown locally and organically—without the use of insecticides, herbicides, artificial fertilizers, or growth-stimulating hormones.[3] The shining truth is that when it comes to variety and freshness, the home garden surpasses commercial giants like grocers. When harvesting your food-forest produce, look for fruits and vegetables at the peak of their ripeness. These contain maximum nutrients.

FOOD PREP

The food you harvest from your permaculture garden will offer you more culinary variety than you've ever imagined. Just think of the satisfaction of serving a glass of wine to a friend and saying, "I made that!" When deciding what food to grow, you'll want to acknowledge your interest level in the kitchen. Some foods will need preparation, while others won't. If you like being in the kitchen, then you'll be in good company! Great chefs will tell you that delicious meals are simple to make when you have fresh ingredients to celebrate in a dish.[4] That's exactly what you have with a food forest: fresh produce. Learning to cook your crops will be a lifelong journey if you want it to be, and one with many rewards. Wholesome, fresh foods promote health and provide pleasure. As health enthusiast and author Jason Manheim puts it, "[A]lthough you can't feel your body 'not' getting cancer, . . . you can feel your energy levels increase, your focus intensify, your hunger satiate, and your body shift into overdrive—ready to take on any tasks. . . . [T]hese are measurable, motivational and gratifying results that you can feel almost instantly."[5]

Using wisdom from blue zones, if you create simple recipes from just 6 of 20 versatile plants you've grown, then you can create *tens of thousands* of different meals. Surprisingly, though, most families repeat meals every few days, so it isn't difficult to grow enough food to provide all daily meals with variety over a week.[6] Creating a two-week menu and then growing the foods to produce the meals on that menu is a good way to stay organized. Appendix B provides an example menu, meal plan, and harvest schedule.

On top of having fresh produce handy, a well-stocked pantry can help you cook on the fly in today's busy world. This means regularly harvesting and stocking spices, oils, vinegars, sauces, marmalades, sweeteners, flours, powders, dried beans, noodles, nuts, seeds, and dried fruit. As your harvest comes in, prepare these pantry items so that when you are in a rush, you can whip up a dish quickly. The following kitchen appliances help immensely.

Omega Juicer and Dehydrator

If I have a big harvest of fruit coming in at once, I'll juice it, then ferment the juice into wine. This process is easy and fun, and the fruit pulp serves as a great leather or even pulled-pork substitute when dehydrated and rehydrated in a savory sauce. I've also made nut butters using my juicer. I soak my nuts and seeds overnight, drain them, sauté to warm the oils, and then juice them. The nut butter accumulates in the mouth of the machine, while the meal or flour from the pulp is separated. I dehydrate the nut and fruit meal as a flour for breads, cakes, and cookies.

Vitamix or Blendtec Blender and Food Processor

Blender and food-processor blades are efficient to quickly infuse spices in oils or vinegars or whip up pesto, ice cream, soups, sauces, marmalades, jellies, and jams. For instance, I make nut milk in my blender by pureeing coconut meat with water. I then strain out the coconut meal and—presto!—I have coconut milk and flour for baking. So delicious! This fresh meal or flour can even be juiced to extract "cream." From there, I have blended the meal with dried fruit and made simple but delicious pie crusts in a food processor. As a side note, if you boil the coconut meal in water, then the oil releases and rises to the surface. Once cooled, it solidifies, and you can scrape it off and save it for later use. This also allows the dehydrated flour to last longer.

Coffee Grinder

A juicer or blender will produce coarse flour, which works great for crackers or even cookies. But for bread or pasta, the coffee grinder can help create finer flour. I also grind my dried moringa and lemongrass leaves in the coffee grinder to make a powder to sprinkle over eggs and popcorn. Some invest in a mill to grind their flour, but I haven't found one worth mentioning yet.

EATING NEW FOOD-FOREST PRODUCE

Learning to cook from the garden is a journey. Some of the plants listed in the Chapter 4 plant profiles will be completely new to you. Always taste small quantities of new foods and then wait 24 hours to be sure you do not have an allergy, even if the plant isn't known to cause adverse health effects. Every person is unique, and allergies can develop over time.[7] Pay attention to your body and its responses to foods.

Choose the healthiest plant and fruit specimens to eat, and use the rest as "chop and drop" green manure or nitrogen to amend the soil. A good rule of thumb is "If in doubt, throw it out." Because you may be foraging, you need to know some highly poisonous plants so you can remove them from your food forest, including rosary pea (*Abrus precatorius*), oleander (*Nerium oleander*), gloriosa lily (*Gloriosa superba*), king sago (*Cycas revoluta*), and spotted water hemlock (*Cicuta maculata*). Additionally, be sure to know if an edible plant has a poisonous lookalike. That way, you can be extra cautious when identifying these species. For instance, dill, fennel, parsley, carrot, and parsnip have very poisonous lookalikes that even smell like the real thing, so be careful![8]

Some plants require a specific cooking method to eat safely. Even common foods bought at the grocery store are like this. Just consider a white potato—it is toxic until cooked. Likewise, cashews and raw spinach should be consumed in moderation due to oxalic-acid content. You'll want to learn how to prepare each plant safely to maximize the nutritional value for you and your family. In Chapter 4, on the health section of the profile, I list cautions and preparation steps to enhance safety. However, please combine my research with your own for extra safety. Additionally, I mention historical, folk-healing uses for many plants, but this does not mean the plant will cure or heal an ailment. Please always consult a physician.

Safety is among the most important considerations when creating a food forest. I've had friends visit my garden and pop berries or greens in their mouths without asking me what they were. They did not know what they were eating, which is extremely dangerous! Enthusiasm is great, but a healthy dose of caution is so much safer. I have a young son, so I am very cautious about what I allow in my food forest and how I prepare food for my family. Please do the same for you and your family's safety. I've had mom friends say, "Are you growing ackee? I've heard it's a staple crop in Jamaica." Ackee is delicious and beautiful but is also associated with child fatalities. I have a young, curious child, so that is one crop I will not be adding. Ackee has to be carefully cooked to be made safe and is just one example of many you can find in the cautionary notes of the Chapter 4 profiles.

Food-processing methods that can lower toxicity risk are peeling, drying, grinding, soaking, boiling, cooking, fermenting, and roasting.[9] Boiling and dumping the water (i.e., blanching) is really effective at reducing most environmental contaminants and antinutrients, including lectins, tannins, protease inhibitors, and oxalic acid.[10] Most toxins are water-soluble. For instance, seeds, grains, and beans should be presoaked (water discarded) and then boiled, cooked, or roasted to make the nutrients more available and to decrease antinutrients like phytic acid.[11]

If a plant is safe to eat raw, then always thoroughly rinse and wash it because there may be mold, insects, or bird droppings that aren't easily seen. Wash produce by soaking 15 minutes in 1:1 solution of vinegar and water to remove parasites and pathogens, like mold or salmonella. Follow with a rinse. Thorough washing of plants before consumption will also remove some of the metal (like lead!) deposited on leaves through air, water, or soil contamination.[12]

START WITH LEVEL 1: LOW-RISK PLANTS

In Chapter 4, the plant profiles have a color-coded dot in the upper-right corner: green for Level 1—no known health risks and easy to cultivate; yellow for Level 2—some known health risks or cultivation challenges, such as being dioecious; or red for Level 3—known

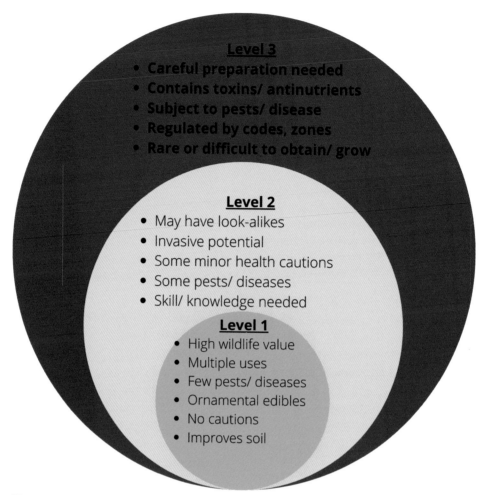

Level 3
- **Careful preparation needed**
- **Contains toxins/ antinutrients**
- **Subject to pests/ disease**
- **Regulated by codes, zones**
- **Rare or difficult to obtain/ grow**

Level 2
- May have look-alikes
- Invasive potential
- Some minor health cautions
- Some pests/ diseases
- Skill/ knowledge needed

Level 1
- High wildlife value
- Multiple uses
- Few pests/ diseases
- Ornamental edibles
- No cautions
- Improves soil

Figure 3.1. Levels and Color Codes Referenced in Chapter Four

health risks and knowledge, careful preparation, and cautious cultivation needed. I suggest prioritizing mostly Level 1 plants for your first 20 crops and then integrating Level 2 and Level 3 plants once your skill and confidence grow. Figure 3.1 puts these levels into a visual guide.

The easiest way to introduce Level 1 plants into the food forest is to buy them from a grocer, eat portions, and then regrow them. As Michael Neimes, a Florida food forester in a hydric hammock and wetland, explains, "Learn what you can grow from the grocery store. Sweet potatoes, malanga, tomato—a lot of plants can be grown cheaper buying from the grocery store."[13] Other examples of garden starter plants include pineapple, which can be regrown from the green tops, and shallots, which can be regrown from the bulb. Additional crops that can be grown from the grocery store aisle are pigeon pea, chia seed, rosemary, thyme, mint, sage, ginger, turmeric, nopal, sugarcane, lemongrass, jackfruit, and sunchoke. Finding international grocery stores may provide a wider selection of produce that can grow in your area. Also, keeping a small hydroponic in the kitchen can help you propagate quickly. This can be as simple as putting mint cuttings in a glass of water (called the Kratky method). For a more formal system, simply buy a $20 fish tank bubbler or aerator, and place it in a tupperware container with drilled holes in the top for plants to fit down into the aerated water. Keep the hydroponic by a bright, ideally southern window or add a growth light. Many plants root quickly that way.

When moving beyond Level 1 plants, though, understanding risk is important. For example, a mango tree is a Level 2 plant because some people are allergic to both the sap and pollen and the plant may suffer from fungal diseases in Florida. I bought my property with 25 mature mango trees established onsite. If I am not careful in spring, I am one itchy and blotchy mama because I am so allergic! I wish I had known mango was in the poison ivy family earlier, but I do love the fruit (carefully washed of all sap, of course), and the cooling shade the mature trees offer is so delightful. Chaya is a Level 3 plant and requires boiling to remove toxins, but it should not be boiled in aluminum pans because a toxic broth forms.

Safe preservation of food is equally important. Many crops grown in a food forest are not in the grocery store because they don't travel well. Quickly perishable or poor shelf life means you'll want to quickly dehydrate, can, freeze, and freeze-dry harvests to maintain year-round supplies and avoid mold, indoor fruit flies, and other annoyances. The Chapter 4 plant profiles reference preparation and storage methods. Lonny Reid, in a Zone 9b, two-acre, high and dry (oaks and pines) food forest, describes, "[W]e eat from our farm at every meal. . . . [P]robably 50% of our food comes from here or is bartered from other local farmers."[14] Yet Lonny believes that he could eat much more than this percentage, but harvesting and preparing is a "time issue, with more time to harvest and prepare, we would definitely be eating more, . . . but . . . we're getting that under control so more and more of our diets are home grown."[15]

His wisdom suggests the importance of scheduling harvests and food preparation on a weekly, if not daily, basis. That way, we can eat more of the nutritious food we are growing, saving ourselves money and maximizing health benefits.

SOIL AMENDMENT AND COMPOSTING

Maximizing nutrition by consuming fresh produce is a goal easily achieved in a food forest with a bit of practice. Amending the soil can improve nutrients available to plants and therefore make the food you are eating more nutritious. I "lasagna compost," meaning I layer food scraps, cardboard, and manure or mulch on top of weeds to amend soil and prepare it for planting. I keep a five-gallon bucket by the trash and add food scraps throughout the day as I meal prep. Once a week, I dump the kitchen scraps on weeds, cover them with cardboard, and bury the cardboard with mulch. Thick paper bags, brown corrugated cardboard, and mulch are an effective weed barrier while also preserving moisture and soil nutrients.[16] Large cardboard from appliance stores or agricultural or farm stores are especially efficient. Avoid glossy, highly printed, waxed, or otherwise coated cardboard, paperboard, and papers.

This lasagna-composting technique can build remarkable soils quickly because it helps restore nutrients.[17] Most compost qualifies as a fertilizer because it is rich in N-P-K (nitrogen, phosphorous, and potassium).[18] Nitrogen, phosphorous, and potassium are considered the three mineral elements most plants need to grow[19]:

- Nitrogen promotes leaf growth. Add manure, chop and drop, and mulch with leaf litter.

- Phosphorous encourages seeding and fruiting. It also encourages root growth and disease resistance. Sources include hair, bone meal, nuts, and beans.
- Potassium makes plants more vigorous and resilient to weather, like wind. The stalks become more rigid. Sources include banana peels, coffee grounds, and hardwood ashes.

Today's US gardeners collectively spend more than $500 million each year on special soils. Making your own by composting is well worth the savings! Plants prefer soil that's every bit as alive as they are, and compost soil outperforms even potting soil in research studies.[20]

Compost anything that can decompose, like leftover fruit, peelings, coffee grounds, leaves, and eggshells.[21] If you cook often and eat at home, then your kitchen will produce a surprising bounty of compostables that will enrich the soil. Companies can also contribute to your efforts for free! For example, Starbucks promotes recycling through Grounds for Your Garden and will gift you spent coffee grounds.[22]

SAFETY WITH SOIL AND PLANT INTERACTION

Mike Elson, a food forester in Zone 9b and a soil scientist and agronomist with decades of growing experience, recommends you "get your soil tested for nutrient levels. It is definitely not uncommon for Florida soils to be deficient in some of the important nutrients, micro-nutrients and trace minerals plants need for optimum growth, health, and pest resistance."[23] You can have soil tested through your Cooperative Extension Service or by Soil Testing or Agricultural Colleges, sometimes for free. If you are actively amending soil with mulch, manure, and compost, then the three-year mark is a good time to have a soil test.[24]

Nutrients are not the only consideration when it comes to soil, though. As you get started, you may want to evaluate the site's history. For instance, is the food-forest location a former industrial area? Were any onsite buildings painted prior to 1970, when lead paint was common? If you cannot afford testing and simply want to err on the side of caution, then plant large trees, which remove large quantities of toxins. Also prioritize high-growing fruit and nuts with thick skins and shells, which typically harbor fewer contaminants.[25] Deciduous trees also help to amend the soil quickly through leaf mulch. For tubers and tender greens planted near buildings, establish nontoxic, geotextile bottom layers in raised beds filled with soil from certified sources.

AIR CIRCULATION AND HEALTH-RISK PREVENTION

When it comes to health and safety in a food forest, one little-known fact is that plants, animals, and humans can share fungal diseases. Don't walk through the garden when plants are wet, such as in early morning with dew or after a rain or irrigation, and avoid walking barefoot on moist mulch. Many diseases need water to spread, so allow plants to dry out completely between waterings when possible and avoid watering in severely cold weather.[26] To avoid watering out in the food forest, consider simply planting nurse plants, like bananas, as edible irrigation; these plants sop up excess water and then release it to other plants via root systems in times of drought. This limits moisture on leaves caused by sprinkler systems.

Plant bananas throughout the food forest, but be sure to prune them regularly, and remove decomposing leaves to limit disease.

Another element of health and safety relates to preventing injury. Gardening is highly physical. Although creating a food forest is wonderful exercise, you may want to take extra care to prevent injury, such as by exercising outside of gardening time to build dynamic strength. Stretching can help prevent injury, as well. My husband and I do 10 minutes of yoga using YouTube tutorials nearly every morning, and I do four simple stretches each evening before bed. Thankfully, we have not had any serious pulls, strains, or injuries while working in the garden despite the fact we are out there *a lot*.

Also, when moving mulch, consider covering your nose and mouth with a cloth mask to prevent inhaling mold spores, which can cause congestion and other symptoms.[27] While working with compost or mulch does more to improve your health than hurt it, there are a few potential health threats that fall into two broad categories: skin and lung issues. For example, consider farmer's lung, histoplasmosis, or legionnaire's disease. To prevent these issues, wear a mask when moving dusty mulch or compost, and change clothes immediately after; also consider dampening compost to limit airborne spores. Skin issues include paronychia or tetanus. To prevent these issues, wear gloves without holes, and replace gloves if they get wet with dry ones. Also, get regular medical checkups.

Additionally, in hot, humid climates, ears can suffer congestion much like a nose, so make a point to keep your ears especially dry to prevent issues.[28] I swab my ears with a bit of coconut oil before moving mulch to help trap dust and prevent it from getting embedded. When planting or harvesting, immediately disinfect any cuts. Cover cuts before handling dirt or mulch. Also, wash hands and tools often by keeping a spray bottle filled with alcohol, and giving tools and gloves a squirt before moving on.[29] Finally, leave garden shoes outside when possible. Appendix C has a checklist of safety items that can be used when training a team to create a permaculture garden in settings with higher liability, such as at schools and businesses.

SUMMARY TIPS TO SAVE EFFORT

Although there are safety considerations, starting a food forest is a fun adventure. Enjoy the process! With planning, the time and effort to create a food forest can be minimal.[30] The health advantages far outweigh the risks. As you dive into the process, I hope the following summary of tips from the previous chapters help you to get started efficiently:

- Plant trees and large shrubs first.
- Select native edibles that host high numbers of soldier bugs to prevent pests (e.g., oaks).
- Prioritize 20 Level 1 crops to start.
- Develop a schedule to harvest and cook. Stock the fridge on a specific day.
- Root cuttings in water after you harvest to increase your crop count.
- Learn to cook with crops safely based on research.
- Taste small amounts of new foods, and wait 24 hours to ensure you don't have allergies.

- Dedicate direct sun to staple starches and carbohydrates. Most leafy greens like part shade.
- Plant evergreen trees and shrubs along north property edges to block cold winter wind.
- If near the coast, plant windbreaks (e.g., bamboo) in the direction of prevailing winds.
- Locate short plants on the south side of tall ones to create a "sun trap."
- Utilize all nine layers of a food forest to create a polyculture within small "zones."
- Use trellises as arches over mowed paths for vines.
- Space plants with chop-and-drop pruning for increased airflow and speed drying and to prevent fungal diseases.[31]

4

200 PLANTS FOR YOUR FOOD FOREST

Plant Profiles

The love of nature, plants, and delicious foods are often a few reasons people create a food forest. But the most significant reason is enjoyment. Watching a food forest mature is so gratifying and fulfilling! That said, this chapter is the fun part for most gardeners. This chapter will help you streamline your food forest. Plants are in alphabetical order by the plant's common name to keep the language reader-friendly. The plants included are those vetted by fellow Floridian food foresters throughout the state. Some plants in the profiles are very aggressive, invasive, or even noxious, and I mention if a plant is prohibited or a Category 1, meaning the plant has had a negative environmental impact. Some examples of highly edible Category 1 invasives in Florida include mimosa (*Albizia julibrissin*), winged yam (*Dioscorea alata*), Surinam cherry (*Eugenia uniflora*), water spinach (*Ipomoea aquatic*), sapodilla (*Manilkara zapota*), sword fern (*Nephrolepis cordifolia*), strawberry guava (*Psidium cattleianum*), guava (*Psidium guajava*), and kudzu (*Pueraria Montana*, var. *lobata*). Many of these are highlighted in the plant profiles.

Because these plants may show up in the food forest on their own, it's important to know them. Also, some well-meaning food foresters plant highly aggressive crops or even Category 1 invasives not knowing the impact. For instance, I know many people who plant hoja santa without knowing that it should be contained to a pot in an enclosed area or that tindora should be planted indoors or be the sterile variety. Likewise, kudzu is highly nutritious and edible and will likely show up on the property without being planted. Digging the tubers to eat is a very effective means of controlling its spread.

Three symbols found in the upper-right corner of each plant profile are important to know:

- **Florida Natives, Host Plants, and/or Cultivars:** indicated by a Florida peninsula symbol
- **Historical Staples:** indicated by a shield with a star in the middle
- **Safety Colors:**

  Level 1 = green
  Level 2 = yellow
  Level 3 = red

Each plant profile also includes a simple recipe with a maximum of six ingredients. I prioritized cross-cultural recipes. Around the world and throughout history, three nutrient-dense foods have sustained people and maintained health: bread, soup, and ferments, so the profiles feature these foods.[1] Soups are an easy way to cook seasonally and are a part of every culture's diet.[2] In terms of bread and ferments, I frequently mention "sourdough starter." Sourdough is a natural leavening, and the process has been a part of human history for thousands of years. For generations, people have begun each day with the prayer "Give us this day our daily bread" in reference to wholesome sourdough.[3] Sourdough bread is considered more nutritious and less-allergy-provoking because the fermentation process can remove antinutrients, reduce allergenic qualities, and promote better digestion.[4] Sourdough bread also can have less gluten (1% of normal white bread).[5] Feed the starter what you have in the garden, whether it's boiled and pureed cassava, green banana, pigeon pea, or coconut. Just keep it alive by pureeing the starch or carbohydrate source with an equal amount of water and then stirring it into the starter. The following is an easy sourdough recipe:

> Add 1 cup of flour and 1 cup of water to a mason jar. Mix. Cover with cotton cloth. Airborne yeast will colonize. Stir daily for uniform fermentation. After 3 days, the starter is ready. Loosely cover with a lid and store in the fridge. Feed once a week or more frequently if you bake often. *Note:* Never use a metal container to store ferments. The yeast produces carbon dioxide and alcohol, which can corrode the metal and contaminate the starter.

Each recipe in this chapter is self-referencing, meaning all ingredients can grow in a Florida food forest. I strongly believe that if there is any place in the United States that could become a new blue zone, it is a community of Floridian food forests. I've decided that living according to blue-zone tenets is a worthwhile, lifelong experiment. Although my original goal with creating my garden was simply to foster sustainable food, so far, the friendship part has been the most fun and unexpected reward! The food forest is already helping me to live a more full and meaningful life, and I am so grateful for that. I hope the same for you and your family. Happy gardening!

Achira
Canna Edulis

HARDINESS ZONES: 7 TO 13

An easy-to-grow, high yielding, attractive, adaptable, perennial with edible rhizomes (raw or cooked). In one of the most popular ornamental plant families, Cannaceae! Resembles a small banana. Attractive bright red to orange flowers attract butterflies, bats and hummingbirds. A traditional staple food! Rhizomes starch yields range from 12% to 16%. Makes great noodles! Pretty red flowers can be cut for flower arrangements. A fast windbreak, hedge & shade plant!

SIZE h*w	SUN	SOIL	WATER	EDIBLE
6ft*1ft	full to partial	deep; neutral to acidic	continuously moist	roots, seeds, leaves, sprouts

PROPAGATION METHODS

- SEEDS: <u>Not recommended.</u> Hybrid: not true to seed; reverts to small rhizomes.
- RHIZOMES: Divide clump in spring when temperatures are at least 78F; grown from vegetative clones for large starchy tubers.

RECIPE

BAKED ACHIRA: Boil roots for 45 min or until very soft; slit the skin and scoop out the shiny, starchy content. Add oil, salt, & pepper to taste.

Alternatively, puree boiled, peeled roots & dehydrate at 115 F to form a "gel sheet." Fold, and cut into noodles.

CULINARY USE

Roots
Harvestable in 5 months. Color varies - often white. Refrigerate & eat within 3 weeks. Can be steamed or baked like a potato, formed into cakes, noodles or dehydrated & made into a powder to thicken foods. Easily digestible. Rhizomes grow for years without becoming woody.

Young shoots
Cooked and eaten as a green vegetable. High in potassium and protein.

Seeds
Immature seeds are ground and made into tortillas. Rarely sets seed. NOTE: If seeds are prolific, the type is not edulis.

Leaves
Leaves used as food wraps (e.g., tamale) or plates and can be steamed; contain 10% protein.

CULTURAL SIGNIFICANCE

- Andean cultures buried it with the dead in graves for 3500 years. Food source during the Great Chinese Famine of the 1950s-1960s
- Pollinator plant. High nitrogen fodder
- In Thailand, cannas are a traditional gift for Father's Day
- Leaf fiber used for paper making or to wrap parcels. Seeds used as buck shot, for purple dye, as beads in jewelry or for music rattles

CAUTIONS & CONSIDERATIONS

Health
No known hazards. Taxonomy debate: Canna indica is considered "conspecific" (the same species - only wilder & more invasive). Syn. C. discolor. May cross-pollinate with ornamentals.

Pests
Minor pests: Slugs, aphids, fungus "rust", virus spots.

Landscape design
Excellent green manure & erosion control. Able to fit sixteen plants in a six-by-six ft block; aggregate yield is high. Compare with Canna coccinea & Canna 'Musifolia.'

Adam's Needle

Yucca filamentosa

HARDINESS ZONES: 4 TO 10

This evergreen, Florida native is very drought resistant, thriving even with neglect and competition. Low maintenance and fast-growing. Very ornamental & free flowering. Butterflies & hummingbirds flock. Striking sword-like leaves & dramatic hanging, bell-shaped flowers. Native Americans relied on the plant, eating the flowers, stalks, and fruits. In the Asparagaceae family.

SIZE h*w	SUN	SOIL	WATER	EDIBLE
4ft*2ft	full to part	poor - OK	drought tolerant	flower, fruit, stem

PROPAGATION METHODS

- SEEDS: Germinate at 82-90F. Pre-soak seed for 24 hours in warm water.
- DIVISION: Can be propagated easily from basal offsets.

RECIPE

YUCCA PUREE: Pick the fruit when 4 inches long. Wash and spread on a baking sheet. Roast at 400 F for 20 to 30 minutes, or until soft. Cool. Pull apart/ peel back the sections. Scrape out the inside and separate from the seeds. Puree and use as a side dish (similar to applesauce).

CULTURAL SIGNIFICANCE

- Attracts hummingbirds. Larval host for Yucca Giant-Skipper and Cofaqui Giant-Skipper
- In African communities, leaves were tied above doorways to protect homes & graves
- Leaf fiber used for making tinder, hats, shoes, paint brushes, ropes, cloth, baskets, paper, mats. Listed in Thomas Jefferson's Garden Book for garden rope
- Pulpy root mashed with water for soap; contains saponins

CULINARY USE

Fruit

Large and fleshy. Most often roasted until tender. A somewhat sweet, molasses or fig-like flavor. The fruit can also be dried and ground into a sweet meal. The pulp, sweetened, can be used for pies or dried into a paste or fruit leather sheet. Remove seeds prior to eating.

Stem

Cooked/ roasted like asparagus or baked into bread.

Flowers

Often boiled and added to eggs. Used as a flavoring in salads. The edible flowers taste somewhat like bitter artichoke and can be used raw/fresh in salads, cooked in soups or stews, or roasted. Only eat the petals. Watch out for moth larvae as it is uses yucca as a host. Summer blooms.

CAUTIONS & CONSIDERATIONS

Health

No known adverse health effects. Not to be confused with "yuca"/ cassava. Leaves are spiny.

Pests

No serious insect or disease problems.

Landscape design

Do not collect from the wild. May be protected. Will form a small colony over time from basal offsets. Compare with Yucca baccata, a related, highly edible plant; some varieties have variegated leaves.

African Basil

Ocimum kilimandscharicum × basilicum

HARDINESS ZONES: 10 TO 12+

As a cross between camphor and dark opal, this fast-growing basil is one of a few types which are perennial, towering as a woody shrub up to 5 feet tall. Use the rich, mellow anise flavor from leaves, stems, and flowers in pesto, salads, cocktails and more! Has a reputation as a pest repellent! Attracts bees, & beneficial soldier bugs like ladybugs.

SIZE h*w	SUN	SOIL	WATER	EDIBLE
5ft*4ft	full	sandy; well-drained	average	flower, leaves, stems

PROPAGATION METHODS

- CUTTINGS: Sterile variety. Never goes to seed. Roots readily in water - cut a 4-inch portion. Ideal temperature: 80F+. Take cuttings summer/ spring.

RECIPE

BASIL VINIAGRETTE: 1 cup African basil leaves, 1 tsp sea salt, 2 ½ cups oil, 1/4 c vinegar, 1 tbs honey.

Boil 6 c of water; drop basil in, stir, blanch for 45 sec, drain, & squeeze out water. Puree basil with salt, adding oil progressively. Add vinegar and then honey. Store refrigerated one week.

CULTURAL SIGNIFICANCE

- Symbolism has opposing associations: love/hate, danger/ safety, & life/ death
- Basil is part of many religious traditions. The scorpion is historically associated with basil
- The British at one time used basil instead of a Bible upon which Hindu Indians would take an oath in a court of law
- Used in folk healing (e.g., as an anti-inflammatory and anti-microbial)

CULINARY USE

Leaves

Small leaves can be added whole to dishes or made into pesto. Harvest in the morning when the essential oils are strongest. To keep: chop, combine with olive oil in a food processor or mortar/pestle and freeze in ice cube trays; The leaves contain aromatic oils often extracted commercially.

Flowers

Flowers can be candied, added to sour cream for baked potatoes, floated in ice trays or added to ginger ale, champagne or white wine spritzers. Flowers do not need to be pinched back to keep the plant growing – it's sterile.

Stems

Non-woody stems and branches can be steeped in liquids for poached fruit, beverages, soups and meat.

CAUTIONS & CONSIDERATIONS

Health

Good source of vitamin K & A, iron, calcium. CAUTION: Use in moderation. Camphor and camphene in higher proportions – medicinal.

Pests

Subject to a variety of pests like Japanese beetles, grasshoppers, slugs, aphids, mites, whiteflies, nematodes.

Landscape design

Efficient rooting system may prevent soil erosion. In spring, prune back dead wood to promote growth.

African Marigold

Tagetes erecta

HARDINESS ZONES: 2 TO 11

Long consumed worldwide for culinary & medicinal purposes. A low maintenance annual that self-seeds, behaving as a perennial. Used for its root secretions - insecticidal effect against nematodes, & slugs. Petals said to repel insects when grown amongst crops. Unaffected by summer heat & often blooms throughout the year for pollinators. In the Asteraceae family.

SIZE h*w	SUN	SOIL	WATER	EDIBLE
3ft*3ft	full to partial	sand, clay - OK	drought tolerant	flowers

PROPAGATION METHODS

- SEEDS: Germinates at 70 - 75F within 2 weeks. Sprouts readily from seed; simply cast on bare or mulched ground. Flowers within 3 months.

RECIPE

MARIGOLD TEA: Wash and rinse 1 tbs of petals. Place petals in 1 cup of lukewarm water using a tea infuser or cheesecloth for two hours. Strain out the solids and refrigerate for up to 3 days. Sweeten to taste.

NOTE: Considered medicinal.

CULINARY USE

Flowers
The petals eaten once separated from sepals. A yellow dye obtained from petals used as a saffron substitute and food coloring. Used in lettuce salads and soups to add color and flavor. Pungent, bitter, astringent taste. The flowers are rich in carotenoids. Always wash flowers well before eating. Introduce one flower at a time to identify any potential allergies. Used as garnishes on cakes or cupcakes, baked in cookies, preserved in oils or vinegars or tossed in salads. Marigold extract is used mainly in western Europe as a yellow to orange food colorant in salad dressings, ice cream, dairy products, soft drinks, bakery products, jams and confectionery.

CULTURAL SIGNIFICANCE

- Represented in Aztec art (e.g. monolith of Coyolxauhqui). In Mexican festivities (Day of the Dead) used to decorate altars and tombs; hence the name "flower of the dead." Used to wash corpses in Honduras; commonly planted in cemeteries
- Yellow dye from flowers. Ground petals added to poultry feed for good coloration of egg yolks
- Believed to have antioxidant & neuroprotective properties

CAUTIONS & CONSIDERATIONS

Health
No known health hazards. Consume in moderation. May contain phototoxic thiophene derivatives/ skin irritant. CAUTION: Not all Tagetes are edible. Identify carefully.

Pests
Susceptible to powdery mildew, leaf spot, and rots. Watch for spider mites or thrips.

Landscape design
Cultivar 'Inca Orange' gained the Royal Horticultural Society's Award of Garden Merit. Compare with Mexican Tarragon (Tagetes lucida)- high edibility.

African Potato Mint

Coleus rotundifolius

HARDINESS ZONES: 10 TO 12+

Known as a kaffir potato. The egg-shaped tubers of this perennial groundcover are nutritious and productive. This plant is said to offer household food security. An under-researched staple crop although it may need fermentation to enhance digestibility. An edible ornamental in the mint, Lamiacae family.

SIZE h*w	SUN	SOIL	WATER	EDIBLE
1ft*3ft	partial	sandy loam	moist	tuber, leaves

PROPAGATION METHODS

- CUTTINGS: Roots readily in water.
- TUBERS: Plant at the beginning of wet season
- SEED: Doesn't typically produce seeds but germinates best around 75F.

RECIPE

BOILED POTATO MINT: Wash and scrub tubers - clean off any dirt. Boil for 30 minutes or until very soft. Let cool. Peel off skin. Toss peeled tuber in oil and salt to taste.

Alternatively, puree peeled, boiled potato mint and feed to a sourdough starter to increase digestibility. Bake as a bread or pancake.

CULTURAL SIGNIFICANCE

- Also called Plectranthus rotundifolius, Solenostemon rotundifolius, or Coleus tuberosus
- In Africa: improves nutrition and income and reduces food insecurity at the household level
- Efforts by National Root Crops Research Institute (NRCRI) in Nigeria, to boost production
- Intercropped with groundnut, yam, okra, and sorghum

CULINARY USE

Tuber

Takes 5-7 months from planting to harvest the tubers. Tubers are varying shapes and sizes. Typically boiled, but may also be roasted, baked, or fried. Cooked with spices, but can also be roasted or fried and eaten as relish. May have a subtle mint essence but generally the tubers are bland like a potato. Flour is milled from dried tuber. When there is too much rain, the tubers tend to split - then difficult to peel. Plant on inclines to aid drainage in rainy seasons. The white, starchy, slightly aromatic tubers become dark with age. Refrigerate after digging. Consume within a week. Best consumed in small quantities.

Leaves
Cooked as a vegetable but considered medicinal.

CAUTIONS & CONSIDERATIONS

Health
CAUTION: Literature provides few nutritional details. Numerous taxonomic problems in the naming. Benign but somewhat indigestible - like corn.

Pests
Various caterpillar species feed on the leaves. Pests are rarely of economic importance.

Landscape design
Piling earth around base of plants encourages tuber development. Foliage shades out the competing species. Compare with C. esculentus and C. edulis.

Agastache
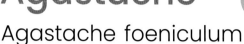
Agastache foeniculum

HARDINESS ZONES: 4 TO 10

Also called, Anise Hyssop or Lavender Hyssop. Popular as an ornamental but has a strong history in traditional uses such as an herbal/ medicinal tea. When crushed, its leaves give off a distinct odor of anise. Deadhead spent flowers to promote additional bloom. Easily started from seed and often blooms the first year. Adds eye-catching, vertical lines to the landscape. In the mint family, Lamiaceae.

SIZE h*w	SUN	SOIL	WATER	EDIBLE
3ft*1ft	full	well-draining	drought tolerant	flowers, leaves, seeds

PROPAGATION METHODS

- SEEDS: Germinates at 68-75F in 1 - 3 months. Sow early spring; barely cover seeds.
- CUTTINGS: Basal cuttings of young shoots in spring. Roots within 3 weeks.

RECIPE

HYSSOP TEA: Steep 2-3 tbs of bruised fresh leaves in 2 c of steaming hot water for 5 minutes covered. Strain and drink hot or iced.

Alternatively, triple the quantity of leaves to make concentrated version. Freeze in ice cube trays to infuse water and make tea on demand.

CULTURAL SIGNIFICANCE

- Flowers are attractive to bees, hummingbirds and butterflies. Goldfinches and other birds may feed on the seeds
- Dried leaves can be added to potpourris
- Used in folk healing & by Native Americans to treat coughs & diarrhea. Poultice of leaves & stems used to treat burns/ wounds. Tea used to induce sweating to reduce fever/ fight against colds; believed good for heart health with antimicrobial & antifungal properties

CULINARY USE

Flowers & Leaves

Leaves and flowers enjoyed raw or cooked. A sweet aniseed flavor. Good in salads. Used to flavor cooked foods, especially acid fruits. Aromatic leaves can be used to make herbal teas or jellies. The best time to harvest leaves & flowers is when the flowers are just past full bloom, as the oil content is the highest at that time, but they can be used at any time. May be used to decorate cakes. Research indicates that freeze-drying is the best solution to prolong the shelf life of the flowers. A great substitute for tarragon, fennel, anise, and chervil. Flowers have a milder anise flavor than the leaves.

Seeds

Seeds can be added to cookies or muffins.

CAUTIONS & CONSIDERATIONS

Health

No known adverse health effects. Leaves may produce a drying effect in the mouth and so cannot be eaten in quantity.

Pests

No significant pest problems; crown/root rot may develop in poorly drained soils.

Landscape design

Plants will spread by rhizomes and will easily self seed in optimum growing conditions. Grow in dappled light in zones higher than 9a.

Agave
Agave tequilana

HARDINESS ZONES: 9B TO 10B

Also called "Blue Agave" & considered by some to be the finest agave in the world. An evergreen perennial offering a low glycemic index sweetener! Living up to 50 years but dies after flowering. A rapid grower & prolific off-setter with many permaculture advantages. A staple crop (roasted heart is pure starch like banana, taro, cassava, or yam). Low maintenance! These plants need little or no maintenance. Gorgeous bluish leaves. In the Asparagaceae family.

SIZE h*w	SUN	SOIL	WATER	EDIBLE
6ft*6ft	full to partial	poor - OK	drought tolerant	stem/ sap

PROPAGATION METHODS

- SEEDS: Germinates at 77F+. Takes years for flowering to occur; plant dies after flowering.
- PUPS: Plants are surculose/ create suckers around the base of the parent plant.

RECIPE

ICECREAM: ½ cup agave syrup, ½ cup coconut milk, 3 frozen ripe bananas, ¼ tsp vanilla extract, ¼ tsp. sea salt.

Blend all ingredients and serve immediately. Alternatively, freeze in an ice cube tray and re-blend prior to serving.

CULTURAL SIGNIFICANCE

- Pollinated by bats
- Tequila is made from a cultivar of Agave tequilana called 'Weber Azul'
- Suggested as a potential source of ethanol (biofuel)
- Soft leaf fiber known as 'Jarsia' used for yarn
- The nectar is 1.4 to 1.6 times sweeter than sugar; used as a vegan alternative to honey
- Some reports that flowers, nectar, immature flowering stem & center of rosette is edible

CULINARY USE

Stem/ Sap
To harvest agave syrup: Leaves are cut off to reveal the base of the plant 1/2 above and 1/2 below the ground. The agave base/ "pineapple" is then dug up & heated to no more than 118F in a giant "pressure cooker" to release juices. The base is then chopped up, and the liquid filtered and simmered into a syrup. This liquid is extracted before the plant flowers but after the plant has been growing for seven to fourteen years.

NOTE: Syrup produced from several species (e.g., A. tequilana & A. salmiana). A. salmiana nectar extraction differs. Stalk is cut off before it fully grows, creating a hole in center of plant which fills with liquid ("aguamiel"). The liquid is collected daily, heated & concentrated into syrup.

CAUTIONS & CONSIDERATIONS

Health
CAUTION: Spines on leaves/ tips. Blue agave syrup is not recommended for people with fructose intolerance. Excessive consumption of agave syrup can result in insulin resistance.

Pests
Agave snout weevil (A. americana is more susceptible). Clonal propagation results in more disease vulnerability.

Landscape design
200+ agave species. Compare with endangered Florida native, Agave neglecta (wild century plant).

Aibika

Abelmoschus manihot

HARDINESS ZONES: 7A TO 10

A robust shrub quickly growing over 10ft in height. Easy to propagate. Relatively disease-resistant and highly nutritious! One of the highest yielding leafy vegetables known. A good vegetable protein with vital micro-nutrients! Considered by some to be the world's most nutritious leafy vegetable. Recommended by the World Health Organization as a good baby-food: young leaves are easy to mash. In the okra/ hibiscus family, Malvaceae. A good container plant!

SIZE h*w	SUN	SOIL	WATER	EDIBLE
6ft+*3ft	full to partial	neutral to alkaline	continuously moist	buds, leaves, sprouts

PROPAGATION METHODS

- SEEDS: Germinates at 80-86F in 2 weeks if nicked or abraded and soaked overnight. Seeds ripen from August to October.
- CUTTINGS: Stem cuttings root in soil or water.

RECIPE

EGG DROP SOUP: Sauté 2 c mushrooms, 1/2 c chopped scallions, & 1 tbsp fresh grated ginger in 1 tbsp oil. Add 2 c aibika. Wilt covered. Add 4 c water (or coconut water) with 1 tsp sea salt. Bring to a boil over medium-high heat. Whisk two eggs in a bowl. Turn off stove. Stir soup with wooden spoon to swirl. While swirling, pour in whisked eggs in a thin, slow stream. Cover and allow to cool 5 min.

CULTURAL SIGNIFICANCE

- The most important leafy vegetable in New Guinea and Irian Jaya
- Good source of folate, and essential amino acids. Used in folk healing to increase lactation in new mothers
- Used to make Japanese neri, a starchy substance used in making washi or handmade paper similar to Korea hanji
- Seeds used to make perfume - musky smell

CULINARY USE

Flowers
Flower buds eaten raw or cooked.

Leaves
Short succulent tips are usually cooked but can be eaten fresh. Sweet and mucilaginous. Leaves become slimy upon cooking and are used as a lettuce or spinach substitute. High in vitamins A and C, and iron. Slightly older leaves are best steamed, boiled, fried, baked or added as a tasty addition to an omelette. Ideally served with or cooked in coconut cream, which increases the uptake of betacarotene and conversion to vitamin A. Large soft leaves can be used to wrap food, similar to grape vine or cabbage leaves. Can produce up to 60 tons of leaves per hectare. Environmental factors affect micronutrient content.

CAUTIONS & CONSIDERATIONS

Health
No known adverse health effects.

Pests
Susceptible to root nematodes. Like all malvaceous plants, aibika is very attractive for insects.

Landscape design
Cut to ground in winter to rejuvenate. Varied leaf shape, color, production & flavor but usually palmate & 4 in across. Cultivars include: Kiko's clump, Chief Kubo's Prize, & Autie Lilli's/ South Sea Salad Tree. Compare with Common Mallow (Malva neglecta).

Akee
Blighia sapida

HARDINESS ZONES: 10 TO 12

A very decorative, vigorous species. The foliage and bright red fruit of ackee are beautiful. In Jamaica, Akee is one of the most common backyard trees and is the national fruit of Jamaica. Extreme caution is needed when using the fruit through. Deadly poisonous if improperly prepared. Yet, considered a staple as it is over 16% protein and over 16% fat - equivalent to soybean. Technically, it's a fruit, but it's cooked and used as a protein vegetable. In the soapberry/ Sapindaceae family.

SIZE h*w	SUN	SOIL	WATER	EDIBLE
65ft*65ft	full to partial	poor - OK	drought-tolerant	fruit

PROPAGATION METHODS

- SEEDS: Germinates at 75-80F. Propagates easily by seed. Fruits in 3 – 4 years.
- CUTTINGS: Roots quickly; yields in 1 – 2 years.

RECIPE

SAUTEED ACKEE: Select firm, fresh, ripe "cheese" ackee naturally split open on tree. Remove seeds & jacket/ all attaching tissue & veins. Simmer half an hour in salted water. Remove from heat when flesh turns from cream to bright yellow. Strain. Sauté in oil with diced onions, tomatoes, peppers. Top with a sprinkle of cinnamon, salt & pepper to taste.

CULTURAL SIGNIFICANCE

- Brought to Jamaica in 1793 as slave food
- Outlawed in Trinidad after fatalities
- U.S. imports banned in 1970s but resumed in 2000 after safety issues addressed
- Green fruits produce lather in water, used for laundering. Seeds used for oil content, and the jacket valued for potash content when burned; ashes used in making soap
- Fragrant flowers used as decoration, cologne

CULINARY USE

Fruit
Pick ONLY after fruit naturally opens (e.g., sometimes called awned). When ripe, all chambers reveal shiny seeds with the fleshy/ edible aril. All parts of unripe & overripe fruit are highly poisonous (hypoglycin A and B toxin). Red tissue & veins attaching aril to seed must be removed before eating. Arils are parboiled in salted water or milk, and often fried in butter. Ackee and saltfish is considered the unofficial Jamaican national dish. Often cooked with onions & tomatoes; added to stew with scallions & thyme; curried with rice. Two main tree varieties: "butter" – soft & yellow arils and "cheese" – hard & cream arils. Latter preferred: fruit retains shape in cooking. If harvested correctly & prepared properly, akee is nutritious & rich in fatty acids, vit A, & protein.

CAUTIONS & CONSIDERATIONS

Health
CAUTION: Negatively impacts human health. Toxic peptide, hypoglycine A, in the unripe aril; pink raphe is deadly toxic. Hypoglycin A, present in the aril, seed, base of aril - said to cause Jamaican vomiting sickness, encephalopathy in children, & death.

Pests
Fungal diseases, sooty mold, wilt disease, scale insects.

Landscape design
48 cultivars of ackee grouped as either "butter" or "cheese" types. Can withstand hurricane-winds. Ripens Dec-May.

Aloe Vera

Aloe barbadensis miller

HARDINESS ZONES: 9 TO 11

Also called First Aid Plant. In the Asphodelaceae (Liliaceae) family. Popular as an edible, medicinal & ornamental; even used for hair gel & was reportedly used by Cleopatra as part of her beauty routine! An essential ingredient in food, cosmetics & pharmaceuticals. Cultivation is expected to expand worldwide. An economically significant plant! Promising in medical, dental and health care fields. Wonderful houseplant for beginners.

SIZE h*w	SUN	SOIL	WATER	EDIBLE
2ft*3ft	partial/ dappled	poor - OK; well-draining	drought tolerant	leaf gel (avoid latex)

PROPAGATION METHODS

- DIVISIONS: Divide offsets in spring. Produces dense rosettes with creeping rhizomes that spread from basal offshoots colonizing areas.
- SEEDS: Germinate at 75-78F. Sprouts in 4 weeks.

RECIPE

ALOE VERA GLAZE: Wash a large aloe leaf, cut off spikey ends & filet it. Scrape out 1/3c of clear gel; avoid colored content. Soak in water to leech latex. Strain, rinse gently. Puree with 1 c distilled water. (1:3 ratio of aloe to water). Paint on 3c of fruit such as in a tart to add shine & to help preserve. Allow to air dry. Refrigerate tart up to 1 week.

CULTURAL SIGNIFICANCE

- Folk healing/ medicinal history dating back to 400 BC (e.g., as anti-inflammatory, laxative; to reduce blood glucose levels; topically for burns, acne, psoriasis & eczema; to stimulate immune system)
- Grown indoors to remove toxins from air
- In 2002, the U.S. FDA ruled to remove aloe from laxative products due to lack of safety data
- Considered the 'plant of immortality' according to Ancient Egyptians

CULINARY USE

Leaf Gel

Aloe vera gel is used commercially as an ingredient in yogurts, smoothies, beverages, and some desserts like jellies and ice cream. Increasingly used to preserve fruit tarts as an edible coating to improve the appearance (shine), as a gas exchange barrier, to promote moisture, serve as an antimicrobial and antifungal layer, and therefore extend shelf life. Prevents browning in fruits and vegetables prone to oxidation. Preserves the quality and safety of fruits during cold storage.

Contains compounds such as polysaccharides, glucomannan, tannins, organic acids, minerals.

CAUTIONS & CONSIDERATIONS

Health
CAUTION: Aloe latex can be toxic. Leech in water. May be confused with inedible varieties (e.g., Aloe vera Chinensis). Avoid if pregnant or have a bleeding disorder. May interfere with certain medications.

Pests
Spider mites, mealy bugs, scale, and aphids.

Landscape design
May behave invasively. Nurse nearby species via arbuscular mycorrhiza (i.e., symbiosis granting access to nutrients in soil). Three years for harvestable size; yields 7 years.

Amaranth

Amaranthus caudatus

HARDINESS ZONES: 3 TO 11

Love-Lies-Bleeding cultivar is used as both a food crop and ornamental plant. A fast-growing crop with edible leaves harvestable within 50 days! With no frost, it behaves as a perennial. Showy summer color & hot weather spinach substitute. Offers a protein-packed grain which can be a gluten-free flour substitute! A dietary staple for over 6,000 years! Flowers have been used in food coloring. Beautiful in dried flower arrangements!! In the Amaranthaceae family.

SIZE h*w	SUN	SOIL	WATER	EDIBLE
4ft+*2ft	full	acidic, poor - OK; well-draining	drought tolerant	seed, leaves, stem

PROPAGATION METHODS

- SEEDS: Germinates at 68F-70F. Seeds ripen from August to September. Seed types for vegetable use have better tasting leaves than the grain types. Plant in spring.

RECIPE

POPPED AMARANTH: Cut off stalks, hang to dry. Once dry, roll crisp flowers between your hands massaging the seeds into a bucket. Blow off chuff. Soak overnight, drain, dry. Store excess.

Preheat pot over medium-high heat, add 3 tbs spoon of seeds in 1 tbs oil. Cover. Shake pot until all seeds pop. Continue in batches. Salt to taste.

CULTURAL SIGNIFICANCE

- Historical food source dating back to 4000 BC
- Zuni people ground flowerhead with seed into a fine meal & used to color ceremonial bread red
- "Protein complement" of amaranth grain surpasses wheat according to FAO/WHO
- Crushed leaves and blossoms are also moistened and rubbed on cheeks as rouge
- Seed oil used in sunscreen, lotion, lipstick, eye makeup

CULINARY USE

Leaves/ Stem
Cooked/ blanched as a spinach for 5 minutes, then strained to remove any oxalates or nitrate. Mild-flavored. Rich in vitamins and minerals. Crisp interior of large stems makes a tasty vegetable, eaten raw or cooked as an asparagus substitute. Used in pesto.

Seeds
Yields a nutritious staple grain. Easy to harvest: simply dry, thresh, winnow. Soak and discard water to remove saponins. Grind into flour, pop like popcorn, cook into a porridge, or make into granola. Gluten-free flour substitute! Easily replaces up to 75% of flour in recipes while still maintaining functional properties and flavor. Use for pie crusts, breading chicken, and in crackers.

CAUTIONS & CONSIDERATIONS

Health
CAUTION: Grow organically: nitrates in leaves when exposed to chemical fertilizers. Oxalic acid present.

Pests
Resilient: Aphids, leaf-chewing insects.

Landscape design
A. caudatus is a grain species adapted to tropical zones. A. hypochondriacus & A. cruentus also grown for grain. A. tricolor grown for the leaves. Celosia argentea, vegetable amaranth, is pest resilient. Compare with Americas-native: Globe Amaranth (Gomphrena serrata).

Apio

Arracacia xanthorrhiza

HARDINESS ZONES: 8 TO 11

Considered a staple food in some parts of South America and is in the same family as celery and carrot (Apiaceae). Often intercropped with maize, beans, and coffee. One of the most ancient, tuberous crop plants of South America. Grows best in the tropical highlands or when grown in a heap of mulch. Swallowtail butterfly host plant. Up to 25% starch! High in calcium & vitamin A!

SIZE h*w	SUN	SOIL	WATER	EDIBLE
3ft*3ft	dappled	poor, sandy - OK; well-draining	consistently moist	tuber, stem

PROPAGATION METHODS

- TUBER: Each tuber grows a new plant; base of tuber is slashed to stimulate shoots/ lateral roots. Vegetatively propagated from off-sets (colinos) or shoots on crown of main rootstock (cepa). Prefers 70F.

RECIPE

CREAMED APIO SOUP: Sautee 2 cloves of garlic in a pot with 2 tbs sunflower oil and 1 tsp coriander seeds. Once browned and fragrant, add 3 cups coconut water and 2 cups coconut milk. Boil 2 lbs of apio roots until tender.

Puree. Add sea salt to taste and top with chopped chives.

CULINARY USE

Tuber
Eaten cooked. Tastes like blend of celery, cabbage and roasted chestnuts; soft and aromatic. Roots are between 2-10 inches long. Harvested in fall. Short storage life. Use soon after harvesting. Mashed into purées, formed into dumplings and gnocchi, used as an ingredient in pastries, chopped and boiled in stews, or creamed into soups. Also made into fritters, biscuits, & ground into flour. 3 main varieties/colors: yellow, white, and purple-colored roots.

Stem & Leaves
Leaves used as a flavoring the same way as celery in raw or cooked salads. Young stems eaten raw or cooked as a vegetable, blanched and used like celery in salads. Leaves of arracacha are similar to parsley, and vary from dark green to purple.

CULTURAL SIGNIFICANCE

- One of the oldest cultivated Andean plants (even than potato -Solanum tuberosum). Crop provides income to thousands of families
- Has naturalized in Cuba - tendency to spread
- Rich in resistant starch - promotes smooth digestion and a healthy intestinal flora
- Some companies use arracacha powder in baby food formula
- Underexplored in research - untapped opportunity to boost commercial importance

CAUTIONS & CONSIDERATIONS

Health
No known hazards. Excessive consumption may cause yellowing of the skin due to high vit A.

Pests
Slugs and voles; surround with mashua to repel; Potyvirus.

Landscape design
Preventing the plant from flowering can increase yields. Some varieties ready to harvest in seven months. Up to 10 carrot-sized tubers, 6lbs of edible roots. Frequently rotated with banana and plantains.

Arrowroot
Maranta arundinacea

HARDINESS ZONES: 9 TO 12

A Florida native in the Marantaceae family. One of the earliest plants to be domesticated as a staple, dating back to 8200 BC. Not just edible but also medicinal. Found growing wild on moist stream banks. Cultivars with colorful leaves have been developed but these cultivars may not offer same nutritional value. Often grown as a ground cover and ornamental in sub/tropical gardens.

SIZE h*w	SUN	SOIL	WATER	EDIBLE
5ft*1ft	part sun/ shade	well-draining	flood tolerant	root

PROPAGATION METHODS

- Rhizome: Ready for harvesting in 10–12 months; as leaves of the plant begin to wilt and die, divide and replant.
- SEED: Germinates at 70-90°F within 30 days.

RECIPE

ARROWROOT POWDER: Peel the roots and cut into cubes. Purée with a bit of water and place a strainer in a large bowl. Pour purée through strainer into bowl and agitate the pulp in the strainer to separate the starch from the fiber. Remove fiber/pulp with strainer. Allow starch to settle to bottom of bowl (15 to 20 min). Pour off top liquid. Scrape out starch and dehydrate at 115F.

CULTURAL SIGNIFICANCE

- Powdered root has traditionally been made into a poultice in folk medicine. Boiled tubers used to relieve constipation - mild laxative
- Industrial applications such as cosmetics and glue. Used as a base for face powders
- Highly digestible starch fed to infants and to people with specific dietary requirements
- Commercial potential for arrowroot fibers in textile, biofuel, papermaking, bioenergy, packaging, and automotive industries

CULINARY USE

Root

Twin clusters of small white flowers bloom about 90 days after planting, indicating tubers are ready for harvest. Replaces wheat flour in gluten-free recipes! High quality, readily digestible starch, obtained by grinding the root into a fine powder. Used in pastries, biscuits etc. Preferred to flour for thickening soups, sauces and gravies as it does not add a mealy taste. Excellent gelling property. Must be processed within 48 hours of harvest - prone to rotting. To process: rinse and peel off the outer layer and slice. Rhizomes will keep in the refrigerator for up to two weeks. Can also be baked until soft and added to soups or porridge. The powder of the arrowroot plant will keep almost indefinitely if kept in a cool location in an airtight container. Root may also be pickled when harvested early.

CAUTIONS & CONSIDERATIONS

Health
No known adverse health effects. Easy to digest, high fiber, iron, potassium, folate - higher in protein than most tubers.

Pests
Poor drainage conditions leads to Rosellinia bunodes.

Landscape design
Can be grown in the same spot for 5 - 6 years. Re-sprouts easily and can be difficult to eradicate. May behave invasively. Forms thickets. 3–6 lbs of tubers per plant per year. Compare with Calathea allouia & Thaumatococcus daniellii - similar in growth and edibility.

Asparagus
Asparagus officinalis

HARDINESS ZONES: 2 TO 10

Considered gourmet! Widely used as medicine and food since ancient times and has gained reputation as "king of vegetables." Easily grown in any good garden soil. A long-lived perennial, producing over 20 years! Asparagus spears can grow up to 2 inches per day, producing bountiful harvests for gardeners. Plant on the north or east side of the garden so it will not shade out other crops. Give it plenty of room to spread. In the Asparagaceae family.

SIZE h*w	SUN	SOIL	WATER	EDIBLE
5ft*2ft	full to partial	acidic -OK; well-draining	average	shoots, stem

PROPAGATION METHODS

- SEEDS: Germinates at 70-80F within 8 weeks.
- DIVISIONS: Rhizomatous; underground stems send out shoots. Harvest 2 yrs after planting crowns.

RECIPE

BLANCHED ASPARAGUS: Bring a large pot of water to a boil with 2 teaspoons of salt. Immerse the asparagus in the water and blanch up to 10 min. The asparagus should still be crisp and brightly colored.

Once blanched, season with salt & garlic.

CULINARY USE

Shoots/ Stem
Harvest the immature shoots which eventually become the bushy foliage/ ferns the third year after planting from seed. Multiple colored cultivars (e.g., green, white, purple-green). In the third year, harvest only 2 to 3 weeks. In years after, harvest no longer than 6 weeks when 6 to 8 inches tall. Either snap or cut the spears off at ground level. Avoid injuring spears beneath the soil surface. Normally blanched/ steamed and used as a vegetable. Keeps fresh when standing in an inch of water in the refrigerator. Store up to a week. Rinse asparagus under a stream of cool water and snap off the bottoms at their natural breaking point before cooking. Discard the bottoms or use in vegetable stock. Most edible portions are 7-9 inches long.

CULTURAL SIGNIFICANCE

- One of the world's top 20 vegetable crops
- Used in folk healing (e.g., to restore & cleanse bowels, kidneys & liver)
- A museum dedicated solely to asparagus: European Asparagus Museum (Europäisches Spargelmuseum)- Schrobenhausen, Germany
- Contains asparagusic acid, which has nematocidal properties
- Depicted on Egyptian tombs dating from the 4th century BC

CAUTIONS & CONSIDERATIONS

Health
CAUTION: Consume in moderation. Large quantities can irritate kidneys. Do not consume berries: mildly poisonous. Contact dermatitis from raw shoots - wear gloves.

Pests
Prone to fungus, crown rot, rust, & Stemphylium purple spot; beetles.

Landscape design
Don't cut back ferns until completely dead & limit harvesting to under 6 wks to ensure yield following spring. Compare with Florida native Sarsaparilla (Smilax aspera).

Atemoya

Annona chermiola x annona squamosa

HARDINESS ZONES: 10 TO 12

A fast-growing hybrid created in Florida. A cross between cherimoya (Annona cherimola) and sugar apple (A. squamosa). Believed to be one of the best Annonas! Often sweeter and fruitier-flavored than the cherimoya. 'Geffner' variety does not require hand pollination. The Florida native "pond apple" Annona glabra tolerates wet soil and can be use as root stock for grafting Atemoya. In the Annonaceae family.

SIZE h*w	SUN	SOIL	WATER	EDIBLE
25ft*25ft	full to partial	poor - OK	dry/ drought tolerant	fruit

PROPAGATION METHODS

- GRAFTING: Hybrid - therefore not reproduced by seed. Graft near the end of the winter (dormant period) when buds start to break at around 85F.

RECIPE

ANNONA MILK: Press open 1 ripe fruit skin and squeeze out pulp covered seeds into a bowl with 1 cup of water. Gently massage off the pulp. Strain to remove seeds and puree. Use in place of coconut milk in recipes or drink fresh.

OPTIONAL: Allow to ferment at room temperature 24 hrs.

CULTURAL SIGNIFICANCE

- The name "atemoya" is a combination of "ate", an old Mexican name for sugar apple, and "moya" from cherimoya
- The seeds, leaves, and limbs contain alkaloids used to kill lice
- In Florida, nine species of native and exotic nitidulids (sap beetles) visit the flowers
- In Jamaica, the dried Annona cherimola flowers have been used as flavoring for snuff
- Living trellis during dormant months

CULINARY USE

Fruit

The fruits must be clipped from the branch with a small stalk intact to prevent injury to skin. Harvest daily as fruit ripens. Ideal ripeness for harvest is when creamy lines appear around the areoles showing widening spaces. If picked too soon, the fruit will not ripen but will darken and shrivel. Fruit should be picked and allowed to further ripen (soften) at room temperature until soft to touch. Then refrigerate. Ripe atemoya stores 2-4 days refrigerated. Fruit often served chilled and may be simply cut in half or quartered and the flesh eaten from the "shell" with a spoon. Slices or cubes of the pulp may be added to fruit cups or salads or various dessert recipes. Some people blend the pulp with citrus juice and coconut cream and freeze as ice cream.

CAUTIONS & CONSIDERATIONS

Health
CAUTION: Seeds toxic. Blindness from seed juice contact with eyes. Avoid ingesting seeds, leaves or stems: Contain annonacin. Consume fruit in moderation.

Pests
Collar rot (Phytophthora sp.), seed borer, mealy bugs.

Landscape design
Deciduous. Fruit harvested August - October & December -January. Fruiting is improved if the flowers are hand pollinated; Annona cherimola, Annona mucosa, Annona squamosa are related with excellent edibility.

Avocado
Persea Americana

HARDINESS ZONES: 9 TO 12

A large evergreen & perfect summer shade tree. One of the healthiest sources of mono-unsaturated fats. A staple! Responds well to a thick leaf mulch and grows quickly. By getting several varieties with different fruiting seasons, you can have avocado all year! Good office plant with lustrous green leaves but doesn't bear fruit without ample sunlight. Boosts the absorption of antioxidants in other foods. In Lauraceae family.

SIZE h*w	SUN	SOIL	WATER	EDIBLE
80ft*30ft	full to partial	well-draining	average	fruit, leaves

PROPAGATION METHODS

- SEEDS: Germinates at 70-80F within 8 weeks. Sow within 7 days. Seedlings take 6- 8 years to produce fruit. <u>Self-sterile; need 2+ trees for fruit.</u>
- GRAFT: Can start fruiting in their second year.

RECIPE

GREEN GODDESS DRESSING: 1 ripe avocado, peeled/de-seeded, ¾ c coconut milk, 3 tbs vinegar or citrus juice, 1 tbs agave syrup, ½ tsp salt, ¼ tsp black pepper.

Blend all ingredients together until smooth. Keeps in the fridge 2-3 days in an airtight container. Drizzle on torn aibika leaves for a delicious salad.

CULTURAL SIGNIFICANCE

- Fruit is poisonous to some animals; American Society for the Prevention of Cruelty to Animals (ASPCA) lists it as toxic to horses & birds
- "Avocado" is an Aztec Náhuatl word meaning "testicle" given shape
- Pulp used in cosmetic industry as cooling and soothing skin remedy & in soaps and skin moisturizer products. Oil used on scalp and hair as a vitamin-rich hair tonic to restore and promote hair growth

CULINARY USE

Fruit
Fruit matures on the tree but ripens off the tree (like bananas). Commonly eaten raw and used as a sandwich spread. Also added to smoothies, ice creams, and used as a main ingredient for avocado soup. A non-drying oil obtained from the fruit has a mild, pleasant taste. The fruit is pureed as a salad dressing, especially with strong tasting leaves such as chicory. Citrus juice can be mixed with avocados after peeling to prevent browning. Rich source of nutrients and phytochemicals.

Leaves
A tea can be made from the leaves. Toasted leaves are used as a flavouring in stews and bean dishes. Flavor somewhat reminiscent of anise, Consume in moderation: contains persin.

CAUTIONS & CONSIDERATIONS

Health
Provides important monounsaturated fats. CAUTION: May trigger tree-pollen allergy or latex-fruit syndrome. Unripe fruit is poisonous. Ground seed used as a rat poison.

Pests
Scale insects; root rot; Anthracnose; Laurel wilt.

Landscape design
Brittle wood prone to wind damage. Mexican, Guatemalan, West Indian, & Hybrid avocado types. Varieties fruit by season (e.g., Fall-Lula; Winter/Spring-Choquette & Mexicola; Summer-Russell).

Banana

Musa spp

HARDINESS ZONES: 7A TO 10

A powerhouse of nutrients and an instant energy booster. Banana is the world's largest herbaceous perennial. Considered the most important tropical fruit crop. Ranks with rice, wheat, & maize in importance as a staple. Valued since the dawn of recorded history. A banana "tree" is actually an herb related to ginger; the fruit is actually a berry! Flour from green bananas is a gluten-free substitute for wheat! Ideally suited for home gardens. Dwarf varieties are more wind resilient. Compare with Plantain (Musa balbisiana).

SIZE h*w	SUN	SOIL	WATER	EDIBLE
16ft* 5ft varies by type	full to partial	acidic - OK	continuously moist	fruit, flowers, stem

PROPAGATION METHODS

- SUCKERS: Vegetatively propagated in spring from shoots growing from bud at base of plant. Sword suckers preferred to water suckers.
- CORM: Bulbs/ rhizomes divided in winter.

RECIPE

GREEN BANANA "GNOCCI": Slice green banana peels lengthwise. Boil 10 min. Strain. Cool. Peel. Boil 5 min. Strain. Top with favorite pasta/ curry sauce.

Alternatively, Slice & dehydrate at 115 F until crisp. Pulse into flour. OR puree 1 peeled, green banana with 2+ TBS water (aim for gravy consistency). Feed to a sourdough starter to ferment for bread.

CULTURAL SIGNIFICANCE

- Many uses: 'Nurses' crops as living irrigation. Potable water in stump. Fermented peels used as fertilizer "tea." Leaves used as fodder or to waterproof food containers. Stem/ leaf fiber used for papermaking & textiles. Boiled peel yields black dye
- The song "Yes! We Have No Bananas" (1923) was the best-selling sheet music in history
- In India, banana trees are tied to form wedding arches. Symbol of fertility & prosperity

CULINARY USE

Flowers
Typically steamed but also fried. Rich in vitamins and minerals. Used like artichoke; bracts and heart edible. Eaten with dip, in soup.

Fruit
Eaten ripe or unripe. Ripe banana consumed as a fruit or in desserts like ice-cream, bread, or candy. Unripe banana used as a vegetable & processed into starch, beer, vinegar or flour. Cooked like potatoes – boiled, poached, stewed, or smashed and fried. Hang rack upside down to ripen best. Some cultures consume the peels.

Stem
Typically cooked as a vegetable in stew like endive.

Leaves
Employed as a food wrap such as during grilling to add a subtle sweet flavor.

CAUTIONS & CONSIDERATIONS

Health
No known adverse health effects. Fruit is a rich source of vit A, B complex, C, manganese, & potassium.

Pests
Aphids, weevil, beetles, fruit flies, thrips, scales; fungus lesions. NOTE: disease-resistant hybrids developed.

Landscape design
Remove dead leaves to prevent disease. Plantations thrive 25+ years if managed. Spacing based on cultivar. Protect from wind. Often planted in a "banana circle." Divide pups when 3ft+ tall & clump has 4 plants.

Barbados Cherry

Malpighia glabra

HARDINESS ZONES: 10 TO 12

This butterfly host plant makes a perfect food forest hedge! Produces up to three crops per year. Extremely high in vitamin C. Outstanding ornamental. Bears for about 15 years with little care. Produces a dependable crop in South Florida. Consider the FL cultivar: 'Florida Sweet' given its large fruits, thick skin, apple-like flavor. In the Malpighiaceae family.

SIZE h*w	SUN	SOIL	WATER	EDIBLE
13ft*13ft	partial	well-draining	drought tolerant	fruit

PROPAGATION METHODS

- CUTTINGS: 1/4" thick, 8" long hardwood cuttings when not flowering/ fruiting; roots in 60 days. Plant 50% in soil. Air layering also effective.
- SEEDS: Germinates at 70-85F within 12 months with 5-50% success. Not preferred.

RECIPE

CHERRY JELLY: 4 cups Barbados Cherry puree; 4 tbs sweetener of choice; 1/2 cup chia seeds.

De-seed fruit. Cover with water. Simmer until the fruits are soft. Puree. Add sweetener, chia seeds, and fold gently. Let cool and solidify. Refrigerate for up to 1 week. Serve on crackers or with yogurt.

CULINARY USE

Fruit

Mature over the course of 3 weeks. Eaten raw or stewed; made into juices, sauces, jellies, jams, wines or purée. As raw dessert, the fruits are picked when fully ripe. For processing or preserving, they can be harvested when slightly immature, when they are turning from yellow to red. Picking is done every 1-3 days to avoid loss by falling. Some growers shake the tree & allow the ripe fruits to fall onto sheets spread on the ground. Harvested fruits should be kept in the shade & stored indoors within 3 hours to prevent loss of ascorbic acid. The juice & purée should be kept no longer than one week in fridge to optimize nutrients. Freezing/ freeze-drying preserves nutrients well. Cooked fruit purée utilized as a topping to prevent browning such as on sliced banana.

CULTURAL SIGNIFICANCE

- Deer sometimes eat the leaves & birds, racoons & coyotes feed on fruits
- Larval host for four species of native butterflies including skippers
- Wine made from Barbados cherries in Hawaii was found to retain 60% of the ascorbic acid
- Widely used in the preparation of vitamin tablets and other nutritional supplements
- Used to control erosion on terraces
- Bark has 20-25% tannin; used in leather industry

CAUTIONS & CONSIDERATIONS

Health

CAUTION: intestinal inflammation and obstruction may occur if seeds are ingested. Minute hairs on plant may irritate skin.

Pests

Nematodes, anthracnose, whiteflies, scale; long-term health usually not affected by pests.

Landscape design

Brittle branches. Can train into single or multi-trunks. Space 5ft for hedges. Compare with Grumichama (Eugenia brasiliensis) & Cherry of Rio Grande (Eugenia aggregata).

Basket Vine

Trichostigma octandrum

HARDINESS ZONES: 9 TO 11

An interesting & ornamental Florida native. Critically imperiled and considered endangered by the State of Florida. Has wildlife value as birds eat the berries. Habitats generally include shell mounds, tropical swamps, rockland hammocks, and bayheads. Traditionally, used by natives as a potherb and basket weaving material. In the Petiveriaceae family.

SIZE h*w	SUN	SOIL	WATER	EDIBLE
up to 30ft*20ft	partial	sand - OK	flood tolerant	leaves

PROPAGATION METHODS

- CUTTINGS: Place two nodules into soil ensuring that 50% is submerged and 50% is exposed. Keep humid until rooted.
- SEEDS: Germinates at 80F. Birds often disperse.

RECIPE

CREAMED BASKET VINE: 1c basket vine leaves. 2c coconut milk; sea salt to taste.

Wash. Boil for 40 minutes changing the water at the 20 min mark. Strain with coconut milk and salt to taste. Serve over vegetables such as mashed cassava.

NOTE: Review cautions & health notes.

CULTURAL SIGNIFICANCE

- Purple juice from berries used as a dye
- Neotropical folk medicine. Colombians use the leaves to help cure wounds and as a medicinal tea
- Discovered in 2007 in the FL Everglades by IRC biologist. Abundant in parts of the West Indies including northern coast of Cuba
- A large sturdy plant, trainable into bowers and enclosures. Split stems and bast fibers used to make barrel hoops, baskets, crafts

CULINARY USE

Leaves

Young leaves are boiled in two water changes. Reportedly a nutritious vegetable. Vinegar-based salad dressing decreases bitterness. Fill pot, boil and discard water two separate times to remove bitterness and increase edibility. Similar potherbs are often served with butter or cream sauce, added to soups after chopping finely, or pureed within a pesto. Considered medicinal.

CAUTION: More research may be needed to safely consume this plant as it is currently endangered and has an indigenous rather than European history of use. As a result, nutrition and other data is not readily available.

CAUTIONS & CONSIDERATIONS

Health

CAUTION: Formerly placed in the pokeweed family. Taste carefully. Confused with Rivina humilis.

Pests

Generally resistant; grows aggressively without maintenance.

Landscape design

Grows in tropical swamps near the edges of hammocks and brakes. Weak taproots, extensive lateral roots - promotes soil stability. Fast-growing (10ft a year). Lives decades.

Beautyberry

Callicarpa americana

HARDINESS ZONES: 6 TO 11

American Beautyberry, sometimes called French Mulberry, is a fast-growing, Florida native deciduous shrub with jewel-like fuchsia-colored berries, cascading down branches of vibrant green leaves. A stunning perennial/ ornamental used to make jam! Showy flowers and fruit. May fruit year-round, although summer and fall are the peak seasons. Beaded branches make beautiful dry arrangements. Berries used as a dye. In the Lamiaceae/Verbenaceae family.

SIZE h*w	SUN	SOIL	WATER	EDIBLE
6ft*4ft	partial	acidic - OK	drought tolerant	berries

PROPAGATION METHODS

- SEED: Viable for years. Lightly cover with soil. Germinates in 1 - 3 months at 65F.
- CUTTING: Cuttings of half-ripe wood 4 inches long around time of new growth: July/August.

RECIPE

BEAUTYBERRY SYRUP: 4 cups of beautyberries, 4 cups agave syrup, 4 cups water.

Simmer berries in water until soft (20 min). Strain through cheese cloth to remove seeds/ pulp. Mix juice with Agave syrup. Refrigerate up to 3 weeks. Drizzle on yogurt, ice-cream, cake, fruit salads, and more.

CULTURAL SIGNIFICANCE

- Attracts birds, bees, butterflies. Larval host for spring azure butterflies & snowberry clearwing moths. Leaves favored by deer
- Pioneer species. Hurricane-wind resistance
- Used medicinally by FL natives (e.g., berries for fevers, dysentery. Crushed leaves used to repel mosquitoes, flies, ticks). 60% of the leaf oil is terponoids (e.g., callicarpenal); comparable to DEET in research

CULINARY USE

Fruit

Berries, also called drupes preferred cooked or fermented. Juicy, zesty, slightly aromatic when cooked. Tart and astringent when raw/ fresh. They make a very fine jelly, and the flavor is mild and pleasant. Good as syrup on vanilla ice cream, homemade yogurt or angel food cake. 10-15 branches typically yield 1.5 quarts of berries.

To consume in mass: Place berries in a pot cover with water and boil until berries burst (e.g., 20 min). Strain. Mash/ press berries through a colander or cheese cloth to remove seeds. Add sweetener to taste. Mild bitterness suitable for wine and an antioxidant-rich tea. Fermentation removes bitterness.

CAUTIONS & CONSIDERATIONS

Health
No known adverse health effects.

Pests
Resilient; leaf spots and black mold.

Landscape design
Main bloom time is spring. Typically planted in masses. Transplant in autumn. Blooms on new wood so prune in late winter to a foot tall. Add 5-inch layer of mulch in fall. Native beautyberries have berries held to stem; non-natives have berries held away from stem. Lives 10 years. Callicarpa americana var. lactea produces white drupes.

Bee Balm
Monarda didyma

HARDINESS ZONES: 4 TO 10

Also called Scarlet Beebalm or Bergamot. This perennial is not only beautiful, but also valued for healing properties since antiquity. The flower is often used as a folk medicine, as well as added to foods as a spice. In the Lamiaceae (or mint) family. Good plant for butterfly & bird gardens. Native to eastern North America & typically occurs in moist woods and streambanks. Important food source for bees, hummingbirds & butterflies.

SIZE h*w	SUN	SOIL	WATER	EDIBLE
up to 4ft*1ft	partial	well-draining; clay - OK	seasonal flood - OK	flowers, leaves, shoots

PROPAGATION METHODS

- SEEDS: Germinate at 70F in 20 – 30 days. Ripen from August to October.
- DIVISIONS: Rhizomes; underground stolons.

RECIPE

TEA BOMB: Cut 20 calamondins in half. De-seed. Place cut side up. Into each half place, stuff with fresh bee balm petals & leaves.

Place halves into the dehydrator or oven at 115F until thoroughly dry. Can take up to 24 hours. Store in an airtight container. Steep in steaming hot water as a tea on demand.

CULTURAL SIGNIFICANCE

- Oswego Indians made tea from dried leaves; early colonists substituted in place of British tea (e.g., "Oswego tea")
- Used in folk healing: (e.g., as a poultice - headaches & stings; tea to boost immunity for anti-inflammatory, antibacterial, & antioxidant effects; for flatulence, colds, & flu)
- Larval host to multiple species of moth (e.g., hermit sphinx, orange mint moth, & raspberry pyrausta). Supports specialized bees

CULINARY USE

Leaves & Shoots
Leaves and young shoot tips eaten raw or cooked. Leaves have a minty aroma when crushed. They are used as a flavoring in salads, fruit salads, drinks, jellies, soups, & stews. Aromatic foliage is the result of essential oils produced by the leaves of the plant. Can be used as a substitute for Mediterranean herbs. NOTE: Central stem, branches and leaves are covered with fine hairs. Can be blanched off.

Flowers
Flowers eaten raw; added as an attractive garnish to salads or used as a tea made from fresh or dried flower heads. Blooms from July to September. The blooming time lasts around 2 months during summer. The flowers do not have any scent.

CAUTIONS & CONSIDERATIONS

Health
No known adverse health effects. Contains thymol much like thyme and oregano.

Pests
Fungal leaf diseases, powdery mildew; ensure air circulation.

Landscape design
Can become weedy. Monarda genus contains over 20 species, all with spicey, fragrant foliage. Pinch new growth for bushier growth habit. Compare with Monarda fistulosa and the Florida native, Monarda puntata.

Betony
Stachys floridana

HARDINESS ZONES: 8A TO 10B

A perennial, Florida native and one of the most common plants found throughout the state! Square stems characteristic of the Lamiaceae (mint) family. Flowers, emerge in late spring & are pinkish-purple in color. A charming, highly adaptable wildflower with trumpet-shaped blooms. Almost entirely edible with an incredibly crunchy, radish-like tuber. A pleasing & sweet taste.

SIZE h*w	SUN	SOIL	WATER	EDIBLE
1.5ft*1ft	partial	poor - OK	seasonal flooding - OK	tuber, seeds, leaves, stem

PROPAGATION METHODS

- DIVISION: Small segments of rhizome can be sprouted into new plants or the entire tuber may be transplanted to a new area.
- SEEDS: Germinates at 70F in 30 days with less than 20% success. Not preferred.

RECIPE

BLANCHED BETONY: Wash tubers well. Bring a pot of water to a boil with salt to taste. Immerse tubers in water and blanch for 3 minutes. The tubers should still be crisp & bright white. Plunge into ice cold water to stop the cooking process.

Once blanched, use to scoop hummus, guacamole or other dips as a delightful snack.

CULTURAL SIGNIFICANCE

- Commercial nursery trade dispersed the plant across the Southeast in the mid-1900s
- Attracts bees and butterflies
- An excellent addition to a freedom lawn; can be mowed over without inhibiting growth
- Used in folk healing (e.g., High content of stachyose promotes healthy gut-flora; used by some diabetes patients as a pharmaceutical plant; aerial parts used for headaches, anxiety, and nervous system health in teas & tinctures)

CULINARY USE

Tuber
Root tubers resemble a snake rattle. A special & traditional Chinese starchy vegetable; sometimes boiled like peanuts. Mild and crispy. Eat raw or pickled, but harvest in spring when white. In summer, it turns tan and soft, losing flavor and texture. Tubers can be shaved over a salad or eaten straight out of the hand. Radish or jicama-like texture. Offers a source of a sugar called Stachyose. Used to scoop hummus or guacamole.

Leaves & Stem
Young leaves and stems can be cooked like pot-herb greens or dried and made into a tea; musty flavor.

Seeds
Some reports that seeds can be eaten raw or cooked.

CAUTIONS & CONSIDERATIONS

Health
No known adverse health effects. Harvest from non-contaminated soil. Dig to confirm identity - Stachys is one of the largest genera. CAUTION: Under-researched. Called wild artichoke but not related to Cynara cardunculus.

Pests
Resilient.

Landscape design
Aggressive growth in fall & spring. Dormant in summer. Find nurseries with tubers at PlantRealfForida.org. Compare with Stachy affinis - sells for ca. $150 per lb, a gourmet delicacy.

Bidens Alba

Bidens alba

HARDINESS ZONES: 8A TO 11

Excellent at attracting pollinators! Prolific enough to grow as a crop. Used as food and medicine throughout the world. In the absence of heavy frost, plants can live 3-5 years. Many butterfly & bee species would starve without this incredibly versatile plant! Monarch butterflies – among others – depend upon its nectar along migratory routes. Considered an immune booster in traditional medicine. In the Asteraceae family.

SIZE h*w	SUN	SOIL	WATER	EDIBLE
4ft*3ft	full	well-draining	drought tolerant	flowers, leaves

PROPAGATION METHODS

- SEEDS: Germinates at 75-85F. A single plant can produce 3,000+ seeds which attach to clothing. Viable for 3 to 5 yrs.

RECIPE

BIDENS ALBA TEA: Pick 1 tbs of young leaves and freshly opened flowers. Steep in 1 c steaming hot water for 5 minutes, uncovered.

Sweeten to taste.

CULTURAL SIGNIFICANCE

- Larval host plant for the Dainty sulphur butterfly and an important nectar source for bees. In Florida, B. alba is the third most common reliable source of nectar (behind saw palmetto and orange blossom)
- Used in folk healing (e.g., as an antimicrobial against infections that are inflammatory to the mucous membranes or as a poultice for skin infections; infusions made for coughs, and fever)

CULINARY USE

Leaves & Flowers

Young tender leaves eaten cooked. Shoots, tips and young leaves are good potherbs. Dried leaves are favored in Hawaii for tea. Nutrient dense, wild plant, boasting a similar nutrient profile to kale - high in fiber and proteins, carotenes, folate, and magnesium. People in South Africa, Zulus, and Indians consume the fresh or dried leaves by boiling them. Wine is made from leaves or blooms. Almost always available fresh throughout the year. Excellent at drawing up-toxins from the soil; pay close attention to where you harvest. Harvest in soils free from contaminants.

NOTE: Be sure to correctly identify. There are 250+ species within Bidens genus. Herbalists consider, B. alba the all-star.

CAUTIONS & CONSIDERATIONS

Health
CAUTION: Look alikes. Capable of interbreeding within genus (e.g., with B. pilosa). Considered medicinal. High concentrations of phenylheptatriyne in fall - believed antifungal and antiviral effects.

Pests
Resilient; Uromyces bidenticola — rust.

Landscape design
Reproduces prolifically. Forms colonies in disturbed areas. Blooms nearly all year. An excellent green manure/ chop & drop. Compare with Bidens pilosa - also edible.

Blackberry

Rubus trivialis

HARDINESS ZONES: 5 TO 9

Also called Southern Dewberry. This native deciduous, vine produces sweet, juicy fruit. Easy to grow and prolific. A pioneer species! It will grow in any soil as long as it's not permanently soggy. In the Rose family (Rosaceae) and serves as an effective groundcover. Digging suckers is a very easy way to propagate this plant. Thornless varieties exist as well.

SIZE h*w	SUN	SOIL	WATER	EDIBLE
3ft*1ft	full to partial	well-draining; acidic	average	fruit

PROPAGATION METHODS

- CUTTINGS/ LAYERING: Roots at nodes. Flowers/ fruit appear on last season's growth - don't prune aggressively.
- SEEDS: Germinates at 77-85F. Stratify and sow in early autumn. Hybridizes.

RECIPE

BLACKBERRY COBBLER: Fill a pie crust with 3c blackberries. Drizzle with 1/3 c maple syrup, & 3 tbs melted coconut oil. Sprinkle with sea salt. Top with a "crumble": 2 c flour mixed with 1/2 c sourdough starter, 1/3 c melted coconut oil, 1/4 c of maple syrup, 1/4 tsp cinnamon & 1/2 tsp salt. Bake at 350F for 20-35 min or until golden brown and bubbly.

CULTURAL SIGNIFICANCE

- Hosts bees from the Halictidae family
- Root and leaves used in folk healing (e.g., for astringent, stimulant and tonic properties)
- In some traditions, cane berry's deep purple color has religious symbolism
- Purple to blue dye obtained from the fruit
- Stabilizing groundcover - banks, eroded sites
- Young leaves steeped for tea. Pick in the morning to preserve essential oils in leaves
- Fermented for wines and cordials

CULINARY USE

Fruit

Fruit eaten raw, cooked or used in jams, preserves etc. Large and well-flavored. Edible blackberry-like fruits, known regionally as dewberries, are produced in spring to early summer. Botanically, they are an aggregate of single seeded drupelets. Initially green, then red and finally black-purple at maturity. When harvesting, bring a long stick to poke around in the brambles to scare off creatures which might be hiding or foraging. Wear gloves to protect your hands from prickles. Seeds contain oil rich in omega-3 (alpha-linolenic acid) and omega-6 (linoleic acid) fats.

CAUTION: Wetter conditions may produce molds on fruit (e.g., Botryotinia) - toxic effects. Discard moldy fruit.

CAUTIONS & CONSIDERATIONS

Health

No known adverse health effects. Contains numerous phytochemicals/ nutrients; CAUTION: May have thorns; poison ivy (Toxicodendron radicans) often intertwines with Dewberry in thickets.

Pests

Red neck cane borer, crown gall, thrips, honey fungus.

Landscape design

Aggressive in mixed plantings. Compare with other blackberry varieties: R. Floridus, R. pensilvanicus and especially R. cuneifolius.

Blueberry
Vaccinium spp.

HARDINESS ZONES: 7 TO 11

A deciduous shrub which may fruit nearly year-round. Beautiful fall color! Leaves turn brilliant red, orange, yellow, and/or purple. Sharpblue and Shineshine blue (self-pollinating) cultivars require the fewest chill hours. Shiny Blueberry (Vaccinium myrsinites) is a good native option. Bushes live up to 60 years! A growing market: Blueberry acreage in Florida has more than doubled over the past decade! In the Ericaceae family.

SIZE h*w	SUN	SOIL	WATER	EDIBLE
4ft*4ft	full to partial	well-draining; acidic	average	fruit

PROPAGATION METHODS

- CUTTINGS: Hardwood or rhizome cuttings in winter. Mother rhizomes result in a large patch of genetically distinct plants. Plant two varieties/ cross pollinate for better yield.

RECIPE

BREAKFAST SMOOTHIE: 1 c blueberries, 1/2 cup coconut milk, 1 tbs chia seeds, 1 tsp vanilla extract, 1 tsp coconut oil, 1 cup water.

Puree and serve immediately.

CULINARY USE

Fruit
Eaten fresh or are processed as frozen fruit, purée, juice, or dried or infused berries. These may then be used in a variety of goods, such as jellies, jams, pies, muffins, snack foods, or as an additive to breakfast cereals. Can be incorporated into a variety of basic stews. Added whole to puddings and cakes or ground and added to flour, soups and meat as flavoring. Used as a rub for meat. Fruit blended with water & used to cool fevers and quench thirst. In recognition of Native American Heritage Month, sautauthig pudding is made: berries are mixed with meat to make pemmican, and then further mixed with cornmeal, honey and water to make a pudding called "sautauthig." Commonly used to make wine.

CULTURAL SIGNIFICANCE

- During the Civil War soldiers drank a blueberry beverage to improve their health
- US Highbush Blueberry Council supports research on folk medicine uses (e.g., leaf tea; as a muscle relaxant or anti-spasmodic for women during childbirth; a syrup to treat the coughs and sore throat)
- Juice yields excellent dye for baskets, cloth
- Economically important: U.S. leads world production as of 2019

CAUTIONS & CONSIDERATIONS

Health
No known adverse health effects. High content of antioxidants.

Pests
Resilient but host to 17 species of viruses.

Landscape design
Prune late winter 3rd year. Low-chill, southern highbush (SHB) cultivars best for FL. Compare with Vaccinium corymbosum x Vaccinium darrowii or related hybrids. Comparable FL natives: Huckleberry (Gaylussacia spp) or Darling Plum (Reynosia septentriolalis).

Breadfruit

Artocarpus altilis

HARDINESS ZONES: 10 TO 12

An easy-to-grow staple crop in the mulberry (Moraceae) family. Can be cooked or eaten during all stages of its development! Valued as a source of starch but also protein, iron, calcium, and potassium. Fast growing! Trees usually produce two crops per year when 3 - 6 years old, eventually producing up to 200 fruits per tree annually! Grown as an evergreen ornamental. Showy flowers! Fruit matures within three months. Offers food security amidst climate change concerns.

SIZE h*w	SUN	SOIL	WATER	EDIBLE
50ft*30ft	full to patial	well-draining; saline - OK	seasonal flooding - OK	flowers, fruit, leaves, seed

PROPAGATION METHODS

- SEEDS: Germinates at 80-85F about 2 weeks after sowing; lose viability quickly.
- ROOT CUTTINGS: Seedless breadfruit is grown from suckers.

RECIPE

BREADFRUIT PUDDING: 1 breadfruit (8in diameter), 2 c coconut milk, 3 tbs honey, sea salt and cinnamon to taste.

Before cutting the fruit, wash to remove sap from skin. Quarter, remove core, slice off peel and cube. Boil for 20 min until soft. Drain. Drizzle coconut milk and honey over. Sprinkle sea salt & cinnamon.

CULINARY USE

Fruit
Fruits 2x a year. The unripe fruit - even as small as 2 inches in diameter, is cooked as a starchy vegetable - tastes similar to artichoke hearts. Ripe fruits are somewhat sweet and are occasionally eaten raw but are more often cooked as a starchy vegetable or fermented into a cheese-like food. A potato texture. Can be eaten steamed, boiled, baked, and fried. Mature fruit (e.g., 8+ inch diameter) is dried and ground into a flour or made into hummus. Baked fruit has the aroma & texture of baked bread. Often fermented.

Seeds
Eaten cooked boiled or roasted; taste similar to chestnuts, Rich in niacin.

Leaves & Flowers
Male inflorescence are cooked and used as a vegetable.

CULTURAL SIGNIFICANCE

- Used as a windbreak or shade tree
- Bast makes good cordage. Milky sap/ gum used as a caulk, adhesive, sealant, or gesso
- Wood is used to construct houses, canoes, & surfboards - resistant to termites & worms
- 'Mutiny on the Bounty' is a movie on breadfruit when a 1780s West Indies famine lead British plantation owners to import breadfruit trees
- Listed as top crop in International Treaty on Plant Genetic Resources for food security

CAUTIONS & CONSIDERATIONS

Health
No known adverse health effects. NOTE: contains a milky latex sap.

Pests
Leaf rust, fruit rot (Phytophthora spp); scales, mealy bugs.

Landscape design
Two main forms of the breadfruit: Seeded and seedless. Can naturalize in tropics. Trees shed leaves when soil is too dry; shed fruit when the soil is too wet. Productive for many decades. Compare with Breadnut (Artocarpus camansi).

Butterfly Pea
Clitoria ternatea

HARDINESS ZONES: 9B TO 11

An easily maintained, perennial. This showy vine produces deep blue-purple flowers which bloom nearly year-round. Deemed a high-quality, protein-rich legume and a "tropical alfalfa." Preferred by livestock as fodder. Used to improve soil quality and attract pollinators. In the Fabaceae family. A tea from the flowers is used in Ayurvedic medicine and changes color with pH changes. For instance, the tea color changes from blue to pink by adding lemon juice!

SIZE h*w	SUN	SOIL	WATER	EDIBLE
8ft*1ft	full to partial	any poor - OK	drought tolerant	flowers, leaves, young shoots, tender pods

PROPAGATION METHODS

- SEED: Germinates at 80-85F. Requires scarification prior to sowing (e.g., abrasion, hot water or peroxide/ water mix).
- CUTTINGS: Root in the vermiculite or moist sand.

RECIPE

BUTTERFLY PEA TEA: 1/2 c of dried butterfly pea flowers, 1 tbs dried lemongrass, 2 c of water.

Add steaming hot water to butterfly pea flowers & lemongrass. Let rest 5 min, covered. Strain.

OPTIONAL: Add honey to taste. Add citrus juice to turn pink. Add fresh coconut milk to turn green.

CULTURAL SIGNIFICANCE

- Flowers used as dye. At normal pH (blue), lowered pH (purple/pink), raised pH (green)
- Revered as holy in India for puja rituals
- Flowers likened to female genitals/ Latin name "Clitoria", from "clitoris". Chinese medicine practitioners associate impact on female libido
- Folk healing use (e.g., as brain tonic for mood & memory; for antioxidant, diuretic, anti-inflammatory, antimicrobial properties)

CULINARY USE

Flowers
Used to color rice, starches & desserts like shaved ice. Increasingly researched as an edible, non-toxic food coloring source. Has a longer shelf life than comparable plant-based food coloring. Drinking butterfly pea tea in some Asian countries is believed to promote younger skin complexion and defend against skin aging. Often paired with pandan syrup. Also used as a garnish. Frozen into ice cubes for "mood ring cocktail." Taste is sweet and mildly "earthy." Sometimes dipped in batter and fried.

Pods, Leaves & Shoots
Young pods are eaten as a vegetable when tender and pliable. Blanched 10 minutes. Then added to stir-fries, stews, or rice. Very palatable. High digestibility and protein content. Popular for vegetable dishes in the Philippines.

CAUTIONS & CONSIDERATIONS

Health
No known adverse health effects. CAUTION: May be confused with FL native Clitoria mariana which has poisonous features.

Pests
Leaf-eating insects; root nematode, fungal diseases.

Landscape design
May behave invasively. Nitrogen fixing; improves crop yields. Valuable cover crop in coconut plantations. Competes well; can cover the ground in 6 weeks. Plant 1 seedling per sq ft. Low tolerance of flooding or waterlogging.

Cabbage Palmetto

Sabal palmetto

HARDINESS ZONES: 8 TO 11

One of the most ubiquitous and hurricane-proof, native plants in FL. One of 12 Florida native palms and named our state tree! Ornamental and actually a grass! This evergreen is in the Arecaceae/ Palmae family, and although it's slow-growing, it has so much to offer including fragrant flowers many edible parts. A protected species in the wild.

SIZE h*w	SUN	SOIL	WATER	EDIBLE
40ft*13ft	full	sand - OK; well-draining	drought tolerant; maritime - OK	fruit/ seed, leaves heart,

PROPAGATION METHODS

- SEEDS: Germinates at 86°F–95°F at 50% rate within 4 months. Scatter seed over surface of soil and barely cover. Seedlings form a long tap-root long before forming a shoot; shoots look like grass initially.

RECIPE

PALMETTO CRACKERS: In a food processor, coarsely grind 1 c of ripe fruit/seed pods. Soak overnight in water. Strain. Puree with 1 tbs of water until a thin paste forms. Mix in 1/4 tsp of salt and 2 tbs of oil. Press onto a greased or silicone sheet-lined pan and bake at 325F for 30 min or until thoroughly dried into a cracker. If needed, decrease to 250F after 30 min and bake 20 more min to dry out.

CULTURAL SIGNIFICANCE

- Host for monk skipper (Asbolis capucinus)
- Fronds are waterproof; leaf stalk fiber used to make stiff-bristle brushes; leaves are woven to make hats, mats and baskets
- In swamps and wet areas, Cabbage Palms are a signal of higher, dryer ground
- Plant ashes used as a salt substitute
- Palms considered 3rd most important plant family for human use
- Yields sweet sap; blossoms result in rich honey

CULINARY USE

Fruit/ Seed ("Beans/pods")
Huge annual yield/ crop. The sweet fruit lining tastes like prune & covers a pea-sized seed (1/2 inch). The fruit is deep purple when ripe. Fruit & seed are soaked, dried, and ground into meal for bread. Nutty flavor. Ground into a pulp resembling peanut butter.

Heart
The heart of the tree (top 3ft) can be harvested as "swamp cabbage" but kills the tree. Mild and crunchy. Pith of the upper trunk is chewed for the sweetish juice.

Leaves
The young leaves are eaten raw or cooked and the large, white succulent leaf buds are cooked and eaten as a vegetable but removing too many can kill the tree.

CAUTIONS & CONSIDERATIONS

Health
No known adverse health effects.
Pests
Palmetto weevil (grubs are edible), Ganoderma butt rot, Thielaviopsis trunk rot, Texas phoenix palm decline (TPPD); Lethal Bronzing Disease (LBD).

Landscape design
Deep penetrating root systems - plant seedlings. Mature transplants require removal of leaves to prevent water loss. 20+ yrs to mature. Compare with Saw Palmetto (Serenoa repens), Bush Palmetto (Sabal minor), & Jelly/ Pindo Palm (Butia capitata).

Calamondin

Citrofortunella microcarpa

HARDINESS ZONES: 8A TO 10B

An ornamental, evergreen, in the Rutaceae family & hybrid between an orange & a kumquat. A staple fruit juice in the Philippines & popular house plant grown in 10-gallon pots. Can live for more than 50 years & bears nearly all year! Better cold tolerance than any other true citrus. Introduced to Florida in 1899; vintage cookbooks feature it very creatively! Immune to citrus canker and scab!

SIZE h*w	SUN	SOIL	WATER	EDIBLE
13ft*8ft	full to partial	acidic, sand, clay - OK; well-draining	drought tolerant	fruit/ peel

PROPAGATION METHODS

- SEEDS: Germinates at 60-70F. Produce within 2 years. Self-fertile. Easily grown from seed. Polyembrionic/typically "true to type."
- CUTTINGS: Half-ripe wood in July/August.

RECIPE

CALAMONDIN POPSICLE: 1c calamondin puree (10 deseeded fruits, blended with pulp & peel, mixed with 2 tbs water), 1 tbs agave syrup, 3 c water. Combine all ingredients and pour into popsicle molds. Freeze overnight.

OPTIONAL: Add in 1/4 c pureed aibika leaves to boost nutritional content.

CULTURAL SIGNIFICANCE

- Called "Kalamansi" in the Philippines and is used as a condiment in almost in every famous local dish
- Juice used as a deodorant; hair & scalp tonic; when combined with pepper, the juice is used in folk medicine to expel phlegm
- Valued as a rootstock for the oval kumquat
- Used in Florida before limes became available
- Rinds used in research to remove lead from water

CULINARY USE

Fruit
Orange when ripe. The small, 1-inch, round, juicy & acidic fruit is edible raw or cooked. Used in pickles, drinks, teas, marmalades, preserves, soups, and chutneys - in all the ways that lemons or limes are used. Tastes like a sour tangerine. The skin has a sweet, tart flavor and is also edible. The whole fruit with the peel is fried in coconut oil and is eaten with curry. Peel is candied. Juice can be squeezed over fruit salad or sliced over cooked seafood dishes.

Harvest continuously. Use scissors to cut the fruit from tree to keep the stem end attached which prolongs the shelf-life. Best eaten within a few days or refrigerated up to 10 days.

CAUTIONS & CONSIDERATIONS

Health
No known adverse health effects. Positive antioxidant effects.

Pests
Fruit fly, crinkly leaf, exocortis, psorosis, xyloporosis, tristeza.

Landscape design
Fragrant blooms resemble gardenias. Shelter from winds. Hand-pollinate the flowers if indoors. An attractive hedge plant. Deep tap root and spiny stem. The fruit ripens slowly (can take up to a year); stays fresh on tree for weeks.

Calendula

Calendula officinalis

HARDINESS ZONES: 2 TO 11

A member of the daisy family (Asteraceae). In milder climates, calendula is a short-lived perennial. Elsewhere, it is one of the most reliable cool season annuals, and among the best-known flowers in Western herbal medicine! Quite popular in England during Shakespeare's time. Once used to forecast rough weather. A beautiful cut flower and among the easiest edible varieties.

SIZE h*w	SUN	SOIL	WATER	EDIBLE
2ft*1ft	full to partial	well-drained	average	flower, leaves

PROPAGATION METHODS

- SEEDS: Germinates at 60-70F. Direct sow early spring & early fall. Blooms longer in cool but frost-free weather. Will not bloom long in intense heat - intolerant of hot, humid weather.

RECIPE

CALENDULA-INFUSED OIL: Stuff a mason jar full of dried calendula bloom heads. Cover blooms with oil. Place mason jar in a pot filled partially with water. Simmer in this "bain marie" for 6 hours.

Drizzle on salads or soups; use as a dye for icing or doughs; employ as a base for salves.

CULINARY USE

Flower

Harvest the whole flower tops when the flowers are fully open. Pick after dew has dried and dry in a well-ventilated spot out of direct sunlight. Store in air-tight containers. Fresh petals are chopped and added to salads. The dried petals are used as a seasoning in soups, cakes etc. High in vitamins A & C and lutein. Inexpensive substitute for saffron; used to color and flavor rice, soups etc. A tea is made from the petals and flowers.

Leaves

Leaves are typically bitter and often are added to leafy salads. Blanch to decrease bitterness; imparts a viscid sweetness and mild salinity. Rich in vitamins and minerals - similar to Dandelion in nutritional value.

CULTURAL SIGNIFICANCE

- Ancient Greek, Roman, Middle Eastern, & Indian cultures used as a medicinal & dye for hair, fabrics, foods, and cosmetics. Considered antiseptic, antispasmodic, anti-viral, astringent. Used as a tea to improve circulation and varicose veins & as a poultice and skin tonic for wound healing properties
- Host plant for numerous moths (e.g., gothic moth, large yellow underwing, and setaceous Hebrew character)

CAUTIONS & CONSIDERATIONS

Health

CAUTION: Possible allergen - in daisy family. Often called, "pot marigold." May be confused.

Pests

Resilient but susceptible to powdery mildew, slugs and Snails.

Landscape design

Has a taproot. May self-seed in the garden. A spicy aroma. Showy. Deadhead to prolong blooming. Plant in masses. Compare with other edible flowers: Cosmos sulphureus, Antigonon leptopus and Bougainvillea glabra.

Cardamom

Elettaria cardamomum

HARDINESS ZONES: 10 TO 12

A pungent, aromatic, herbaceous, evergreen perennial of the Zingiberaceae/ ginger family. Crop of fruits are hand-picked and perfect for the home garden! Can serve as a house plant: loves hot, steamy bathrooms! The third most expensive spice by weight behind saffron and vanilla. Worth the effort to grow! Cultivated since 4th century BC! Grew in the gardens of Babylon in 720 BC. A beautiful functional food! Called 'queen of spices' - black pepper (Piper nigrum) being 'king.'

SIZE h*w	SUN	SOIL	WATER	EDIBLE
11ft*7ft	partial to full shade	loamy	flood tolerant	seeds, pods, shoots

PROPAGATION METHODS

- SEEDS: Short viability. Germinates at 70-85F within 30 days.
- DIVISION: Rhizome division. <u>Self-sterile</u> - plant a mixture of clones. Flowering in 2-3 yrs.

RECIPE

CARDAMOM-PAPAYA PUDDING: 1 large ripe papaya, 1 tbs coconut oil, 4 tbs agave nectar, 3 green cardamom pods, 2 tbs coconut milk.

Puree all in a blender, chill, and serve.

CULTURAL SIGNIFICANCE

- Host plant for the moth Endoclita hosei
- Used in folk healing: Ancient Egyptians chewed to sweeten breath. Employed in Ayurvedics for skin complaints. Recommended by Roman epicures to aid digestion; used as a stimulant/ aphrodisiac & for coughs or colds; believed to have antioxidant, antimicrobial, antidiabetic, gastro-protective & insecticidal properties
- Infused into perfume, soap, & massage oils
- Ornamental: Reed-like with orchid-like flowers

CULINARY USE

Seed/ Pod
Harvest when seed pod begins to split. Pod should pull away easily. Both the seeds & pods are used to flavor dishes and drinks. Seeds are more aromatic than the pericarp. Frequently used in Indian and Asian cuisines; also popular in Middle Eastern countries for tea and coffee and in Scandinavia countries for baked goods. Primary contributor to the flavor of tea/ "masala chai." Orchid-like flowers September-February; pods follow. Dry pods for 6-7 days and store in an airtight container in a cool, dry place, away from direct sunlight to be preserved.

Shoots/ Leaves
Young shoots eaten raw, steamed or roasted. Leaves are used as a wrap.

CAUTIONS & CONSIDERATIONS

Health
No known health hazards as a spice. Use essential oil with caution.

Pests
Fungal, bacterial and viral diseases pose threats along with thrips, borers, root grubs, and whiteflies.

Landscape design
Grows on somewhat cane-like stems. Several varieties of seed plants are known as "cardamon" - be sure of variety. Prune by removing flowered stems in spring. Compare with Alligator pepper (Aframomum melegueta).

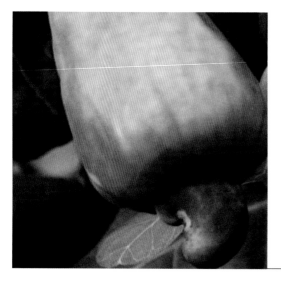

Cashew

Anacardium occidentale

HARDINESS ZONES: 9 TO 12

A fast-growing evergreen tree with many edible features. Attractive to bees, butterflies and/or birds due to its fragrant flowers. A valuable cash crop and ideal for smallholder farms! Low-maintenance tree with high culinary potential, but processing the nuts requires expertise given the allergenic oils. Considered a staple due to being over 16% protein & fat, equivalent to soybean. Nuts yield 36% DV of protein; significant magnesium, iron. Anacardiaceae (poison ivy) family.

SIZE h*w	SUN	SOIL	WATER	EDIBLE
40ft*65ft	full to partial	poor, sandy - OK	drought tolerant	fruit, nut/seed, leaves, shoots

PROPAGATION METHODS

- SEEDS: Germinates at 90-95F. Sow within 4 months. Soak in water for 24 hours. Fragile transplants. Fruits are produced after three years.

RECIPE

WINE: Separate fruits from seed. Wash. Juice in a masticating juicer and pour juice into a jar and cover with cheese cloth. Stir several times a day for 3-5 days until bubbling becomes rigorous & then subsides. Re-cover top with cloth after stirring. Refrigerate after 5 days. Allow sediment to settle 2 days. Then enjoy.

CULTURAL SIGNIFICANCE

- Brazil has highly developed cashew industry
- Tannic cashew apple juice is a prescribed folk remedy for sore throat in Cuba
- Seed oil for cosmetics, cooking, salad dressing
- Components of the bark gum acts as a vesicant and has insect repellent properties
- One homesteading method of roasting seeds involves burying in sand-filled, covered pot; placing in fire pit for 10 min @ 250 degrees, then washing, shelling, and peeling

CULINARY USE

Fruit
High in Vit C. Made into syrup for colds or coughs. Eaten fresh, cooked in curries, or fermented into vinegar or wine. Steeped in boiling, salt water for 5 min removes astringency. High pectin content - great for jam & jelly. Yields of fruit is 10x weight of nuts.

Seeds
Requires high heat processing. Must be: 1.) cleaned & soaked to prevent scorching, 2.) roasted to remove corrosives, 3.) shelled, dried, & peeled. CAUTION: Use gloves and mask when processing. Made into cashew milk, cheese, butter, curries, sweets & meat-alternatives.

Leaves & Shoots
Described as edible but see health notes. Picked in rainy season, dried & added as astringent seasoning in curries.

CAUTIONS & CONSIDERATIONS

Health
CAUTION: Nutshell contains corrosive allergens like poison ivy; destroyed by heat. Roasting seeds/ burning wood releases caustic chemicals into air. Sap may cause dermatitis. All nuts can become contaminated by aflatoxins. Dry thoroughly. Store in freezer.

Pests
Few diseases or pests; borer insects, anthracnose disease.

Landscape design
Red considered superior to yellow fruit. Dwarf cultivars yield in 1 yr. Deep taproot system. Provides erosion control.

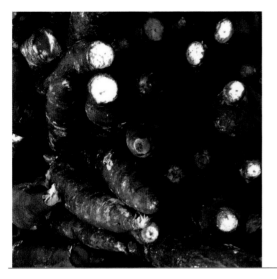

Cassava
Manihot esculenta

HARDINESS ZONES: 8 TO 11

Ready to harvest in as little as 6 months! Attractive! Many nutritional benefits if properly prepared. The most important vegetatively propagated food staple in Africa and a prominent industrial crop in Latin America and Asia. 3rd largest source of carbohydrate in the tropics. Good economic potential! Grows well even in poor soils. Demand has steadily increased. In the Euphorbiaceous family.

SIZE h*w	SUN	SOIL	WATER	EDIBLE
10ft*3ft	full	poor	dry; drought tolerant	tubers, leaves

PROPAGATION METHODS

- STEM CUTTINGS: 80F+ is ideal temperature. Select plants at least 10 months old. Cut stems into 6-inch pieces with 3+ nodes. Submerge in soil with 2+ node buried in spring.

RECIPE

CASSAVA SOURDOUGH: Peel, core, & dice cassava into 1-inch pieces. Cover with ample water (5x the amount of cassava). Soak from 5 hours to 6 days, based on preference - see health notes. Discard/change water daily. Fill pot with fresh water (5x the amount of cassava). Boil <u>uncovered</u> 30-45 min/ until very soft. Drain. Purée and feed to a sourdough starter. Makes delicious crackers!

CULTURAL SIGNIFICANCE

- Staple for more than 800 million people in the world. 4th supplier of dietary energy in the tropics (after rice, sugar & maize)
- Cassava chips and pellets are used in animal feed and alcohol production
- Provides food security during conflicts; the invader cannot easily destroy crop
- Cassava bread is the main staple in the diet of many people in the Amazon Basin

CULINARY USE

Tubers
To maximize health benefits, harvest same day as processing. Soaking followed by boiling is more effective to remove cyanide than soaking or boiling alone. Wash, peel, remove inner woody stem, dice, soak/ discard water, & boil with lid off (e.g., 45 min)/ discard water. Often dehydrated at 95F into flour. Prepared into a mash, fermented as with sourdough & spread on a hot griddle to make a tortilla-like cake. Dehydrated into crackers for long-term storage. Harvest cassava at 10 months for tender roots with lower cyanogenic glucosides. Short shelf-life: discoloration or streaking a few days after harvesting.
Leaves
Young leaves are eaten as a vegetable after pounding & boiling (45 min). CAUTION: 10x more cyanogens than roots.

CAUTIONS & CONSIDERATIONS

Health
CAUTION: Contains cyanogenic glucosides & goitrogens. Toxins can be lethal, cause paralysis or Tropical ataxic neuropathy (TAN) & epidemic spastic paraparesis (konzo).
Pests
Whitefly, mite, grasshopper, mealybug, root rot.
Landscape design
Flesh color varies. "Bitter" or "sweet" varieties from environmental/genetic conditions (e.g., drought). Bitter has more anti-nutrients. Compare with native coontie (Zamia integrifolia) or spurge nettle (Cnidoscolus stimulosus).

Cattails

Typha latifolia

HARDINESS ZONES: 3 TO 10

A highly edible wild native with many ecosystem benefits! Tolerates flooding, poor soil, moderate salinity; used in water & soil remediation - absorbs lead, pesticides, nitrogen, potassium. Rich in vitamins! Championed by survivalists - can be eaten throughout the year. Eaten as a staple for thousands of years. A popular vegetable in traditional Chinese cuisine. A good container plant. Attracts songbirds! Beautiful in fresh or dried in flower arrangements! Typhaceae family.

SIZE h*w	SUN	SOIL	WATER	EDIBLE
9ft*3ft	full to partial	Poor - OK	flood tolerant	roots, shoots, flower, pollen, seeds

PROPAGATION METHODS

- SEEDS: Germinates at 85-90F. Seeds viable 5 months. Surface sow in a pot & stand in 1 inch of water. Self-seeds readily.
- DIVISIONS: Divide young shoots under 1 ft with some root attached.

RECIPE

CAT-ON-THE-COB: 30-40 peeled cattail flowerheads.

Boil cattail flowerheads in water for 10-15 minutes; Drain. Drizzle with salt, pepper, and oil to taste. Eat as a "corn on the cob."

CULINARY USE

Flower, Pollen, Seeds
Flower stalks, boiled & eaten like corn on the cob. Seed typically roasted & has a pleasant nutty taste; also ground into a flour for cakes etc. Pre-pollen flower stalks have an olive/ artichoke flavor. Pollen tastes nutty.

Shoots
Young shoots in spring (under 16 inches long) are eaten raw, cooked, or pickled as an asparagus substitute; tastes like cucumber. Base of mature stem often eaten cooked with outer part removed.

Roots
Most often boiled, baked, or roasted like potatoes. Also, macerated, then boiled to yield a sweet syrup. Can be dried & ground into a protein-rich flour for bread, biscuits, muffins. 80% carbohydrate (30 - 46% starch).

CULTURAL SIGNIFICANCE

- Tubers contain more calcium, iron, and potassium than potatoes or rice
- May create blocks in sewer and stormwater drains, spreads aggressively
- Flowering spike used for dab painting. Stems/ leaves used for thatch, paper, mats, baskets, chairs, hats, rush lights (oiled & lit as a candle)
- Hairs of the fruits are used for stuffing pillows; WWII, US Navy life-vests

CAUTIONS & CONSIDERATIONS

Health
No known adverse health effects. Avoid eating from polluted water. Pollen is highly inflammable, used in fireworks. May be mistaken for poisonous iris species - harvest with corn-dog like fruit to identify correctly.

Pests
Highly resilient.

Landscape design
Forms clonal colonies. Harvest roots in late autumn or early spring. Compare with T. angustifolia, and T. domingensis.

Chaya

Cnidoscolus aconitifolius

HARDINESS ZONES: 9B TO 11

Known as "tree spinach." This specimen is a fast-growing perennial shrub. One of the most productive vegetables, nutritionally out-performing most other greens; packed with protein, vitamins, calcium, iron and antioxidants! Perfect for a xeriscape! Evergreen with showy white flowers. Lives up to 20 years. One of the most nutritious vegetables in the world. A historical staple food of the Mayans. Year-round production! Attracts butterflies! In the Euphorbiaceae family.

SIZE h*w	SUN	SOIL	WATER	EDIBLE
12ft*12ft	full to partial	poor	dry; drought tolerant	leaves & stems

PROPAGATION METHODS

- STEM CUTTINGS: Take woody stem cuttings about 6-12 inches long and submerge in soil with 2+ nodes buried when 80-90F. NOTE: Few varieties go to seed. 'Picuda' goes to seed.

RECIPE

CHAYA QUICHE: Wash, finely chop, and boil 4 c of chaya leaves uncovered for 25 min. Strain. Sauté with 1 minced garlic clove in 1 tbs oil. 5 min. Allow to cool. Mix with 5 beaten eggs, 1 c sourdough starter, & ¼ tsp salt. Oil & heavily flour a pie dish. Pour mixture into to dish. Bake at 350F 30-50 minutes until a toothpick comes out clean.

CULTURAL SIGNIFICANCE

- Pre-Hispanic historical food: first used in indigenous cultures (Mexico, Central America)
- Used in folk healing (e.g., for fertility, diabetes, arthritis; for anti-microbial properties)
- Leaves serve as a pleasant aromatic herb
- Serves as shade trees for coffee or fencing
- Sought after ornamental; shaped as hedge, artful "living labyrinths", mandala circles
- Believed to hold promises as a means to tackle malnutrition, hunger & food scarcity

CULINARY USE

Leaves
Chop leaves and boil for 25 minutes with lid off in well-ventilated area. Toxin removed as gas during boiling. Can be harvested continuously as long as no more than 50% of the leaves are removed from the plant at any time. For maximum leaf production, harvest leaves every 2 to 3 months. Cooking in aluminum cookware can result in a toxic broth, causing diarrhea. Dump water to be safe/ Do not cook in aluminum. Leaves take on flavors from whatever seasonings are added. Can be used in all of the same ways as cooked kale, collards, spinach or other dark leafy greens but much more nutritious (2-3x). Once boiled, puréed chaya can be added to masa to fortify tortillas. Can be dried into a powder after being boiled for a quick addition to smoothies. 33% of DV of calcium, 51% of iron, 27% Vit A! Rich in antioxidants & phyto-chemicals.

CAUTIONS & CONSIDERATIONS

Health
CAUTION: Raw leaves are toxic: glucoside/ cyanide. Boil 25 min. Some varieties have stinging hairs dissolved in cooking. Wash hands after handling. Do not get sap in eyes.

Pests
High resistance to pests and disease.

Landscape design
C. aconitifolius is star-leafed. C. chayamansa is maple-leafed, both edible. Debate on whether they're same species. 4 varieties: Estrella, Picuda, Chayamansa & Redonda. Compare with Stinging Nettle (Urtica dioica).

Chayote
Sechium edule

HARDINESS ZONES: 9 TO 12

A vigorous, perennial vine, an important commercial vegetable and an excellent staple crop! Although it looks like a green pear, the taste is a cross between potato and cucumber. The fruit even suites those in hurry since it does not need to be peeled prior to eating! Used to make curries, stir-fries, or even pies! Loved by beekeepers because it flowers abundantly throughout the year! Cultivated since pre-Columbian times. A functional food in the Cucurbitaceae family.

SIZE h*w	SUN	SOIL	WATER	EDIBLE
30ft*1ft	full to partial	well-draining	average	flowers, fruit, seed, leaves, root, shoots

PROPAGATION METHODS

- SEEDS: Germinate at 80-85F in ripe, mother plant; keep seed inside fruit when sowing. Plant narrow end in soil with wide end facing up and out of soil. Produces within 4 months.

RECIPE

CHAYOTE CURRY: 2 chayotes, 4 tbs oil, 2 c coconut milk; 4 cloves garlic, 3 red peppers, 6 tropical almonds or cashews; Optional: 2 tsp palm sugar, salt and pepper to taste.

Puree spices with nuts. Roast puree in oil until fragrant on medium heat. Add chayote and sauté until soft. Mix in coconut milk and serve warm.

CULTURAL SIGNIFICANCE

- Mild flavored: Used as dietary food in nursing homes & in baby food
- An Australian urban legend claimed restaurant "apple" pies were actually chayote pies
- Leaves/ tea used in folk healing (e.g., to relieve headache/ anxiety; promote cardiovascular and kidney health. Believed diuretic properties of the leaves & seeds & anti-inflammatory properties of the leaves & fruits)
- Stem fibers used to make baskets, hats

CULINARY USE

Fruit
Eaten raw julienned in salads, but more often lightly boiled to retain crispy consistency. Also roasted, stuffed, mashed, baked, fried, or pickled. Mild cucumber/ zucchini flavor. Can be used as a substitute for apples in pies. Peeling optional.

Seeds
Eaten cooked. Nutty flavor. When deep-fried they taste like french-fries (potato). Good source of protein. Considered a delicacy.

Leaves, Flowers, Shoot
Young leaves/ stem tips cooked as a vegetable like asparagus; often eaten in salads and stir-fried.

Root
Typically boiled, baked, fried and candied in syrup. Rich in starch.

CAUTIONS & CONSIDERATIONS

Health
No known health hazards. Rich in amino acids. Good source of iron, carotene, thiamine, riboflavin and niacin.

Pests
Very susceptible to pests & diseases in wet climates. Plant on slopes.

Landscape design
Many varieties - some with spiny fruits. A cheap, easy-to-produce vegetable, both for home consumption and for city markets. Invasive potential - can form dense colonies. Compare with milkweed vine (Morrenia odorata).

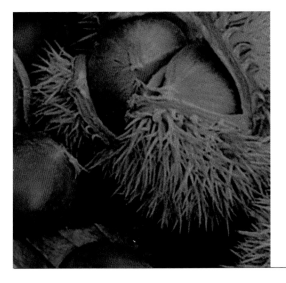

Chestnut

Castanea pumila ashei

HARDINESS ZONES: 6 TO 10

Produces the largest nut of all Chinquapins! A starchy staple & delicious Florida native shrub. Deciduous. Also called dwarf chestnut. On the endangered species list. Propagate to promote population sizes. Harvesting is typically in early September. An ornamental valued for rapid growth, productiveness, and delicious little nuts. Good fall color!! In the Fagaceae family.

SIZE h*w	SUN	SOIL	WATER	EDIBLE
13ft*8ft	full to partial	poor, acidic - OK	drought tolerant	seed

PROPAGATION METHODS

- SEEDS: Germinates at 70-75, typically in fall. Fruits at 4+ years.
- DIVISIONS: Underground suckers. Divide in winter.

RECIPE

CHESTNUT BUTTER: Cut a deep "x" on the rounded side. Roast for 35 min at 350F or until skins pull back & the nut has softened. While warm, place in damp towel to steam and cool for 15 min to aid peeling. Peel. Purée 1 lb with 1/2c water. Add honey and salt to taste.

Store, refrigerated, in an airtight container 3 weeks.

CULINARY USE

Seeds

Seed edible raw but most often cooked. Sweet, nutty flavor. 45% starch and 2.5% protein. To enhance the sweetness of the nut, it is often recommended to hang the nuts in a porous/paper bag, to allow them to dry and for the starches to break down into sugars. Then roast.

Roasting requires scoring the fruit beforehand to prevent explosion. After roasting, the seeds are eaten whole as a snack. Roasting enhances the chocolatey undertones in flavor. Texture is slightly similar to that of a baked potato and serves as a substitute.

NOTE: Seed is half the size of C. dentata

CULTURAL SIGNIFICANCE

- High fire tolerance. Wood/husks - suitable fuel
- Base of plant is cut to ground level to prompt multiple stalks as a thick cover for turkeys
- Nuts consumed by squirrels and rabbits while white tail deer graze upon the foliage
- Larval food for the Orange-tipped oakworm moth (Anisota senatoria), attracts butterflies
- Leaves and bark contain tannins for dying
- Native Americans used leaf infusions for headaches/ fevers as an astringent and tonic

CAUTIONS & CONSIDERATIONS

Health
No known adverse health effects.
Pests
Chestnut blight fungus, weevils.

Landscape design
Bloom odor. Thicket-forming. For zones 8+: Plant in shade of oak. Also, consider blight-resistant varieties: Dunstan chestnut (Castanea dentata x mollissima) or other cultivars: "Fuller", "Rush"; Compare with Tahitian chestnut/ Inocarpus fagifer. May be confused with the horse chestnut (Aesculus hippocastanum).

Chia

Salvia hispanica

HARDINESS ZONES: 9 TO 11

This pretty flowering plant has recently gained popularity as a "superfood." It's a good source of protein, easily digested fats, soluble fiber and antioxidants. An ancient Aztec staple and a low-maintenance crop. Compared to maiz/ corn in cultural significance and value throughout history. Seeds stay fresh for 4-5 years without refrigeration. Initially sold in the U.S. for 1980s Chia Pets! Annual in all zones. Perennial in zones 9-11. In the mint family (Labiatae).

SIZE h*w	SUN	SOIL	WATER	EDIBLE
3ft*1ft	full to partial	sandy, acidic-ok	drought tolerant	seed

PROPAGATION METHODS

- SEEDS: Germinates at 77-86F. Direct sow in spring. May be grown year-round in areas with mild winters. Ensure seed-to-soil contact. Plant in May-June. Harvesting is typical in October.

RECIPE

CHIA PUDDING: 1/2 c of coconut water, 2 tbsp of chia seeds; (topping) 1 ripe mango pureed.

Mix chia seeds and coconut milk. Leave overnight in the fridge for the seeds to absorb the liquid. Top with mango puree.

CULTURAL SIGNIFICANCE

- A staple food for Mesoamerican cultures
- Offered to Aztec gods in religious ceremonies
- Pressed seed oil used as base for face paint
- Fresh mucilage used as stabilizer in ice cream and other frozen desserts
- Like guar gum and gelatin, used as thickener in various stages of food preparation
- Replaces egg or oil content (e.g., in cakes) - a common substitute in baking

CULINARY USE

Seeds
A complete protein, containing all nine essential amino acids. Hydrophilic, absorbing up to 10 times their weight in liquid; can be prepared as a gruel or pudding. As with most seeds, optimally nutritious when eaten soaked or sprouted. Sprouted seeds eaten in salads, sandwiches, soups, stews. Guidelines recommend no more than 48 g/day (5 tbsp). The European Commission approves chia seed in bread if under 5% (more may increase acrylamide content).

A good source of protein and easily digested fats. Seeds may be soaked to make Mexico's chia fresca. May be added to other foods as a topping (e.g., yogurt). Gluten free! A "chia egg" = 2 tbs chia seeds 1/2 c water. Used as an egg substitute in vegan recipes.

CAUTIONS & CONSIDERATIONS

Health
No known adverse health effects. Great source of calcium, iron, zinc, magnesium, phosphorus, & selenium. Rich in omega-3, 6, 9. Unlike flax, no need to grind - readily bioavailable. Don't eat dry seeds. NOTE: May increase acrylamide if baked in bread.

Pests
No major pests or diseases.

Landscape design
Related perennials include S. officinalis, S. elegans, and S. apiana. Compare with Chan seeds (Hyptis suaveolens).

Chicasaw Plum

Prunus angustifolia

HARDINESS ZONES: 5 TO 9B

A deciduous, easy-to-grow, Florida native and host plant in the Rosaceae family. Also called Florida Sand Plum. Showy, fragrant flowers make this shrub a delightful addition to the food forest. First cultivated around 1874 but long used by Native Americans and early settlers. Attracts bees, butterflies and birds!

SIZE h*w	SUN	SOIL	WATER	EDIBLE
25ft*25ft	full to partial	well-draining	average	fruit, seed

PROPAGATION METHODS

- SEEDS: Germinates at 80-86F within 18+ months. Sprout in moss. Not true to type.
- DIVISION: Suckers freely; divide runners.
- CUTTINGS: Softwood in spring, 65-70F.

RECIPE

PLUM WINE: Remove all stems and ferment fruit for 1-2 days in water until easily removed from seed. Strain. Cover pulp with water. Puree. Place puree in a glass vessel covered with cloth for 3 days, stirring vigorously 2-3 times a day. When actively bubbling, strain. Allow to ferment 1-2 days longer. Bottle and refrigerate.

CULTURAL SIGNIFICANCE

- Used as a shelterbelt hedge plant; has an extensive root system and can form thickets useful for erosion control on stream banks
- A bonsai plant: Attractive bark, small leaves and thin branches
- Larval host for many moth species (e.g., black-waved flannel moth, blinded sphinx, the cecropia moth, coral hairstreak, elm sphinx, the hummingbird clearwing moth, imperial moth, striped hairstreak, and tiger swallowtail)

CULINARY USE

Fruit
The thin-skinned, 1-inch diameter fruit has a soft juicy, tart/sweet pulp and is eaten raw or cooked. Fruits change from red to yellow when fully ripe in the spring. Also, dried for later use. Used in pies, preserves, jellies, wine, etc.

NOTE: Increasing interest in the fruit as a high-value specialty crop.

Seeds
Described as edible raw but likely safest cooked. Do not consume if bitter as a toxin may be present. See health notes. Remove shells from the sunflower-sized kernels. Boil 20 minutes, discard water and dry/ roast. Native Americans ground the kernels and formed into cakes/ crackers. Consume with caution.

CAUTIONS & CONSIDERATIONS

Health
CAUTION: Stems, leaves, seeds produce hydrogen cyanide, particularly toxic in the process of wilting. Shoots can become thorny.

Pests
Resilient. Leaf spot, canker and black knot, aphids, scale, borers and tent caterpillars.

Landscape design
Colonizes an area - thicket forming. May grow in zone 10 under an oak. Consider varieties like "Guthrie" or "Bruce." Compare with Flatwoods Plum (Prunus umbellatus).

Chicory
Cichorium intybus

HARDINESS ZONES: 3 TO 10

In the aster family (Asteraceae). Attracts beneficial insects like lady bugs & bees. Highly ornamental. Cultivated for centuries for edible & medicinal leaves, buds and roots. Believed to be one of the oldest cultivated vegetables in human history. Long history of herbal use especially for believed tonic affect upon the liver, spleen, digestive tract. Rich nutritional composition! Widely used as a coffee substitute, especially in France and New Orleans.

SIZE h*w	SUN	SOIL	WATER	EDIBLE
3ft*1ft	full to partial	well-draining	drought tolerant	roots, leaves, flowers

PROPAGATION METHODS

- SEEDS: Germinates at 65-75F. Direct sow - broadcast. Forms a large taproot quickly.
- ROOT: Grows from pieces of root.

RECIPE

CHICORY 'COFFEE': Harvest in winter in the 2nd year of growing. Separate. Wash and freeze leaves for later use. Rinse and wash roots in water/vinegar bath. Chop in 1/4-inch-thick rounds. Dry in oven at 170F until crisp (e.g., 2 hrs), then brown at 350 for 5-10 min stirring occasionally. Grind in a coffee grinder and steep as with coffee.

CULTURAL SIGNIFICANCE

- The plant is used in Bach flower remedies - the keywords for prescribing it are "possessiveness" and "self pity"
- Inspiration for romantic, European folklore of "Blauwarte" and to cure 'passions of the heart'
- Grown as a forage crop for livestock, believed to reduce intestinal parasites
- Beer brewers use roasted chicory to add flavor to stouts and strong blond ales
- Traditional Chinese medicine (e.g., diuretic)

CULINARY USE

Roots
Fleshy root can grow 2ft long! Wildly cultivated as a coffee substitute. Roots are also baked, roasted, ground & steeped. Young roots have a slightly bitter, caramel flavor when roasted. Young roots (under 2 years) are cooked/boiled with raisins. Also candied. Harvest after flowering.

Leaves & Flowers
Leaves and flower edible raw. Leaves are often blanched/boiled to remove bitterness. Less bitter in winter or when continuously covered by leaf mulch to deprive of sunlight. In Greece, leaves are cooked in a wild-greens pie. In the Apulian region, wild chicory leaves are combined with fava bean puree in the traditional local dish "fave e cicorie selvatiche." In ancient Rome, a dish called "puntarelle" was made with chicory sprouts.

CAUTIONS & CONSIDERATIONS

Health
CAUTION: Medicinal. Consume in moderation. Excessive use may impair retina function. Significant amounts (more than 20% of the Daily Value) of vitamin K, A, C; rich in inulin. High polyphenol & flavonoid content.

Pests
Generally, disease and pest resistant; rabbits may forage. Fungus and bacterial/ watery soft rot may decrease yield.

Landscape design
As a perennial, chicory produces only leaves the first year. May behave invasively.

Chocolate Pudding Tree

Diospyros digyna

HARDINESS ZONES: 10 TO 12

Also called Black Sapote. Actually, a species of persimmon and member of the Ebenaceae family. This slow-growing evergreen is quite the novelty and conversation starter! The flesh is dark chocolate brown and rich in flavor! Used as ornamental! A nice alternative for those who do not like citrus: offers Vit C, A, E and fiber. Good source of calcium and phosphorus.

SIZE h*w	SUN	SOIL	WATER	EDIBLE
50ft*50ft	full to partial	well-draining	flood tolerant	fruit

PROPAGATION METHODS

- SEEDS: Germinates at 77-86F easily but slowly – not true to type. <u>Generally dioecious</u>. Need male & female to yield fruit.
- GRAFT: Can fruit when 2 - 3 years old.

RECIPE

"CHOCOLATE PUDDING" MOUSSE: 1 cup of strained sapote pulp, 1/2 cup coconut cream, 2 tbs agave syrup, 3 tbs cocoa powder, 1 tbs chia seeds, 1/4 tsp vanilla extract. OPTIONAL: pinch of salt.

Combine all ingredients using a handheld mixer. Refrigerate 2 hours. NOTE: Add additional chia seed to make firmer as for a pie.

CULTURAL SIGNIFICANCE

- Considered an 'energy booster' fruit
- Good shade tree: grows fairly slowly for the first 4 years but then grows much more rapidly
- Folk healing use: (e.g., leaf poultice for blisters. Fruit believed to offer anti-inflammatory, antiviral & antioxidant properties)
- Towns called "Zapotlán" occur frequently in regions of western Mexico, referring to an abundance of "Zapote" (Diospyros spp.) trees, known as "Tlilzapotl" in the Nahuatl language

CULINARY USE

Fruit

Prune-flavored fruit eaten raw like an avocado – the fruit is split into two halves and the pulp eaten with a spoon. Ripens in October-March when there are few tropical fruits to enjoy. Turns a duller color when ripe and should be very soft before eating. Fruits soften 1 - 14 days on the counter if picked. Frozen and pureed into an ice-cream. Also cooked and used as a chocolate substitute in pies, mousse, liquors, bread and milkshakes. In Mexico, the pulp is mashed, strained and mixed with citrus juice and served with whipped cream. Used as a base for "moles" – pronounced "MOH-lay" from Nahuatl mōlli, meaning "sauce."

NOTE: Common varieties in Florida include 'Merida' (aka 'Reineke') and 'Bernecker' (aka 'Berniker').

CAUTIONS & CONSIDERATIONS

Health

CAUTION: Unripe fruits are astringent, caustic, bitter and irritating; unripe fruit is used as a fish poison.

Pests

Hardy but does attract spider mites, scales, cochineals.

Landscape design

Some varieties may require cross-pollination. Shelter from strong winds. Compare with Canistel/ Yellow sapote (Pouteria campechiana), Caimito/ Star Apple (Chrysophyllum cainito), Mamey (Pouteria sapota) or Florida native, persimmon (Diospyros virginiana).

Chufa

Cyperus esculentus var. sativus

HARDINESS ZONES: 8 TO 10

One of the oldest cultivated plants dating back to 4,000BC Egypt! 30% starch! Cultivated for its edible tubers. A fast-growing perennial productive for up to 5 years. A single plant can produce up to a hundred "nut" morsels! Considered the #1 food in a NASA bio-regenerative life support systems analysis! Excellent for container growing! Cyperaceae family.

SIZE h*w	SUN	SOIL	WATER	EDIBLE
2ft*1/2ft	full	sandy loam	continuously moist	tubers

PROPAGATION METHODS

- Tubers: Germinates at 65-75F. Collect seed in fall. Broadcast seed in late fall or early spring on moist or bare soil and cover with a shallow layer of soil (1.5 inch). Seed 35 to 50lbs per acre.

RECIPE

HORCHATA/ NUT MILK: 1 c chufa, 4 c water (x2).

Soak chufas overnight in 4 c of water. Discard water. Refill 4 cups of water and puree with chufa nuts. Strain to obtain milk.

Optional: add honey, cinnamon, vanilla to taste.

CULINARY USE

Tubers
Sweet, nutty flavor - a cross between fresh coconut, almonds, and raisins. 3 ingredients derived from tigernut: milk, flour & oil. Cooked tubers go well in soups and stews. The tubers are the primary ingredient in "horchata de chufa" (Spain) and kunnu aya (Nigeria and Mali), a sweet, milk-like beverage. After harvesting tiger nuts, wash with water to remove sand and small stones. If preparing a beverage, soak overnight, strain, add water, grind & sweeten. Dried & ground tiger nuts are an excellent flour sometimes added to biscuits and other bakery products. Roasted tubers are a coffee or cocoa substitute. Pressed tubers yield a superior oil comparable to olive oil used for salads or deep frying. May be baked as a vegetable or grated and used to make ice cream or sherbets.

CULTURAL SIGNIFICANCE

- Leading food plot for turkeys. Also feeds ducks, sandhill cranes, crows, waterfowl; Larval host for Dun Skipper
- In Spain, horchata is a popular beverage competing with carbonated drinks. Fermented for alcohol in Sicily
- Tuber used in making oil, soap, and starch extracts. Leaves used to make baskets, paper, hats, matting. Folk healing use: antiflammatory

CAUTIONS & CONSIDERATIONS

Health
No known adverse health effects. High in vitamin E & iron.

Pests
Florida negro bug, Thyreocoris pulicaria, reported to damage crop; larvae develop inside the tubers.

Landscape design
Allelopathic. Can be invasive & resembles grass. Erosion and slope control. Grow in beds for easy ID & harvest. Discounted seed sold by National Wild Turkey Federation: seedstore.nwtf.org. Compare with Water Chestnut (Eleocharis dulcis), Indian Potato (Apios Americana).

Cilantro

Coriandrum sativum

HARDINESS ZONES: 2 TO 11

An annual well-worth your time! Repels aphids - a good companion plant. Root-to-seed edible. Sow seeds in the fall and winter a few seeds at a time every few weeks to have a steady supply. Pairs well with citrus and fruits like mango. When planted in mass, it resembles Baby's Breath flowers! One of the most widely used herbs! In Apiaceae family.

SIZE h*w	SUN	SOIL	WATER	EDIBLE
1.5ft*1ft	full to partial	well-drained	drought tolerant	leaves, stem, flowers, seeds, root

PROPAGATION METHODS

- SEEDS: Germinates at 60-70F within 10-45 days. Autumn sown plants will grow bigger & produce more seeds. Bolts in hot summer climates (85+F). Self-seeds readily.

RECIPE

CORIANDER SEED BISCUITS: 3/4 tsp toasted & ground coriander; 1/3 c coconut meal, 1/4 c sourdough starter, 1/2 c coconut oil, 3 egg whites.

Purée into a paste. Cover. Let rest 4 hrs in fridge. Shape into 2 in flattened balls on oiled pan. Bake 15-30 min at 350. Dry out in oven 30 min-2hrs.

CULTURAL SIGNIFICANCE

- Seed used in folk healing (e.g., for calming effect on digestive system, treating flatulence, etc. Chewed to stimulate the flow of gastric juices and to cure foul breath; believed to be an aphrodisiac. Leaf believed to detox body)
- A spray from boiling coriander leaves used to repel mites & aphids
- Oil from the seed used for making soap
- Grows wild in Asia and Europe. Long history of cultivation dating back to ancient Egypt

CULINARY USE

Leaves, Stem & Flowers
Leaves eaten raw or cooked. Used as a flavoring in salad, soup, pesto, curry and more. Good source of Vit K. Leaves have a different taste than the seeds. Added to the dish immediately before serving as heating, freezing and drying diminish aroma. Snip off stems before flowering to prolong leaf production. Stems diced finely. Flowers used as garnish.

Seeds
Mature seed often eaten cooked. Pleasantly sweet-spicy fragrance. Used in cakes, bread, curries, and liquors. Becomes increasingly fragrant when dried. Used in brine for pickling vegetables, beer and wine making. Substitute for caraway. Egyptians called it: "Spice of happiness."

Root
Delicate flavor & moist texture for curry pastes.

CAUTIONS & CONSIDERATIONS

Health
CAUTION: Consume in moderation. Powdered coriander may cause allergic reactions (asthma) & photosensitivity.

Pests
Wilt and bacterial blight; grasshoppers, leafhoppers.

Landscape design
Cilantro plants yield about 1¾ tonnes per acre of seed! Very productive! Compare with perennial cousin: culantro (Eryngium foetidum), Vietnamese coriander (Persicaria odorata), Epazote (Chenopodium ambrosioides), or Cutting Celery (Apium graveolens var. secalinum).

Cinnamon
Cinnamomum verum

HARDINESS ZONES: 10 TO 12

Among the earliest, most popular spices historically used!! A small, slow-growing evergreen tree which can be grown as a leafy bush. Produces well for over 40 years! Also called Ceylon cinnamon. Grows easily in South Florida's subtropics. A luxury spice in the 16th century: Explorers, like Christopher Columbus set out on cinnamon discovery missions. In the Lauraceae family.

SIZE h*w	SUN	SOIL	WATER	EDIBLE
40ft*20ft	partial	well-draining	average	inner bark, leaves

PROPAGATION METHODS

- SEEDS: Germinates at 65-70F within 6 months. Short viability. Remove fruit pulp.
- CUTTINGS: Soft-wood roots in soil. Root cuttings in spring.

RECIPE

CINNAMON VEGGIE MARINADE: 3 cinnamon sticks, 1 tbs ginger, 1 hot pepper, 4 c vinegar mixed with 1 c honey, salt/ pepper to taste.

Place chopped herbs in a jar. Pour in vinegar/ honey. Steep 4 weeks. Stir often. Strain. Drizzle marinade on veggies prior to serving.

CULINARY USE

Inner Bark
Small side branches (under 2 in diameter) are removed from the trees. The outer bark is scraped off along with green layer. The inner bark is loosened by rubbing with a rod. Then, it is split with a knife, and peeled off. These 'quills' are dried over several days. Used in coffee drinks, desserts, curries, spice combinations (e.g., garam masala). Used as a spice for both savory and sweet cooking. Widely employed in cakes and breads. An important ingredient in Jerk Seasoning. Store quills whole. Grind just prior to use to keep it fresh and aromatic.

Leaves
Leaves can be used for flavor in cooking as with bay leaves. Steep in stew, soups, or teas. A source of phytonutrients.

CULTURAL SIGNIFICANCE

- Twigs, leaves & berries/ seeds are pressed for oil & widely used in food and industrial products like candies, chewing gums, mouthwash and toothpaste
- Used in folk healing (e.g., bark is said to aid in digestion, relieve headaches/ heavy menses; offer anti-inflammatory properties & serve as circulatory stimulant)
- Oil is effective in killing mosquito larvae
- Fruits are eaten by birds and spread widely

CAUTIONS & CONSIDERATIONS

Health
Good source of beta-carotene; contains antioxidants called proanthocyanidins. CAUTION: Ground cinnamon is not water soluble. Do not ingest or respire without mixing into other ingredients.

Pests
Bacterial and fungal leaf spot and dieback; canker.

Landscape design
Ready to harvest in 3 years. Compare with Chinese cinnamon (C. cassia), Allspice (Calycanthus floridus) or FL native: Wild Cinnamon (Canella winterana)- endangered.

Clumping Bamboo

Nastus elatus

HARDINESS ZONES: 10 TO 12

Sold as an ornamental and prized for its use in cooking, this variety is edible and delicious raw, unlike most other bamboos. Rarer variety sought by enthusiasts and collectors. You will never eat bamboo shoots from a can again! Excellent in stir-fries! Plant on a mowed island: Forms dense thickets. In the Poaceae family.

SIZE h*w	SUN	SOIL	WATER	EDIBLE
60ft*4in	full to partial	sandy, clay - OK	average	shoots

PROPAGATION METHODS

- DIVISIONS: Propagated most frequently by divisions of clumps in the ground. Seed is not typically produced.

RECIPE

BAMBOO CHILI SLAW: 1 c boiled julienned bamboo, drained, 3tbs oil, 1/3 cup chopped hot pepper.

Purée hot pepper with oil. Toss with cooked bamboo. Use as a topping for tacos, eggs, or avocado or as a side condiment. Keeps 1 week in the refrigerator.

CULTURAL SIGNIFICANCE

- Culms used for building, musical instruments, flattened to weave house walls/ floors or split to make arrow-points, utensils. Stems are hollow between internodes - used as water containers
- Symbolic of strength, resilience, humility, prosperity and grace
- The Japanese proverb says "a bamboo that bends is stronger than the oak that resists"
- Common food throughout Asia, harvesting is said to be a poetic meditation on gentleness

CULINARY USE

Shoots
Edible raw or cooked. Smells of sweetcorn & makes a delicious wonton filling. Generally harvested in early spring by carefully digging around the underexposed culm beneath the ground, just as the tips start to poke through. Sweetest before the shoot is exposed to sunlight or air when no more than two weeks old. Any older and they can be fibrous and tough. The bamboo shoot can be stored raw (whole & unpeeled) in a refrigerator crisper for two weeks. To cook: Peel & trim root end. Slice, dice, or julienne the shoots, then boil in fresh water. After cooking, rinse in cold water, drain, and store in a covered container in the refrigerator until ready to use. The cooked shoots can also be drained and frozen. Mulch heavily for sweeter shoots.

CAUTIONS & CONSIDERATIONS

Health
CAUTION: Be sure of variety. Unless you know positively that your bamboo is edible raw, cook the shoots for at least 20 minutes but ideally for an hour. Discard water.

Pests
Highly resilient: aphids occasionally but do little damage.

Landscape design
One of the fastest-growing species. New shoots produced nearly year-round. Compare with FL native and medicinal, Horsetail (Equisetum hyemale) or FL native bamboos: Arundinaria gigantea & Lasiacis divaricate.

Cocoa
Theobroma cacao

HARDINESS ZONES: 10 TO 12

Cultivated since 400BCE! An important staple which also yields one of the world's most popular products - chocolate! The seed contains up to 50% fat. An understory, evergreen in the Malvaceae family is often interplanted with bananas and coconuts! After 5 years, trees can yield up to 7 lbs of cacao per year. Interesting, small, ornamental tree! Flowers directly on its trunk and branches (cauliflory).

SIZE h*w	SUN	SOIL	WATER	EDIBLE
25ft*25ft	part to full shade	well-draining	flood tolerant	fruit, seed

PROPAGATION METHODS

- SEEDS: Germinates at 80-85F within 4 weeks. Short viability. Plant out at 6 months.
- CUTTINGS: Greenwood cuttings should have 2– 5 leaves and 1 or 2 buds. Roots in soil.

RECIPE

GLAZED COCOA NIBS: 2 c nibs, 1/3 c maple syrup, 1/8 tsp sea salt.

Soak seeds 24-48 hrs. De-pulp/ discard water (use as plant fertilizer). Dehydrate at 115 F/ 45 C until crisp. Crack, discard husks. Mix nuts, syrup and salt. Pour into a skillet on medium-high heat stirring until caramelized (3 min). Cool. Refrigerates 2 wks.

CULINARY USE

Fruit
The fruit contains about 30 seeds engulfed in a thin, succulent, mildly sweet pulp which is sucked as a sweet snack or made into juices and jellies. Has a tropical taste like passion fruit and mango.

Seeds
Widely used in the confectionery industry to make chocolate, cakes, ice cream, drinks etc. Seeds are fermented 2-7 days, slowly dehydrated and then roasted. Seeds are then cracked to separate the kernels/nibs from the shell (shelled beans are called "nibs"). The nibs can be ground such as to make a chocolate bar, which usually takes 30-35 cacao beans. Historically, nibs were mixed with chile as an Aztec drink. Many health benefits - beans are rich in antioxidants.

CULTURAL SIGNIFICANCE

- Used in folk healing (e.g., to relieve depression symptoms & as antiseptic, diuretic)
- Fat from unfermented cocoa beans and burnt husks extracted for soap making. Cacao butter also used in skin creams, cosmetics
- In Mexico, Central America and South America seeds were used as a monetary currency
- The Latin name "Theobroma" means "food of the gods" - Mayans and Aztecs used chocolate in engagement, marriage and religious rituals

CAUTIONS & CONSIDERATIONS

Health
CAUTION: Chocolate can cause allergies and migraine in some people; contains caffeine. Dehydrate the beans covered/ indoors to prevent air/ rain contamination (e.g., heavy metals).

Pests
Borer insects, anthracnose, rot, dieback, canker.

Landscape design
Plants dislike temperatures below 40 degrees- intolerant of frost. Compare with Cupuacu (Theobroman grandiflorum) & Carob bean (Ceratonia siliqua).

Coconut
Cocos nucifera

HARDINESS ZONES: 10 TO 12

A member of the palm tree (Arecaceae) family, the fruit is actually a drupe, not a nut. One of the most useful trees in the world and is often referred to as the "tree of life" or "the tree of a thousand uses." Provides a wide range of foods and commodities. Grown as both an ornamental and commercial plant. The inner flesh of the coconut fruit, as well as the oil and milk are staples throughout the tropics and subtropics.

SIZE h*w	SUN	SOIL	WATER	EDIBLE
98ft*10ft	full to partial	poor, salinity - OK	flood, drought tolerant	fruit, water, sap, sprout, root, stem

PROPAGATION METHODS

- SEEDS: Germinates at 80-85F; no dormancy. Soak nut, plant with the pointed end down/ attached part upward, 1/3rd above soil. Water often.

RECIPE

GLUTEN-FREE, COCONUT FLOUR: Purée coconut with water and strain to separate. Freeze the liquid as a diluted coconut milk (good to ferment into yogurt). Boil shredded coconut in water briefly. Oil will float to top. Refrigerate to skim off. Save for later. Strain. Dehydrate shredded coconut at 115 F/ 45 C until crisp. Pulse into flour. 1 c white/wheat flour = ¼ c coconut flour.

CULTURAL SIGNIFICANCE

- Folk medicine uses: (e.g., emollient/ moisturizer, laxative). Used in infant formulas
- Many uses: Rare 'coconut pearl' (lime, calcium carbonate) prized for jewelry. Coir used to make ropes, mats, brushes, sacks, or highly valued compost. Leaves - baskets, thatch, mats, skewers. Roots - dye, mouthwash, toothbrush. Shells - bowls, musical instruments, charcoal. Oil - soaps, cosmetics, candles

CULINARY USE

Fruit/ Water
Water drank fresh. Meat used fresh or dried (e.g., in buko pie, macaroons). Coconut milk pressed from grated meat. Coconut flour obtained from dehydrated meat. Oil extracted by boiling grated meat in water; oil skimmed after cooling.

Flower Sap
The sap derived from incising the flower clusters serves as a tea, alcohol (if fermented), or syrup/ sugar (if reduced).

Sprout/ Stem
Newly germinated coconuts contain an edible fluff of marshmallow-like consistency. Stem pith made into bread, added to soups or pickled.

Roots
Roots are roasted and used as a substitute for coffee.

CAUTIONS & CONSIDERATIONS

Health
CAUTION: Falling/ flying coconuts are a liability esp. in hurricanes.

Pests
Phytoplasma disease; Lepidoptera species; leaf beetle, eriophyid mites.

Landscape design
Can yield 30-75 fruits per year. Produces within ten years. Varieties include Dwarf, Maypan , King, and Macapuno. Intercropped with cassava, sweet potatoes, bananas. Compare with African Oil Palm (Elaeis guineensis).

Cocoplum

Chrysobalanus icaco

HARDINESS ZONES: 10 TO 12

Also called Paradise Plum. This Florida native has a lot of loveable features: Showy flowers & fruits, interesting foliage, hurricane wind resistance. Pollinators and birds are attracted to this plant and as an evergreen, it lends a tropical look. Considered a staple thanks to its nuts' high protein and oil content. In the Chrysobalanaceae family.

SIZE h*w	SUN	SOIL	WATER	EDIBLE
10ft*15ft	full	sandy loam	flood and drought tolerant	fruits, seed

PROPAGATION METHODS

- CUTTINGS: 8-inch terminal, non-fruiting stem cuttings in spring. Mist daily. Roots in 6 months.
- SEEDS: Germinates slowly at 85-95F. De-pulp. Short viability. Plant when ripe in summer.

RECIPE

"UMBOSHI" PLUMS: 10lbs of fruit, 1.5 c salt. Wash fruit, pierce the fruit/ seed with a knife so water enters kernel. Soak fruit/seed overnight in water. Drain. Deseed. Toss fruit with salt. Ferment 3 days in a glass container, covered with cloth. Shake & strain out moisture daily. A spin on traditional Japanese pickled plums - a breakfast and lunch side dish! OPTIONAL: Dry seeds & de-husk to eat.

CULTURAL SIGNIFICANCE

- Found as an invasive species on islands; seeds are transported by birds, tortoises
- Nectar from the flowers produces a dark-colored honey
- Potential source of construction timber and industrial oils. Seeds are rich in oil; can be strung on sticks and burnt like a candle
- Fruits and leaves yield black dye. Root, bark, fruit and leaves all contain tannins

CULINARY USE

Fruit

The purple or red-skinned fruits are superior in flavor to white forms. Fruit is consumed raw or cooked into jams and jelly by stewing in sugar. Fruits may also be dried like prunes. Fruiting is abundant from late spring through summer.

Seed

When preparing, the fruits are pierced right through the center, including the seed. This allows the juice of the fruit to penetrate the seed for soaking. After soaking 24 hrs, the brown, almond-flavored seeds are strained, de-pulped, roasted, de-husked & eaten or ground into a flour. Also yields edible oil. Seed's kernel is ground into a powder as a West African spice (called gbafilo or itsekiri).

CAUTIONS & CONSIDERATIONS

Health
No known adverse health effects.

Pests
Scales, sooty mold, canker, blight.

Landscape design
Typically used as a hedge. Can be shaped into box shapes as a border. Common cultivars are 'Red Tip' (purple fruit), 'Green Tip' (white or purple fruit) and 'Horizontal,' (whitish pink or purple fruit). Compare with FL native, Pigeon Plum (Coccoloba diversifolia).

Coffee
Coffea arabica

HARDINESS ZONES: 10 TO 12

An understory, evergreen in the Rubiaceae family. Can be grown as an ornamental houseplant and kept small! Indoor plants like bright sunny windows and offer fragrant flowers with the aroma of jasmine. Wild arabica coffee is endangered due to deforestation and climate change. Allowing plants to self-seed and be "wild" can ensure disease and pest-resistant varieties. Bears up to 100 years! Easy and fast growing!

SIZE h*w	SUN	SOIL	WATER	EDIBLE
12ft*6ft	part to full shade	well-draining	average; high humidity	fruit, seed, leaves

PROPAGATION METHODS

- SEEDS: Germinates at 80-85F within 90 days. Plant out at 6 months in rainy season. Yield in 3-4 yrs. Budding, grafting, air layering, & cuttings used too but genetic diversity is increasingly valued.

RECIPE

ROASTED COFFEE BEANS: Ferment fruit covered beans in water for 2 days. Once soft and bubbly, remove pulp. Dry the "beans" in a dehydrator or oven at 115F or lowest possible temperature. Once completely dry, remove hull/ skin and roast beans at 350F for 5-10 minutes stirring frequently. Store in the fridge. Grind on demand.

OPTIONAL: Ferment fruit pulp into wine or vinegar.

CULINARY USE

Fruit

Berries have a pulpy grape-like texture. Harvest in fall/ winter when red. In Arabia, the pulp is fermented in water as a drink. The fruits are a mild stimulant.

Seeds/ Beans

Berries are picked by hand when ripe and depulped, with the extracted seeds/beans then dried in the sun before roasting. 100 to 200 lbs of fruit produce 20 to 40 lbs of "beans." In Ethiopia, the beans are cooked in butter to make rich flat cakes. Used as a masticatory since ancient times. Used to flavor ice cream, pastries, candies, liqueurs. Roasted green seeds used as an appetizer.

Leaves

Contain caffeine. Leaves are steeped to make a tea. When cooked, the leaves are brown with a neutral flavor.

CULTURAL SIGNIFICANCE

- Hybridization between diploids Coffea canephora and Coffea eugenioides - an allotetraploid. One of 124 species of "coffee"
- In the 17th century, when water often wasn't safe, coffee was a viable alternative to alcohol
- Coffelite is a type of coffee-bean plastic
- Wood is good for furniture: termite-resistant
- Used in folk healing (e.g., coffee with iodine used as a deodorant; leaf poultices used on sores)
- After oil - world's most traded commodity

CAUTIONS & CONSIDERATIONS

Health

CAUTION: Beans contain caffeine. Excessive caffeine intake can have negative health effects. Chlorogenic acid may cause rhinitis/dermatitis during roasting or grinding.

Pests

Bacterial blight, fungal leaf spot, rust; coffee berry disease (CBD) Colletotrichum kahawae, borers.

Landscape design

Leaf-drop when below 55F. Trim to 6' tall for best production. Compare with C. canephora and Kola Nut (Cola acuminata) & FL native, Wild coffee (Psychotria nervosa).

Cordyline
Cordyline fruticosa

HARDINESS ZONES: 9 TO 13

Also called, "Ti" and "Tree of Kings." Highly ornamental - Very colorful leaves! An evergreen shrub and commonly grown houseplant in humid, brightly lit bathrooms. Considered pet- and child-safe. Considered a "good luck" plant & symbol of high rank and power. Among the most sought-after tropical plants. Wide range of uses in food, medicine, textiles and religious ceremony. Popular in flower arrangements! In asparagus (Asparagaceae) family!

SIZE h*w	SUN	SOIL	WATER	EDIBLE
10ft*3ft	partial to full shade	well-drained	average	leaves, tuber

PROPAGATION METHODS

- CUTTINGS: Use 6-8in cuttings. Place 2-3 nodes in the soil.
- SUCKERS: Divide plant every few years. NOTE: Rarely goes to seed.

RECIPE

BAKED CORDYLINE: Wash thoroughly, steam until knife inserts easily and desired sweetness is achieved. The longer the rhizome is steamed, the more starch is converted into sweet fructose.

Historically, steamed in pit ovens for 24 hours or more to get a molasses-like syrup.

CULTURAL SIGNIFICANCE

- Leaves used in Hawaii to make hula skirts, rain "jackets," thatch, plates for food
- Planted densely as a living fence also known as a "fedge" - fence/ hedge
- Often planted near sacred spots; highly regarded spiritually & common in cemeteries
- Used in folk healing (e.g., for fever, headache, coughs, skin eruptions & joint pains)
- Funded by FAO of United Nations (FAO) to enhance Asian household food security

CULINARY USE

Tuber

Starchy rhizomes store sugar in the form of fructose. The root is sweet and when baked, it has molasses-like flavor. Used as a sweetener. Roots can weigh up to 14lbs. Can be fermented into a drink. Considered a special-occasion food. Thick fleshy rhizomes grow vertically or obliquely downwards. Rhizomes are boiled or baked. Made into beer by baking & then fermenting, later distilled into liquor called, okolehao!

Leaves

Young leaves are cooked as a potherb and used to wrap foods - the same way that corn husks are used in Mexico to make tamales; neutral flavor. Dried leaves should be soaked to soften before using. Also used medicinally.

CAUTIONS & CONSIDERATIONS

Health

CAUTION: The red berries are inedible. May be confused with inedible Dracaena. Identify carefully.

Pests

Aphids, scale, spider mites and mealybugs; sensitive to flouride in water; hosts palm weevil larvae (human food).

Landscape design

Often intercropped with sugarcane. Cultivars have diversly colored leaves: Red, pink, purple, maroon, yellow, rose, orange. Compare with C. australis.

Cowpea
Vigna unguiculata

HARDINESS ZONES: 10 TO 12

Also called black-eyed peas! A butterfly host plant with a pretty flower, and fantastic summer ground cover. Grown as an annual in colder regions or perennial in areas with mild winters. A "nitrogen fixer" in the Fabaceae family. Grows even in poor soil & offers erosion control! First domesticated over 5,000 years ago & considered one of the oldest crops! Can produce all year round in the tropics. Fast growing!

SIZE h*w	SUN	SOIL	WATER	EDIBLE
10ft*1ft	full to partial	well-drained; sand, clay - OK	drought tolerant	leaves, seed/pea

PROPAGATION METHODS

- SEEDS: Germinates at 70-80°F. Direct sow; cast seed over bare ground at the beginning of the rainy season to use as a ground cover.

RECIPE

COLLARD GREENS WITH BLACK-EYE PEA: 1 lbs mature cow peas, 2.5lbs washed & chopped collards with rib removed, 5 shallots, 2tbs vinegar, 2 hot peppers; OPTIONAL: honey, salt, pepper to taste.

Soak peas overnight. Strain. Boil until tender. Drain. Stir fry with remaining ingredients.

CULTURAL SIGNIFICANCE

- Plant's defense against insects, the cowpea trypsin inhibitor, (CpTI) is trans-genically inserted into other crops as a pest deterrent
- In Africa, cowpea paste is used in infant formula when weaning babies
- "Black-eye peas" are a traditional Southern dish served on Jan 1st
- Cowpea starch is digested more slowly than cereal starch - beneficial to human health

CULINARY USE

Seeds

Immature seeds are used as a vegetable - steamed, boiled, or stir-fried. Mature seeds are added to soups, stews, purees, casseroles and curries or ground into powder and used like coffee or a flour. Cowpea flour used for making cakes, bread etc., or fermented into "dosa"/pancake batter. Seeds can also be sprouted, then eaten raw or cooked. A pod can contain 6-13 seeds - usually kidney-shaped. As the seeds reach maturity, the pod changes color to tan or brown. Range of seed sizes and colors. Young seed pods are harvested about 2 months after sowing; mature seeds take 3 - 5 months. Rich in folate.

Leaves

Leaves are blanched like spinach or sweet potato greens.

CAUTIONS & CONSIDERATIONS

Health
No known adverse health effects.

Pests
Susceptible to nematode, fungal, bacterial, and virus diseases like cowpea mosaic virus (CPMV).

Landscape design
Many named varieties. Can either be short and bushy or grow as a vine. Although insects can greatly decrease yield, it serves the food forest well when grown as a ground cover, host plant, & nitrogen fixer. Compare with FL native, V. luteola - hosts 35 species of butterflies and moths.

Cranberry Hibiscus

Hibiscus acetosella

HARDINESS ZONES: 8 TO 11

A striking & colorful, short-lived perennial shrub with delicious crimson leaves branching out from the multi-stemmed base. The red leaves resemble maple leaves. Pleasantly tart! Young leaves are commonly used as a vegetable, either raw or cooked. In Malvaceae family. A beautiful, functional food. Popular as a jam and tea.

SIZE h*w	SUN	SOIL	WATER	EDIBLE
6ft*4ft	part sun	prefers acidic	moist; drought tolerant	leaves, flowers

PROPAGATION METHODS

- SEEDS: Germinates at 70-75F within 2-3 weeks. Self-seeds easily. Allow seed pods to dry while still on the plant, then harvest.
- CUTTINGS: Roots readily in water or soil.

RECIPE

PINK "LEMONADE": 5 red leaves, 30 flower blossoms, 1/2 c honey, 5 c water.

Boil 5 cups water and 5 leaves for 15 min to obtain a red color. Strain, puree colored water with flower blossoms. Add honey to taste.

CULINARY USE

Flowers
Pink blossoms may be used to make a beverage. Pick about 30 blossoms in the evening after they have folded up. The petals add a smooth texture and intense color, more than any special flavor. Popular for jam: petals & leaf juice are mixed - First leaves are boiled for 15 min & filtered. Then petals are added to the juice and boiled for 10 min. Sweetener, salt & citrus juice are then added.

Leaves
Fleshy leaves and young shoots may be eaten raw or cooked; Leaves become slimy if cooked too long; leaves may be dehydrated and pressed into white chocolate to create a seasonal "bark." Additionally, the leaves may be soaked in water, pureed, strained, and mixed with honey to create a tart tea.

CULTURAL SIGNIFICANCE

- Members of the genus Hibiscus support the specialized bee, Ptilothrix bombiformis
- Highly resistant to root-knot nematodes; plant after tomatoes/ solanaceous vegetables
- Stem yields quality fiber. Leaves yield red dye
- Colorful temporary hedge; can be pruned & harvested simultaneously. Great indoor plant
- Used in folk healing (e.g., for antioxidant & antibacterial activities; also for anemia)

CAUTIONS & CONSIDERATIONS

Health
CAUTION: Wear gloves when removing seed pods due to irritating hairs. Leaves have oxalic acid, consume raw in moderation.

Pests
Resilient but may succumb to soil pathogens.

Landscape design
Cut to the base after it finishes flowering for perennial behavior. Compare with FL native: H. grandiflorus - hosts 37 species of butterflies and moths.

Creole Garlic

Allium sativum

HARDINESS ZONES: 7 TO 10

One of the best-known herbs around the world and member of the lily family (Amaryllidaceae). The Creole variety (a softneck) is tolerant of hot climates! Stores up to 12 months! Gorgeous deep red clove coloration. Wonderfully nutritious! Believed to confer strength and protect from disease - widely used by the Romans! Typically grown as an annual but actually a perennial.

SIZE h*w	SUN	SOIL	WATER	EDIBLE
2ft*8in	full to partial	well-drained	drought tolerant	bulb, seed, leaves

PROPAGATION METHODS

- BULB: Plant bulbs in the early fall and wait for stems to emerge in early spring. Harvest in late spring/ early summer. Bulb formation at 60°F. Maturation/ halted growth at 90-91°F.

RECIPE

GARLIC AIOLI: 3 peeled, roasted garlic cloves, 1 cup oil, 1 egg, 3 tsp citus juice, 1/4 tsp sea salt.

Slowly blend egg, lemon juice and salt. Gradually, add in 1 tbsp of oil at a time until mixture emulsifies. Add in garlic at the end. Keeps up to a week in the fridge.

CULINARY USE

Bulb
Eaten raw or cooked. Has an initial sweetness that builds to heat. Described as earthy. Flavor is influenced by local environment. Ready to harvest when half of the leaves have turned brown. Dig the bulbs with the shoots still attached. Cure 3-4 weeks or until roots and remaining shoots should have dried. Store as whole bulbs in an area with 45-55 percent humidity & a temperature of 50-70F. Loses pungency when cooked. Sautéing is the easiest method of cooking & yields a mellow nutty, savory taste; stir constantly – garlic burns easily.

Seeds
Sprouted seed added to salads.

Leaves
Used as a flavoring.

CULTURAL SIGNIFICANCE

- Used by nomadic tribes to ward off evil spirits
- Long history of folk healing use (e.g., to expel phlegm from lungs and as circulatory tonic; antiseptic, diuretic, febrifuge, stimulant, stomachic. Ancient Israelis called garlic a "parasite-killer" & Hippocrates documented use for intestinal parasites)
- Used in the treatment of plant blight & mold or fungal diseases. Said to repel pests
- China leads the world as a supplier of garlic

CAUTIONS & CONSIDERATIONS

Health
CAUTION: Avoid eating while on with anticlotting medication or prior to surgery. May cause contact dermatitis. Botulism risk when preserved in oil in an airtight container.

Pests
Rots in poorly-drained soils, nematodes, thrips, mites.

Landscape design
Inhibits growth of legumes. Many Creole varieties - choose one based on hardiness zone. Compare with Society Garlic (Tulbaghia violacea) & Garlic Vine (Mansoa alliacea).

Cuban Oregano

Coleus amboinicus

HARDINESS ZONES: 9A TO 11

A fast-growing, herbaceous succulent with attractive serrated leaves and a deep glossy green color. Produces a number of delicate flower heads in white, lavender and pale pink. Comes in variegated colors including those with purple stems. A semi-succulent perennial plant in the family Lamiaceae. Said to offer natural antioxidants, and health-promoting phenolic & flavonoid content!

SIZE h*w	SUN	SOIL	WATER	EDIBLE
3ft*3ft	semi-shade	loamy	well-drained	leaves

PROPAGATION METHODS

- CUTTING: Root in water or soil.
- SEEDS: Germinates at 65-75F. Sow as soon as they are ripe. Older seeds will not germinate.
- DIVISION: Cut the root-ball into pieces.

RECIPE

OXYMEL DIP: Infuse 1c vinegar with 20 dried oregano leaves for 4-6 weeks in a cool, dark place. Strain. Mix into 2c honey. Stores up to 1 year.

Use as a vegetable dip or add into pickle brine, stew, chutney or drizzle on bread.

CULINARY USE

Leaves

Use fresh aromatic leaves as a tea, food additive or spice to flavor meat, soups, fish, and beer. Dry & crush the leaves and store in an airtight container. Use the leaves within cocktails and cold drinks for a mild spicy and earthy undertone. Leaves are also eaten as a vegetable. In Indian subcontinent, the leaves are combined with coconut, dhal, red chilies, cilantro and curry leaves for Sambarpalli Chutney. Eaten raw with bread and butter. Used as fried snack or as beer and wine flavoring. It is also used as a condiment for sour soup in Vietnam (called canh chua), and the Indian salad (called bajeh). Principal flavoring in Cuban black bean soup. Popular in salads in Caribbean. Phytochemicals: Carvocrol & thymol.

CULTURAL SIGNIFICANCE

- Used in folk healing (e.g., to relieve spasms, aid digestion & wound healing; as a breast milk stimulant, for cough & inflammations; anti-bacterial properties)
- Food labelled "oregano-flavored" may contain this herb
- Used for washing clothes, hair, and laundry due to its fragrance
- Use in magico-religious rituals in Brazil
- Allelopathic inhibition of water hyacinth

CAUTIONS & CONSIDERATIONS

Health

CAUTION: Some cases of handling allergy (skin). Syn. Plectranthus amboinicus.

Pests

Resistent to pests; noon sun burns leaves.

Landscape design

Leaves and stems also have a tendency to trail & root. Has a beautiful structure that will look fantastic within any herb garden or pot. Compare with other "Oregano" shrubs, Poliomintha longiflora & Lippia graveolens.

Curry Tree

Murraya koenigii

HARDINESS ZONES: 9 TO 12

An attractive evergreen shrub in the Rutaceae family. Showy, fragrant flowers attract butterflies. Can serve as a kitchen house plant for convenient leaf harvest! Sometimes called sweet neem. Leaves are used a similar way to bay leaves – as an aromatic in stews and soups. Valued as a flavoring for stews, breads, & vegetables since 4th century AD!

SIZE h*w	SUN	SOIL	WATER	EDIBLE
13ft*9ft	full to partial	well-drained	drought tolerant	fruit, leaves

PROPAGATION METHODS

- SEEDS: Germinates at 70-75F. Short viability. Remove pulp before planting.
- DIVISION: Divide root suckers.
- CUTTING: Half-ripe wood.

RECIPE

CURRY LEAF PESTO/ SOUP-BASE: 1 c de-stemmed curry leaf, 1/2 inch ginger, 2 garlic cloves, 2 large green chillies or 1/4 c chives, 3tsp vinegar, salt/pepper to taste

Puree all ingredients. Leave for an hour so that the natural oil from the curry leaves permeate

CULTURAL SIGNIFICANCE

- Can be grown as a hedge
- Leaves are considered a hair tonic in India to prevent grey
- Leaf oil can be extracted and used to make scented soaps
- Used in Ayurvedic and Siddha medicine for antimicrobial & antioxidant properties; used as a poultice, and digestive aid
- Branches are popular for cleaning the teeth- said to strengthen gums and teeth

CULINARY USE

Fruit
A peppery flavor. Berry pulp is eaten as a dessert. Black berries contain a single large seed. Typically fruits July-August. Good source of Vit C. Characteristic odor. Avoid eating seeds.

Leaves
Leaves are cooked to release a pungent, aromatic for curries, chutneys, stews etc. First fried in oil until crisp, then added to the recipe. Best used fresh as older leaves quickly lose their flavor. Can be picked about one year after planting but more prolific after 3 years. Added to vegetable dishes. Leaves are roasted and used as an ingredient in a Cambodian soup (called maju krueng). Nutty, yet citrus-like flavor. A warming herb said to improve appetite and digestion. Rich in vitamins & minerals.

CAUTIONS & CONSIDERATIONS

Health
No known adverse health effects. Leaves are rich in antioxidant, folic acid & iron; source of carbazole alkaloids.

Pests
Hardy. Root rot, citrus mealy bug.

Landscape design
Leaves may drop in colder areas. Vigorous suckering - may spread quickly & send up shoots dozens of feet away from mother. Shelter from strong winds. Typically, flowers April-May. Gamthi variety most fragrant but slow growing.

Daikon Radish

Raphanus sativus var. longipinnatus

HARDINESS ZONES: 2 TO 11

"Daikon" is a Japanese word meaning 'big root,' and that is exactly what you'll get. Milder, sweeter flavor than ordinary radishes. Perfect for children's gardens and ideal companion plants. Few pests! Versatile! Great winter cover crop. Suppresses weeds, prevents erosion, and used in folk art for carved figures. In the Brassicaceae family.

SIZE h*w	SUN	SOIL	WATER	EDIBLE
2ft*2ft	full	sandy; clay - OK	drought tolerant	tuber, leaves, seeds, pod, oil, flowers

PROPAGATION METHODS

- SEED: Germinates at 65-85F. Direct sow outdoors in succession from late winter to the middle of spring. Fast germination; sow seed every 2 weeks to have constant supply.

RECIPE

SAUTEED RADISH STIRFRY: 3 bunches of daikon greens, blanched & chopped, 3 daikon roots peeled & diced, 2 tsp oil, 2 garlic cloves - minced, 1 tbs vinegar or citrus juice, sea salt to taste.

Sauté roots & garlic in oil and then add greens. Cook, covered on low 3-4 minutes. Add citrus/vinegar and sprinkle with sea salt.

CULTURAL SIGNIFICANCE

- One of the first European crops introduced to the Americas
- Included in Japanese Festival of Seven Herbs (Nanakusa no sekku) - 7th day of new year
- Citizens of Oaxaca, Mexico, celebrate the Night of the Radishes on December 23
- Third-century B.C. Greeks wrote of radishes
- Folk healing use (e.g., stimulate appetite & digestion; laxative effects)
- Pressed to extract radish seed oil/ biofuel

CULINARY USE

Tuber
Most often thinly peeled, sliced or diced and put into soups. Popular pickled as a crunchy salad vegetable or cooked. Crisp texture and a pungent, peppery flavor. Blended with fruit juices. Sliced as a garnish in Mexican cuisine such as in tostadas, sopes, enchiladas, & posole stew. Heat increases with age. Woody after bolting. Prized as a relish.

Seed/ Pod
Young seedpods eaten raw. Seeds offer a crunchy, sharp addition to salads and are sprouted like mung bean.

Leaves/ Flowers
Tops can be used as a leaf vegetable. Typically, blanched like spinach. Young flower clusters eaten raw or cooked. Broccoli substitute.

CAUTIONS & CONSIDERATIONS

Health
CAUTION: Roots contain glucosinolate. Decrease by peeling tuber skin. Cook. May be confused with toxic butterweed (Senecio glabellus). Harvest greens along with tuber for positive identification.

Pests
Larvae of flea beetles; cabbage root fly; swede midge.

Landscape design
Breaks up compacted soils, recovers nutrients if not harvested. Compare with Rat-tailed radish (Raphanus sativus var. Caudatus) & summer radishes.

Daylily
Hemerocallis fulva

HARDINESS ZONES: 3 TO 10

An edible, flowering ground cover in the Liliaceae family! Also called the "perfect perennial." All parts have culinary value! Low-maintenance, and hardy. Beautiful for cut flowers and attracts pollinators. Very popular ornamental. Vigorous and adaptable. Plant in an area where you can contain its rhizomatic spread.

SIZE h*w	SUN	SOIL	WATER	EDIBLE
3ft*3ft	full to partial	well-draining; poor - OK	drought tolerant	flowers, root, leaves, shoots

PROPAGATION METHODS

- SEEDS: Germinates at 60-70°F within 2 months. Sow in spring. High germination rates but almost never sets seed.
- DIVISION: Divide rhizomes in spring or after flowering in late summer or autumn: Aug – Oct.

RECIPE

SAUTEED FLOWER BUDS: Pick unopened flower buds and save in the fridge until you have 3 cups.

Quickly sauté in oil until crisp on the edges. Sprinkle with sea salt. Eat as a side or add to soups.

CULINARY USE

Flowers
Flowers open one at a time and only for one day each. Eaten raw or cooked. Petals are thick and crunchy - sweet-peppery flavor with sweet nectar at base. May be stuffed for hors d'oeuvres or made into fritters. Also dried and used as a thickener in soups etc. - picked when withered and closed. Rich source of iron. Flower buds also eaten raw or cooked and have a pea-like flavor - dried as a relish.

Root
Potato-like roots. A sweet, radish-like flavor. Cook until soft.

Leaves & Shoots
Sword-like young leaves and shoots are eaten cooked as an asparagus or celery substitute. Leaves become fiberous with age

CULTURAL SIGNIFICANCE

- Tough dried foliage is plaited into cord and used for making footwear
- Provides erosion control along streambanks
- Year-round food potential. Flowers and tubers are high in protein and oils. The flower buds are good sources of beta carotene and vitamin C
- Flowers used in Chinese medicine as an anodyne, antiemetic, antispasmodic, depurative, febrifuge and sedative

CAUTIONS & CONSIDERATIONS

Health
CAUTION: Always blanch/ cook the leaves and roots; toxin present. May be confused with inedible tiger lily (Lilium lancifolium). Carefully identify when in flower.

Pests
Few problems with pests and foliar disease.

Landscape design
Consider cultivar 'Kwanso Flore Pleno' variety. Spreads rapidly by rhizomes, can be invasive; H.fulva, H. lilio-asphodelus = edible varieties. Plants take a year or two to become established after being moved. Hybridizes.

Dragon Fruit
Hylocereus undatus

HARDINESS ZONES: 9B TO 12

Also called Pitaya. A beautiful, fast-growing, vine-like cactus with triangular stalks and aerial roots enabling it to climb. Great for xeriscape. Used as a flowering hedge such as atop of fence posts. 4-6 fruiting cycles per year! A night-flowering ornamental with decorative fruit boasting bright red skin, speckled with green scales. Naturalized in tropical and subtropical regions worldwide. May be terrestrial or epiphytic. Great for a 10+ gallon container! In the Cactaceae family.

SIZE h*w	SUN	SOIL	WATER	EDIBLE
13ft*6ft	full to partial	poor - OK	drought tolerant	fruit, flower buds

PROPAGATION METHODS

- CUTTINGS: Stem segment of 6" or longer; dry in shade for a week. Once calloused, stake upright in well-draining potting medium. Plant shallow. (Also grown from seed but with more difficulty).

RECIPE

DRAGON FRUIT SORBET: 3 pitayas (red fleshed), 3tbs agave syrup, 1 tbs coconut milk (if needed); mint as a garnish.

Cut fruit in half, spoon out pulp. Deseed by pressing through a strainer. Puree with agave. Freeze in ice cube trays. Blend ice cubes into a frozen puree and spoon into bowls. Top with mint.

CULINARY USE

Fruit

The outer skin is not eaten. Chilled and cut in half so that the flesh can be eaten with a spoon - like an avocado. The inner fruit has a sweet, pleasant flavor - eaten raw or cooked. The juicy flesh is either white or red with tiny black seeds. Seeds may be pressed out by straining through mesh but reportedly high in essential fatty acids: linoleic/ linolenic acids; prebiotic properties. Has a texture similar to prickly pear and kiwi. Good source of vitamin C, calcium, potassium and fiber. The pulp is blended as a drink or used for sherbets, salads, juice, wine. Frozen pulp is used to flavor ice cream, yogurt, jelly, preserves, candy and pastries.

Flower Buds

Unopened flower buds can be cooked and eaten as a vegetable. Steeped as a tea.

CULTURAL SIGNIFICANCE

- Fruit used as ornament on banquet tables
- Considered the showiest cactus - fragrant flowers last dusk-dawn. Night nectar for bats
- Peel yields betacyanin & coloring pigments
- The mucilage employed in cosmetics
- Colony-forming: weight can topple trees
- Used in folk healing (e.g., wound healing/ antibacterial peel). Researched in food preservation - antibacterial activity against food-borne pathogens. Rich in phytochemicals

CAUTIONS & CONSIDERATIONS

Health

CAUTION: Spines & sharp edges. Tiny black seeds are edible but indigestible - mild laxative effect.

Pests

Hardy: Fruit flies, Cactus virus X (CVX), thrip, sooty mold.

Landscape design

Yellow type is sweeter than the red. Bleaching may occur with excessive sunlight. Can be productive for more than 20 years. Prune 1-3x per year. Compare with apple-dragon (Cereus peruvianus).

Duck Potato

Sagittaria latifolia

HARDINESS ZONES: 7 TO 11

A flowering, wetland perennial and Florida native! Primarily found in marshes, bogs, and ponds. One of the largest and showiest of the emersed Sagittarias. This is a low-maintenance, starchy staple used since ancient times as a food and a major trading commodity among Native Americans. Long lived! Great in containers as well! In the Alismataceae (Water-Plantain) family.

SIZE h*w	SUN	SOIL	WATER	EDIBLE
3ft*2ft	full to partial	waterlogged; wet/ loamy	flood tolerant	tuber

PROPAGATION METHODS

- SEEDS: Germinates at 70-86F. Sow on soil in pot standing in 2" of water. Requires light
- DIVISION: Divide tubers in spring or autumn. Pot up runners any time.

RECIPE

ROASTED DUCK POTATO: Wash and slice the tubers in half. Coat lightly with oil. Place open-side down on a baking sheet and bake at 350F for 20 minutes.

Peel off skin and sprinkle with sea salt.

CULINARY USE

Tuber

Tubers are delicious roasted with a potato-like texture and a taste like sweet chestnuts. Light and airy consistency! Remove skin after the tubers have been cooked. The tubers can also be dried and ground into a powder for making bread or thickening stews. The egg- shaped tubers are golf-ball sized and are approximately 12-inches deep in the soil. Best harvested when the leaves die back. High in starch and phosphorous.

NOTE: The tubers cannot be harvested by pulling on the tops; the leaves break off easily. Dig with a pitchfork. Tubers usually float to the surface once detached.

CULTURAL SIGNIFICANCE

- Widely cultivated as an ornamental pond plant in Europe
- Extensively cultivated to supply Chinese markets
- Used for wetland restoration. Important as food and cover for aquatic wildlife like fish, birds, beavers, porcupines & muskrats
- In folk healing, an infusion of arrowhead roots is used to clean and treat wounds

CAUTIONS & CONSIDERATIONS

Health
CAUTION: Cross-pollination can impact edibility. Ensure water is not contaminated. Harvest during flowering - may be confused with arrow alum (Peltandra virginica).

Pests
Resilient; aphids and spider mites.

Landscape design
Helps prevent erosion. Dormant in winter/ dry season. Compare with Sagittaria sagittifolia and S. lancifolia (salt tolerant). May behave invasively. Prefers water up to 5 inches deep.

Echinacea

Echinacea purpurea

HARDINESS ZONES: 3 TO 10

A Florida native and beautiful cut flower in the Asteraceae family! A perennial and low maintenance ornamental. Considered rugged and hardy. In a genus valued as the most effective detoxicant in Western herbal medicine. Adopted by Ayurvedic medicine. Commonly used for colds and infections. Beneficial insect attractor. Competes well with weeds! Excellent choice for borders! Uses date back to the 20th century.

SIZE h*w	SUN	SOIL	WATER	EDIBLE
3ft*1ft	full	well-draining	drought tolerant	leaves, petal

PROPAGATION METHODS

- SEEDS: Germinates at 68-75F within 10 - 21 days. Freely self-seeds.
- CUTTINGS: Root cuttings, and basal cuttings. NOTE: clump divisions also recommended.

RECIPE

ECHINACEA OXYMEL: 4 tbs dried echinacea leaf, 2 tbs dried elderberries (boiled 15 minutes, strained), 4 tsp grated ginger root, 1 c vinegar, 1/2 c honey.

Infuse vinegar for 4-6 weeks. Strain. Mix with honey. Store in the refrigerator. Drizzle over warm roasted vegetables or stir into warm water as tea.

CULTURAL SIGNIFICANCE

- In Germany, over 200 pharmaceutical preparations are made from Echinacea
- Rich in nectar. Very popular with bees, butterflies, hummingbirds and birds which eat and spread the seeds
- Used in folk healing (e.g., Root considered adaptogen, antiseptic, aphrodisiac, digestive; believed to decrease inflammation and increase the body's immune system)

CULINARY USE

Leaves & Flowers
The beautiful purple petal is edible and serves as an excellent salad garnish. Although all parts of the plant are considered medicinal, the leaves and flower petals are most commonly harvested such as for herbal tea. NOTE: Compare with other varieties used to brew tea including E. angustifolia, and E. pallida.

USE IN MODERATION: All parts of the plant but especially the roots have been used in tinctures and other medicinal methods. Plant contains a wide variety of chemicals such as cichoric acid, caftaric acid, echinacoside, and various fat-soluble alkylamides. Fresh plant matter is believed to have higher active constituents.

CAUTIONS & CONSIDERATIONS

Health
CAUTION: Possible immune suppression with long term use. Only use a max of 7 consecutive days. Don't take with caffeine or if you have an auto-immune disorder. May interact with medications like those for liver treatment.
Pests
Japanese beetle and leaf spot.
Landscape design
Often planted with black-eyed Susans (Rudbeckias). Long taproot. Compare with Toothache Plant (Acmella oleracea) & Echinacea angustifolia - preferred by herbalists.

Eggplant Pea
Solanum torvum

HARDINESS ZONES: 8 TO 11

Also called Turkeyberry. An evergreen, perennial shrub considered to be a wild edible. Can flower and produce fruit all year round! Forage rather than plant! Listed as a U.S. federal noxious weed as birds eat and disperse the seeds creating dense, thorny thickets. However, you may find it growing on your property and there are valuable edible qualities. So hardy, it serves as an outstanding rootstock. Be sure to carefully identify. In the nightshade family (Solanaceae).

SIZE h*w	SUN	SOIL	WATER	EDIBLE
8ft*5ft	full to partial	well-draining	drought-tolerant	fruits

PROPAGATION METHODS

NOT RECOMMENDED UNLESS FOR ROOTSTOCK
- SEEDS: Germinates at 65-93F. Fresh seeds display dormancy. Seedlings are root stock.
- CUTTINGS: Half-ripe wood.

RECIPES

TURKEY BERRY FLATBREAD: 1/3 c eggplant peas, 1 tbs oil, 1 tsp coriander seeds, 1 tsp fennel seeds, 1 c sourdough starter (discard) or 50/50 mix of flour/water, pinch of salt.

Fry peas, salt and seeds in oil on medium-high covered until fragrant and peas have burst. Pour in starter to form a flatbread. Once bubbling, flip.

CULINARY USE

Fruit
Fruit is edible raw but is more frequently cooked. Juicy with many small seeds. In Asia and West Indies, it is often served as a side dish with rice, or added to stews, soups, curries etc. The immature fruit is green, turning yellow then orange as it ripens. The globose berry typically measures 1/2 inch in diameter. Utilized as a vegetable and regarded as an essential ingredient in the South Indian population's diet. Often cooked in a tamarind sauce with spices. Boiled to reduce bitterness. High calcium content. Good source of iron and manganese.

Reports of edible leaves and shoots, however research shows primarily medicinal use of those parts.

CULTURAL SIGNIFICANCE

- Used in folk medicine (e.g., pulp is applied topically for insect bites; also used to improve digestion, as antihypertensive & antidiabetic; a store house of minerals, vitamins, antioxidants)
- Ongoing scientific attempts to incorporate its genes into other vegetables for disease resistance (e.g., for Verticillium wilt) & ability to exclude uptake of environmental toxins
- In 14th century, eggplant was imported into Italy from China - initially thought to be poisonous

CAUTIONS & CONSIDERATIONS

Health
CAUTION: Consume only with positive identification. Can be confused with poisonous Solanums. Plants in the Solanaceae family contain alkaloids/ anti-nutrients.

Pests
Highly resilient to pests and diseases; leaf-eating chrysomelid beetle (Leptinotarsa undecimlineata).

Landscape design
Used as a rootstock for tomatoes or eggplants to improve resilience to pests and disease. Compare with hardy Ichiban Eggplant (Solanum melongena).

Egyptian Spinach

Corchorus olitorius

HARDINESS ZONES: 9 TO 11

A historical staple among ancient Jewish and Egyptian communities given its high protein content. Part of the national dish of Egypt! Also called "Molokia," derived from the Arabic word Mulukia meaning "Royal" - additional names include Jew's Mallow and Nalta jute. Member of Malvaceae family.

SIZE h*w	SUN	SOIL	WATER	EDIBLE
8ft*1ft	full to partial	well-draining	drought tolerant	leaves

PROPAGATION METHODS

- SEEDS: Germinates at 80-90F. Broadcast on soil in situ in mid-spring. Self-seeds readily. May behave as a perennial in areas with mild winters.

RECIPE

EGYPTION SPINACH STEW: 3 c washed molokia, 2 garlic cloves minced, 2 tsp coriander seeds, 1tbs oil.

Remove molokia leaf stems and chop. Boil 5-10 min. Strain. Sauté garlic & coriander seeds in oil until fragrant. Combine with boiled/ strained leaves. Stir-fry 2 min. OPTIONAL: Add rabbit meat. Cover. Simmer 30 min. Sprinkle with vinegar.

CULINARY USE

Leaves

Young leaves and stem tops eaten after boiling/ discarding water to remove anti-nutrients. Sticky leaf mass used as a spread for breads - mucilaginous when cooked. Leaves also dried for tea or as a soup thickener. Harvest after about six weeks. In Egypt, leaves are usually harvested green and once the leaf spine is removed, the leaves are finely chopped with garlic & coriander and served as a stew with rabbit. Thought of as a spinach substitute. Cooked in oil/ fried to decrease mucilage. Rich in amino acid and essential minerals.

NOTE: Reports that seeds and fruit are also edible but information lacking.

CULTURAL SIGNIFICANCE

- Used in folk healing (e.g., Leaves are considered demulcent, diuretic, febrifuge and tonic. A remedy for aches and pains)
- The coarse fiber is used for yarn, twine, sacking, carpet backing, sackcloth, paper
- Once known as the golden fiber of Bangladesh - the most important cash crop
- Legend tells of an early Egyption Pharaoh who became very ill and consulted a healer who cured him with a diet of Molokia

CAUTIONS & CONSIDERATIONS

Health

CAUTION: Contains HCN toxin and several cardiac glycosides. Cook prior to eating. Rich in potassium, iron, vitamin B6, A and C. Do not grow in contaminated soil; accumulates heavy metals.

Pests

Highly resilient, nematodes, fungus when overcrowded.

Landscape design

Clipping increases branching for leaf harvesting. Compare with Chipilín (Crotalaria longirostrata), Lamb's Quarter (Chenopodium album), & FL Lettuce (Lactuca floridana).

Elderberry
Sambucus nigra ssp. canadensis

HARDINESS ZONES: 4 TO 10B

A deciduous, fast-growing Florida native with showy white, lacy flowers. A perennial, and pioneer species with economic potential; demand is growing! Full production takes 3-5 years. This plant is rich with history and folklore. Widely employed as a medicinal herb by many native North American tribes. A good hedgerow-based crop. In the Adoxaceae family.

SIZE h*w	SUN	SOIL	WATER	EDIBLE
12ft*12ft	full to partial	well-drained, mildly acidic	flood tolerant	fruit, flowers

PROPAGATION METHODS

- CUTTINGS: Hardwood in early spring; previous season canes. Roots in 4-6 wks. Take softwood cuttings before flowering.
- DIVISION: Divide root suckers when dormant.

RECIPE

ELDER FLOWER TEA: 1 tsp dried elder flower petals, 1 c boiling water, ½ tsp honey.

Pick off the flower petals (avoid all stems). Dry. Steep petals in boiling water for 10 minutes, strain and add sweetener to taste.

CULINARY USE

Fruit

Must be fully ripe. Examine fruit clusters and remove any unripe berries. Best cooked after being dried. Boil and then press juice from berries, straining out seeds with mesh or cloth. Fruits used for wine, preserves, tinctures, and teas. Very high in Vitamin C & anthocyanins/ antioxidants. Good source of iron. Cultivar 'Adams' fruits in dense clusters - excellent for baking.

Flowers

Often covered in batter and made into fritters. Flowers can be picked when unopened, fermented/pickled and then used as a flavoring in candies or soups. Also steeped into tea. Blooms on 2nd year wood. WARNING: flowers look similar to water hemlock. Identify carefully.

CULTURAL SIGNIFICANCE

- Fruit yields a reddish-purple dye for food and textiles; black dye from bark. Branches can be bent into ornamental arches/ shapes
- Attracts butterflies, bees, and birds
- Flowers used in cordial like St-Germain (French liqueur) & Hallands Fläder (Swedish akvavit)
- Thought to ward off evil; "Elder" Wand is pivotal in the final Harry Potter book
- Provides riverbank stabilization

CAUTIONS & CONSIDERATIONS

Health
CAUTION: All parts contain cyanogenic glucosides - dry thoroughly. Cook. Confused with toxic plants like water hemlock. Red elderberry (Sambucus racemosa var. melanocarpa) is toxic.

Pests
Resilient: mites, borers, stink bug; fungal diseases.

Landscape design
Short-lived. Cross-pollination for better fruiting. Cut to ground/ coppice in spring while dormant to make bushy. Provide shelter from wind - stems break. Don't grow in pots long-term. Produces fruit on both new and old wood.

Elm

Ulmus americana

HARDINESS ZONES: 5 TO 10

Also called "Florida Elm" or "American Elm." A picturesque Florida native in the Ulmaceae family! This deciduous tree is fast-growing, useful and attractive, offering fall color and much needed shade in the heat of summer! Butterfly host plant! Lives 300+ years & is a gorgeous legacy to leave future generations. Increasingly rare! Ulmus americana var. floridana does not get Dutch Elm Disease. Grown in urban areas to decrease air pollution.

SIZE h*w	SUN	SOIL	WATER	EDIBLE
70ft*30ft	full to partial	well-drained	flood tolerant	leaves, inner bark, fruit

PROPAGATION METHODS

- SEEDS: Germinate at 68-86F within a few days to several months (epigeal).
- CUTTINGS: Softwood cuttings in June treated with indolebutyric acid. Leaf bud cuttings.

RECIPE

SAUTEED SAMARAS: 2c samaras, 1tbs soil, pinch of sea salt, pepper.

Soak samaras overnight. Strain. Stir fry samaras in a pan over medium-high heat with oil. Add a dash of vinegar and salt and pepper to taste.

CULINARY USE

Leaves
Pointed oval leaves are typically 4" and 6" long, 2.5" with serrated edges. The very young leaves of all Ulmus species can be eaten, and generally have a mild flavor. Cooked as a pot-herb. Boil and strain.

Fruit
Elm fruit are called samaras or the winged seed pod. Pea flavor. Typically stir-fried.

Inner Bark
The red inner bark has been used to make a coffee-like drink; mostly used medicinally. An infusion of the bark has been used in the treatment of coughs. Also used in a bath for skin issues.

CULTURAL SIGNIFICANCE

- Larval host for butterflies: Eastern Comma, Question Mark, Painted Lady
- Fiber from branch stems harvested in spring & used in making paper
- Wood is harvested for flooring, archery bows, furniture, and musical instruments. Interlocked grain is durable and pliable
- Used as a honey flavor/ food source for bees
- Pioneer species for restoring woodland or diseased orchards

CAUTIONS & CONSIDERATIONS

Health
No known adverse health effects.

Pests
Susceptible to Phloem necrosis, 'Dutch Elm Disease,' a fungal disease spread by beetles.

Landscape design
Aggressive surface roots & tap roots. Hybridizes freely. Consider Dutch Elm Disease resistant varieties like Ulmus americana 'Valley Forge', 'Jefferson' 'Deleware #2' & 'Princeton.' Trees killed by Dutch Elm Disease can still resprout from root suckers & persist for 20 years or more.

Ensete
Ensete ventricosum

HARDINESS ZONES: 9 TO 11

An attractive evergreen, perennial and staple crop! Offers significant starch! Resistant to droughts & can be harvested at any stage. Considered a classic tropical foliage plant and striking landscape specimen. Provides more foodstuff per unit area than most cereal crops. Although it looks like a banana plant, it is harvested like a root vegetable and tastes like a tortilla. In the Musaceae family. Offers food security & sovereignty!

SIZE h*w	SUN	SOIL	WATER	EDIBLE
19ft*9ft	full	poor soil - OK	moist soil, drought tolerant	trunk, seed, stalk

PROPAGATION METHODS

- SEEDS: Germinates at 75-95F. Soak 24 hrs. May need scarification. NOTE: Rarely produce offsets but cultivated varieties may be more likely to have pups.

RECIPE

KOCHO: Dig corm & cut leaves from stem. Shred pith of stem and corm using a bamboo scraper. Puree with 1 tbs of water at a time until a thick gravy-like consistency forms. Ferment, covered, in a wide-mouth glass or ceramic vessel for several months (3+). Mix fermented ensete with spices and oil to taste. Form into flat discs. Fry as a tortilla.

CULINARY USE

Trunk
The young and tender tissues in the center or heart of the plant (the growing point) are cooked and eaten like the core of palms and cycads. The pulverized trunk and inflorescence stalk are fermenting into "kocho"/ a bread-like food. Regarded as a delicacy. Said to taste like a good quality sourdough. "Bulla" is made from the starchy liquid squeezed out of the ferment and is eaten as a porridge.

Corm
The fresh corm is cooked like potatoes before eating. Called "amicho." Chop into small pieces to speed cooking.

Seeds
Endosperm of the seed is consumed as a food
NOTE: Fruits described as flavorless, housing many seeds.

CULTURAL SIGNIFICANCE

- Ensete disease epidemic in 1984–85 wiped out plantations. An important food security crop for 20 million people
- Gained Royal Horticultural Society's Award
- Fiber from stem used for cordage, sacking. Seeds are made into rosaries, rattles. A brown dye is obtained from the stem
- Erosion control, soil improver and mulch
- Usually harvested for food around 4 years old, before the inflorescence uses up the starch

CAUTIONS & CONSIDERATIONS

Health
No known health hazards.
Pests
Aphids, spider mites, root mealybugs, scale, anthracnose, bacterial wilt disease and mosiac virus.
Landscape design
Can survive light frosts. Shelter from wind. Takes 4-5 years to fully mature. Yields about 88 lb of food. "Soft" and "hard" varieties. Soft requires 1/3 the fermentation time. Stagger plantings. Intercropped with coffee, cocao, sorghum. Monocarpic (flowers, set seeds, then dies). Compare with Sago Palm (Metroxylon sagu).

Everglades Tomato

Solanum pimpinellifolium

HARDINESS ZONES: 9 TO 10

This tender perennial may fruit all year long! Considered by some to be a wild FL native. Offers flavor and aromatics lost in most commercial tomatoes. Can produce multiple pints of blueberry-sized tomatoes each week. Let ramble; roots where plant touches the ground boosting resilience. Contains 40x the lycopene of domesticated tomatoes. In the Solanaceae family.

SIZE h*w	SUN	SOIL	WATER	EDIBLE
2ft*10ft	dappled	well-draining	drought tolerant	fruit

PROPAGATION METHODS

- SEEDS: Germinates at 68-77F. Indeterminate germination. Self-seeds if allowed.
- CUTTINGS: Rooted cuttings directly from plant.

RECIPE

VIRGIN BLOODY MARY: 3 c washed everglades tomatoes, 1 hot pepper, 2 cups coconut water, 1 cup of cilantro, salt & pepper to taste; olives as a garnish.

Blanch and drain tomatoes and peppers. Cool. Add all other ingredients to the blender with ice. Garnish with olives.

CULINARY USE

Fruit
Edible raw or cooked. Garnish salads, wraps, and drinks with the whole, fresh, tomato berries. Useful in any recipe that calls for tomatoes, just add the whole berries before cooking, no need to slice and dice. An old Florida favorite is to add them whole to omelets. Can be dried as an excellent dessert fruit. Used in slices, stewed, incorporated into a wide variety of dishes, or processed into ketchup or tomato soup. Tomato juice is sold as a drink and is used in cocktails such as the Bloody Mary.

Green tomatoes can be pickled or fried. Significant source of umami flavor. Slightly sour when unripe.

CULTURAL SIGNIFICANCE

- Will hybridize with other species, important in breeding for disease resistance
- Showy fruit attracts birds
- Nahuatl (the language used by the Aztecs) word "tomatl" became the Spanish word "tomate" & then the English word "tomato"
- Pulp used as a wash to balance oily skin & in soap-making. Used in folk healing as a first aid treatment for burns, scalds & sunburn
- Mistaken as poisonous by Europeans for 200 yrs

CAUTIONS & CONSIDERATIONS

Health
Good source of lycopine - more concentrated if cooked & absorbed better when consumed with a healthy fat.
CAUTION: All green parts are poisonous. Member of nightshade family. Immature fruit contains tomatine, toxic in large quantities.

Pests
Tomato hornworms; Borage said to repel hornworm moth.

Landscape design
Strong aroma said to repel insects - similar to marigold. Often used as a companion for carrots & asparagus.

Fennel
Foeniculum vulgare var purpureum

HARDINESS ZONES: 3 TO 10

This perennial herb is highly ornamental with feathery frowns. Also prized by the ancient Greeks & Romans for medicine, food, insect repellent and a tea believed to provide courage for warriors prior to battle. A low-maintenance, butterfly host plant. Thought to improve digestion & is even used with babies to cure "wind." In mild winters, leaves are available all year. In the Umbelliferae family.

SIZE h*w	SUN	SOIL	WATER	EDIBLE
3ft*1ft	partial	sandy – OK	drought tolerant	leaves, root, seed, stem

PROPAGATION METHODS

- SEED: Germinates at 64-70F. Self-sows freely. Flowers bloom in mid- to late summer and are followed by aromatic seeds.

RECIPE

GREEN BANANA "POTATO SALAD": Peel 20 green bananas and boil 10 min. Strain. Slice into 1/2-inch-thick discs (should yield at least 5 cups). Toss the boiled, green banana with a dressing made of 1/2 cup mayo, 1 tsp salt, 1 tbs vinegar, 1/2 tsp agave syrup. Top with 2 tbs washed, chopped fennel fronds.

CULTURAL SIGNIFICANCE

- Folk medicine uses (e.g., to reduce intestinal gas. Anti-inflammatory, antioxidant, antibacterial, antispasmodic, antifungal, mosquito repellent properties)
- Attracts beneficial insects (e.g., bees, parasitic wasps). Helps prevent aphids infestation.
- One of nine plants in the pagan Anglo-Saxon 'Nine Herbs Charm' of the 10th century
- Key in absinthe & Chinese 5-spice powder
- Yellow and brown dyes from flowers, leaves

CULINARY USE

Leaves, Stalk, & Flowers
Leaves, stalk and delicate yellow flowers are edible raw or cooked - a delicious aniseed flavor. The young leaves are best as older ones become tough. Use as a garnish on raw or cooked dishes like potato, fish or egg dishes. Small flowers highly valued. Inflated leaf bases and the tender young shoots can be eaten like celery.

Seed
Aromatic. Used in puddings, cakes, bread, stuffing. Sprouted & added to salads. In India, roasted seeds are eaten as an after-meal digestive & breath freshener. Seed yields up to 5% essential oil used in toothpastes.

Root
Larger in annual varieties. Cooked for a parsnip-like flavor. Often sautéed, stewed, braised, grilled.

CAUTIONS & CONSIDERATIONS

Health
CAUTION: Do not confuse with poison hemlock. Identify carefully when flowering. Sap may cause photo-sensitivity, dermatitis. Avoid if diabetic or experiencing liver disorders.

Pests
No serious insect or disease problems.

Landscape design
Some named varieties. May behave invasively. Poor companion; inhibits neighboring plant growth. Fennel and dill can hybridize. Resembles dill, coriander, and caraway.

Fig
Ficus carica

HARDINESS ZONES: 6 TO 10

A deciduous shrub with attractive foliage. Cultivated since ancient times and mentioned in multiple religious texts! In the Mulberry/ Moraceae family. 50-75 year old specimens get a striking, silver-gray bark and often gnarl with age. In cooler areas, trees are grown in containers and brought indoors for winter. May bear twice a year!

SIZE h*w	SUN	SOIL	WATER	EDIBLE
18ft*18ft	full to partial	well-draining; clay, poor - OK	drought tolerant	fruit

PROPAGATION METHODS

- SEEDS: Germinates at 70-81F. Keep in container 1st yr. Produces in 8 yrs. Not preferred method.
- DIVISION: Root suckering. Underground runners
- CUTTINGS: Mature wood, 5 inches with a heel.

RECIPE

FIG "FLOWERS": 12 figs; 24 shelled, tropical almonds. Cut the fruit with 2, "x" snips of scissors to form 4 "petals," opening from the stem apex. Sandwich 2 fig "flowers", flesh-to-flesh. Push 4 almonds 1/3 into the fig sandwich where "petals" connect. Place on cookie sheet. Bake 15 min at 350F. Makes 6 flowers. OPTIONAL: Dust with cocoa powder.

CULTURAL SIGNIFICANCE

- Caducous (or Smyrna) figs have flowers produced inside a "package" (syconium) where fig wasps live and pollinate
- Leaves believed to have medicinal properties: bergaptene and psoralene content
- Fig latex researched as rubber alternative
- Dried seeds contain 30% edible oil with beneficial fatty acids
- Figs were common in ancient Greece; cultivation described by Aristotle

CULINARY USE

Fruit

Fruit eaten raw or cooked and has a sweet and succulent flavor which melts in the mouth when served at room temperature. Often dried for later use. Dried figs used as a coffee substitute or blended with coffee after roasting and pulverizing. Fig syrup is a popular, gentle laxative used for all ages. Sliced for salads or cheese spreads. Also dried, or used in pastries, preserves, and jams. Fig paste is prepared by grinding dried fruits. Harvested fruits are spread out in shade for a day, so the latex dries out. Keep fresh figs refrigerated up to 8 days. Freeze to store several months or dehydrate for longer-term storage. Contain diverse phytochemicals.

CAUTIONS & CONSIDERATIONS

Health
CAUTION: Consume only ripe fruit; sap is a serious eye irritant, and contact phytophotodermatitis may occur from sap.

Pests
Root knot nematodes, scale, aphids, mealybugs and spider mites. Leaf spots, rust and blight may occur.

Landscape design
Grow on S or SW side of property. Mulch heavily. Can spread by seeds/ runners to form thickets. Plant when dormant. Limit pruning; fruits on old wood. Some varieties do not need pollination (e.g., Celeste, Brown Turkey).

Firebush

Hamelia patens

HARDINESS ZONES: 8B TO 11

Originally called the Mayan name "Ix-canan," or "guardian of the forest." Loves heat! Fast growing! A native, evergreen, perennial and semi-woody shrub with bright red to yellow flowers which bloom almost all year! Attracts bees, butterflies & hummingbirds! Has a long history of edible and medicinal use throughout the Americas. A great hedge! Long-lived, charming & nearly indestructible! In the Rubiaceae family. Fall color; leaves turn red in fall.

SIZE h*w	SUN	SOIL	WATER	EDIBLE
11ft*12ft	full	well-drained; poor - OK	drought tolerant	berries

PROPAGATION METHODS

- SEEDS: Germinates at 80-85. Self-seeds.
- CUTTINGS: Take stem cuttings in fall. Develops root suckers - cut from mother plant and relocate in spring or summer.

RECIPE

FIREBUSH & ROSEMARY WINE: Strain out seeds by pressing through a sieve. Place deseeded pulp into a glass fermentation vessel. Add 2, 3-inch sprigs of rosemary. Allow to ferment 2-5 days until bubbling subsides. Refrigerate 1 day to allow lee/yeast to settle to the bottom and then enjoy!

OPTIONAL: Add 1-2 TBS of raw honey to increase the vigor of the fermentation.

CULTURAL SIGNIFICANCE

- Larval host plant: Pluto sphinx moth (Xylophanes pluto)
- Leaves, stems and flowers used medicinally (e.g., for antibacterial, anti-inflammatory, analgesic, diuretic, purgative properties) Choco Indians & Amazonians drink leaf infusions for fevers/ use as a skin poultice such as for wounds, cuts, skin fungus, insect stings and bites
- Stems & leaves used in tanning leather

CULINARY USE

Fruit

Eat fruit when fully ripe. The small berries turn green to yellow to red, and finally, black when ripe. Rounded purplish-black juicy berries are edible raw but are most frequently cooked or fermented. In Mexico, a wine is made from the berries and is believed to have antibacterial properties. Berries can be made into jams or syrups. A refreshing, acidic taste. An initial sweetness and grape-like texture. Seeds may impart a bitter taste. Tannins present in the plant parts. Cooking and fermenting help eliminate tannins/ bitterness. Rich in active phytochemicals, including flavonoids and alkaloids.

Other uses for the berries include chutneys & ketchup.

CAUTIONS & CONSIDERATIONS

Health

No known adverse health effects.

Pests

No serious insect or disease problems; aphids, mites.

Landscape design

Be sure not to confuse with non-Florida native/ exotic relative, H. patens var. glabra. Prune no shorter than 5-8 feet; pruning too hard or too frequently reduces blooming. Can be overwintered indoors as a container plant.

FL Prince Peach

Prunus persica

HARDINESS ZONES: 5 TO 9

A deciduous, Florida cultivar and butterfly host plant. Belongs to the family "Rosaceae." Considered one of the most important fruits worldwide and ranks second only to apple in popularity. Needs only 150 chill hours! A delicious, high quality, and juicy early-season peach with a rapid growth cycle!

SIZE h*w	SUN	SOIL	WATER	EDIBLE
19ft*19ft	full to partial	loamy; nitrogen rich	average	fruit, flower, seed

PROPAGATION METHODS

- CUTTINGS: Softwood cuttings in spring to early summer. Ideal temp: 60-75F.
- GRAFTING/ LAYERING/ BUDDING: Done in Spring.

RECIPE

CARAMELIZED PEACH: Heat an oiled skillet on medium high. Drizzle peach top with maple syrup while pan heats. Turn peach face down onto the pan and allow the maple syrup to crystalize onto the peach (5-10 minutes).

OPTIONAL: Serve topped with coconut ice cream.

CULINARY USE

Fruit
May be consumed fresh or processed into many products such as juice, jam, jelly, or dried. Good source of vitamin A. Easily bruised, and do not store well. Taste best when ripened on the tree and eaten the day they are picked. Medium-sized peach with a firm skin; good blush. Semi-clingstone.

Seeds
Eaten cooked. Shell like walnut. Cut in half; boil 30-45 min. discard water. CAUTION: Do not consume if bitter.

Flowers
Flowers consumed raw and added to salads or used as a garnish. Also brewed into a tea. Used in folk healing (e.g., as diuretic & sedative). Distilled flowers used for flavoring.

CULTURAL SIGNIFICANCE

- Has taken 45 years of research to produce this cultivar; specifically created to produce fruit in warmer climates
- High economic value of peach fruit crops
- Stem gum used for chewing
- Seeds yield up to 45% oil - used in skin creams
- This culitvar is increasingly grown in Egypt
- Decended from wild peaches in China, domesticated over 4000 years ago
- Can be trained to grow in an espalier shape

CAUTIONS & CONSIDERATIONS

Health
CAUTION: Do not eat bitter seeds or fruit - hydrogen cyanide may be present.

Pests
Peach leaf curl, borers; Brown rot (Monilinia spp.).

Landscape design
Hand pollination improves fruit-set. Shelter from N/NE winds. Garlic is a good companion to prevent peach leaf curl. Protect bark from being scorched. Compare with other low-chill variety, Tropic Beauty Peach or Wax Jambu/ Java apple (Syzgium samagarense).

FL Sea Oats

Uniola paniculata

HARDINESS ZONES: 7B TO 11

A Florida native in the Poaceae family. An attractive perennial with showy fruits that turn golden brown in late summer. Excellent hurricane wind resistance. An excellent pioneer species and a great choice for prairies and large acreage locations as it can fill in an area quickly. Adds a delightful texture and movement to the garden. Feathery stalks used in flower arrangements.

SIZE h*w	SUN	SOIL	WATER	EDIBLE
6ft*2ft	full to partial	sandy - OK	drought tolerant; maritime - OK	seed/ fruits

PROPAGATION METHODS

- SEEDS: Germinates at 77-85F. Barely cover the seed. Low viability.
- DIVISION: Spreads freely by rhizomes. Dig forming buds at stem bases in spring.

RECIPE

SEA OAT SOURDOUGH: 2 c dried sea oats, 2 c water.

Boil sea oats in water for 20 min. Allow to cool. Purée in a blender. Add 1 tbs at a time until a thick gravy consistency is formed. Feed to a sourdough starter.

CULTURAL SIGNIFICANCE

- Used for dune stabilization. Illegal to dig up in Florida given its role in protecting dunes; tall leaves trap wind-blown sand aiding dune growth & deep roots/ rhizomes stabilize them
- Florida law protects nurseries which grow sea oats. Consult state laws. Increased restrictions on collection of sea oat seed and rhizomes for propagation in wild
- The pygmy burrowing owl nest within sea oat colonies to protect young

CULINARY USE

Seeds

Drooping wheat-like seed heads. Seed is cooked and eaten as a cereal. Has a reputation as having a very good flavor. Prepared like oatmeal. Also ground into a flour and made into bread, pastries, crackers etc. Strip the seed heads once they are golden in color. Dry thoroughly and store out of direct light in an airtight container. Can be harvested year-round and fed to starter as oats become available. Edibility compares with the increasingly commercial relative: Distichlis palmeri.

NOTE: Don't store oats with ergot - a fungus ranging in colors from black to pink to green. Affects oats only rarely. Commercial oats have been pre-cooked to destroy pathogens making them safe to eat "raw."

CAUTIONS & CONSIDERATIONS

Health

No known adverse health effects.

Pests

No serious pests or diseases.

Landscape design

May be confused with Wood Oats (Chasmanthium latifolium). Sea Oats have the potential to become invasive. Compare with Kernza (Thinopyrum intermedium) or Nipa (Distichlis palmeri), grown commercially in Australia - higher yield to flour than wheat & major food source of the Cocopah tribe in western United States.

Flax

Linum perenne

HARDINESS ZONES: 5 TO 9

Also called "Perennial Flax" or "Bright Eyes." An ornamental and very nutritious plant in the Linaceae family. High in alpha-linolenic acid (ALA), an essential omega-3 fatty acid! Tolerates intense heat, humidity and drought. Showy summer flowers! Naturalized throughout much of North America. Compare with the more commercial annual flax: Linum usitatissimum.

SIZE h*w	SUN	SOIL	WATER	EDIBLE
1ft*8in	full to partial	well-draining	drought tolerant	seeds

PROPAGATION METHODS

- SEEDS: Germinates at 65 - 70F within 30 days. Self-sows freely. Sow in fall.
- CUTTINGS: Basal cuttings taken in spring when shoots are 4" long with substantial underground stem.

RECIPE

FLAXSEED CHUTNEY POWDER: 1/2c dry roasted flaxseeds, 6-10 dried chilis, 4-5 dried garlic pods, 3/4 tsp sea salt.

Polverize all ingredients in a coffee grinder. Store in an airtight container in the fridge. Sprinkle on vegetables or add to stirfries and soups.

CULINARY USE

Seeds

Seed is eaten cooked and has a pleasant nutty taste. High oil content. Eaten on its own or used as a flavoring. Seeds are used in breads, baking and cereals. The oils in the seeds can become rancid, so either harvest just what you need, or store the seeds in the refrigerator or freezer.

To cook/ dry roast the seeds, heat a dry skillet on medium-high. Let the seeds roast 4-5 min. Stir frequently, until the seeds become fragrant. Be careful to continue stirring to prevent burning or scorching! Seeds may pop or jump like popcorn or jumping beans.

CULTURAL SIGNIFICANCE

- Seed oil use parallels commercial variety (i.e., Linum usitatissimum)
- Stem fiber used for making cloth, nets, string, baskets, mats etc., and in paper making; once used in Europe to make linen and rope
- Folk healing uses (e.g., using seed oil in medicines to sore throats, coughs, constipation)
- High wildlife value: Birds use seeds & deer eat foliage

CAUTIONS & CONSIDERATIONS

Health
CAUTION: As with the more commercial variety, flax should not be eaten raw because it contains cyanide. Always cook.

Pests
No serious insect or disease problems; cutworms, grasshoppers, stem rot in areas with poor drainage.

Landscape design
Looks best massed. Effective in rock gardens, border fronts. Plant in a sheltered location. Seeds maintain viability for years. Hybridizes.

Frangipani

Plumeria rubra

HARDINESS ZONES: 10 TO 12

Bring an instant tropical feel to the garden! Sensational in arrangements, or in leis/ flower necklaces. Deciduous and in the Apocynaceae family. Highly aromatic at night. Flower frangrance is believed to be calming and is used in perfume and incense. A good host for dendrobium orchids and trellis for vanilla! Can be kept small or left to become a gnarled giant. A symbol of love, loyality & protection!

SIZE h*w	SUN	SOIL	WATER	EDIBLE
20ft*20ft	full to partial	well-draining	drought tolerant	flowers

PROPAGATION METHODS

- CUTTINGS: Cut a 8-24" branch. Allow the branch to dry out for a few days and stick the branch in the soil. It roots with high rates of success.

RECIPE

PLUMERIA TEA: Pick 1/4 c of flowers in the late evening or early morning May to June when fragrance is strong. Soak for about 10 minutes and rinse a couple of times to remove any latex. Simmer plumeria flowers in 4c of water for 10-20 min. Strain. Add sweetener to taste.

CAUTION: See health notes

CULTURAL SIGNIFICANCE

- Wood used to create drums, bowls, furniture
- When taking cuttings, know if the plant is patented or trademarked for legal reasons
- Plumeria rubra is an important traditional medicinal plant for inflammatory conditions
- Associated with temple worship/ protection
- Bride and grooms give garlands of plumeria flowers at weddings in India
- Flower oil is astringent causing skin contraction
- Larval host for Pseudosphinx tetrio; no nectar

CULINARY USE

Flowers

The flowers are used in traditional medicine for antimicrobial properties (e.g., Chinese Five Flower Tea). Consume with caution and in moderation. Used to flavor cacao, and as an exotic flavoring for coconut oil and beverages including alcoholic drinks. For instance, in Mexico, the flowers are used to aromatize a hot maize-based drink called atole & a chocolate-based ceremonial beverage called bu'pu (meaning 'foam' in Zapotec). The flowers freeze well and are used to garnish ice cream cakes. Petals are also used in hot teas and eaten in sweetmeats. Flowers are also cooked as a vegetable such as by frying.

NOTE: Recipes callling for "frangipani" or "frangipane" likely mean an almond paste - not plumeria flowers.

CAUTIONS & CONSIDERATIONS

Health

Flowers used medicinally in folk healing for cough, constipation, etc. CAUTION: USDA Forestry Service lists Plumeria rubra as a poisonous plant; milky latex irritates the eyes and skin.

Pests

Scales, nematodes; Root rot, rust.

Landscape design

Most economically important of Plumeria species. Shelter from strong winds. Brittle limbs. Phosphorus applications improve flowering. Can overwinter indoors as a potted plant.

Gai Lon Broccoli

Brassica oleracea var alboglabra

HARDINESS ZONES: 7 TO 11

Also called "Chinese Kale" or "Kailaan." An easy-to-grow short-lived, perennial. Deciduous. Thick, erect stems with flat, glossy, blue-green leaves and compact flowerheads. Succeeds in just about any well-draining soil. Heat and frost tolerant! Closely related to broccoli! In Brassicaceae family.

SIZE h*w	SUN	SOIL	WATER	EDIBLE
1ft*8in	full to partial	well-draining; clay - OK	maritime - OK	leaves, flowers

PROPAGATION METHODS

- SEEDS: Germinates at 64-71F. Three months from sowing to harvest. Self-seeds.
- CUTTINGS: Lateral shoots root easily.

RECIPE

GAI LON STIRFRY: 5-7 terminal shoots of gai lon, 2 garlic cloves peeled & minced, 1/2" ginger piece minced, 1 tbs oil.

Heat a skillet on medium-high. Toss all ingredients with oil. Stir-fry 5-7 minutes. OPTIONAL: Add salt and pepper to taste.

CULTURAL SIGNIFICANCE

- One of the top five Asian vegetables sought by Australian supermarkets
- Pollinated by bees
- Most cultivars were developed in warmer parts of China
- High in calcium, iron, and vitamins A and C; rich in antioxidents
- Eaten widely in Chinese, Cantonese, Vietnamese, Burmese and Thai cuisine
- Believed to reduce cholesterol if eaten often

CULINARY USE

Leaves & Flowers
Harvest just as the first flowers begin to open. Young flowering shoots and small leaves eaten raw but more frequently cooked; become tough with age. Peel older stems. Some peel and eat the inner stem cooked. The developing inflorescence is also edible. To prompt perennial behavior, only harvest the terminal shoot which encourages the development of lateral shoots. About three cuts can be obtained from one stem per season. Flavor is similar to broccoli, but more complex & slightly bitter. Cooking reduces bitterness. Very popular for stir-fry dishes. Also steamed or boiled. Harvest in the early morning.

Refrigerates well up to 7 days in an airtight container.

CAUTIONS & CONSIDERATIONS

Health
No known adverse health effects. NOTE: Brassica family has thyroid suppressing goitrogens. Cook/ blanch.
Pests
Flea beetles, diamond-back moth, borers, cabbage looper, aphids, grasshoppers and crickets. Damping off in soil with poor drainage.
Landscape design
Yields up to 4lbs in 10 sq ft. A range of cultivars (F-1 hybrids grow vigorously; Mandy - high yield; Kailaan White - tree structure & Dai Sum - disease resistant). Sow heavily and thin after 3 wks (eat the pulled seedlings).

Geranium
Geranium carolinianum

HARDINESS ZONES: 3A TO 11B

A biennial, FL native which is highly beneficial to a food forest. Hosts 25 species of butterflies and moths and therefore promotes a healthy eco-system with pests in check!! In the Geraniaceae family. Also called, Cranesbill. Used for hundreds of years by Native American tribes, such as the Obijwe, Chippewa and Blackfoot tribes, as a valuable medicinal herb with the shallow taproot being most coveted for herbal remedies.

SIZE h*w	SUN	SOIL	WATER	EDIBLE
1ft*6in	partial	sandy, clay - OK	drought tolerant	leaves

PROPAGATION METHODS

- SEEDS: Germinates at 82-86F. Readily reseeds and spreads forming a groundcover in ideal growing conditions.

RECIPE

MOUTHWASH: 2 tsp fresh leaves. Pour 1 cup of boiling water over the leaves and steep 5 minutes. Strain the leaves out.

Used as a gargle for sore throats. Spit excess. Use in moderation and for short periods of time.

CULTURAL SIGNIFICANCE

- Birds eat the seeds and insects and deer forage on the leaves
- Native Americans would dry the root, grind into a fine powder, then sprinkle the powder into wounds to stop bleeding & promote healing
- Provides nectar for long-tongued bees (Megachile spp.), short-tongued bees (Halictid), and flower flies (Syrphid) which provide cool season aphid control
- Fresh leaves are used to treat insect stings

CULINARY USE

Leaves
Leaves are edible raw, but the taste is strongly bitter & astringent. Used as a medicinal tea or gargle (e.g., for inflammation, wound healing). Like the leaves, there are several reports that the root was infused in water for a medicinal gargle and mouthwash as well.

NOTE: "Geraniums" are often referenced as "edible flowers." The edible flower varieties of geranium generally come from the Pelargonium spp group. For instance, Rose Geranium (Pelargonium graveolens) is an evergreen, 4ft shrub for zones 10-11 and has highly edible flowers, commonly added to salads. The leaves are rose-scented and used to flavor desserts, jellies, vinegars, tea, etc.

CAUTIONS & CONSIDERATIONS

Health
CAUTION: Contains tannins. Medicinal. Consume in moderation and with caution. Low-growing. Don't collect from contaminated sites.

Pests
Generally pest and disease free aside from hosting insects.

Landscape design
Can behave invasively. Compare with culinary "scented geraniums" (Pelargonium spp.), endangered FL native: G. maculatum or popular medicinals: Ashwaganda (Withania somnifera) & Wild dagga (Leonotis leonurus).

Ginger
Zingiber officinale

HARDINESS ZONES: 8 TO 12

A fragrant kitchen spice and medicinal, this herbaceous perennial grows annual pseudostems which offer edible leaves. As a tropical plant, ginger needs plenty of heat and humidity, and will love a partially shady spot of your summer garden. Sprout a few organic grocery store rhizomes for fun! Considered a universal medicine in Ayurvedic & Chinese herbal treatment traditions! Confucius was said to eat ginger every meal. In the Zingiberaceae family.

SIZE h*w	SUN	SOIL	WATER	EDIBLE
4ft*3ft	full to partial	well-draining	flood/ drought tolerant	flower, leaves, oil, root, shoot

PROPAGATION METHODS

- RHIZOME: Ten month growing season. Ideal temp: 70-85F.
- DIVISION: As new growth begins. Harvest when the stalks begin to wither.

RECIPE

GINGERSNAPS: 5 tbs minced ginger, 1/2 sourdough starter, 1c sunflower seed flour, 1/3 c molasses, 1/4 c oil, 1/4 maple syrup; OPTIONAL: 3/4 tsp salt.

Combine all ingredients. Refrigerate overnight. drop tsp sized balls of dough 1/2" apart onto an oiled baking sheet. Bake 12-18 min at 350.

CULTURAL SIGNIFICANCE

- Leaves woven into mats
- Root used in folk healing (e.g., as an anti-inflammatory for reducing arthritis pain; remedy for constipation, nausea & vomiting; to reduce risk of cardiovascular disease)
- Contains two classes of constituents: the essential oils and oleoresins. An essential oil obtained from the root used in perfume
- One of the first exported Asian spices during spice trade, used by Greeks and Romans

CULINARY USE

Rhizome
Very young rhizomes are peeled and eaten raw in salads, pickled, or cooked in syrup and made into sweetmeats; added to dishes such as cakes, curries, chutneys, stir-fry dishes, candies etc. Commonly used in beverages. Roots can be used fresh or dried and ground into a powder - dried root is about twice as pungent as the fresh root; serves as a meat tenderizer. A key ingredient in eastern recipes like: masala chai & kimchi.

Leaves & Flowers
The young, slightly spicy leaves and young shoots can be eaten as a potherb, or pureed and used in sauces and dips. The leaves can also be used to wrap food. Young inflorescences can be eaten raw.

CAUTIONS & CONSIDERATIONS

Health
CAUTION: May interact with some medications.

Pests
No significant problems; bacterial wilt may occur.

Landscape design
Compare with ginger-related, under-story plants which have additional edibility like: Curcuma zedoaria, Alpinia galangal, Alpinia zerumbet, Alpinia nutans, Kaempferia galanga, Curcuma petiolata, Costus speciosus.

Goji Berry
Lycium barbarum

HARDINESS ZONES: 6 TO 10

Also called wolfberry. A deciduous shrub with a long history of medicinal use as energy restoring tonic and also for ailments like skin rashes. In the Solanaceae (nightshade) family. Eaten in Asia for generations in the hopes for a longer life - considered by some to be a fountain of youth. Long used to nourish liver and kidney in China. Deemed a 'superfruit' given the many nutrients and bioactive compounds.

SIZE h*w	SUN	SOIL	WATER	EDIBLE
6ft*6ft	full, partial	well-draining; sand - OK	maritime - OK; drought tolerant	fruit, leaves, shoots

PROPAGATION METHODS

- CUTTINGS: Half-ripe wood, 5 inch in early summer. Full yields within 5 years. Ideal temp: 60-70F.
- DIVISIONS: Suckers divided in late winter & can be planted out in permanent positions.

RECIPE

GOJI-MINT SMOOTHIE: 1 cup sautéed goji berries, 1/2 cup mint leaves, 2+ c water, 1 c ice. Honey to taste.

Wash mint thoroughly in a 1:1 vinegar/water bath. Rinse. Blend all ingredients. Add additional water until desired consistency.

CULINARY USE

Fruit
Bright orange-red berries are elliptical and ½- to 1-inch when ripe. Only eat fully ripe fruits. Traditionally, cooked before consumption or made into juice or wine. Mild liquorice/ sweet-and-tangy flavor. Often dried for later use (like raisins). Chinese cuisine incorporates Goji berries in a variety of soups, teas, and congees. Soak dried berries in water overnight and then strain for nutrient-rich juice. Berries are frozen & thawed and maintain color and flavor. NOTE: Pruning increases yields.

Leaves & Shoots
The leaves are a tea substitute and potherb. Young shoots eaten cooked as a vegetable, the flavor is similar to watercress. Powdered & used as a nutritional supplement.

CULTURAL SIGNIFICANCE

- Used for centuries in traditional Chinese medicine (e.g., for immunomodulation, anti-aging, neuroprotection, endurance, increased metabolism, control of glucose & antioxidant effects)
- Good soil stabilization: Extensive root system
- Dried berries are a good source of potassium, calcium, iron, selenium, zinc, & polysaccharides
- A cash crop suitable for Florida eco-types
- Can tolerate infertile & unfavorable conditions

CAUTIONS & CONSIDERATIONS

Health
CAUTION: Spines on most cultivars. Avoid if on blood thinners; may also interact with diabetes and blood pressure medication.

Pests
Leafhopper, thrips, aphids, spider mites, powdery mildew, runny gum disease, and root rot.

Landscape design
Compare with FL natives, Christmas Berry (Lycium carolinianum - flood tolerant) & Hackberry (Celtis laevigata). Good for informal hedge. Pinch tips for bushy growth. Can grow in 5g pots.

Golden Apple
Spondias dulcis

HARDINESS ZONES: 9A TO 12

A vigorous and fast-growing deciduous tree with crunchy pineapple-mango flavored fruits. Juicy, vaguely sweet, but with a hint of tart acidity. With consistent rainfall, the plant can flower and fruit all year round. Heavy fruit production!! Graceful, rounded branches. A single tree provides a steady supply when most other fruits are out of season. Often grown as a living fence. In the Anacardiaceae family.

SIZE h*w	SUN	SOIL	WATER	EDIBLE
80ft*30ft	full	acidic - OK	well-drained	leaves, fruit

PROPAGATION METHODS

- SEEDS: Germinates at 77-82F within 4 weeks. Can bear fruit in 4 years.
- HARDWOOD CUTTING: Bears fruit in 2 - 3 yrs
- AIRLAYERING: Roots easily.

RECIPE

CHUTNEY: 5 washed golden apples peeled, cored/chopped, 1 c herbs of choice, 1/2 tsp cinnamon, 1/2 cup dried mulberry "raisins," 1/2 tsp salt, 1 tsp minced ginger.

Puree all into a chutney and serve with crackers.

CULINARY USE

Fruit
The fruit may be eaten raw. Good source of phosphorus, calcium, magnesium. Best when golden colored but firm. Fruit fall to the ground while still green & hard, turning golden-yellow as they ripen. If allowed to soften, it becomes difficult to slice. Made into jam, preserves, sauces, soups. Soak in vinegar with chili/ spices to make acharu, a type of relish/pickle. Use green, unripe fruit to make a salad called, nhoam mkak. Stew flesh in water & sugar & strain to create an apple butter-like product (if cooked down).

Leaves
Young leaves are used as seasoning (such as for pepes) or cooked as a vegetable. More mature leaves are also eaten as a salad green though they are tart.

CULTURAL SIGNIFICANCE

- Folk medicine use (e.g., treatment of wounds, sore throats, mouth infection, coughs; believed to have antimicrobial, antioxidant & thrombolytic properties)
- Widely grown in Somalia's agriculture belt
- U.S. Dept of Ag received seeds from Liberia in 1909
- Potable water can be derived from the roots
- Sometimes cooked with meat to tenderize it
- Unripe fruit contains about 10% pectin

CAUTIONS & CONSIDERATIONS

Health
CAUTION: seeds have very sharp spines. The fruit may present a choking hazard if the core and fibers are not properly removed. Contact with foliage and sap may cause dermatitis in some individuals.

Pests
Few pests; nutritional problems on highly alkaline soils.

Landscape design
Branches are brittle; shelter from winds. For European apples, consider Florida cultivar, low-chill-hour varieties like 'TropicSweet', 'Anna', and 'Dorsett Golden.'

Goldenrod

Solidago spp

HARDINESS ZONES: 5 TO 10

A Florida native! 82 species of butterflies and moths use it as a caterpillar host including ladybirds, lacewings and hoverflies which help to control insect pests. In the family Asteraceae. A showy, low maintenance plant. Flowers explode into bursts of long-lasting yellow blooms in late summer. Beautiful in cut arrangements as a filler. A versatile plant: 75 species of goldenrod exist in the U.S.!

SIZE h*w	SUN	SOIL	WATER	EDIBLE
6ft*3ft	full to partial	clay - OK	drought tolerant	seeds, leaves, flowers

PROPAGATION METHODS

- SEEDS: Germinates at 68-70F. Sow in spring. Barely cover the seed.
- DIVISIONS: In spring or autumn. Pot and grow in a lightly shaded position, once well-established plant out in summer.

RECIPE

GOLDENROD TEA: 2 tbs thoroughly washed flowers; 2c boiling water.

Allow to steep 2-5 minutes covered. Add sweetener to taste. Store in the refrigerator up to 3 days.

CULINARY USE

Seeds

Seed is used as a thickener in soups, stews and porridge.

Leaves & Flowers

Sweet smell and anise-like taste (especially S. odora - considered most delicious variety). Young leaves and flowering stems are eaten cooked. A tea is made from the flowers and leaves. Mixed with packaged berries to prevent mold given anti-fungal/antimicrobial properties and to maintain quality.

NOTE: S. canadensis research used to create this reference sheet. Without regard to a specific species, goldenrod in general is documented as a gentle herb.

CULTURAL SIGNIFICANCE

- Flowers used for dying - yellow, brown & green
- Accused of causing hay fever - does not: pollen is not airborne
- After Boston Tea Party, goldenrod called "liberty tea." Exported (China highly esteemed)
- A sign of good luck & fortune in many cultures
- British believed it pointed toward golden treasure and marked hidden springs
- Used in folk healing (e.g., for colds, kidney/ urinary tract tonic, baths for sore muscles)

CAUTIONS & CONSIDERATIONS

Health

CAUTION: Medicinal (e.g., diuretic). Consume in moderation and with caution. Avoid harvesting plants with fungus on leaves.

Pests

Rust, powdery mildew, leaf spot, root rot, beetles, aphids & gall-forming insects.

Landscape design

Can colonize. Stabilizes soil & revegetates disturbed areas. Compare with FL native goldenrods: S. sempervirens (salt tolerant, marsh-friendly), and S. fistulosa.

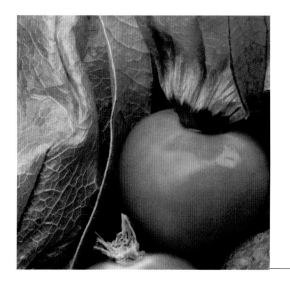

Gooseberry

Physalis peruviana

HARDINESS ZONES: 10 TO 12

Also called Goldenberry, Inca Berry or Peruvian Groundcherry. This ornamental, evergreen plant conveniently wraps up each fruit in its own protective 'paper bag'. If picked with bag/calyx intact, the fruit stays fresh up to 3 months! Cultivated plants live up to 4 years when cut back each year after fruiting. Highly productive even in poor soils!! In the Solanaceae family.

SIZE h*w	SUN	SOIL	WATER	EDIBLE
4ft*4ft	full to partial	poor - OK; well-draining	average	fruit

PROPAGATION METHODS

- SEEDS: Germinates at 75-80F. Low rates but fast germination.
- DIVISION: In spring, remove young shoots from the side of the clump and plant in a pot in the shade until well-established.

RECIPE

GOOSEBERRY ICECREAM: 1 c gooseberries, 1/2 c agave syrup, 1 c coconut milk, 2 tbs chia seed, pinch of sea salt.

Stew gooseberries on medium-high heat with agave syrup until they burst. Add salt, chia seed and coconut milk and allow to thicken (15 min). Puree all ingredients. Freeze.

CULINARY USE

Fruit
Ready to harvest in summer when the husks turn from green to tan and the fruit falls from the plant. Berry-like fruit is edible raw but is more often cooked in pies, cakes, jellies, compotes, jams, puddings, chutneys and for ice cream. Marble-sized. Dried fruit can be used as a raisin substitute, though more bitter-sweet. Tangy pineapple-like flavor. In Colombia, fruits are stewed with honey. British use the husk as a handle, pulling it backwards while still attached for dipping fruit in icing or fondue. Fruit size can vary greatly. Popular in restaurants as a decorative garnish. The fruit is rich in vitamin A, C and B. High protein and phosphorus levels for a fruit.

NOTE: Wet calyx covered berries need drying before storing.

CULTURAL SIGNIFICANCE

- One of the few fresh fruits of the early settlers in New South Wales
- Described enthusiastically by the late Dr. David Fairchild in his well-loved book, 'The World Was My Garden'
- In the 18th Century, the fruits were perfumed and worn as jewelry by native women of Peru
- Used traditionally since Columbian times to treat various diseases given high amounts of antioxidants, vitamins, minerals and fibers

CAUTIONS & CONSIDERATIONS

Health
CAUTION: Unripe fruits are poisonous. All parts of the plant, except the fruit, are poisonous. Calyx is toxic and should not be eaten.

Pests
Cutworms, mites, whiteflies, flea beetle.

Landscape design
Growers shake flowers or spray with water to distribute pollen. May behave invasively. For other hardiness zones, compare with tomatillo, Chinese lantern and with European gooseberry (Ribes uva-crispa).

Gotu Kola
Centella asiatica

HARDINESS ZONES: 7 TO 10

A plant with many common names, including Asiatic pennywort, this low-growing perennial can form a dense ground cover in wet habitats. In the Apiaceae/ Umbelliferae family. Used for medicinal purposes worldwide since ancient times. In Ayurveda medicine, it's believed to prolong life & enhance memory. Increasingly popular as a dietary supplement! Some eat a few leaves a day in hopes of increasing their lifespan.

SIZE h*w	SUN	SOIL	WATER	EDIBLE
8in*3ft	full to partial	poor draining - OK	seasonal flooding - OK	leaves, stem

PROPAGATION METHODS

- SEEDS: Germinates at 77-85F. Sow densely, thin.
- CUTTINGS/ DIVISIONS: Produces stolons up to 3ft in length with roots at the nodes; cut and divide. Plant stem pieces with at least 1 node.

RECIPE

SLEEPY-TIME TEA: 1 tsp thoroughly washed, finely shredded Gotu kola leaves; 1 cup boiling water.

Cover cup and allow the leaves to steep 10-15 minutes.

OPTIONAL: Add warmed coconut milk.

CULTURAL SIGNIFICANCE

- Dried root, stems, leaves, and fruit used in traditional Chinese & Indian Ayurvedic medicine (e.g., as a mental rejuvenator; anti-inflammatory; to improve circulation; topically to aid wound healing & scar prevention; in ointments for skin diseases - supported by clinical data)
- Potential in phytoremediation - removes heavy metals
- Flowers offer pollen for honeybees

CULINARY USE

Leaves & Stem
Fan-shaped leaves are eaten raw or cooked. Can be consumed in soups or salads, and in curries. Treated as a vegetable or aromatic. A mild taste and aroma, similar to asparagus. Discard fruit-bearing structures (intense bitter taste). Beneficial levels of copper. Loaded with vitamins and minerals: B, K, calcium, zinc, and magnesium.

In Burmese cuisine it is made into a salad mixed with onions, crushed nuts, bean powder. In Sri Lanka, it is prepared by pureeing it and mixing that paste with rice and coconut milk. Used in sweet drinks and herbal teas. Served stir-fried in coconut oil. Also blended with grated coconut, shallots, chilies, and lime juice. Occasionally made into fritters with turmeric and flour.

CAUTIONS & CONSIDERATIONS

Health
CAUTION: Medicinal. Consume in moderation. May cause skin irritation. Pollen is an allergen. Some report dizziness/ drowsiness after consuming. Do not consume if grown in contaminated soils. Toxic in large doses/ longterm use.

Pests
Mites, root knot nematode, sap suckers.

Landscape design
Can behave invasively. Compare with the FL native look-alike: Hydrocotyle umbellata "dollar weed" & Bacopa monnieri.

Gramichama

Eugenia brasiliensis

HARDINESS ZONES: 9 TO 11

An attractive evergreen, slender, and erect shrub cultivated as an edible ornamental given glossy foliage and showy trunk structure. Reminiscent of Japanese cherry trees producing thousands of white flowers! A great understory plant! Its canopy stays dense, even in partial shade. Fruits several times a year, providing a delicious, cherrylike fruit. In the Myrtaceae family.

SIZE h*w	SUN	SOIL	WATER	EDIBLE
26ft*26ft	full to partial	clay, acidic - OK; well-draining	average	fruit

PROPAGATION METHODS

- SEEDS: Germinates at 68-86F. Slow growing. Fruits after 4 yrs. Dried seed are not viable. Low germination rates. Most gramichamas in nurseries are grown from seed.
- CUTTINGS: Root easily.

RECIPE

BRAZIL CHERRY JAM: 1 pint of washed, halved, and pitted cherries; 2 tbs chia seed; 1/4 c agave nectar; pinch of sea salt.

Purée cherries and mix with all ingredients. Allow to thicken at room temperature. Refrigerate and use within 2 weeks. Alternatively, freeze in ice cube trays and purée as a sorbet at a later time.

CULINARY USE

Fruit
The small fruits are round and form as clusters on long stems. Can vary considerably in color: black, yellow, or red (sweetest variety color). Thin and delicate skin; grape-like. Soft and melting pulp; a mild subacid taste. Flavor is like Concord grape mixed with cherry and jaboticaba. Fruit ripens over the course of a month and is then harvested over a few days. Fruit is eaten raw or used in jams, jellies etc. Whole pitted fruit are used in pies, cakes and fruit salads. Also employed in ice creams as a flavoring agent. Harvesting fruit by clipping stems and storing in 1-pint containers with no more than double layers prevents damage. Stores refrigerated up to 12 days. Processed purée can be frozen for future use but may lose some flavor.

CULTURAL SIGNIFICANCE

- Wood is compact & ideal for cabinets, boxes, and carpentry; cross-grained
- Used in folk medicine as astringent, diuretic, energizing, anti-rheumatic and anti-inflammatory. An infusion of the leaves or bark is used as a treatment for rheumatism in Brazil
- Bark and leaves contain large amounts of tannins, reportedly among highest (34%)
- Bioactive compounds investigated to reduce chronic diseases

CAUTIONS & CONSIDERATIONS

Health
No known adverse health effects. Pollen may cause mild allergies. Good levels of calcium for a fruit.

Pests
Host for fruit flies.

Landscape design
Narrow crown - recommended for street planting. Shelter from strong winds - shallow roots. Used as hedges, screens, or in shrub borders. Can handle light frosts. Grows well in 5-10g pots as a container specimen. Can be pruned to 6ft to aid harvest. Compare with Jaboticaba.

Guanabana
Annona muricata

HARDINESS ZONES: 10 TO 12

Also called Soursop. This showy, evergreen is a low maintenance plant and bears fruit almost continually throughout the year! Each tree can produce up to several dozen fruit per year. Smells a bit like pineapple, tastes like strawberry-apple and has a banana-like texture! Delicious and healthy. The fruit has many major minerals like calcium, iron, and magnesium! A coveted tropical tree! In Annonaceae family.

SIZE h*w	SUN	SOIL	WATER	EDIBLE
23ft*23ft	full to partial	poor - OK	average	fruit, leaves

PROPAGATION METHODS

- SEEDS: Germinate at 77-86F. True to type. Scarify and soak 24-48 hours. Fast growing and fruiting starts 2nd year.
- CUTTINGS: Semi-ripe wood.

RECIPE

GUANABANA MILK SHAKE: 1 medium guanabana, 1 cup water; 5 frozen coconut milk ice cubes, 3 tbs agave, a pinch of sea salt.

Mash fruit pulp in water, let stand, then strain to remove fibrous material and seeds. Puree with coconut milk ice cubes, salt and agave.

CULTURAL SIGNIFICANCE

- Often used in traditional medicine (e.g., leaves in bath for skin ailments; ripe fruit is believed to relieve liver ailments, eliminate worms and parasites, relieve arthritic pain, & decrease fever). All tree parts have insecticidal properties
- Host plant for tailed jay (Graphium agamemnon)/ swallowtail caterpillars
- Can graft onto other annonas including the FL Native: pond apple (A. glabra)

CULINARY USE

Fruit

The inedible fruit skin becomes yellowish-green when fully ripe. The mature fruit it soft to the touch and has a pleasing fragrance and flavor and is consumed raw or mixed with ice cream or milk. Fruit has a pineapple like aroma, but its subacid to acid flavor is unique and the pulp is very juicy. Rich in vitamin A and C. In Indonesia, fruit pulp is boiled and mixed with sugar to make sweet-cake ('dodol sirsak'). In the Philippines, unripe fruits are eaten as a vegetable by boiling, frying or roasting. Strained pulp is considered a delicacy when mixed with wine.

Leaves & Shoots

Young shoots are cooked and eaten as a vegetable. A tea, called corossol tea, is made from the leaves. Good source of calcium.

CAUTIONS & CONSIDERATIONS

Health

CAUTION: Medicinal. Consume in moderation. Fruit, but mainly seeds, may contain annonacin toxin. Seed powder/ oil used to kill lice and bedbugs. Stem sap is a skin irritant.

Pests

Resilient; scale, borers, fruit flies, mealybug.

Landscape design

Heavily mulch base of the tree to avoid dehydration during dry season. Shallow roots - shelter from strong winds. Loses leaves when stressed by drought. May behave invasively.

Guava
Psidium gujava

HARDINESS ZONES: 9 TO 12

Also called Apple Guava - an excellent pioneer species often grown as an ornamental edible in the Myrtaceae family. However, it is listed as a FL Category 1 Invasive and may present spontaneously as a wild cultivar. Eating the nutritious fruit will help manage its spread. A good source of Vit A, calcium, iron, and phosphorus. Plants may bear heavily for 15-25 years with full productivity achieved after 5-8 years.

SIZE h*w	SUN	SOIL	WATER	EDIBLE
32ft*32ft	full to partial	poor, sandy, clay - OK	drought tolerant	fruit, leaves, seeds

PROPAGATION METHODS

NOT RECOMMENDED
- SEEDS: Germinates at 70-85F. Often self-sows freely. True-to-seed. Can fruit within 3 years. Carefully collect all fruit to prevent spread. Wide variety in wild tree size, yield & fruit quality.

RECIPE

WHITE GUAVE CHUTNEY: 2 guavas de-seeded, puréed, 2 garlic cloves, 1 tbsp moringa leaves, 1 tbsp citrus juice, pinch of salt, 1 tbs oil.

Sautee the garlic, salt, and chopped peppers in oil until fragrant. Add puree until warmed. Mix in citrus juice and top with moringa leaves. Eat with flatbread or crackers.

CULINARY USE

Fruit
Yellow-skinned, apple-sized fruit can be ovoid or pear shaped. Consumed raw or cooked, made into jams or used as an ingredient in desserts like milkshakes. Very delicate in flavor. The popular, Latin American beverage, "agua fresca" is often made with guava. Flavor ranges from sweet to acidic. Also eaten with a pinch of salt, cayenne powder or a mix of spices. Very high in pectin. If fruit ripens during seasonal flooding, it loses flavor and may split.

Seeds
Provides an edible oil rich in linoleic acid.

Leaves
Used in cooking, especially in Asian cuisine.

CULTURAL SIGNIFICANCE

- Wide range of folk healing uses (e.g., considered an antibacterial, astringent, & anti-inflammatory; ripe, fresh fruit is eaten to relieve constipation)
- Wood is used for tool handles, fence posts, carpentry, turnery, firewood, meat smoking, and charcoal
- Leaves and bark may be used for dyeing and tanning; pounded with coconut milk to make a dye that turns silk black

CAUTIONS & CONSIDERATIONS

Health
No known adverse health effects. Moderate levels of folate.

Pests
Host for fruit flies; scales, mealy bugs, leaf-eaters.

Landscape design
Useful for bio-indication/ as a bio-accumulator. Succeeds in harsh, direct sun and provides valuable shade. May behave invasively - can form thickets. Root suckers. Red pulp varieties used as a tomato substitute. Compare with Pineapple Guava (Acca sellowiana) and Strawberry Guava (Psidium cattleianum).

Gumbo Limbo

Bursera simaruba
HARDINESS ZONES: 10 TO 12

Also called "Tourist Tree" or "Sunburn Tree." A FL native and long-lived, deciduous, perennial. A beautiful shade tree & rugged windbreak with striking, red/bronze-colored peeling bark. Protects crops in hurricanes!! Attracts birds, butterflies, & bees! In the Burseraceae family. Aromatic & fast growing! Valued medicinal properties.

SIZE h*w	SUN	SOIL	WATER	EDIBLE
40ft*30ft	full to partial	well-draining	drought tolerant	leaves

PROPAGATION METHODS

- SEEDS: Germinates at 78-90F. Viable 10 mo. 40% germination. Better than cuttings - tap root.
- CUTTING: Even large branches will root. Simply stick branches into the ground - not as wind tolerant.

RECIPE

GUMBO LIMBO TEA: Steep 3 leaves in 2 cups of water. Cover for 2 minutes. Remove leaves.

Tea should be lightly aromatic. Sweeten with agave or honey to taste.

Limit consumption given medicinal use.

CULINARY USE

Leaves

When crushed, the leaves are fragrant. A tea substitute - considered medicinal. Consume in moderation and with caution. Used in folk medicine to treat ailments like colds and flus. Believed to have anti-inflammatory properties.

Some resources report that the bark is used similarly in medicinal teas.

NOTE: Information on edibility is limited to ethnobotanical accounts. Limited published research on safe consumption.

CULTURAL SIGNIFICANCE

- Fragrant resin is used as insect repellent, in glue, canoe paint, and insect repellent; used by Mayans as an incense since ancient times
- Trees used as living fence on ranches. May attract bat species
- Host for dingy purplewing (Eunica monima)
- Used in folk healing (e.g., flowers/ fruit for snake bites; leaves to sooth dermatitis; extract to decrease heart rate/ for vascular protection)

CAUTIONS & CONSIDERATIONS

Health
CAUTION: Underresearched plant; leaves could possibly be confused with Poisonwood (Metopium toxiferum). Some reports that the fruits are edible but information lacking.

Pests
Resilient.

Landscape design
Great pioneer tree. Fast growth. Excellent wind break for other crops. Among the most hurricane-wind tolerant plants if planted by seed. Remove lower branches if close to the ground. Ecological versatility. Great companion plant.

Hemp
Cannabis sativa

HARDINESS ZONES: 8 TO 11

Part of a billion-dollar industry and widely considered one of the most sustainable plants! Thanks to new laws, hemp can be grown in Florida as an annual! Well-worth the time! A good companion plant that repels pests! Cultivated throughout history for fiber, seed oil, food, recreation, and medicine. NOTE: According to s. 581.217(6), F.S., individuals must be licensed to grow hemp in FL. Licensing involves background checks and registration. In the Cannabaceae family.

SIZE h*w	SUN	SOIL	WATER	EDIBLE
8ft*2ft	full to partial	loamy; well-draining	average	leaves, oil, seed

PROPAGATION METHODS

- SEEDS: Germinates at 78-82F. Dioecious. The Association of Official Seed Certifying Agencies (AOSCA) gives seed & propagation materials: https://www.aosca.org. Low-THC varieties.

RECIPE

HEMP MILK: ½ cup shelled hemp seed, pinch of sea salt, 1 tbs sweetener of choice, 2 ½ c water.

Puree all ingredients. Strain through a cheese cloth. Save liquid as milk. Save and dehydrate meal as a flour for bread or crackers.

CULINARY USE

Seeds

Known as hemp nuts are eaten raw or cooked and can be dried into flour and made into cakes and fried. Contains about 27% protein. Non-allergenic alternative to nuts. Oil and flour have a taste reminiscent of hazelnut. Easily digestible. Seed is approximately 26% edible oil, rich in essential fatty acids. Used for hemp milk/ ice cream, hemp butter, hemp protein and even hemp tofu. Sold as a superfood. Hemp seeds are sprinkled over salads, granola, puddings, or other desserts.

Leaves

Bitter but highly nutritous. Leaves are cooked and used in recipes like soups, smoothies, and stir-fries. Good source of iron, zinc, potassium, magnesium, fiber, phosphorous, polyphenols and omega-3 and omega-6 fatty acids.

CULTURAL SIGNIFICANCE

- Chinese medicinal herb used since 3rd millennium BC (e.g., for stress relief & antibacterial and antifungal activities)
- Drying seed oil - used for lighting, soap, paints
- Inscriptions on 13th century Tower in Bologna: "Panis Vita / Canabis Protectio / Vinum Laetitia" – "Bread is Life/ Cannabis is Protection/ Wine is Joy"
- Hemp flowers used in beer making
- Hemp plastic researched to replace oil-based

CAUTIONS & CONSIDERATIONS

Health

CAUTION: Considered an illegal narcotic in some areas.

Pests

Mites, aphids, whiteflies, white powdery mildew / white powdery mold, stem rot.

Landscape design

Compare with Kenaf (Hibiscus cannabinus) and C. indica. While C. sativa is known for cerebral effects, C. indica is known for its sedative effects. Grows rapidly and soon crowds out weeds.

Hickory/ Pecan

Carya illinoensis

HARDINESS ZONES: 5 TO 9

A deciduous, fast-growing species of hickory native to the southern United States. In Juglandaceae family. One of the oldest cultivated tree nuts. A massive, ornamental shade tree. Although it is slow to bear and higher maintenance, it is worth it! Mature trees regularly yield up to 500lbs of nuts! Cholesterol-free and high in unsaturated fatty acids. Very healthy!

SIZE h*w	SUN	SOIL	WATER	EDIBLE
100ft+*50ft+	full to partial	humusy; well-draining	drought tolerant	seed, oil, leaves

PROPAGATION METHODS

SEEDS: Germinates at 86-95F. 8-10 years to bear. Peaks when 75 to 225 years old.

BUDDING & GRAFTING: In spring

RECIPE

CANDIED PECANS: ½ cup pecan halves, 1 tbs maple syrup, pinch of ground cinnamon and a pinch of finely ground sea salt.

Toast pecans in an oiled skillet on medium-low until browed. Add all other ingredients, stirring constantly for 5 minutes. Remove from heat. Let harden. Store in air tight container up to 2 weeks.

CULTURAL SIGNIFICANCE

- Included in state symbols of Alabama, Arkansas, California, Oklahoma, and Texas
- Wood used in furniture-making and flooring, for smoking meats
- Considered the most important horticultural crop native to the United States
- Rich source of dietary fiber, manganese, magnesium, phosphorus, and zinc
- 191 species of butterflies and moths use this as a caterpillar host plant

CULINARY USE

Seeds

Rich, buttery flavored nuts are up to 1.5 inches long and produced in clusters of 3-11. Ripen in fall. Deshelled nuts are eaten raw or cooked. Made into desserts like pecan pie or praline candy. Also added to ice cream, used in cakes, bread etc. A milk can be made from the seed and is used to thicken soups, season cakes or vegetables. When stored in the shell in a cool, dry place, the seeds stay fresh 6 months or longer. An edible oil is obtained from the seed. Consists principally of monounsaturated fatty acids, mainly oleic acid, and the polyunsaturated fatty acid, linoleic acid.

Leaves

Leaves used as a tea substitute.

CAUTIONS & CONSIDERATIONS

Health
No known adverse health effects but nuts are an allergen.

Pests
No serious insect or disease problems: scab, aphids, weevils, webworms, twig girdler.

Landscape design
Aggressive surface roots possible. Plant 3+ cultivars with varying pollination types for cross-pollination. Scab resistant cultivars (e.g., 'Elliot'). Shelter from winds. Compare with FL native hickories: Pignut Hickory/ Carya glabra; Scrub Hickory (Carya floridana).

Hollyhock
Alcea rosea

HARDINESS ZONES: 5 TO 10A

This fast-growing, perennial in the Malvaceae family is a beautiful addition to the food forest as an edible flower. Offers old world charm as a cottage garden favorite! Long history of folk healing uses - all plant parts have been used as traditional medicine! Fuzzy heart-shaped leaves, and huge, 5," bell-shaped, flowers clustered along vertical stalks are a showstopper! Attracts butterflies, bees, and hummingbirds.

SIZE h*w	SUN	SOIL	WATER	EDIBLE
7ft*2ft	full to partial	well-draining	average	flowers, leaves, root, stem, oil

PROPAGATION METHODS

- SEEDS: Germinates at 58-60F within 3 weeks
- DIVISIONS: After flowering.
- CUTTINGS: Root cuttings when dormant in winter. Basal cuttings - any time.

RECIPE

HOLLYHOCK TEA: Gather a handful of fresh flowers. Wash and detach petals. Wrap petals in a cheesecloth tied with string.

Leave overnight in a jar of cool water. Remove cloth and refrigerate. Use within a day or two.

CULINARY USE

Leaves, Stem & Flowers

Young leaves and inner portion of young stems are eaten cooked as a bitter, potherb. Flowers 2nd year. Flower petals and flower buds are eaten raw in salads or stuffed and fried. A tea is made from the flower petals. The flowers are harvested when open and dried for later use. Flower buds were deemed a delicacy. If being used medicinally, preparations of hollyhock flowers are done as cold infusions to maintain mucilage.

Root

Yields a nutritious starch; collect 1st year - otherwise woody.

Oil

Seed contains 12% of a drying oil.

CULTURAL SIGNIFICANCE

- Stem fiber used in papermaking. Flowers act as natural dye
- Official Latin name, "Alcea" originates from Greek "altho" - to cure or heal. Traditionally considered anti-inflammatory, astringent, demulcent, diuretic, emollient, febrifuge; added to cough syrups as an expectorant
- Used as a substitute for common marshmallow (Althaea officinalis) in herbal remedies

CAUTIONS & CONSIDERATIONS

Health
No known adverse health effects. Consume in moderation.

Pests
Rust, leaf spot and anthracnose. Spider mites and Japanese beetle.

Landscape design
White, lavendar, yellow, pink, black, & red blooming varieties. Short-lived but self-seeds; forms colonies. Can live for many years if you cut the stalk off at the base after flowering. Shelter from wind. Plant against walls. Sometimes listed under "Althaea." May behave invasively.

Honeypod Mesquite

Prosopis glandulosa

HARDINESS ZONES: 8 TO 11

A fast-growing, deciduous tree in the Fabaceae family & ideal pioneer species for restoring soil and re-establishing woodland. Described as the most important gum-producing plants in North America! Native to arid and semi-arid areas of the southern USA. Fruits even in drought! A balanced carbohydrate crop like wheat! In Fabaceae family.

SIZE h*w	SUN	SOIL	WATER	EDIBLE
23ft*23ft	full	poor - OK; well-draining	drought tolerant	flowers, roots, seed, seedpod, gum

PROPAGATION METHODS

- SEEDS: Germinates at 86-98F. Scarify before sowing (e.g., pour hot water on the seeds or nick seedcoat) and then soak 24 hours. High level of dormancy.

RECIPE

MESQUITE MILK: ½ cup seedpods, pinch of sea salt, 1 tbs sweetener of choice, 2 ½ c water.

Puree all ingredients. Strain through a cheese cloth. Save liquid as milk. OPTION: Save meal to use as a protein-rich soup base.

CULINARY USE

Seed/Seedpod
The sweet immature seedpods are cooked as a vegetable like string beans or prepared in soup. Cooked immature seedpods are also sometimes boiled, pureed with water and then strained for nut milk. Mature pods are often dried and ground into flour for bread. Contains abundant protein and carbohydrates; used as a substitute for wheat flour.

Gum
White resinous bark secretions used to make candy or chewed like gum.

Root
Used to flavour drinks

Flowers
Used to make a tea.

CULTURAL SIGNIFICANCE

- Supports native pollinator species; favored by bees. Good cattle fodder but thorns injurious
- Resin is used as an adhesive
- Hard timber with desirable color and finish. On par with world's best timbers for flooring and furniture. Excellent firewood/ charcoal
- Thorns used as tattoo needles/ ashes for ink by the Cahuilla and Serrano Indians
- Used in folk healing for antibacterial & antifungal properties

CAUTIONS & CONSIDERATIONS

Health
No known adverse health effects. CAUTION: Some mesquite pods are infected with dangerous aflatoxin-producing fungus. Discard dicolored pods/ seeds. Cook thoroughly. Some varieties are thorny.

Pests
Resilient: Wood-boring beetles, twig girdlers.

Landscape design
Showy racemes of yellow-orange, five-petaled flowers. Attractive grayish, sculptural trunk. Used to provide shade, shelter, erosion control. May behave invasively. Willow-like sprawl. Compare with Yeheb nut (Cordeauxia edulis).

Ice cream Bean

Inga edulis

HARDINESS ZONES: 9 TO 12

A fast-growing, evergreen in the Fabaceae family, living around 30 years - also called Monkey Tamarind. Helps improve food forest soil while also providing deliciously sweet, cottony pulp and high protein seeds! Can flower and fruit 2-3 times per year! Attracts hummingbirds and bats. Historically, Ice cream Bean has been an important food crop of the Incas and many Amazonian peoples. Look for seedlings under established trees. Starts fruiting at just 2 years!

SIZE h*w	SUN	SOIL	WATER	EDIBLE
59ft*59ft	partial	acidic – OK; seasonally wet – OK	flood/ drought tolerant	fruit

PROPAGATION METHODS

- SEEDS: Germinates at 85-90F. Sow as soon as fruit is ripe. Short viability but high germination rates. Self-seeds.
- CUTTINGS: Greenwood after fruiting.

RECIPE

INGA BEAN FLOUR: Soak beans overnight to help dislodge pulp. Drain. Boil beans in water 30 min. Strain. Dry beans at 122-200F until the beans clank and are fully dehydrated (several hours).

Grind into a flour and feed to a sourdough starter or bake as a chickpea flour substitute. Replaces wheat 1:1 in recipes.

CULTURAL SIGNIFICANCE

- Wood is great firewood - burns with little smoke
- Species has a symbiotic relationship with soil bacteria which form nodules on the roots and fix atmospheric nitrogen
- Leave mulch improves soil, reduces soil erosion, & provides dune stabilization
- Symbiosis with ants (e.g. Pheidoles spp.)
- Used in folk medicine (e.g. Leaf decoctions for cough and lip sores)

CULINARY USE

Fruit
The seeds are encased by a white/ translucent, jelly-like pulp. The texture is like a juicy, chewy cotton candy. Some varieties have a slight cinnamon flavor. The seedpod can vary considerably in size and in the quantity of pulp it contains. Beans and pulp are quickly perishable and harvested as needed when ripe. Harvest when thick and soft. Keeps up to a week refrigerated. Eaten fresh or used to flavor desserts and make the alcoholic beverage cachiri. Packed with antioxidants, vitamins & fiber.

Seeds
Inedible unless cooked. Eaten as a vegetable. Seeds are boiled and then dried/ ground into a flour for bread. In Mexico, inga seeds are roasted and sold to movie-goers much like popcorn. Garbanzo/ lima bean flavor.

CAUTIONS & CONSIDERATIONS

Health
No known adverse health effects. Inga seeds reportedly contain trypsin & chymotrypsin inhibitors.

Pests
Very resistant: fruit fly.

Landscape design
Handles extreme pruning. A shade tree for coffee, cacao, tea, & vanilla (or living trellis). Leaf litter is high in nitrogen, lignins and polyphenols. Responds well to coppicing. Compare with other Ingas: I. feuillei, I. rhynchocalyx, I. spectabilis or Coral Shower (Cassia grandis).

Inca Peanut

Plukenetia volubilis

HARDINESS ZONES: 10 TO 12

An evergreen and fast-growing vine. Considered a protein-oil staple crop!! Offers a highly digestible protein and gourmet oil, rich in omegas! In the family Euphorbiaceae. Used as a wild food source for over 3000 years. Contains essential minerals such as iron, magnesium and calcium. Believed to be a means to mitigate food and nutritional insecurity! A well-researched plant with a lot of promise!! A promising plant with high economic value.

SIZE h*w	SUN	SOIL	WATER	EDIBLE
6ft*8in	full to partial	well-drained	average	leaves, seed, oil

PROPAGATION METHODS

- SEEDS: Germinates at 77-86F. Soak 24-48 hours. Germination rates are high - up to 93%; speed up germination by nicking outer shell. Flowers in 5 months & seeds at 8 months.

RECIPE

ROASTED INCA PEANUT: Remove dried seeds from pod, cover with water, soak overnight and dump the water.

Spread in a single layer on a baking sheet and roast at 140F in an oven or dehydrator until thoroughly dried. Crunchy and tasty! Serve with dried banana as a trail mix (1:5 ratio - nut to fruit).

CULTURAL SIGNIFICANCE

- Increasingly grown as a cash crop by small-scale farmers for household use or income
- Contains a high amount of polyunsaturated fatty acids (PUFAs)- beneficial for human health. 2nd only to walnut
- Often marketed as a "superfood," and marketed as a means to reduce excess abdominal fat and promote weight loss 35–
- 60% edible oil comparable to sunflower seeds and peanuts. Rich in vitamins A, E

CULINARY USE

Seeds

Star-shaped pods contain 4-6 seeds. Allow pods to dry on the plant. Rich in fat and protein. Seeds are eaten toasted/roasted and an oil is often extracted. The oil is rich in the essential fatty acids omega-3, 6, & 9 linolenic acid. The oil has a mild flavor with a nutty finish. Roast at a low heat (below 140 °F) to preserve omega fatty acids. Almond-like flavor. Used to make nut butter by blending with honey and salt. The meal which remains after removing the oil is used to make flour or protein powder. A good source of macro- and micronutrients, and phytochemicals.

Leaves

Leaves are cooked and eaten as a vegetable. Roasted leaves are made into a tea. Regarded as highly nutritious.

CAUTIONS & CONSIDERATIONS

Health

No known adverse health effects when cooked/ roasted. Do not consume leaves or seeds raw - toxins present.

Pests

Resilient: Gymnandrosoma aurantianum (citrus fruit borer); Meloidogyne javanica (sugarcane eelworm).

Landscape design

Grow on a trellis for ease of harvest. Prolific! By year 2 can produce 100+ pods giving 400 to 500 seeds several times a year! Compare with Inchi (Caryodendron orinocense).

Indigo Milk Cap

Lactarius indigo var. indigo

HARDINESS ZONES: 8 TO 11

An easy to identify FL native mushroom! A rare blue food and one of the most beautiful mushrooms you can find in the woods. Part of the fungus kingdom's Russulaceae family. A well known edible species due to its unique coloration and peppery taste. Bleeds blue milk - key to identification! Rare but widely distributed.

SIZE h*w	SUN	SOIL	WATER	EDIBLE
3in*6in	partial	well-draining	seasonal flooding - OK	cap, stem

PROPAGATION METHODS

SPORE: Fruits August-November. Cut a small piece of cap with spores and put onto an agar plate or liquid culture mixture and then, once spores drop, transfer to substrate. Await mycelium growth.

RECIPE

MILK CAPS IN HERBED OIL: 2 lb milkcaps cleaned and sliced 1/2 thick, 2 qts water, 1 qt vinegar, 2 tbsp sea salt, 2 cups garlic and rosemary infused oil.

Boil water, salt, & vinegar. Add mushrooms. Simmer 5 min until wilted. Drain. Dry. Pack mushrooms in sterilized jar. Cover with herb infused oil. Use on bread or pasta. Store in refrigerator.

CULTURAL SIGNIFICANCE

- Grows naturally in eastern North America, East Asia, and Central America; also reported growing in southern France
- Sold at the markets in rural Mexico, Guatamela, and China
- When combined with a mordant can create a colorful dye
- Can be used to make a fluorescent dye being investigated as a diagnostic tool in medicine

CULINARY USE

Cap/Stem

Mild, sweet and nutty flavor with a hint of pepper. Course texture. Oozes blue latex when sliced. May fruit singly or in groups from the ground. The cap is 2-6 inches in diameter & convex becoming flat or vase-shaped with age. Colored deep to medium blue when fresh. Fades to grayish or silvery blue with age. The flesh is whitish, turning indigo blue when cut. The milk is a deep indigo blue and becomes dark green on exposure with air. Delicious sautéed in butter but loses color. When prepared in an omelet or with scrambled eggs, it turns the eggs green. To retain the blue color for dishes, blanch quickly in salted water with vinegar. The blue milk may be used to add color to marinades. Cooking in a wet method (like a stew) will also preserve color.

CAUTIONS & CONSIDERATIONS

Health

Be sure to carefully identify mushrooms with the aid of an expert. Several other blue mushrooms exist (e.g. Clitocybe nuda; blue/purple Cortinarius species - does not ooze milk). NOTE: For positive identification - KOH negative or yellowish on cap surface. Spore print: cream to yellow.

Pests

Worms, slugs, birds.

Landscape design

Mycorrhizal with oaks and with pines. Grows alone, scattered, or gregariously usually in summer and fall.

Jackfruit

Artocarpus heterophyllus

HARDINESS ZONES: 10 TO 12

Handsome and stately. This is a fast-growing, prolific, tropical evergreen staple crop. The fruit has a subtle pineapple or banana-like flavor. Because of its abundant yields, some call Jackfruit "miraculous." The nuts provide balanced carbohydrates similar to maize, rice or wheat. Considered one of the most promising solutions for sustainably feeding the world. Timber is resistant to termite attack and fungal/ bacterial decay. In the Mulberry family (Moraceae).

SIZE h*w	SUN	SOIL	WATER	EDIBLE
50ft*50ft	full to partial	well-draining	average	fruit, seed, leaves, flowers

PROPAGATION METHODS

- SEEDS: Germinates at 79-85F within 8 weeks. Expedited by soaking. Can produce within 3 to 8 years. Protect young seedlings from direct sun. Leaves may burn.

RECIPE

JACKFRUIT SEED IN TOMATO SAUCE: 10 seeds, 1/2 c puréed, roasted tomato, 1 cinnamon stick, 1 tbs coriander seeds, 1 c coconut milk, 1 tbs coconut oil.

Boil jackfruit seeds 20 min in water. Strain. Dry on a rack. Peel off husk. Sauté coriander in oil until highly fragrant. Add tomato, coconut milk, cinnamon stick & seeds. Simmer 10 min.

CULTURAL SIGNIFICANCE

- Used in folk healing (e.g., Seeds as an aphrodisiac, cooling tonic; latex harvested for anti-bacterial activity similar to papaya)
- When boiled with alum, heartwood sawdust produces a yellow dye used for Buddhist robes
- Leaves as plates, food wrappers in cooking
- High-quality, rot-resistant timber for furniture and musical instruments. Roots are highly prized for carvings and picture framing

CULINARY USE

Fruit
Turns from green to brown/ yellow as it ripens. Fruit eaten raw or cooked. Inner fiber/ pulp is treated as a pulled pork substitute. The fruit is dried, roasted, added to soups, used in jams, juices, wine, & ice cream. Fruit is capable of reaching 100 pounds. Rind yields a jelly/ pectin. NOTE: Inner perigones & central core not eaten. Ripens summer & fall.

Seeds
Edible cooked: boiled, baked, or roasted. Seed can be ground into a powder; used in biscuit-making; flavor and texture similar to chestnuts or macadamia in taste; treated like baked beans and cooked in tomato sauce.

Leaves/ Flowers
Young male flowers are eaten mixed with chillies, sugar, salt; young fruits and leaf shoots - cooked in soups.

CAUTIONS & CONSIDERATIONS

Health
No known adverse health effects. High nutritional value and reported health benefits. High in protein, potassium and vitamin B6. Ripe fruit is somewhat laxative.

Pests
Mealybugs, stem and fruit borers. May suffer manganese deficiency.

Landscape design
Lives over 100 years. Highly perishable fruit - Pick often. Can be used to control soil erosion - extensive root system. Plant 30 ft from house/ septic. Produces up to 200 fruits per year.

Jamaican Mint
Satureja viminea

HARDINESS ZONES: 9 TO 11

Also called Costa Rican mint. A perennial, tiny-leafed mint relative growing as a woody shrub with a very potent spearmint flavor! Can be trained into a small tree. Produces pretty, little white flowers seasonally. A nice pollinator plant! A rare plant in the Lamiaceae family and related to rosemary and thyme. Can grow well in a pot and overwinter indoors when necessary.

SIZE h*w	SUN	SOIL	WATER	EDIBLE
7ft*5ft	full to partial	well-draining	drought tolerant	leaves, flowers

PROPAGATION METHODS

- CUTTINGS: 5" woody stem cuttings in soil before flowering period. Plant 1/2 in soil in high humidity setting.

RECIPE

MINT SAUCE: 1 tbs minced mint leaves, 1 inch piece of fresh ginger, ¼ cup vinegar, ¼ cup honey, 1 tbs oil.

Sauté mint and ginger in oil on medium heat until fragrant. Puree with vinegar and honey.

Add sauce to soups or use as a tea when diluted with water to taste.

CULINARY USE

Leaves & Flowers

A delicious mint replacement but should be cooked given potent essential oil concentration. Strong, pennyroyal-like flavor & aroma.

Used in soups, salads, sauces, or as a boiled tea. In the Caribbean, particularly in Trinidad and Jamaica, the leaves are ground and used as a spice to season meats. This herb often replaces mint in the Jamaican version of the mojito (made with dark rather than white rum).

Leaves also used to make an herbal breakfast tea, combined with ginger and sugar for added flavor.

CULTURAL SIGNIFICANCE

- Used for making a famous Kama Sutra Luxury Mint Tree Bath Gel and Body Wash
- Traditionally considered to have antioxidant, digestive, expectorant, sedative, stomachic and carminative qualities. Used medicinally for antifungal and antiseptic properties
- Host plant for Lepidoptera (butterflies and moths)
- One of 30+ species in savory genus - least known and among hardest to find

CAUTIONS & CONSIDERATIONS

Health
CAUTION: Contains essential oil, pulegone; sedative & analgesic. Consume in moderation.

Pests
Slugs, root rot in poor draining areas.

Landscape design
A carefree plant - prune to desired shape. Potential topiary plant. Wonderful in an herb spiral. Compare with Pennyroyal (Mentha pulegium), Pineapple Mint (Mentha suaveolens), Winter Savory (Satureja montana) or Yerba Buena (Satureja douglasii).

Jing Okra

Abelmoschus esculentus

HARDINESS ZONES: 2 TO 11

One of the oldest cultivated staple crops; grown in Egypt as long ago as 2,000 BC! The seed is a protein powerhouse!! May produce twice annually & act as a perennial with ratooning. This variety produces beautiful flowers and gorgeous orange fruit. Known as "ladies' fingers," okra is related to cotton, cocoa, and hibiscus. Heat- and drought-tolerant! Called "a perfect villager's vegetable" - seed protein has both lysine & tryptophan amino acids. In the Malvaceae family.

SIZE h*w	SUN	SOIL	WATER	EDIBLE
3ft*2ft	full	alkaline - OK	drought tolerant	fruit, seeds, root, leaves, oil

PROPAGATION METHODS

- SEEDS: Germinates best at 85-95F. Soaked seeds germinate within a week whereas dry seeks can take up to 3 weeks. In flower from July to September. Let seed dry on plant in pod.

RECIPE

CRISPY OKRA: 1lb okra pods, 1 tbs oil, ¼ tsp turmeric, ¼ tsp pepper, pinch of sea salt, ¼ cup water.

Wash pods. Cut off ends; slice thin. Heat oil in skillet and sauté turmeric, pepper, & salt until fragrant. Add okra and ¼ cup of water. Cover and simmer on low 2-5 min. Uncover. Cook 15 min on medium; stir often. Cook until crisp. Dip in pesto.

CULTURAL SIGNIFICANCE

- Native to tropical Africa and Asia but India ranks number one in consumption
- Mitigates malnutrition/ alleviates food insecurity
- Many uses: Fruit is crushed with the young leaves to wash hair & treat dandruff. Stems used as straws. Stem fiber is a jute substitute; makes paper. Roots used as a substitute for marshmallow (Althaea officinalis)
- Mucilage glazes paper, confectionery; researched to expand blood volume & plasma

CULINARY USE

Fruit
Fruit is edible raw, pickled, fried, or cooked. Heat intensifies mucilaginous qualities. Thickens soups/ sauces. Offers pectin for jam. To de-slime okra, cook with an acid like citrus or vinegar. Harvest pods at 3". Picking fruit increases production. Signature ingredient in gumbo.

Seeds
Okra seeds may be roasted and ground to form a caffeine-free substitute for coffee (sudorific properties). Provides a meal for flour or can serve as a 'couscous' or caviar substitute. A source of 'tofu' or 'tempeh'!

Leaves & Flowers
Young okra leaves, flower buds, flowers and calyces can be eaten cooked as greens like beet or dandelion greens. Can be dried, crushed into a powder and stored.

CAUTIONS & CONSIDERATIONS

Health
Fruit rich in calcium & potassium. Seed oil is rich in linoleic acid. CAUTION: Hairs on seed pods can be an irritant - removed by washing. Contains oxalates & solanine.

Pests
Aphids, corn earworms, spider mites, slugs and whiteflies, powdery mildew, root-knot nematodes.

Landscape design
Yields in 4 months. Many named varieties. Rotate crop. 'Clemson's Spineless', 'Emerald Spineless', 'Long Green' and 'Green Velvet' are also noteworthy varieties.

Juanilama

Lippia alba

HARDINESS ZONES: 8B TO 11

Makes an awesome tea! Also called Oaxaca lemon verbena. Used medicinally for thousands of years by indigenous peoples across the Americas. Slow growing but worth the wait! In the verbena family - Verbenaceae. An attractive, perennial, evergreen, small shrub prized for its beautiful white, pink and lavender flowers. Mint and lemon scented, aromatic foliage.

SIZE h*w	SUN	SOIL	WATER	EDIBLE
5ft*3ft	partial	sandy, clay - OK; well-draining	average; drought tolerant	leaves, flowering tips

PROPAGATION METHODS

- CUTTINGS: Very easy to clone; roots in water or soil. Thrives in hydro or aquaponics systems. Basal or nodal softwood cuttings. Lower basal branches can become long rooting suckers.

RECIPE

SLEEPY-TIME TEA: 1 tbs washed and dehydrated juanalima leaves; 1 cup hot water.

Steep leaves in the water. Cover to allow for more concentrated flavor. Allow to sit for 5 minutes. Drink warm at bedtime.

CULINARY USE

Leaves & Flowers
Leaves and flowering tops consumed as tea, fresh or dried. Kickapoo Indians make a hot tea with the plant. Leaves used mainly as a flavoring in soups, bread, or salads, and occasionally used as a cooked vegetable. An intense aniseed aroma. Used in Oaxacan mole sauces. Remarkably high amounts of micronutrients like iron and copper. Dried and blended with salt as a seasoning or with honey as a syrup against cough and bronchitis.

Also used as an ingredient in the Hot Spicy Curry or Jalor Aanja – a dish popular in lower Assam/ northeastern India. The dish is generally prepared during the festival season of Magh Bihu.

CULTURAL SIGNIFICANCE

- One of the most cited medicinal plants in traditional medicine in Central/South America for digestive soothing and sedative antidepressant, and analgesic properties
- Leaves used in soothing, calming herbal baths
- Native to the Americas across Southern USA
- One of the first two overseas plants to be approved by French Drug Agency for inclusion in the French Pharmacopeia
- Used to anesthetize fish

CAUTIONS & CONSIDERATIONS

Health
No known adverse health effects. Researched as antifungal, antimicrobial & anti-inflammatory. Contains essential oils (e.g., Dihydrocarvone, limonene, pinene, linalol, camphor). CAUTION: May be confused with lantana varieties due to similar leaf & flowers. Identify carefully.

Pests
Highly resilient.

Landscape design
Compare with Moujean Tea/ Pineapple Verbena (Nashia inaguensis) and Mexican Oregano (Lippia graveolens).

Jujube
Ziziphus jujuba

HARDINESS ZONES: 5 TO 10

Also called Chinese Date. A fast-growing, easy-to-grow, deciduous tree used in Chinese medicine and culinary delicacies as a tonic to strengthen liver function. Used in Japan to improve immune-system functioning. Historically believed to extend life expectancy by nourishing blood, increasing sleep quality & improving digestive system. Touted in traditional Persian medicine (TPM) - used to treat colds & influenza. In the Rhamnaceae family. Fragrant flowers!

SIZE h*w	SUN	SOIL	WATER	EDIBLE
30ft*20ft	full	poor - OK; well-draining	drought tolerant	fruit, seeds

PROPAGATION METHODS

- SEEDS: Germinates at 80-85F. Slow-to-germinate but fruits in 2-4 yrs.
- DIVISIONS: Root suckers. Divide when dormant.
- CUTTINGS: Mature wood of current season's Growth.

RECIPE

JUJUBE RAISINS/DATES: Remove from the tree fully ripe. Wash in a 1:1 solution of vinegar and water. Then dehydrate at 115F until shriveled like a raisin (usually 20-30 hours).

Store in an air-tight container. Use as a tea, sweetener for nut milk, or as a snack!

CULTURAL SIGNIFICANCE

- Popular worldwide in folk healing (e.g., believed to have blood purifying, anxiety-reducing, aphrodisiac, and sedative properties; also, used to treat anemia)
- Great hedge plant! Provides a thorny screen
- Attracts bees, butterflies, birds, mammals: food for silkworms
- An ancient jujube tree in Al-Qurnah, Iraq (considered original site of Garden of Eden) is described as Biblical Tree of Knowledge

CULINARY USE

Fruit
Olive-shaped, one-inch long, bright red fruit with 1 or 2 seeds. The apple-like textured fruit is eaten raw when green but is preferred dried when ripe. Like dates, sweetness concentrates. Sometimes left on the tree to become wrinkled for increased sweetness and then smoked with fruit tree wood for complex flavoring. Also used in pickle recipes, wine, vinegar or cooked in puddings, cakes, breads, jellies, soups. Dried fruits are ground into a powder used in tea or 'kochujang'/ a fermented hot pepper-soybean paste tasting like miso. Good source of vitamin C, phenolics, flavonoids, triterpenic acids, and polysaccharides.

Leaves
Occasionally eaten cooked.

CAUTIONS & CONSIDERATIONS

Health
Storehouse of numerous required nutrients! Phosphorus, calcium, magnesium and iron. CAUTION: Gnarled, spiney branches. May interact with certain medications - consult physician.

Pests
No serious insect or disease problems: fruit fly, nematodes.

Landscape design
Deep taproot. Responds well to coppicing. Fruit litter. Can behave invasively - thicket forming from root suckers/ self-seeding. Compare with Date Palm (Phoenix dactylifera).

Katuk

Sauropus androgynus

HARDINESS ZONES: 10 TO 12

Also called sweet leaf. This delicious perennial shrub offers a flavor punch with a pleasant taste similar to fresh garden peas. Produces tiny red flowers and cute white berries almost year-round. Katuk can be easily shaped into an attractive landscape feature. Leaves, flowers and berries are very rich in plant proteins. Often grown as an edible hedge in home gardens. Excellent source of vitamins A, B, C, and carotenoid! Up to 10% protein! In Euphorbiaceae family.

SIZE h*w	SUN	SOIL	WATER	EDIBLE
4ft*3ft	shade	loamy; acidic - OK	flood tolerant	leaves, shoot tips, fruit, flowers

PROPAGATION METHODS

- CUTTING: Propagated readily from 6-inch cuttings. Use softwood in spring/ summer.
- SEEDS: Germinates at 68-77F. Viable 3-4 months. Slow germination.

RECIPE

KATUK SALAD WITH MANGO DRESSING: 2 tbs water, 2 mangos/ 2 kimchi peppers puréed for dressing; 4 cups of washed katuk leaves; 12 butterfly pea flowers; 3 tbs sprouted, roasted pumpkin seeds.

Wash katuk leaves, pile onto a plate. Drizzle with the dressing and top with flowers and roasted pumpkin seeds.

CULTURAL SIGNIFICANCE

- One of the most popular leafy vegetables in South Asia and Southeast Asia
- In India, known as 'Multivitamin Plant' - high carotenoid, vitamin B and C, protein, lipid, carbohydrate and mineral content
- Used in folk healing (e.g., for diabetics, cancer, inflammation, microbial infection, cholesterol and allergy for antioxidant effect. Believed to improve the flow of breast milk)
- Used as feed for cattle and poultry

CULINARY USE

Leaves

The more the leaves mature, the higher the nutrient content. Peanut-like taste when eaten raw and resembles spinach when cooked. Young leaves and the top 6 in. of stem tips are normally eaten raw in salads but can be cooked, steamed, boiled, etc.

Shoot Tips

Sold as tropical asparagus. In Vietnam, the locals cook it with crab meat, minced pork or dried shrimp to make soup. In Malaysia, it is commonly stir-fried with egg or dried anchovies.

Flowers & Fruit

Flowers and small purplish fruits can be steamed, boiled or fried.

CAUTIONS & CONSIDERATIONS

Health

CAUTION: Consume in moderation. Katuk extract taken in excess for body weight control in Taiwan in the mid '90s resulted in health issues due to the alkaloid papaverine.

Pests

Mostly resistant; Chinese rose beetle; root rot.

Landscape design

Growth slows in winter/ crops can become unpalatable. Cut close to the ground in late winter. Regular pruning keeps it attractive. Varieties with pink or white fruit; variegated leaves but tougher/ more bitter flavor.

Kimchi Pepper
Capsicum annuum

HARDINESS ZONES: 9 TO 11

Also called Gochugaru pepper - the most important ingredient in kimchi (fermented vegetables) and the most popular of five domesticated capsicums. An ornamental, mild hot pepper with around 1,500 Scoville heat units. As with many plants in the Solanaceae family, it behaves as an evergreen, perennial in areas with mild winters but can be grown as an annual everywhere else. Good companion for basil and okra but avoid planting near fruit trees.

SIZE h*w	SUN	SOIL	WATER	EDIBLE
3ft*3ft	full to partial	acidic, sand/ clay - OK; well-draining	average	fruit/ seeds

PROPAGATION METHODS

- SEEDS: Germinates at 68-86F in 4 weeks. Barely cover seeds with soil. Thin and plant in individual pots once true leaves appear.

RECIPE

HOT SAUCE: Remove stems from 30+ peppers, chop them, and add to 5% brine (i.e., 3 tbs salt per quart of water) add garlic and spices to taste.

Ferment a month or longer. Keep peppers submerged. Shake often. Liquify in a food processor. Store in the refrigerator after fermentation.

CULTURAL SIGNIFICANCE

- In Kimchi, the red pepper powder helps control putrefactive microorganisms to promote lactic acid fermentation
- Used in folk healing (e.g., to improve circulation, to treat the cold stage of fevers, and as an anti-rheumatic, antiseptic, diaphoretic, digestive, tonic, etc.)
- Used as a food in Peru more than 8,000 years ago. Christopher Columbus helped spread them around the world

CULINARY USE

Fruit/ Seeds

Turn from green to red when mature. When green, they are used fresh similar to bell peppers. Considered an ideal gateway chile for those new to hot spices. The mature, red peppers are also eaten fresh but are commonly dried, stewed, stuffed, or in pickling. Eaten raw in salads or added to soups and stews for flavoring. An essential ingredient in Korean cuisine - used as a condiment for nearly every food like kimchi, tofu and eggs. Offers a wonderful level of heat with touches of fruity sweetness. For those who prefer extra spice and heat, seeds are kept in place during cooking. Smoked for added flavor complexity. De-seeded, ground and sprinkled over BBQ as a substitute for paprika. Infused in maple syrup, vinegar and various oils.

CAUTIONS & CONSIDERATIONS

Health
CAUTION: Peppers may cause stomach irritation when used in excess or harm during contact with the eyes. Maya Indians used pepper spray as a weapon. Reports of leaves and flowers being edible but in Solanaceae family - caution.

Pests
Potato tuber moth (Phthorimaea operculella).

Landscape design
Compare with FL native Bird pepper (Capsicum annuum var. glabriusculum), or world's most expensive pepper, Aji Charapita (Capsicum chinense).

Kudzu

Pueraria montana lobata

HARDINESS ZONES: 5 TO 10

Known as "mile-a-minute" and "the vine that ate the South." A staple carbohydrate in Japan! This is a specimen you do NOT plant! Listed as a Category 1 Invasive in Florida. You will likely see volunteers on your property. Dig them! Eat them! Help control the spread. Nutritious! In the Leguminosae family. Chop and drop to improve the soil. Commonly used in Chinese herbalism as one of the 50 fundamental herbs. Flowers have a sweet vanilla scent!

SIZE h*w	SUN	SOIL	WATER	EDIBLE
90ft+*10in	full	well-draining	drought tolerant	tuber, leaves, flowers

PROPAGATION METHODS

NOT RECOMMENDED: Species has escaped cultivation, swallowing forests. Chokes out other plants. Dominates aggressively. Can lead to species extinctions and loss of biodiversity.

RECIPE

KUDZU MASHED "POTATOES": 2 lbs of roots washed, peeled, and chopped into 1 inch cubes; 2 tbs oil, 1 cup nut milk (e.g. coconut), salt and pepper to taste.

Add roots to salted boiling water & cook until tender - 30 min. Drain. Puree with other ingredients.

CULTURAL SIGNIFICANCE

- Used in folk healing (e.g., for alcoholism, menopause, colds, headache, dizziness)
- Stems used as a strong fiber for ropes, cables, coarse cordage, paper, basketry, and textiles
- Introduced to USA during 1876 Philadelphia Centennial Exposition - touted as a sturdy, sweet-smelling, ornamental. 1930-1950, Soil Conservation Service promoted for soil erosion control. WWII military used vine for camouflage
- Animal fodder: hay has up to 23% crude protein

CULINARY USE

Root
Sometimes called Japanese Arrowroot given similar edibility. Eaten peeled & cooked. Rich in carbohydrates & starches. Measures up to 6 ft long & can weigh 77+lbs! Extracted starch used as a crispy coating in fried foods, or for thickening soups. Made into noodles or used as a gelling agent. Harvest in winter. Only a kudzu root from a seedling will produce quality starch. Surface roots are woody but used as a tea.

Leaves & Flowers
Stems and leaves typically cooked like spinach. Very nutritious. Fresh young shoots taste like pea. Flowers are used to make a jelly/ candy which tastes like grape. Flowers also eaten in salads & used for tea and wine.

CAUTIONS & CONSIDERATIONS

Health
CAUTION: Consult physician - possible interaction with medication. Wash thoroughly if plants are sprayed with herbicides. May have three leaf arrangement like poison ivy and poison oak! Carefully identify.

Pests
Fungus: Myrothecium verrucaria.

Landscape design
Can grow a foot a day. Deep tap roots. Compare with water hyacinth (eichhornia crassipes).

Lá Lốt
Piper Sarmentosum

HARDINESS ZONES: 8A TO 11

Also called Wild Betal Leaf - A delicious, ornamental foliage! This plant has attractive shiny, heart shaped, bright green leaves. In the Piperaceae / pepper family. A great understory plant and ground cover. Can be the solution for boggy areas. You may be able to find Lalot cuttings at international grocery stores. Considered a functional food.

SIZE h*w	SUN	SOIL	WATER	EDIBLE
15in*4in	shade	wet; slightly acidic - OK	seasonal flood - tolerant	leaves

PROPAGATION METHODS

- CUTTINGS: Creeping rhizomes and stems, typically on the ground. Mostly dioecious (male/ female needed for seed). Propagate in summer/ wet season.

RECIPE

LEAF ROLLS: Put washed leaf on work surface, matte side up with stem closest to you. Take 1 tbs of filling and spoon content horizontally across upper portion of leaf, below pointy tip. Roll the leaf tip over filling towards the stem. Stick the stem into roll as a "pin" to secure the fold. Broil 5 minutes turning frequently to prevent burning.

CULTURAL SIGNIFICANCE

- Used in folk healing (e.g., as antiseptic, breath freshener, alleviating headaches, toothaches, cough/as an expectorant, inflammation, rheumatism, indigestion, flatulence & diarrhea; tea is said to be a sleep aid. Believed to have antidepressant effects)
- Leaves commonly used to line food platters as a miniature plate or way to grab the edibles

CULINARY USE

Leaves
Leaves have a smoky, peppery flavor and smell when crushed. Leaves are wrapped around vegetables and meat, then grilled. Sometimes used as a raw ingredient in salads - shredded. In Vietnamese cuisine, meat and various finely chopped spices such as garlic, onion and lemongrass are wrapped in lalot leaves and grilled, which brings smokey flavor. It is then served with noodles, fresh herbs, sliced star fruits and pineapples. Other cultures stuff the leaves with stir-fried prawn, green mango, and toasted coconut seasoned with lime, chili, & palm sugar. Used as a replacement for grape leaves, rice paper, and nori in many recipes. Leaves can also be added to curries, or blanched and used as a potherb. Used to add flavor to soup & stews.

CAUTIONS & CONSIDERATIONS

Health
No known adverse health effects, but low growing so susceptible to soil and water contaminants. Also may be confused with other species like Piper betle.

Pests
Highly resilient.

Landscape design
May behave invasively. Taprooted. If planting in a hanging basket or container, use 3g or bigger. Primary stem grows up to 3ft. long, after that it forms creeping stems having heart shaped leaves. Stems are slightly hairy.

Lab-Lab
Lablab purpureus

HARDINESS ZONES: 9 TO 11

Fast-growing! Young pods are ready to harvest just 4 months after sowing - sometimes sooner! Also called hyacinth bean. Showy, fragrant purple flowers attract hummingbirds. Prized for its immature beans as a substitute for French beans. Outcompetes other legumes - drought tolerant! Cultivated in India as early as 2500 BC. An ornamental crop in the cut flower industry valued for late summer blooms & pods. In the Fabaceae family. Underutilized but prime for market!

SIZE h*w	SUN	SOIL	WATER	EDIBLE
6ft+*6in	full	well-draining	drought tolerant	seed, flowers, root, seedpod, leaves

PROPAGATION METHODS

- SEEDS: Germinates at 77-86F within 4 weeks. Pre-soak. A short-day plant; flowers and sets seed when days become shorter than nights - around September.

RECIPES

FRITTERS: Shell immature beans. Boil until tender (about 20 min). Drain & rinse. Purée with onion, chili, salt & pepper to taste. Add water as needed to purée. Ferment 4 hrs to 2 days according to preference. Beat/ whip to impregnate with air until smooth and stiff (like egg whites). Drop by spoonful into hot oil & fry until golden. Drip dry on a rack to cool. Sprinkle with salt. Serve warm.

CULTURAL SIGNIFICANCE

- Often grown as forage for livestock and ornamental
- Considered an "orphan crop;" under colonial rule in Kenya, farmers were forced to give up growing lablab to produce common beans (Phaseolus vulgaris)
- Juice from boiled immature pods is used in folk healing to treat inflamed ears and throats
- In the legume family: 3rd-largest land plant family in terms of a number of species

CULINARY USE

Root

Root is valued for its large size and starch. Boiled or baked

Seeds/ Pods

Rich in protein. Used to make a fried bean cake in Asia. Often prepared as 'tofu' or fermented into 'tempeh' like soy beans. Tender young seedpods and immature seeds are boiled and drained like French beans. Mature seed is edible when soaked overnight and thoroughly boiled 45 minutes or longer in two changes of water to remove the toxins. Drain water after boiling. Most prefer immature seeds to avoid toxin/ labor intensive cooking.

Leaves & Flowers

Leaves eaten cooked just like spinach. Flowers used as a garnish, or added to soups or stews as a vegetable. Young shoots and inflorescences are eaten after boiling.

CAUTIONS & CONSIDERATIONS

Health

CAUTION: Cook thoroughly or sprout. The raw seed has toxin (cyanogenic glucosides). Syn. Dolichos lablab.

Pests

Resilient.

Landscape design

A good green manure and effective ground cover. Often intercropped with maize. 4 varieties with different color flowers. Competes with weeds once established. Compare with Scarlet Runner Bean (Phaseolus coccineus), Common Bean (Phaseolus vulgaris) & Lima Bean (Phaseolus lunatus).

Lemongrass
Cymbopogon citratus

HARDINESS ZONES: 10 TO 12

An easy way to add an appealing, lemony fragrance to the garden! Growing up to six feet tall and four feet wide, the bright and citrusy leaves and stalks enhance teas and curries and are used in folk medicines thanks to its electrolytes and minerals. Among the herbs transported along the original spice route from Asia to Europe. Citral, from the oil, is used in soaps, detergents, perfumes and cosmetics. In the Poaceae family.

SIZE h*w	SUN	SOIL	WATER	EDIBLE
3ft*3ft	full to partial	sandy; well-drained	average; drought tolerant	stalks, leaves

PROPAGATION METHODS

- DIVISIONS: Divide stalks from the rhizome of a well-established plant in spring in areas.

- SEEDS: Germinates at 68-77F.

RECIPE

LEMONGRASS ELECTUARY: 2 tbs powdered lemongrass, 1 c raw honey.

Wash and dehydrate lemongrass at 115F until crisp. Grind into a powder. Stir into honey. Allow to sit 24 hours. Add to hot water for tea, drop dollops into soup, or mix into curries.

CULINARY USE

Leaves

Tougher leaves are used to flavor dishes but are typically removed before serving. Leaves may also be used to make lemon grass tea. Weave into a mini-wreath for dunking.

Stalks

Heart of young shoots may be cooked and consumed as a vegetable. Lemongrass can be harvested at any time once the stalks have reached 1/2 in diameter. Cut at ground level with a sharp knife at the bulb and remove the tough outer leaves. Cut or "bruise" the inner stalk and use it to add fresh flavor to your cooking like in the Thai soup, tom kha. Used in baked goods, confections, Thai-style soups, curries, and more.

CULTURAL SIGNIFICANCE

- Used in folk healing (e.g., In the Caribbean, the tea is brewed to boost immunity & bring good luck in love affairs. Considered an insect repellent. Believed to be antimicrobial)
- In beekeeping, lemongrass oil imitates a queen pheromone (attracts bees)
- Essential oil researched as safe natural preservative & food spoilage inhibitor
- Leaves used for incense, potpourri, baskets

CAUTIONS & CONSIDERATIONS

Health
No known hazards; Handling plant may cause mild skin irritation.

Pests
Fungus causes brown elongated streaks on leaves; dark brown pustules on underside of leaves; death of leaves and plant; prune to allow healthy regrowth.

Landscape design
Often used in mass plantings. Compare with shade & water-loving, pandan (Pandanus amaryllifolius), citronella (Cymbopogon Nardus) or lemon balm (Melissa officinalis).

Lipstick Tree
Bixa orellana

HARDINESS ZONES: 10 TO 12

Also called Annatto or Achiote. An evergreen shrub with gorgeous flowers. Blooms & fruits all year in tropical climates - planted as an ornamental. Dried fruit pods are attractive in floral arrangements. Fast-growing and long-lived. Seeds contain a pleasant-smelling oil. Rich in carotenoid pigments - global economic significance! 2nd most economically important dye. One of the most widely used natural dyes to color food, cosmetics & pharmaceutical products! In the Bixaceae family.

SIZE h*w	SUN	SOIL	WATER	EDIBLE
16ft*13ft	full to partial	well-draining; very alkaline - OK	drought tolerant	seed/ pulp

PROPAGATION METHODS

- SEEDS: Germinates at 77-86F in 10 days. Plant in the rainy season. Bears fruit in 2 yrs; full crop in 3-4 years; declines after 12 years.
- CUTTINGS: Hardwood cuttings 1/4 in or larger in diameter - roots in soil within 9 weeks.

RECIPE

ACHIOTE PASTE: 1/3 cup annatto seeds, 4 garlic cloves minced, 2 tbsp vinegar, 2 tsp dried oregano.

Mix all ingredients in a food processor until a paste forms. Store in the fridge in an airtight container up to 2 wks. Mix with broth as needed to thin. Use as a rub on meats; drizzle on vegetables; or blend into batters.

CULINARY USE

Seeds/ Pulp
Dozens of seeds inside each pod. Each fruit capsule resembles the bur of a chestnut. The capsule splits open when ripe to reveal seeds covered with orange pulp: Annatto. Seeds are often steeped in hot oil to remove pulp and create a flavoring or dye. Astringent. Used for coloring butter, ghee, margarine, & cheese, etc. Highly stable color since it binds with proteins.

Whole seeds are also ground into a red paste as a coloring or a base for other spices. High nutritive value: 5% fatty oil, 13% protein. Ground seeds widely used in traditional dishes in Central and South America, Mexico, and the Caribbean (e.g., cochinita pibil, chicken in achiote, caldo de olla, and nacatamal).

CULTURAL SIGNIFICANCE

- Red or yellow dye from seed used to color cloth, paint hair & skin, to repel biting insects & prevent sunburn - annatto paste filters out ultraviolet rays; also used as a lipstick & blush
- Used in folk healing (e.g., leaves are used as a poultice for headaches; a decoction is gargled for mouth and throat infections)
- Substitute for paprika
- Used in Mayan religious or war rituals

CAUTIONS & CONSIDERATIONS

Health
CAUTION: Seed coat extract has paralytic action on mammalian intestinal parasites; slightly purgative.

Pests
Very hardy. Few problems. Fungus and root rot in wet areas.

Landscape design
Used as an informal hedge. Place 20ft from structures: fire can be started by the friction of 2 pieces of the soft wood. Pruning yearly (early morning) is important for better yield. A cross-pollinated plant.

Live Oak

Quercus virginiana

HARDINESS ZONES: 6 TO 10

Oak is the United States' national tree! One of the most important landscaping trees in South Florida. Provides valuable shade, reducing temperatures up to 20 degrees. Provides an internationally recognized staple food. Large quantities of acorns are easily harvested from the ground for weeks in fall - a great source of calories with minimal effort. Low in tannin, live oak acorns have among the sweetest flavors. Taste like chestnuts! In the Fagaceae family.

SIZE h*w	SUN	SOIL	WATER	EDIBLE
60ft*60ft	full to partial	acidic, poor - OK	short-term flooding - OK	seed/ acorn

PROPAGATION METHODS

- SEED: Germinates at 70-80F. Hybridizes. Quickly loses viability if allowed to dry out. Plants produce a deep taproot and need to be planted in situ.

RECIPE

ACORN CANDY: 2 cups de-shelled, leached, dry acorns, 1/3 c maple syrup, 1/2 tsp. vanilla extract, 1/4 tsp. ground cinnamon (more if desired), 1/8 tsp. sea salt, 1 tbsp oil.

Combine ingredients in an oiled pan over medium heat. Stir. Simmer. Reduce to low heat. Continue stirring and simmering until syrup has crystallized - 20 minutes. Store in fridge 1-2 weeks.

CULTURAL SIGNIFICANCE

- USS Constitution/ oldest U.S. naval ship has oak frame; helped it survive cannon fire
- Dyes of various colors obtained from bark
- Significant food & cover for wildlife. 395 species of butterflies/ moths use as host
- Acorn-foods popular in Korea & Spain
- Excellent source of protein, carbohydrate, healthy fat & calcium. Starchy tubers on seedlings historically fried like a potato

CULINARY USE

SEED/ ACORNS
Shelled, dry acorns can stay fresh for over a year. Ripe acorns are tan to brown in color. Green acorns are not edible. Must be ripe. The larger the cap, the more tannins present. To prepare acorns. Wash and remove acorns that float in water. Wash, dry, grind, leach. In other words, wash and then oven dry the acorns at 200 degrees for two hours; de-shell with hammer. Grind/ crush. Boil 30 min, dumping the water and refilling hot water until bitterness is gone (12+ water changes) OR soak in cold water, changing water each morning for 3 to 14 days: taste-test. There should be no bitterness. Cold water leaches without breaking down starches. Use acorns as a soup thickener, make into sweet pudding, as a flour substitute for bread or cookies, or as a coffee substitute.

CAUTIONS & CONSIDERATIONS

Health
CAUTION: Consuming excessive tannic acid can result in kidney failure. Leach out tannic acid; do not eat if bitter.
Pests
Acorn weevil grubs; look for heavy acorns without drilled holes or black spots, a sign of insect infestation/ mold.
Landscape design
Freshly fallen leaves can inhibit plant growth. Broad-spreading habit countered by planting other trees around it, so it competes for light. Evergreen or partially deciduous.

Longan
Dimocarpus longan

HARDINESS ZONES: 9 TO 12

Also called Dragon's Eye. This plant is a fast-growing, evergreen. In the Sapindaceae family. Can produce a massive crop of up to 500 lbs! Rich in antioxidants including polyphenols. An ornamental shade tree and easily digested fruit. Economically important in southeast Asia and increasing in importance in Florida! Sweet and refreshing!

SIZE h*w	SUN	SOIL	WATER	EDIBLE
40ft*40ft	full to partial	well-draining	average	fruit

PROPAGATION METHODS

- SEEDS: Germinates at 77-86F in 2 weeks. Often grown from seed. Seeds lose viability quickly. Dry fresh seeds and immediately plant 3/4 in deep. Produces fruit after 6 yrs.

RECIPE

LONGAN SWEET POTATO SOUP: 2 1/2 cups peeled, diced sweet potato; 1 bunch/ 7 stalks lemongrass leaves washed & tied into a knot. 1/4 c thinly sliced, bruised ginger, 3 tbs light molasses, 1 c de-seeded longan, 5 1/2 c water.

Boil sweet potato until soft. Strain. Add all other ingredients to pot. Simmer on low 8 minutes.

CULINARY USE

Fruit
The round, juicy fruits average an inch in diameter, with a thin, brittle, brown rind which cracks open with pressure. Harvest fruit in morning; cut bunches off while still attached to the branch to maximize freshness. Will not ripen off the tree! Eat raw or cooked. The flesh is translucent and somewhat sweet. Often dried, preserved in syrup, cooked in sweet and sour dishes or in dessert soups. For drying, the fruits are heated to shrink the flesh and facilitate peeling. Seeds are removed and the flesh dried over a slow fire resulting in a black, leathery and smoky product used to prepare a beverage infusion. In Chinese medicine, the fruit is typically brewed as a tea to aid sleep. Pulp has abundant nutritional phytochemicals.

CULTURAL SIGNIFICANCE

- In Chinese medicine, longans are believed to have memory boosting & relaxation effects; fruit is administered as a stomachic, febrifuge and vermifuge
- Introduced to Florida from southern China by the United States Department of Agriculture in 1903
- Seeds high in saponin content & used like soapberries for shampooing the hair.
- Seeds & rind burned for fuel

CAUTIONS & CONSIDERATIONS

Health
CAUTION: Consume ripe only. Avoid consuming on an empty stomach. Do not consume if fasting. Hypoglycemic amino acids present.

Pests
Relatively free of pests and diseases. Oomycete disease. Mineral deficiencies, lychee webworm & scale insects.

Landscape design
Good wind resistance. Remove strong vertical branches and encourage lateral growth. Most longan trees grown in Florida are 'Kohala' cultivar. Compare with Lychee.

Longevity Spinach

Gynura procumbens

HARDINESS ZONES: 9 TO 12

Nicknamed, "Leaves of the Gods" and 'Continuation of Life' thanks to its many purported health benefits such as with lowering blood sugar, inflammation, and cholesterol. This perennial ground cover will exceed your expectations! A superfood acknowledged in scientific circles! In the Asteraceae family. Vigorous enough to farm as a commercial crop!

SIZE h*w	SUN	SOIL	WATER	EDIBLE
12in*6in	partial	sandy; well-drained	moist	leaves, young stems

PROPAGATION METHODS

- CUTTINGS: Cuttings of half-ripe wood root in water or soil. Insert fresh cuttings directly into the soil about five inches, very easy to propagate; hardy and prolific.

RECIPE

LONGEVITY OMELETTE: 1 c longevity spinach, 5 eggs, 1 minced garlic clove, pinch of salt.

Wash leaves thoroughly. Chop. Beat eggs and mix with all ingredients. Pour onto a hot, oiled pan. Allow to cook 2 minutes. Fold over and the cover. Turn off heat and allow to steam 5 minutes.

CULINARY USE

Leaves & Young Stems

High nutritional value. Leaves have a mild raw taste, a slight fuzzy texture and are a thick, semi-succulent leaf. In many Asian countries, leaves are eaten fresh, cooked, dried or powdered. Used in salads, smoothies, stir fries, soups, sauces, stir-fry, or made into tea. The new shoots have the highest concentration of beneficial phytocompounds. They can also be used in sandwiches as a healthy snack. The most effective way to obtain nutritional value and benefits is to eat it raw, but the possibilities are endless. Use it any way you would use any other leafy green and enjoy health perks. A whole potful boiled with salt and butter is similar to eating southern collard greens. Can be freeze-dried as "chips."

CULTURAL SIGNIFICANCE

- In Thailand, used topically for inflammation, rheumatism, body aches, and viral ailments
- An ornamental plant, especially when in flower (purple). Used as an edible house plant
- Referred to as "cholesterol spinach" due to its reputed cholesterol-reducing effects
- Leaf/ stems studied for medical applications (e.g., anti-aging, inflammation and rheumatism; encapsulation/ supplements)

CAUTIONS & CONSIDERATIONS

Health
No known hazards.

Pests
Mostly pest-free aside from occasional mealy bugs, slugs or aphids; Whiteflies & mites in summer.

Landscape design
Efficient ground cover. May be staked upright. Stems may develop purple or have purple spots depending on soil conditions. Compare with Perennial Peanut (Arachis glabrata), Hoan Ngoc (Pseuderanthemum palatiferum) and Beijing Grass (Murdannia loriformis).

Loofah
Luffa cylindrica

HARDINESS ZONES: 10 TO 12

A vigorous vine in the in the cucumber (Cucurbitaceae) family. This annual is well-worth the time. With at least 6 hours of full sun, this plant will produce many gourds. Multiple uses! A great cucumber substitute when young. A wonderful a body scrub when mature! Attracts pollinators! A repertoire of beneficial and health-promoting phytochemicals. The fruits are packed with protein-rich seeds when mature.

SIZE h*w	SUN	SOIL	WATER	EDIBLE
50ft*1ft	full	poor - OK	well-draining	young shoots, leaves, fruit, flower buds, and seed

PROPAGATION METHODS

- SEEDS: Germinates at 68-87F. Direct seeding is fast throughout a frost-free season. Distance plants 3 feet. Approximately 120 days to harvest.

RECIPE

LOOFAH PICKLES: Make a brine by combining 2 c vinegar mixed with 4 c water, 2 tbsp salt, & 2 tbsp agave in medium saucepan. Boil until blended. Cool. Pack 12 loofah, 3 inch "cucumbers" cut into 1/4 spears in a jar. Add 1 head of peeled, smashed garlic, 10 coriander seeds. Top with brine to cover. Store in the refrigerator for one week to pickle. Consume within 6 weeks.

CULTURAL SIGNIFICANCE

- Used in folk medicine (e.g., for inflammation & rheumatism; leaves for wound healing)
- Dried fruits used as bath sponges for skin care (stimulate peripheral circulation); table mats, insoles, sandals, gloves, soundproofing, army helmet insulation, mattress stuffing, filters for engines/ motors & panels for furniture/ housing
- Fruits portrayed on Israel church and synagogue mosaics in Byzantine era

CULINARY USE

Leaves, Shoots, & Flower Buds

Young shoots, leaves and flower buds - cooked. Steamed and served with rice. Used medicinally in folk healing.

Fruits

Picked young (about 3" long) - similar to courgettes. Eaten raw but more often cooked, as you would squash or eggplant. Used in salads, diced like cucumber. Also known as "Chinese okra." Preferred as a vegetable in curries, but equally enjoyed as a snack when dipped in batter and deep fried. In Asian and specifically, Vietnamese cultures it is a common ingredient in soups and stir-fried dishes.

Seeds

Roasted, salted and eaten as a delicacy; cooking oil is obtained from the seed. High proportion of essential amino acids. Good source of protein, carbohydrate, & fiber.

CAUTIONS & CONSIDERATIONS

Health

No known adverse health effects. Clean mature "sponge" thoroughly; controversy exists about whether it can harbor potentially harmful microbes.

Pests

Fruit rot and leaf-leafminers.

Landscape design

May behave invasively. The Luffa genus encompasses 7 species. Luffa aegyptiaca and Luffa acutangula need a sturdy trellis to prevent rot. Can bear about a dozen fruit in ideal growing conditions.

Loquat
Eriobotrya japonica

HARDINESS ZONES: 8 TO 10

An evergreen shrub/ tree in the Rosaceae family. One of the most popular cough remedies in the Far East. Cultivated in Japan for over 1,000 years! Fragrant clusters of white flowers are produced in fall, followed by the delicious, brightly colored, winter fruit. A beautiful ornamental with neat compact growth. Plants live 20- to 30 years.

SIZE h*w	SUN	SOIL	WATER	EDIBLE
30ft*15ft	full	well-draining	maritime exposure - OK; drought tolerant	fruit

PROPAGATION METHODS

- SEEDS: Germinates at 68-75F in 4 mo. Not true from seed. Bears in 8-10 yrs.
- AIR-LAYERING: 80 to 100% of the layers root in 6 weeks with 3% NAA (2-naphthoxyacetic acid). NOTE: Cuttings difficult to root.

RECIPE

FERMENTED HOT SAUCE: 5-6 cups of loquat pulp, 6 fresh chili peppers, 2 garlic cloves, 1 tsp fresh turmeric, 2 tbs spoons vinegar, 2 tsp salt.

Place into a glass container, covered with cloth, stirring daily for up to a week at room temperature. Move into the fridge and consume within 1 month.

CULINARY USE

Fruit

White, yellow, or orange pulp when ripe (green when unripe - toxic). Tastes sour or sweet depending on environmental conditions. Fruit is often peeled, but the peel is edible and not overly thick. Eaten raw in smoothies or cooked such as in pies, sauces, jellies, chutney, and is often served poached in light syrup. Some prepare spiced loquats (with cinnamon, and vinegar) in glass jars. Compared to apples in flavor but not texture. Fruit is produced in winter and early spring.

Good antioxidant properties and source of vitamin A, pectin, potassium & iron. Fruits reach maturity in 90 days from full flower opening.

CULTURAL SIGNIFICANCE

- Fruit is used in folk healing (e.g., for astringent, expectorant and sedative properties. Mature leaves dried into tea to keep skin young & healthy - avoid young leaves due to toxins)
- Seeds are rich in starch (20%) but may contain toxins (cyanogenic glycosides)
- Flowers used as perfume & insect repellent; extracted in oil for cosmetics
- Mentioned in medieval Chinese literature (e.g., poems of Li Bai)

CAUTIONS & CONSIDERATIONS

Health
CAUTION: Avoid consuming seeds and young leaves. Some individuals suffer headache from flower blooms.

Pests
Resilient. Aphids, scale, fruit flies, caterpillars, cankers, scab, leaf spot and blight.

Landscape design
Can be grown as a house plant or trained into an espalier. Planted in mass as a hedge. Self-fertile varieties (e.g., 'Gold Nugget' & 'Mogi'). Compare with Kumquat (Fortunella margarita) or American Persimmon (Diospyros virginiana).

Lychee
Litchi chinensis

HARDINESS ZONES: 10 TO 12

In Chinese, "lychee" means "donor of the joy of living." This highly valued, attractive, evergreen is a perfect shade tree. Trees can produce for 100 years or more! In the soapberry family, Sapindaceae. Cultivation dates back to 1059 AD, when the fruit was used as a delicacy in the Chinese Imperial Court. A nice hedge plant or container specimen. The red fruits are striking. Beautiful, rounded & symmetrical canopy extends nearly to the ground. Showy, spring flowers! Called 'Queen of fruits.'

SIZE h*w	SUN	SOIL	WATER	EDIBLE
40ft*40ft	full to partial	well-draining; acidic, clay - OK	average; seasonal flooding - OK	fruit

PROPAGATION METHODS

- GRAFTING: Fruiting within 5 years, but full production in 20 - 40 years. NOTE: Greenwood cuttings may root.
- SEED: Germinates at 80-95F. Short viability. Fruiting may take 10 years.

RECIPE

LYCHEE MILKSHAKE: 1 ½ c / 15 peeled, de-seeded lychees, 2 c coconut milk, 2 tsp agave, handful of ice.

Add all ingredients to the blender and puree until smooth. Serve cold. Alternatively, for a richer flavor, freeze lychee pulp and omit ice.

CULINARY USE

Fruit
The 1-inch diameter fruit is covered by an inedible pink leathery rind that is pinched off prior to eating. Fruits form in loose clusters. The edible translucent arils are sweet, juicy and subacid, with a flavor similar to Muscat grapes.

Seed is not consumed. Fruit flesh is eaten raw or cooked. Also dried, smoked, spiced, pickled, canned in syrup, used in jams, sauces, cakes, tarts, ice creams / sorbets, & fruit salads etc. Rich in vitamin C.

Poor shelf-life (rind prone to cracking) unless frozen immediately after harvest. Can remain fresh up to 12 months once frozen.

CULTURAL SIGNIFICANCE

- Described by Spanish explorer & sinologist, Juan González de Mendoza in his "History of the Great and Mighty Kingdom of China" (1585)
- Used as a functional food in traditional medicine. Contains flavonoids, anthocyanins, phenolics, sesquiterpenes, triterpenes, & lignans; decoctions of flowers used for throat gargle
- Excellent thirst quencher and believed to serve as a tonic for brain, heart and liver
- Seed used in soap & shampoo-making

CAUTIONS & CONSIDERATIONS

Health
CAUTION: Consume ripe only. Avoid consuming on an empty stomach. Do not consume if fasting. Hypoglycemic amino acids present.

Pests
Resilient. Scales and mushroom root rot if near oaks.

Landscape design
Many named varieties. Cultivars have differing winter chilling requirements. Brittle: Shelter from wind. Fruit litter. Requires very little pruning.

Macadamia ⭐

Macadamia spp.

HARDINESS ZONES: 9 TO 12

An ornamental staple crop grown for glossy, evergreen foliage and attractive flowers. Slow growing but so delicious! Fine, crunchy texture, ivory color and buttery flavor. Considered the world's finest dessert nut! Productive for more than 50 years! Bear reliably year after year. Low maintenance and easy! Can fruit even in poor soil! Known as the "King of nuts" due to its popularity & valuable nutritional value. In the Proteaceae family.

SIZE h*w	SUN	SOIL	WATER	EDIBLE
35ft*35ft	full to partial	muck - ideal; well-drained	drought tolerant; seasonal flooding - OK	nut/oil

PROPAGATION METHODS

- SEEDS: Germinates at 77-86F. Produces within 8-12 years. Variable quality.
- GRAFTING: Production after 3 years.
- CUTTINGS: Softwood has moderate success.

RECIPE

MACADAMIA MAYO: Blend 2 cups macadamia nuts (soaked overnight & strained) with a pinch of sea salt, 5 cloves of garlic, 1.5c coconut water, & 2 tbs citrus juice.

Puree until smooth. Store in the refrigerator and use within 1 week.

CULTURAL SIGNIFICANCE

- The seed contains the highest level of oil yet found in a nut - up to 75% - used in cosmetics
- Shells used as fuel
- Korean Air Flight 86 from John F. Kennedy International Airport in New York City had a macadamia "nut rage incident"
- Often fed to pet hyacinth macaws parrots
- Host plant for Lepidoptera (moth) species
- Resistant to fungus - used to replant infected orchards infected with fungus

CULINARY USE

Seeds/ Nut & Oil

Harvest fallen nuts from late fall to spring. Remove husk, spread & dry at 115° F for about 12 hours. Then cure 3 weeks. The 1-inch diameter nut is de-shelled and occasionally eaten raw but more often cooked since the flavor quality is enhanced by lightly roasting it in oil and salting. Also added to cakes, biscuits, ice cream etc. Added to roasts and casseroles and ground into flour. The seed oil contains 80% monounsaturated fats and 8% omega-6 fatty acids. Provides significant amounts of numerous essential nutrients (e.g., thiamine, vitamin B6, manganese, iron, magnesium, and phosphorus). Can be fermented into an excellent vegan cheese!! NOTE: Refrigerate for the longest shelf life. If kept at room temperature, nuts may go rancid.

CAUTIONS & CONSIDERATIONS

Health
No known adverse health effects in humans. Toxic to dogs. Kernels from M. integrifolia and M. tetraphylla can be eaten raw - other species contain toxins & need to be processed.

Pests
Thrips, mites and scale; canker.

Landscape design
Macadamias inhibit the growth of nearby papaya trees. Naturally have multiple stems but trained to have a central lead. Pruning is not normally necessary. Brittle branches - shelter from wind. Noteworthy cultivars include Beaumont.

Magnolia

Magnolia grandiflora

HARDINESS ZONES: 6 TO 10

An evergreen Florida native & believed to be one of the most ancient flowers on earth! Delights the senses - one of the most strongly scented flowers in the world! Very ornamental! Great for shading children's recreational areas in the food forest. Low maintenance! High wildlife value! Leaves & flowers used in decorations & floral arrangements. The wood is even used in furniture making! In the Magnoliaceae family.

SIZE h*w	SUN	SOIL	WATER	EDIBLE
60ft+*40ft+	full to partial	well-draining; sandy - OK	average; drought tolerant	flowers, leaves

PROPAGATION METHODS

- SEEDS: Germinates at 85-95F within 18 months. Plant out when 6 inches tall and mulch heavily.
- LAYERING: In early spring; semi-hardwood cuttings taken in summer.

RECIPE

MAGNOLIA SYRUP: Remove petals. Simmer 1 cup of chopped petals in 1 cup of agave for twenty minutes. Strain and bottle.

Makes 1.5 cups. Refrigerate up to 6 months. Dilute in tea, drizzle on cakes, cheese, or salads.

CULTURAL SIGNIFICANCE

- Fruits are eaten by squirrels, opossums, & birds
- Beetles are primary pollinators & flowers have a hard carpel to manage beetle mandibles
- State flower of Louisiana & state tree of Mississippi -"the Magnolia State"
- In China, magnolias were considered symbols of womanly beauty & gentleness. Used in bridal bouquets to emphasize purity & nobility
- Folk healing use (e.g., bark for rheumatism & fever)

CULINARY USE

Flowers
Although the primary historical uses are medicinal, magnolia flower petals can be eaten raw or pickled (like like peaches or pears). In some parts of England, the flavor is considered exquisite - a delicacy; used as a spice and a condiment. Paired with sushi or bread and cheese. The fragrant white blossoms can measure twelve inches across. Strong, sweet, floral flavor. Prepared in a sweet and sour pickle recipe like a relish so the floral taste integrates with the sweetness. Also, diced and added to salads, sandwiches, stir-fries, honey, syrups, & other dessert dishes. Base of the flower is bitter and best removed.

Leaves
Used as a substitute for bay leaf to flavor soups & stews. Cut into smaller pieces because of their strong flavor.

CAUTIONS & CONSIDERATIONS

Health
No known adverse health effects. Traditionally used to treat circulatory system disorders.

Pests
Generally regarded as pest and disease free: scale, canker, borers, and weevils.

Landscape design
Drops leaves throughout year. Aggressive surface roots. Relatively wind-tolerant. Can be pruned into an espalier. Flowers open intermittently throughout summer. Compare with flood tolerant, Sweetbay (Magnolia virginiana).

Malabar Spinach

Basella rubra

HARDINESS ZONES: 9 TO 11

This hardy perennial vine produces semi-succulent greens at a time when most greens die back - the heart of summer. Grows well under full sunlight in hot, humid climates. Grown as an ornamental! Beautiful glossy green leaves, red stems, & deep-purple berries. Ready for harvest in less than two months. In the Basellaceae family.

SIZE h*w	SUN	SOIL	WATER	EDIBLE
6ft*6in	full to partial	poor - OK	flood tolerant	leaves, stem tips, sap

PROPAGATION METHODS

- SEEDS: Germinates at 70-80F. Soak overnight/ scarify. Collect from robust plants to ensure progeny adapt. Seed can be saved 4 years.
- CUTTINGS: Root in moist soil; 8-10" cutting.

RECIPE

CREAMED SPINACH: 4 cups leaves, 3 tbs oil, 3 minced garlic cloves, 1/2" minced ginger, 1 pepper, 2 c coconut milk or cream, 1/4 tsp salt, 1 thinly sliced scallion, 4 fresh kaffir lime leaves.

Sauté garlic, ginger, pepper, salt in oil until soft and fragrant. Add all other ingredients and simmer while stirring 3 minutes.

CULTURAL SIGNIFICANCE

- Folk medicine uses: Shoots - febrifuge, diuretic, laxative; leaf poultice - to treat stings, wounds
- Considered anti-inflammatory
- Some recognize three different species, B. alba, B. rubra and B. cordifolia: Basella alba - high in phenols, vitamins A and C. Basella rubra - high in alkaloids, tannins. Basella cordifolia - highest content of anthraquinone among all 3 species
- Suitable as an edible house plant

CULINARY USE

Leaves/ Stem tips
Eat fresh. Pick as needed for use in soups, salads, stir-fry or as a pot herb for stews. Stores up to 4 days refrigerated. Eat raw or cooked. Mild flavor and mucilaginous texture. Main ingredient in Philippine's dish, called, utan. In India, fresh big and tender leaves are washed, dipped in batter and deep-fried. The mucilaginous qualities of the plant make it an excellent thickening agent in stews, soups, & casseroles. Overcooking increases mucilage while acidic foods can decrease the mucilage. Rich in vit A & C, iron and calcium. Contains phenolic phytochemicals; antioxidant properties.

Sap
The purple sap from fruit is a food coloring in sweets (also inks/rouge). Color enhanced with lemon juice.

CAUTIONS & CONSIDERATIONS

Health
No known adverse health effects. Do not grow in contaminated soil - may uptake heavy metals.

Pests
No serious insect or disease problems.

Landscape design
Train on a trellis. Grows well in hydroponic systems. Part shade increases leaf size. Compare with bushier succulant types: Surinam Spinach (Talinum triangulare) and Jewels of Opar Spinach (Talinum paniculata).

Mango
Mangifera indica

HARDINESS ZONES: 10 TO 12

One of the most popular fruits worldwide! A multi-purpose shade tree. The tree itself is highly attractive in the home landscape. The ripe fruit is prepared in many ways and the tangy, raw green mango is a delicacy in its own right. Mango trees can live for hundreds of years and continue to produce fruit at 300 years! 5th most produced fruit crop in the world! One of the best sources of beta-carotene, a powerful antioxidant. In the Anacardiaceae family.

SIZE h*w	SUN	SOIL	WATER	EDIBLE
82ft*82ft	full, partial	well-drained	average; moderately flood tolerant	fruit, seed, leaves

PROPAGATION METHODS

- SEEDS: Germinates at 80-95F. Yields in 8 years. 2 distinct varieties: polyembryonic-identical to parent tree; monoembryonic- hybrid mix of parents. Self-seeds.
- GRAFTING: Yields more predictable fruit flavor.

RECIPE

MANGO SOUFFLE WITH SAUCE: 2 medium mangos, 1 tsp oil, 2 tsp water, 3 large egg whites.

Peel and pit the mangos. Puree mangos with water and divide puree in half. Beat egg whites until stiff. Add half of stiff whites to 1/2 puree; fold in. Fold in 2nd half of whites. Pour the batter into an oiled 4-cup soufflé dish. Bake 25 min at 375 until puffed and golden. Serve drizzled with remaining puree.

CULTURAL SIGNIFICANCE

- National fruit of India and Pakistan, and the national tree of Bangladesh
- A basket of mangos is considered a gesture of friendship in India; leaves hung for luck
- Is relied upon for daily nutrition in many developing tropical nations
- Flowers used to repel mosquitos; bark/leaves yield yellowish-brown dye used for silk; timber used for boats, flooring, furniture; leaves used as mulch and fodder

CULINARY USE

Fruit
Wash and peel before consumption to remove oils. Can be eaten raw, processed into juice, jams, candies, etc., or dried and ground into powder as a flavoring. Sour, unripe mangoes are rich in starch & used in chutneys, pickles, and salsas. Pectin in mango pulp serves as a gelling agent. Good source of iron & vitamin A.

Seeds
Seeds are sources of starch and edible fat. Astringency must be removed by boiling, roasting and soaking. In India, flour is made from mango seeds. Rich in oleic acid and stearic acid.

Leaves & Flowers
Young leaves are cooked as a vegetable or used to make tea but see health notes.

CAUTIONS & CONSIDERATIONS

Health
CAUTION: Contact with oils in mango leaves, stems, sap, and skin can cause dermatitis and anaphylaxis. In Anacardiaceae family along with poison ivy & poison oak.

Pests
Anthracnose fungus, powdery mildew, mites/scale insects.

Landscape design
May flower irregularly - expect one good crop every 3 - 4 years. Several hundred cultivars - vary in size, shape, sweetness, skin color, and flesh color.

Marula

Sclerocarya birrea

HARDINESS ZONES: 10 TO 12

A fast growing deciduous tree in the Anacardiaceae family which has fed people since ancient times. A socio-economically important & protected multipurpose tree throughout Africa and increasingly Australia, India and Oman. Contains four times as much vitamin C as oranges! A protein-oil staple crop. A female tree can yield thousands of fruits in a season. A great windbreak, shade tree, food provider and pioneer plant.

SIZE h*w	SUN	SOIL	WATER	EDIBLE
42ft*42ft	full	poor, acidic/ saline soils - OK	drought tolerant	fruit, seed

PROPAGATION METHODS

- SEEDS: Germinates at 80-90F. <u>Dioecious. Some bisexual flowers.</u> Seed viable for years. Produces fruit 3rd or 4th year.
- CUTTINGS: Preferred since sex can be identified. <u>NOTE: Male & female required for fruit.</u>

RECIPE

MARULA FLOUR: De-pulp nut by soaking in water (note the fermented fruit may be used for "beer.") Remove nuts from water and dry in an oven or dehydrator at lowest setting (e.g. 115F). Crack open nuts to remove edible kernels. Grind into a flour using a coffee grinder.

CULTURAL SIGNIFICANCE

- Edible seed oil has 64% oleic acid, and 17% myristic acid; comparable to olive oil but with greater stability. Seeds burn like a candle. Oil used in cosmetics
- Host plant for edible insects & several butterflies & moths like the African Moon Moth
- Used in traditional medicine (bark: chewed for toothache; fruit: for dry cough & as a laxative)
- Wood used for making drums, bowls, canoes, furniture, and carvings

CULINARY USE

Fruit
Plum-sized stone fruits fall while still green and ripen on the ground. Pale yellow when fully ripe. The 1.5-inch diameter round fruits have a mango/ sub-acid, sweet flavor & mucilaginous texture. Pulp is eaten raw or prepared into shortbread or pie often with pecan. Also made into jam & wine. Boiled down to a thick black syrup and used as a sweetening agent. The leathery rind is removed prior to eating. The expressed juice is often fermented.

Seeds
The nut contains 2-3 seed kernels inside 1-inch long seed. Tastes similar to pine-nut. Can be ground into flour, made into "milk," or cooked and mixed with vegetables as a protein. A delicate nutty taste. Rich in minerals: iron, magnesium, zinc, phosphorus and copper.

CAUTIONS & CONSIDERATIONS

Health
No known adverse health effects. NOTE: Water can collect in the tree & act as a breeding ground for mosquitoes.

Pests
May host fruit fly; hosts numerous insects which may defoliate the tree.

Landscape design
Taproot. Three subspecies - all with similar uses. Decaying fruit has a strong smell. Commonly found in semi-arid regions. Compare with Brazil Nut (Bertholletia excelsa).

Maya Nut

Brosimum alicastrum

HARDINESS ZONES: 10 TO 12

Also called Breadnut. A large, evergreen that can produce two or three harvests per year! Considered a staple crop given its balanced carbohydrate nut. Historically, the principal food of pre-Hispanic cultures. Comparable to corn, rice and wheat in nutrition. In the Moraceae family along with figs & mulberries. A single tree produces around 300lbs of fruit annually & remains productive up to 150 years. Promising economic value.

SIZE h*w	SUN	SOIL	WATER	EDIBLE
98ft*82ft	partial	acidic/saline -OK; well-draining	drought and flood tolerant	fruit, seed

PROPAGATION METHODS

- SEEDS: Germinates at 80-90F. Produces fruit in 5 - 6 yrs. Viable up to 5 years. Dioecious, monoecious or hermaphroditic varieties.
- CUTTINGS: Greenwood roots in soil. Preferred method.

RECIPE

MAYA MASHED "POTATO": Boil the seed for 2+ hours in heavily salted water until it has the flavor of a potato. If it does not taste like a potato it is not ready! When it tastes like a potato, drain, and rinse well with water. Take off the papery covering on the outside of the seed. Mash with oil and spices to taste.

CULINARY USE

Fruit
Sweet, yellow or orange thin edible flesh surrounding the large seed. Smells like citrus.

Seeds
Marble-sized seed eaten cooked. Roasted seed develops a nutty, cacao-like flavor. An agreeable and nourishing food with a flavor similar to hazel nuts. Can also be boiled and mashed like potatoes but lower in carbohydrates. Ground seed made into tortillas. A substitute for wheat flour! Steeped like coffee. High in fiber! When the breadnut is green, it's stewed like a vegetable.

Sap
The milky latex flows freely when the trunk is cut and resembles cream. When diluted with water is said to afford a substitute for cow's milk; used medicinally.

CULTURAL SIGNIFICANCE

- In the Yucatan, seeds are eaten by nursing women to increase the flow of milk
- Wood used for carpentry, flooring, furniture
- Considered a threatened species due to de-forestation
- Planted by Maya civilization 2000 years ago
- Considered a pioneer species - great potential to restore degraded areas
- Aided human survival during the 1980s Contra war in Nicaragua

CAUTIONS & CONSIDERATIONS

Health
No known health hazards. Not a true nut. Contains tryptophan as well as protein, calcium, potassium, B vitamins, antioxidants, iron, and foliate.

Pests
Fruit fly host.

Landscape design
Provides good shade and reduces the impact of strong winds. Helps prevent erosion & stabilize riverbanks. Requires no agricultural input. Abundant leaf litter improves soil fertility. Two sub-species. Prune to encourage branching.

Moringa
Moringa oleifera

HARDINESS ZONES: 10 TO 12

Considered a top-10 plant to end world hunger! A fast-growing, deciduous, drought-resistant tree easily reaching 35ft in height and is nearly completely edible. The feathery leaves alone pack a powerful protein punch exceeding legumes. Multipurpose tree with economic potential. A valued staple! Worldwide list of moringa's medicinal uses is long! In the Moringaceae family.

SIZE h*w	SUN	SOIL	WATER	EDIBLE
35ft*20ft	full	prefers sandy	drought tolerant	leaves, pods, seeds, flowers, roots

PROPAGATION METHODS

- SEEDS: Germinates at 75-90F. High germination rate. Allow seed pods to dry while still on the plant.
- CUTTINGS: Roots readily in soil.

RECIPE

MORINGA GUAC: 1 tsp moringa powder, 1 peeled, seeded avocado, 3 chives minced, 2 tbs citrus juice or vinegar; salt & pepper to taste.

Combine all ingredients and mix well.

To create moringa powder, dehydrate leaves at 115 F/ 45 C until crisp. Pulse into powder.

CULTURAL SIGNIFICANCE

- Used for bee forage, soil conservation, shade, windbreak, live fence
- Powdered seeds help clarify water, honey and sugar cane juice without boiling
- Blue dye from wood; pulp for paper-making
- Bark fiber used for ropes, mats, and tannins
- Mature seed oil used as machine lubricate or for salad oil, soap and cosmetics
- Gum used in calico printing

CULINARY USE

Leaves
Most nutritious when blanched to remove saponins. High concentrations of beneficial polyphenols. Leaves used as a protein and iron supplement.

Pods
Immature seed pods cooked similar to green beans with a slight asparagus taste. Also made into pickles.

Seeds
Green immature seeds eaten cooked like peas, boiled or fried. Mature seeds are 40% oil. The oil is extracted with a hand press or boiled off after grinding. Meal used as flour. A mature tree can yield 1000 or more pods!

Flowers
Eaten raw or cooked. Often fried or used in tea. Contain quercetin. Considered medicinal. Consume in moderation.

CAUTIONS & CONSIDERATIONS

Health
No known adverse health effects. Known for its antimicrobial properties. Root & bark are strongly medicinal - Consume with caution.

Pests
May suffer from rot, canker, pod fly, budworm, hairy caterpillars, or red mites.

Landscape design
Prune shoulder height for easy harvesting. Trees bloom 8 months after planting. Heat-loving. Dwarf varieties. Compare with African Moringa (M. Stenopetala).

Mulberry

Morus nigra

HARDINESS ZONES: 5 TO 10B

Living for hundreds of years in favorable locations, this very ornamental tree is regarded as the most flavorful variety and is high in antioxidants. This self-fertile, small, deciduous version will exceed your expectations in fruit production and can be pruned to stay under 6 feet tall. A staple with leaves producing more protein per acre than soybeans. Wood can be used for smoking meats! In Moraceae family.

SIZE h*w	SUN	SOIL	WATER	EDIBLE
30ft*30ft	full to partial	well-draining	drought tolerant	fruit, leaves

PROPAGATION METHODS

- SEEDS: Germinates at 65-70F. Stratify. Yields in 10 yrs. Better health than cuttings.
- CUTTINGS: Half-ripe wood readily root.
- GRAFTING: Produce stronger root systems.

RECIPE

MULBERRY CHUTNEY: 1/2c dried mulberries, a handful of nuts - minced, 1/4 c blanched moringa leaves.

Grind all ingredients coarsely, adding a bit of oil or water as needed. Spread on toasted sourdough bread slices.

CULTURAL SIGNIFICANCE

- Attracts wildlife - birds, opossums, silkworms; imported to Britain in 17th century for the cultivation of silkworm
- A Babylonian etiological myth attributes color of fruits to the tragic deaths of lovers
- Nursery rhyme: "Here We Go Round the Mulberry Bush" and "Pop Goes the Weasel"
- Vincent van Gogh featured tree in paintings
- Used in agroforestry as windbreak & live fence

CULINARY USE

Fruit
Ripe fruit is succulent, plump, and juicy, resembling a blackberry. Don't consume unripe - toxic. The fruit must be used as soon as it is ripe. Mulberries are used in pies, cobblers, syrups, tarts, wines, cordials, jam, and herbal teas. Can be dehydrated as with raisins or ground into a powder for tea, bread, or food coloring. Mulberries freeze very well and have many uses. Iroquois and Cherokees mashed, dried, and stored the fruit to make sauces they mixed into cornbread to make sweet dumplings.

Leaves
Very young leaves edible when boiled 20 min and strained. Many folk-healing uses as a tea. Can be dried for salads or stuffed like grape leaves.

CAUTIONS & CONSIDERATIONS

Health
No known adverse health effects. Long history of use in Chinese medicine. Nearly all parts of the plant are used.

Pests
Susceptible to fungal and bacterial spot diseases.

Landscape design
Can be kept under 6 feet. Compare with Pakistan mulberry. NOTE: FL native Morus rubra is less disease prone. Some mulberry varieties are dioecious. White Mulberry is considered invasive.

Muscadine Grape

Vitis rotundifolia

HARDINESS ZONES: 6 TO 10

A Florida native and butterfly host plant sometimes called 'Scuppernongs.' More vigorous than most other grape cultivars! Naturally resistant to Pierce's disease! Deciduous. Can produce up to 15 tons of muscadines per acre!! Part of a multimillion-dollar industry in the United States. Larger berries draw the highest prices. Productive for several decades. In the Vitaceae family.

SIZE h*w	SUN	SOIL	WATER	EDIBLE
60ft+*2ft	full	well-draining; sandy loam best	average	fruit

PROPAGATION METHODS

- SEEDS: Germinates at 80-90F. Some varieties are <u>dioecious</u>. Select a self-fertile variety.
- CUTTINGS: Select 2-node-long cuttings 1/4" in diameter. Preferred to ensure self-fertile.

RECIPE

ROASTED GRAPES: 4 cups, de-seeded muscadine, 2 tbs oil, 2 tbs vinegar or wine; 2 sprigs of fresh rosemary.

Toss all ingredients and roast in the oven at 425F for 30 minutes. Serve on toast, ice cream, yogurt, cheese etc.

CULTURAL SIGNIFICANCE

- Host for nessus & mournful sphinx moths
- Muscadine has 40 chromosomes; other grapes have 38
- Ohio considers grapes a noxious weed if number of vines exceed 100 and are unattended for 2+ years
- Seeds can be pressed for oil
- If you cut the vine & invert it, can get a quart or more of water from a one-foot piece
- Blue dye from grape skins

CULINARY USE

Fruit
Hundreds of muscadine grape varieties with bronze, pink, purple, red, or black colored fruit. Harvesting of fruit should begin in the third season. Thicker-skinned, somewhat spicy-sweet as compared to supermarket grapes. Picked individually from the vine rather than in bunches. Fruit matures in August through September. Enjoyed fresh, made into jelly, jam, raisins, fruit leather or wine. High polyphenols/antioxidants and anti-inflammatory compounds especially in skins. Described as the next potential "superfruit." Refrigerate after harvest. Shelf life of about a week.

Leaves
Young leaves boiled and also used as an edible wrapping.

CAUTIONS & CONSIDERATIONS

Health
No known adverse health effects. NOTE: high in acid. Don't crush them bare-handed or footed.

Pests
Highly resilient. Deer, grape root borer moth, fungal disease.

Landscape design
FL self-fertile cultivars (e.g., 'Carlos', 'Polyanna', 'Florida Fry', & 'Southern Home'). Some seedless cultivars. Space plants 15ft+ on lateral trellis. Tie one strong shoot to straight support; prune off other shoots in spring. Allow 2-4 nodes per 6 in of cordon. Shallow roots.

Nasturtium
Tropaeolum majus

HARDINESS ZONES: 9 TO 11

Also called Indian Cress. Popular with chefs! One of the tastiest and easiest to grow edible flowers. An attractive addition to salads! Thrives on neglect! Used as companion plants for biological pest control. Grows well with fruit trees, improving their growth and flavor. Blooms spring to fall. Good source of micro-nutrients! Popular in folk healing for anti-bacterial, anti-fungal and antiseptic qualities. In the Tropaeolaceae family.

SIZE h*w	SUN	SOIL	WATER	EDIBLE
3ft+*1ft varies by cultivar	full to partial	well-draining	average	leaves, buds, flowers, pods and seeds

PROPAGATION METHODS

- SEEDS: Germinates at 68-75F. Self-seeds readily. Direct sow seeds ½" deep. Space 10-12" apart. Avoid transplanting.
- CUTTINGS: Root in water or damp soil.

RECIPE

NASTURTIUM CAPERS: 1 cup washed nasturtium pods/seeds, 1/3 c vinegar, 1/3 c water, 1 tbs sea salt, 1/2 tsp sweetener of choice.

Boil water, vinegar, salt, and sweetner. Pour over the pods into a glass mason jar. Seal and place in a dark, cool, spot for 3 weeks. Shake often.

CULINARY USE

Leaves, Buds, & Flowers
Flowers & leaves have a peppery taste reminiscent of watercress. Spicier when grown in sunnier, hotter weather. Use in stir-fries, cook with pasta, and stuff the flowers! Use entire flowers to garnish platters, salads, & open-faced sandwiches. Add flowers to vinegar to infuse color and flavor. Place flowers on top of tacos as a salsa replacement. The poorer the soil, the more flowers are produced. Young seed pods are pickled as a caper substitute.

Pods & Seeds
Unripe green seed pods eaten raw or pickled in vinegar or salt water - similar to capers. Dried seeds are ground as a pepper substitute and in flavored oils. Contains 25% protein and 10% oil. Pods develop 4 months after seeding.

CULTURAL SIGNIFICANCE

- Nasturtiums inhibit bacterial & mold growth in ferments; used as an antiseptic
- Monet planted at home in Giverny, France
- "Nasturtium" means "nose-twister" due to peppery flavor; believed to relieve nasal & chest congestion - expectorant
- Flowers simmered down to various dyes
- Antioxidant properties; high in phenolic compounds & lutein
- Applied in dermatology to improve skin & hair

CAUTIONS & CONSIDERATIONS

Health
CAUTION: Small children and those with gastrointestinal ulcers or kidney disease should avoid. May cause irritation of the mucous membrane of the gastrointestinal tract.

Pests
Resilient. Cabbageworm (Pieris rapae), slugs/snails, aphids.

Landscape design
Compare with 'Canary Creeper' nasturtium (T. peregrinum) or Mashua (Tropaeolum tuberosum) - the cultivar, lineamaculatum 'Ken Aslet' gained Royal Horticultural Society's Award of Garden Merit.

Neem
Azadirachta indica

HARDINESS ZONES: 10 TO 12

A fast-growing, evergreen tree with more uses than any other known herb. Considered a "village pharmacy" and "Miracle Tree." The edible olive-like fruits occur in large numbers, but the seed is most coveted for its multipurpose oil. With strong light, neem trees may be suitable as indoors plants and handle hard pruning very well. In the Meliaceae family. Offers low-cost alternatives to agrochemicals! Compares well with commercial pesticides!

SIZE h*w	SUN	SOIL	WATER	EDIBLE
50ft*50ft	full, partial	acidic, poor - ok	drought tolerant	flowers, shoots

PROPAGATION METHODS

- SEEDS: Germinates at 80-90F. Produces seed prolifically. Depulping/ cleaning improves the germination rate. Seeds lose viability quickly.
- CUTTINGS: Root and softwood stem in soil.

RECIPE

NEEM TEA: Boil a cup of water. Add five washed neem leaves (fresh or dried). Allow to steep for five minutes covered. Strain.

OPTIONAL: Add sweetener to taste.

CAUTION: See health notes.

CULINARY USE

Flowers, Shoots, Leaves
Bitter unless cooked, tender shoots and white aromatic flowers eaten as a vegetable in India. A soup-like dish called, "veppampoo charu" is made from flowers. In Myanmar, young neem leaves and flower buds are boiled with tamarind to soften its bitterness and eaten as a vegetable. Pickled neem leaves are also eaten with tomato and fish paste sauce in Myanmar. In Vietnam leaves are used in the salad, "goi sau da." In Thailand, leaves and flowers are eaten blanched, often with a chili sauce. Some make a fermented alcoholic drink from sap.

Fruit
Fully ripe fruit pulp cooked and used for drinks as a dessert or lemonade-type drink.

CULTURAL SIGNIFICANCE

- In India, the flowers are used in festivals like Ugadi & trees border streets, temples, & schools
- Wood valued in Africa; grown as hedges to make wardrobes, bookcases, toothbrushes - believed to prevent periodontal disease
- Seed oil used as fuel, for cooking, medicinal soap, hair conditioner. Important source of azadirachtin/ insect repellent. Key in pollinator-friendly, pest management

CAUTIONS & CONSIDERATIONS

Health
CAUTION: Use sparsely. Medically active substances. Not recommended for children, elderly or the frail. Used in folk healing extensively for antiviral, antifungal, antibacterial and insecticidal properties.

Pests
Remarkably pest free.

Landscape design
May behave invasively. Excellent shade tree. Prevents erosion. Green manure. Anti-desertification properties. Intercropped with grains.

New Zealand Spinach

Tetragonia tetragonioides

HARDINESS ZONES: 8 TO 11

Also known as, Sea Spinach. A fast-growing, evergreen but short-lived perennial in the Aizoaceae family. Easy to grow! Excellent spinach substitute! Its natural habitat is sandy shorelines and bluffs - perfect for Florida. Rich in vitamin K!! Used as a vegetable since at least the 18th century AD. An important commercial crop among Australian's native edible plants.

SIZE h*w	SUN	SOIL	WATER	EDIBLE
1ft*3ft	full	well-draining	drought tolerant; maritime - OK	leaves

PROPAGATION METHODS

- SEEDS: Germinates at 60-74F. Ripen from September to October. Mature plant will self-seed. Soak 24 hrs. Space 15 inches apart.
- CUTTINGS: Root easily in soil or water.

RECIPE

SEA SPINACH ON TOAST: Blanch leaves for 1 minute in boiling water. Strain, rinse and dry briefly on a towel. Toast a sourdough slice in a pan with oil and garlic. Place the leaves onto the toasted slice.

Garnish with porterweed flowers for a mushroom-like flavor.

CULINARY USE

Leaves

Ready for harvest about 2 months after seeding. A mild flavor and a hint of salt - leaves store salt in tiny hairs over the leaves. Cooked as a spinach substitute. Harvest shoot tips when 3 inches or shorter to encourages tender side growth. Older leaves develop an acrid taste. Substitute for spinach, chard, or bok choy.

Contains oxalates, like many leafy vegetables. Blanch in boiling water for one minute, then rinse in cold water. Use in stir-fries. Takes the heat beautifully in soups, stews, pies, quiches. Use in fruit and vegetable juices and smoothies (after blanching). High in antioxidants.

NOTE: Some reports that the yellow flowers are also edible.

CULTURAL SIGNIFICANCE

- Mentioned by Captain Cook to help fight scurvy among crew of the Endeavour ship
- Offers soil erosion control
- One of the better known Australian native edible plants.
- A halophyte! A plant-based source of a "salty" flavor
- Known to have been part of Maori cuisine
- Aboriginal name "Warrigal" (Dharug language) meaning "wild"

CAUTIONS & CONSIDERATIONS

Health
No known adverse health effects but like many greens, contains oxalic acid (locks-up other nutrients like calcium). Blanch before eating.

Pests
Resilient. Root rot in wet areas.

Landscape design
Will form a thick carpeting groundcover. Suitable for containers. May behave invasively. Compare with Longevity Spinach (Gynura procumbens), Sisso Spinach (Alternanthera sissoo) or Purslane (Portulaca spp).

Noni

Morinda citrifolia var. citrifolia

HARDINESS ZONES: 10 TO 12

In the coffee/ Rubiaceae family. Also called Cheese Fruit. Widely used in folk healing since ancient times. A natural pioneer species & hedge plant. Flowers & fruits year-round. Significant economic importance - many health & cosmetic products from leaves & fruits! May live 25 years or longer. Attracts fruit bats, honeybees & birds! Great for home gardens - 1 plant provides for a family of 5.

SIZE h*w	SUN	SOIL	WATER	EDIBLE
20ft*20ft	dappled to 80% shade	well-draining; poor - OK	drought tolerant; seasonal flooding - OK	fruit, leaves, shoot, seed

PROPAGATION METHODS

- SEEDS: Germinates at 95-100F in 9 months. Viable 6 months. Floats in water aiding dispersal. Scarify. Flowers & fruits in 3 years
- CUTTINGS: Roots in 2 months. Not as resilient as seedlings.

RECIPE

NONI "CHEESE": Soak 2 c macadamia nuts overnight in the refrigerator. Drain. Juice 1 ripe noni Place nuts & noni juice in a blender along with 3 tbs citrus juice & 1 tsp sea salt (add 2 tbs of water if needed). When silky smooth, place in a cotton fabric secured with string or a rubber band. Hang in refrigerator overnight to drain out excess liquid. Have a bowl underneath to catch liquid.

CULTURAL SIGNIFICANCE

- Used in folk healing (e.g., medicinally active anthraquinone derivates. Believed to be antibacterial, antiviral, antifungal, anti-inflammatory & immune enhancing. Leaves used as medicinal tea; poultice)
- A red dye is obtained from the root bark
- Fruit pulp used to clean hair, iron & steel
- Wood used for poles & plant supports
- Believed to repel ghosts ("ghost medicine")

CULINARY USE

Fruit

Harvested when white (unripe), or fully soft, translucent, and characteristically odorous. Unripe fruit used in Indian sambal & curry recipes. Ripe fruits have an odor similar to strong smelling cheese. Savory flavor. Ripe fruit is often made into vegan cheese, or dressings, sauces and marinades. Contains a number of phytochemicals.

Seeds

Seeds of some varieties are roasted & eaten. Tastes like a sunflower seed ~30% husk.

Leaves & Shoots

Young leaves & blanched shoots are often added to curries. Bitter. Used to wrap foods. Around 5% protein; rich in vitamin A. Often cooked with coconut milk.

CAUTIONS & CONSIDERATIONS

Health

CAUTION: Can interfere with some medication. Those with potassium-restricted diets should avoid.

Pests

Resilient. Fruit fly, whitefly, aphids, leaf miners, sooty mold.

Landscape design

Erosion control. Deep taproot. May behave invasively. Brittle wood but regenerates quickly. Planted as windbreak & support for pepper vines & as a companion with coffee, breadfruit, papaya, mango, coconut, & bananas.

Okinawa Spinach
Gynura bicolor

HARDINESS ZONES: 9 TO 11

A perennial leafy green with a striking purple underside. Beautiful and nutritious! Also known as, Hung tsoi. Low-maintenance and abundantly producing! A nutritious vegetable! Tiny blossoms attract a constant stream of butterflies. Belongs to the family Asteraceae (known to possess medicinal properties). Year-round harvest! Considered both a vegetable and a medicinal herb.

SIZE h*w	SUN	SOIL	WATER	EDIBLE
1.5ft*1.5ft	partial	well-draining	average	leaves, shoots

PROPAGATION METHODS

- CUTTINGS: Rooted in water or moist soil. Stem cuttings 4-6 inches in length root best. Suitable for hydroponic rooting.

RECIPE

OKINAWA TEA: Steep washed leaves and stems in boiling water covered for 5 minutes. Strain.

Serve with sweetener of choice.

Enjoy for broad spectrum of nutrients and plant bioactives.

CULINARY USE

Leaves & Shoots
Eaten raw or cooked. Young leaves and young shoot tips used as garnishes and in salads. Rich in iron, potassium, & calcium. Taste is described as crispy & nutty taste with a hint of pine. Mucilaginous texture, especially when cooked. Purple color is lost when cooked. Cut stem tips when harvesting to keep plants bushy and productive. The top four to six inches are harvested. The more you harvest, the more is produced. Can also be steamed or juiced, and used in stir fries, soups, curries, smoothies, quiches. Brings a faintly spicy, lemon pepper taste. Pairs well with ginger! Use the leaves on sandwiches in place of lettuce. Can be made into a tea. Leaves are ready to harvest after 35-40 days. Stores well in a bag in the refrigerator for up to a week.

CULTURAL SIGNIFICANCE

- Used in folk healing (e.g., for antioxidant properties, anti-inflammatory benefits. Hypoglycemic effects. High amount of phenolic and flavonoid content in the leaves; presence of lipophilic antioxidant compounds such as carotenoids)
- Edible reddish-purple dye/ food coloring
- Commercially grown vegetable green in China
- Indigenous to Indonesia but is also cultivated in Japan, Malaysia, and India

CAUTIONS & CONSIDERATIONS

Health
No known adverse health effects. Consume in moderation - medicinal. Often confused with Gynura crepioides.

Pests
Resilient.

Landscape design
Used as an edible ground cover or border plant. Keeping it dense also helps to stop weeds coming through. Mulch often to maintain moisture. Compare with Longevity Spinach (Gynura procumbens) or Daun Dewa (Gynura segetum)

Olive

Olea europaea var. Arbequina

HARDINESS ZONES: 8 TO 10

A slow-growing, evergreen tree in the Oleaceae family first cultivated 7,000 years ago in the Mediterranean. Because FL climate and soils are similar to the Mediterranean, olives can grow locally! Arbequina is the most popular FL olive tree. Beautiful silvery foliage! Great potential as a landscape ornamental! Thrives in long, hot summers. Yields for hundreds of years!

SIZE h*w	SUN	SOIL	WATER	EDIBLE
30ft*20ft	full	poor - OK	average	fruit, oil

PROPAGATION METHODS

- SEEDS: Germinates at 68-80F. High germination rates. Seedlings used as a rootstock.
- CUTTINGS: Half-ripe wood, 5 inch in summer; usually bears in 4 years.

RECIPE

CURED OLIVES: Wash olives. Cut in the meat of the olive (top to bottom) without cutting the pit. In a pan, soak the olives in brine (1 part salt to 10 parts water). Weight olives to submerge and cover. Cure for 3 weeks, stirring daily and changing the brine water weekly. Taste. May take up to 5-6 weeks to remove bitterness. Then, jar olives in fresh brine, add 4 tablespoons of vinegar and top with a layer of oil.

CULTURAL SIGNIFICANCE

- More than 80 olive groves in Florida (as of 2018) ranging from small back yard plots to 20-acre high density groves
- Rich history—included in ancient mythology and used as a symbol of peace. Among the oldest known cultivated trees; tended before written language. One of the first plants mentioned in the Hebrew Bible (the Christian Old Testament); a dove with an olive branch symbolized the flood ended (Genesis, 8:11)

CULINARY USE

Fruit
Described as alternate-year-bearing species: a year of heavy fruit production followed by a year of light production. Olives must be cured or are otherwise toxic (e.g., with water, brine, oil, salt). Florida growers, often brine Arbequina olives and enjoy them year-round. Cured fruits eaten as a relish, or stuffed for use in breads, soups, salads etc. The Arbequina oil is mild, buttery and very flavorful. Low polyphenol levels and high polyunsaturated fat results in relatively low stability and short shelf-life though.

NOTE: 'Extra Virgin' olive oil is produced by cold pressing the seeds without using heat or chemical solvents.

CAUTIONS & CONSIDERATIONS

Health
CAUTION: Olives must be cured or are otherwise toxic. Good source of Vit. D.

Pests
Relatively pest- and disease-free trees: Olive fly, iron chlorosis, nematodes, scale and verticillium wilt.

Landscape design
Fast growing & self-pollinating but yield benefits greatly from co-planting (e.g. with Mission, Arbosona or Koroneiki varieties). Only prune in low-yield years.

Oyster Mushroom

Pleurotus citrinopileatus

HARDINESS ZONES: 7 TO 11

This tropical "Golden" oyster thrives in warm weather and produces colorful clusters of daffodil-yellow caps visible from afar. A great mushroom for beginners and can be grown in garden beds on straw or on mulch around perennials! Grows quickly and is one of the most spectacular of all gourmet mushrooms! In the Pleurotaceae family.

SIZE h*w	SUN	SOIL	WATER	EDIBLE
2in*2in	partial to dappled	well-draining	needs constant moisture to fruit	fruit/ caps & stem

PROPAGATION METHODS

- SPAWN: Optimum fruiting temperatures 75-90F. Inoculated sawdust or grain on straw. Fruit within a few weeks. Biological efficiency rating: 25-75%.

RECIPE

STUFFED EGGS WITH MUSHROOMS: 6 large hard-cooked eggs, peeled; 1 ½ cup coarsely chopped mushrooms, 1tsp oil, 3 tsp chives, ½ salt, ¼ tsp pepper.

Saute mushroom in oil until limp, add herbs, salt, pepper, mix in with yolks, fill the whites.

CULINARY USE

Fruit

A widely used edible mushroom. Cook thoroughly. Can easily replace button mushrooms in most recipes. Although they resemble a bouquet of yellow flowers, the caps smell like fresh watermelon with fruity, wine-like notes, and taste like roasted cashews when sautéed in oil. Considered a choice edible mushroom. Good sources of potassium, vitamin B2, vitamin B3, and vitamin B5. Cut forming clusters at base for easy harvesting. Cook thoroughly. Do not drink alcohol 48 hours before or after eating mushrooms - gastrointestinal upset may occur.

FEATURES: Gills: white. Stem: short, asymmetrically placed, white. Spore Print: Pale lilac.

CULTURAL SIGNIFICANCE

- Research suggests role in treatment of tumors & high cholesterol
- In far eastern Russia, P. citrinopileatus, are called il'mak, and are one of the most popular wild edible mushrooms; 'tamgitake,' in Japanese - popular with hobbyist growers
- Most commonly decays hardwoods such as oak, beech, elm; a saprophytic fungus
- Species shows potential in mycoremediation and clean up of contamination

CAUTIONS & CONSIDERATIONS

Health
CAUTION: Don't eat any mushroom unless you are absolutely certain of its identity! Similar-looking mushrooms may be toxic (e.g., Jack O'lantern/ Omphalotus olearius: gills = bioluminescent; stem= orange; digestive upset).

Pests
Many insects and mammals consume mushrooms.

Landscape design
Compare with Pink Oyster (Pleurotus djamor).

Papaya
Carica papaya

HARDINESS ZONES: 10 TO 12

This plant resembles a tree but is actually an herb. Adapts to practically any well drained soil. Just be sure to select a hermaphrodite variety. Prolific, fast growing, and space efficient. Nearly all parts of the plant are edible or medicinal. The fruit is one of the first Kenyan kids eat when they wean and is part of the daily diet. First transgenic/ polygamous fruit tree to have its genome sequenced! Can produce 100-200 lbs of fruit yearly! In the Caricaceae family.

SIZE h*w	SUN	SOIL	WATER	EDIBLE
10ft*3ft varies by type	full sun	well-draining	moist but dry in winter	fruit, seeds, leaves, flowers

PROPAGATION METHODS

- SEEDS: Germinates at 75-85F. Plant in large containers to limit transplanting. Dioecious varieties. Seek out hermaphroditic seeds for guaranteed harvest (e.g., Solo Sunset).

RECIPE

SWEET & SPICY GREEN PAPAYA: Peel, de-seed, chop, and boil 1 large green papaya in water for 20 min. Drain. Over low heat, combine 1/3 c nut butter with 2 tbs water & 1/4 c maple syrup. Toss in papaya and add chopped chili pepper, salt & pepper to taste. Cover, and simmer on medium-low until fragrant and flavors meld (about 10 minutes).

CULTURAL SIGNIFICANCE

- Folk healing uses (e.g., Leaves used as a purgative. Skin of the papaya used externally as treatment for skin wounds; seeds are a strong anti-parasitic)
- Green papaya fruit latex is rich in papain for tenderizing meat and other proteins
- Enzymes dried as a powder to aid digestion
- Anti-aging soaps made from fruit extracts
- Stems used as straws

CULINARY USE

Fruit
Edible raw when ripe or cooked when unripe. Usually boiled when green but raw, green papayas are used to make a type of salad resembling coleslaw: Spiralize, soak in water, drain and top with preferred dressing.

Flowers
Male flower buds are sautéed and stir-fried.

Seeds
Black seeds of the papaya have a sharp, spicy taste; grounded for use as black pepper.

Leaves
In some parts of Asia, the young leaves of the papaya are steamed and eaten like spinach given their high protein content. See health notes.

CAUTIONS & CONSIDERATIONS

Health
CAUTION: Older leaves contain the alkaloid carpaine. Unripe papaya releases a latex fluid (a potential allergen).

Pests
Ringspot virus, fungus (anthracnose), papaya wasp, whitefly, mite, fruit fly, root rot - wet soil is lethal.

Landscape design
Some pinch the seedlings to encourage multiple trunks. Compare with FL native: PawPaw (Asimina triloba).

Passionflower

Passiflora incarnata

HARDINESS ZONES: 7 TO 11

A Florida native, butterfly host plant, and short-lived perennial. Also called, "Maypop"! A fast-growing, deciduous vine with a history of use in folk healing, especially to counteract insomnia & anxiety. Showy and fragrant flowers! Hardiest and arguably the prettiest of the passionflower vines! Also, the most commonly used in phytomedicine. Does not have to climb to produce flowers & fruit. In the Passifloraceae family.

SIZE h*w	SUN	SOIL	WATER	EDIBLE
6ft+*1ft	full	well-draining	drought tolerant	fruit, flowers

PROPAGATION METHODS

- SEEDS: Germinates at 70-85 in 12 months. Soak.
- CUTTINGS: 6" young shoots in spring. Fully mature wood in early summer - 3 months to root but high success rate.
- DIVISION: Spreads by root suckers.

RECIPE

PASSIONFRUIT CORDIAL: 1 c passion fruit pulp, 3/4 c agave, 3 c water.

Add ingredients to a glass jar and stir until agave dissolves. Cover jar with cloth secured with a rubber band. Stir daily. Within 3-4 days, bubbles will appear. After 7 days, bottle & store in fridge for up to 6 months. Served as an aperitif.

CULINARY USE

Fruit
Peeled & eaten raw or cooked in jellies, jams. Natives made a beverage by crushing and straining the seeds from the pulp. This juice was also thickened with flour into a pudding. Fruits appear July to October and mature to a yellowish color in fall. Fruit starts out green and eventually fill with a kind of jelly while also turning yellow. Only consume fully ripe. Allow to ripen on vine. Plants grown from seed can vary considerably in the flavor & texture of their fruit. Blooms and fruits on new growth. The flavor is similar to muscadine. Rich source of vitamins A, C, B1, & B2, as well as calcium, phosphorus, niacin, and iron.

Flowers
Flowers are often cooked as a vegetable or made into syrup. Used as a garnish. Considered medicinal.

CULTURAL SIGNIFICANCE

- Folk healing use (e.g., Leaves used to calm nerves/ as sedative) but Cherokee also boiled leaves as food source. Flowers used for anxiety, insomnia
- Genus name from Latin "passio" - "passion" & "flos" - flower. Symbolism: Christ crucifixion
- Larval host for butterflies (e.g., Gulf Fritillary & Zebra Longwing - state butterfly of Florida)
- Flower extract used in cosmetics to soothe, protect the skin or act as a conditioner

CAUTIONS & CONSIDERATIONS

Health
CAUTION: Flammable in drought. Consume in moderation. May be confused with other species with lesser edibility. Identify carefully.

Pests
Resilient. Root rot in flood prone areas.

Landscape design
Grow on a trellis away from home. Prune in early spring. Bears in 2 yrs. Aggressive spread in ideal conditions. Many other (50-60) edible varieties; can cross-pollinate. Compare with Passiflora coccinea, P. edulis, or P. ligularis.

Pepper
Piper nigrum

HARDINESS ZONES: 10 TO 12

A fast-growing, perennial vine in Piperaceae family. Widely cultivated for peppercorns as a spice. Regarded as a stimulating expectorant in Western, Chinese, and Ayurvedic medicine. Used in Indian cooking for over 4000 years! Not yet grown commercially in the U.S. - A potential opportunity! World's most traded spice! Lives over 30 years! Considered king of spices! Used in perfume! Historically referred to as "black gold."

SIZE h*w	SUN	SOIL	WATER	EDIBLE
19ft*3ft	partial	well-draining	average	fruits, seed

PROPAGATION METHODS

- SEEDS: Germinates at 80-90F in 3 weeks. Remove mesocarp and shade dry.
- CUTTINGS: 8in shoot after flowering with leaves.
- DIVISION: Suckers in spring.

RECIPE

PEPPERCORN SAUCE: 2 tbs green peppercorns, 1 tbs shallots, 1 c nut milk, 2 tbs oil, 2 tsp flour, salt to taste

Heat oil in skillet over medium heat. Add shallots & peppercorns; stir until softened (3 min). Add flour; stir until integrated (1 min). Add milk, increase heat to medium-high. Simmer, stirring, until sauce reduces by half. Salt to taste. Drizzle on veggies.

CULTURAL SIGNIFICANCE

- Inhibits mold growth in ferments; anti-microbial
- Used in folk healing as a pungent, aromatic, warming, antiseptic herb (e.g., fruits to lower fever, improve digestion; a circulatory stimulant; to decrease nasal congestion, skin inflammation)
- Essential oil used in Ayurvedic massage for rheumatic pain, to relieve toothache

CULINARY USE

Fruit & Seed

Known as peppercorns. Typically dried, & ground into a powder known as black pepper. Spicier when freshly ground due to the volatile oils. Used as a condiment. Harvested when fruits begin to turn red (before fully ripe). Each fruit turns black after about 3 days of drying. Grinding the peppercorns produces black pepper. White pepper is obtained when the fruits are allowed to turn red and fully ripen. The red outer covering is removed and the kernel ground. Unripe green fruits are pickled in vinegar as a relish.

Believed to increase absorption of minerals, vitamins, herbs, and supplements.

CAUTIONS & CONSIDERATIONS

Health
No known adverse health effects.

Pests
Root rot, pepper weevil, pepper flea beetle, aphids and mealybugs.

Landscape design
Shield from wind. Trellis using an 26ft × 26 ft spacing. After main stem is established, many side shoots create a bushy column. Grown as a houseplant but won't fruit indoors. Not to be confused with Brazilian peppertree (Schinus terebinthifoliais) - the Category I invasive plants in Florida.

Phenomenal Lavender

Lavandula x intermedia

HARDINESS ZONES: 5A TO 9A

Also called, "Lavandin" or "Province." The silvery foliage adds fall interest to the food forest. A new, highly fragrant hybrid growing as a dense clump. Believed to be the best lavender for Florida! Able to withstand summer heat and humidity! Edible, medicinal, & aromatic! A sub-shrub in the mint (Lamiaceae) family.

SIZE h*w	SUN	SOIL	WATER	EDIBLE
18in*18in	full	well-draining	drought tolerant	leaves, petals, flowering tips

PROPAGATION METHODS

- CUTTINGS: Cut tender shoots 2-4 in long with 3-5 nodes. Avoid woody stems. Cut below last node. Roots in soil. Place cuttings in full sun to avoid fungal problems.

RECIPE

LAVENDER VINAIGRETTE: Immerse 3 tbs lavender springs in water to remove any insects or soil. Then lay on cloth to dry. Combine lavender, 1c vinegar and 3c oil in a glass jar. Cover. Shake until well combined. Allow to infuse for 4-6 weeks at room temperature. Shake daily. Strain. Add honey, salt & pepper to taste. Store in the fridge.

CULTURAL SIGNIFICANCE

- Grown commercially for antiseptic, skincare oil
- Mass planted as a low-growing hedge
- Used for mummification & perfume by ancient Egyptians, Phoenicians, & Arabians
- Greeks and Romans bathed in lavender scented water - named after Latin word "lavo" - "to wash." WWI nurses bathed soldiers' wounds with lavender washes
- Queen Elizabeth I drank lavender tea for migraines; believed to ease anxiety

CULINARY USE

Leaves, Petals, & Flowering tips
Sweet, floral flavor, with lemon and citrus notes. Can be eaten raw as a condiment, or in stews, soups, and salads. Use in moderation - potency increases with drying. Too much will make your dish bitter. Use the spikes or stems for making kabobs. Just place your favorite fruit, veggies, or meat on the stems and grill. Add as a garnish for champagne, chocolate cake, sorbets or ice creams.

The flowers, both fresh and dried, can be used for making tea. Oils from the blooms are used as a food flavoring. Substituted for rosemary in bread recipes. Can be put in sugar, salt, vinegar, or oil to infuse it for cake, buns or custards. Often ground in a coffee grinder or mashed with mortar and pestle.

CAUTIONS & CONSIDERATIONS

Health
No known adverse health effects. Believed to have calming effects and relax muscles. Antioxidant activities.

Pests
Excess moisture causes foliage diseases.

Landscape design
Needs air circulation. Don't crowd. Avoid fall trimming - new growth may not be cold hardy. Use gravel or rocks as mulch to reflect sunlight & heat. Prune after flowering to encourage more blooms. Over 450 lavender varieties.

Pickerelweed
Pontederia cordata

HARDINESS ZONES: 3 TO 11

Also called, "Tuckahoe," this pretty and deciduous Florida native is in the Pontederiaceae family. Showy 1/3 inch-long purplish flowers attract hummingbirds, butterflies and native bees! A good companion plant for cattails! Eaten by Mayans, cultivated as an ornamental, and granted the Royal Horticultural Society's Award of Garden Merit.

SIZE h*w	SUN	SOIL	WATER	EDIBLE
3ft*1ft	full	wet	seasonal flooding - OK	seed, stalk, leaves

PROPAGATION METHODS

- SEEDS: Germinates at 77-85F. Sow in pots standing in 1 inch of water. Barely cover. Submerge in 2 in of water after seedlings emerge
- DIVISION: Can be planted out directly.

RECIPE

PICKEREL PORRIDGE: Tap seeds out of flower stalk into a bowl. Lift and gently toss seeds while blowing off any husks. Soak in water overnight. Discard water. Boil equal parts water and seed for 10 minutes. Add sweetener and salt to taste.

Alternatively, feed the unsalted porridge to a sourdough starter.

CULTURAL SIGNIFICANCE

- A valuable wildlife food source. Dragonflies & damselflies lay eggs on plant stems. Fish (e.g., pickerel) seek shelter in plant clumps; hence the name "pickerel weed." Ducks consume the seeds; muskrats and nutria consume rhizomes. The bee (Dufourea novae-angliae) visits this plant and no other
- "Cordata" means "heart" in Latin in reference to the leaf, but shapes vary significantly
- Helps stabilize pond banks to prevent erosion

CULINARY USE

Seed
Starchy seeds are cooked/ boiled like rice or dried and ground into a flour for bread or cakes or to thicken stews and soups. Nutty flavor & texture. Can be roasted and eaten as nuts. Added to granola cereals. In Florida, it can bloom from March - November. Seeds are gathered in late summer or early autumn off the mature fruit spikes. Described as an enjoyable and filling food.

Stalk & Leaves
Young leafstalks and unrolling leaves are cooked like spinach or added to soups. Best gathered in early summer before they have fully unrolled.

NOTE: It is always best to cook water plants to kill any bacteria or other water-born parasites.

CAUTIONS & CONSIDERATIONS

Health
No known adverse health effects. Only consume from plants grown in non-polluted water.

Pests
No serious insect problems or diseases. Spider mites.

Landscape design
Plant around margins of a pond or bogs. Seldom grows in water more than three feet deep. Can spread rapidly to form colonies. Plant 4 feet apart. Can behave invasively. Dormant in the winter.

Pigeon Pea

Cajanus cajan

HARDINESS ZONES: 9 TO 12

A fast-growing, petite tree producing peas for several years. Provides high levels of protein and the important amino acids methionine, lysine, and tryptophan. Hardy and widely adaptable, pigeon peas are a critical, staple crop for food security. Cultivation dates back at least 3,500 years. First seed legume plant to have its complete genome sequenced!! In the Fabaceae family.

SIZE h*w	SUN	SOIL	WATER	EDIBLE
10ft*6ft	full	prefers sandy	drought tolerant	seeds, seedpods, leaves, and young shoots.

PROPAGATION METHODS

- SEEDS: Germinates at 75-86ºF. High germination rate. Allow seed pods to dry while still on the plant.
- CUTTINGS: Roots readily in soil.

RECIPE

HUMMUS: ½ cup dried peas, pinch of sea salt, ½ tsp black pepper, 2 tsp oil, 1 tsp citrus juice, 1 tbs sunflower butter.

Wash shelled peas, soak 12-24 hrs. Discard water. Rinse. Boil 45 min. Add all ingredients and blend to a paste. Serve on crackers or veggies.

CULTURAL SIGNIFICANCE

- Peas make a well-balanced meal favored by nutritionists
- Grown to host scale insects for lac/ shellac
- Planted as green manure
- Stems are used as material in making baskets and in thatching
- Wood is used in light construction
- Nitrogen fixing soil improver and fodder
- Contour hedge in erosion control

CULINARY USE

Seeds/ Peas
Prepared green as peas. Also used dried in stew or for flour. Dried peas may be sprouted briefly, then cooked, for a rich flavor. Sprouting also enhances digestibility. Seed may be used instead of soy bean to make tempeh or tofu. Popular pigeon pea dishes include arroz con gandules (Latin America - rice and green pigeon peas, Christmas dish). Contains amino acids often missing in vegetarian diets. Seeds are similar to soy in protein content - 28 to 36%.

Leaves & Young Shoots
Leaves and young shoots cooked and used as a vegetable imparting a strong, spicy odor. Commonly consumed in Ethiopia.

CAUTIONS & CONSIDERATIONS

Health
No known adverse health effects. Dried seeds are best soaked, then cooked to remove phytic acid. Avoid discolored seeds - may be contaminated with ergot.

Pests
Pod-sucking bugs - affected seeds become shriveled with dark patches.

Landscape design
Crop can last three to five years (although the seed yield drops considerably after the first two years); harvest begins when about 75% of the pods have turned brown.

Pine
Pinus elliottii

HARDINESS ZONES: 7 TO 11

A long-lived evergreen in the Pinaceae family. Pines are among the most commercially important trees, valued for timber & pulp. Seeds eaten since Paleolithic period. An attractive wildlife habitat. 171 species of insects use this as a host plant! Seeds are eaten by birds & deer browse seedlings. Slash Pine (Pinus elliotii) has the widest distribution in Florida! Pinus elliottii var. densa listed as 'Near Threatened'. 7 FL native pines, many with edibility. Find your local species: www.nwf.org/NativePlantFinder

SIZE h*w	SUN	SOIL	WATER	EDIBLE
80ft*60ft	full to partial	acidic, sandy - OK	seasonal flooding - OK	needles, bark, seeds

PROPAGATION METHODS

- SEEDS: Germinates at 80-90F in 15 - 20 days with 80 - 95% success. Can hybridize which may impact edibility. Self-seeds. Used as rootstock for grafting more productive species. Viable for years.

RECIPE

PINE NEEEDLE TEA: Pour 1c steaming hot water onto 1/4c washed, chopped, pine needles (greens only) stir until needles lose color. Strain and serve. A refreshing decongestant!

OPTIONAL: Add sweetener of choice.

CULINARY USE

Leaves
Fragrant needles are 8-10" long grouped in 2-3. Sold commercially for tea! High in vitamins A & C (4x citrus!). Used as a folk remedy for colds. Infused in cocktails & desserts. Needles placed on grills to imbue flavor. NOTE: Additional edibility (bark, seeds) applies to pine species as a whole. No info specific to Slash Pines found.

Bark
Soft, moist, white inner bark (cambium) edible. Best eaten dried and ground into a flour for "bark bread" or thickeners in stews, soups.

Seeds
Shell must be removed before the pine nut can be eaten. Nearly all pine seeds are edible, but most species have very small nuts - slash pine has very tiny cones. Used in salads, sauces, puddings, cookies, cakes, & more.

CULTURAL SIGNIFICANCE

- Cones used in crafts; nut shell for jewelry; boughs for wintertime aroma & greenery; needles for baskets, trays, pots & essential oil
- Adirondack Indians named from "atirú:taks,"- "tree eaters"; pollen & cambium used for flour
- Pine resin has many uses - a glue to close wounds, start fires/ make candles; once a major industry in Florida; vanillin flavoring
- Choctawhatchee sand pine considered best native Christmas tree

CAUTIONS & CONSIDERATIONS

Health
CAUTION: Resin may irritate skin. Flammable. Some poisonous look-alikes (e.g., Yew -Taxus; Australian Pine - Araucana heterophylla; Ponderosa - Pinus ponderosa).

Pests
Resilient: Nematodes, borers/ miners, canker, chlorosis, rust.

Landscape design
Horizontal branches break easily. Compare with Monkey Puzzle Tree/ Bunya Bunya (Araucaria bidwillii), Stone Pines (P. cembra & P. monophylla), Digger Pine (P. sabiniana), Nut Pine (P. edulis) & Umbrella Pine (P. pinea).

Pineapple
Ananas comosus

HARDINESS ZONES: 9 TO 11

Named for pine-cone-like shape. This terrestrial bromeliad actually produces a composite fruit consisting of 100-200 berries. A fast-growing and drought tolerant succulent. The plant may continue to live and fruit for over 50 years, reproducing abundantly. Many named varieties are suitable for growing indoors. 3rd most important tropical fruit in the world! Fruits within 3 years. In the Bromeliaceae family.

SIZE h*w	SUN	SOIL	WATER	EDIBLE
3ft*3ft	full to partial	acidic - OK	drought tolerant	fruit, buds, shoot, stem

PROPAGATION METHODS

- CUTTINGS: Propagated by crowns (fruit tops), slips (peduncles below fruit), suckers (along stem) or via old stems.
- SEED: Germinates at 64-75°F. Sprout in agar.

RECIPE

GRILLED PINEAPPLE WITH MINT SAUCE: Cut 4, ½ thick slices of fresh cored and skinned pineapple. For sauce: Collect any excess juice and remaining pulp; puree with 1 tps maple syrup & 2 tbs finely shredded fresh mint leaves. For grilled portion: Place slices on grill for 1-2 minutes on each side to mark and flavor. Plate & drizzle sauce over them.

CULTURAL SIGNIFICANCE

- 17th century European icon of luxury, hospitality
- King Charles II posed with pina in portrait
- Woven into lustrous lace-like nipis or pina cloth among Filipino upper class
- Fiber made into cordage for nets, hammocks, jewelry
- Folk healing uses (e.g., sour, unripe fruit - ease sore throats; strong purgative; ripe fruit - relieves constipation; tea from peel - arthritis)

CULINARY USE

Fruit
Pick when ripe as starch may not convert to sugar off plant. Do not refrigerate (chill-sensitive plant). Peeled, cored slices with a cherry serve as a garnish for ham. Popular on pizza. A jelly-like dessert is made by fermenting juice. Some dip slices in mild salt-water solution to intensify the pineapple flavor. Thin slivers with core are dehydrated over cupcake tin forms to create pineapple "flowers" - mini, edible serving bowls. Used for cocktails: tepache, chicha & guarapo. Juice is a meat tenderizer. Good source of manganese, potassium!

Buds, Shoot and Stem
Terminal buds and flowering stem are cooked as a vegetable; added to soups or eaten raw. Young shoots are eaten in salads or curries.

CAUTIONS & CONSIDERATIONS

Health
CAUTION: Spines on some varieties. Bromelain enzyme aids digestion/ anti-inflammatory but is hazardous in those who are protein deficient; some react with hives.
Pests
Wilt disease vectored by mealybugs; Heart-rot from fungi/ wet conditions.
Landscape design
Groundcover in mass planting. Pollinated by hummingbirds or bats. Space 2ft. Five main varieties: ananassoides, bracteatus, comosus, erectifolius, parguazensis.

Pistacio
Pistacia vera

HARDINESS ZONES: 7 TO 10

One of the most important commercial nut crops worldwide! A deciduous tree in the cashew/ Anacardiaceae family that loves long hot summers. Among the oldest flowering nut trees. Domesticated about 8000 years ago. A good source of vitamin K, which is necessary for good bone health! In Assyria & Greece, pistachio was considered a powerful aphrodisiac. Can live several hundred years - 300 is common! A desert plant highly tolerant of saline soil.

SIZE h*w	SUN	SOIL	WATER	EDIBLE
30ft*20ft	full	well-draining; poor, saline - OK	drought tolerant	fruit, seed

PROPAGATION METHODS

- SEEDS: Germinates at 75-85F. <u>Dioecious.</u> Plant one male plant for every five females.
- CUTTINGS: Half-ripe wood from juvenile trees
- LAYERING: In spring or summer.

RECIPE

PISTACIO ICE CREAM: Slice 2 very ripe bananas. Freeze overnight. De-shell & soak 1 cup of pistachios overnight in the fridge. Drain. Blend into a butter. Add frozen bananas. Puree all, adding 1 or 2 tbs of coconut milk as needed to create a smooth ice cream.

OPTIONAL: Add salt & sweetener to taste.

CULINARY USE

Fruit

Matures in clusters that resemble grapes. Made into marmalade.

Seeds

Seed is rich in oil & has a mild flavor. Widely used in confectionery, ice cream, cakes, pies etc. Gaining popularity as a nut butter. Edible oil obtained from seed - yields up to 40% of non-drying oil. Nutrient-dense; high concentrations of unsaturated fatty acids and low concentration of saturated fat. Shells typically split naturally prior to harvest, with a hull covering the intact seeds. The hull protects the kernel from invasion by molds and insects.

NOTE: Avoid eating any pistachios with gray to black filament-like growth: Unsafe to eat; mold-infected.

CULTURAL SIGNIFICANCE

- Cultivated in the gardens of Babylon under King Merodach-Baladan II around 700 BCE
- Male trees yield high grade resin used in paints, lacquers etc.
- Persian couples would wait under pistachio trees in the moonlight & to hear cracking pistachio shells - considered romantic
- Used in folk healing (e.g., Seed believed to be sedative, stomachic & a tonic for the brain)

CAUTIONS & CONSIDERATIONS

Health

CAUTION: As with other tree seeds, aflatoxin, a carcinogenic chemical produced by molds, is found in poorly harvested pistacios. Pistacio in bulk containers are prone to self-heating/ spontaneous combustion. Related to poison ivy - contains urushiol, an irritant/ allergen.

Pests

Panicle & shoot blight; anthracnose fungus.

Landscape design

Requires 1k chilling hours. Matures slowly. Bears 7-10 years. Maximum production after 20 years. In the wild - classified as 'Near Threatened' in the IUCN Red List (2007).

Pomelo
Citrus maxima

HARDINESS ZONES: 9 TO 11

Sometimes spelled, "pummelo" but originally called "shaddock" after the captain of an East India Company ship who brought it to Jamaica in 1696. A luscious food and showy evergreen in the Rutaceae family. Huge fruit average 8" in diameter - reportedly the largest citrus in the world! Fruits year-round in ideal conditions! 70 - 100 fruit per tree per year! Excellent source of vitamin C & A, dietary fibers and minerals like potassium, iron & calcium. Grown as an edible, ornamental shade tree.

SIZE h*w	SUN	SOIL	WATER	EDIBLE
20ft*18ft	full to partial	sandy - OK	average	flowers, fruit

PROPAGATION METHODS

- SEEDS: Germinates at 65-77F. Long spines if grown by seed. Polyembryonic: genetically identical to parent if no cross-pollination/hybridization occurred.
- CUTTINGS: Half-ripe wood. Root easily.

RECIPE

CANDIED POMELO PEEL: Peel 3 pomelos. Cover peels with cold water, bring to a boil, then reduce to a simmer. Simmer until soft. Drain. Cool. Using a spoon, remove white rind from peels. Cut peel into thin strips. Place peels back into pot with 1.5 cups of maple syrup. Bring to a boil, then reduce to simmer. Simmer until peels are transparent (30min). Strain. Cool. Coat with maple sugar.

CULTURAL SIGNIFICANCE

- The juice used in the TANG breakfast drink
- Flowers are highly aromatic - made into perfumes in North Vietnam
- In China, pomelo is an auspicious gift at religious & cultural festivals like the New Year
- Wood is heavy & fine-grained - suitable for carving & tool handles
- Folk healing uses (e.g., decoction of fresh leaves used for headache by inhalation of vapor)

CULINARY USE

Fruit

Very popular fruit in Southeast Asia and China. Taste is reminiscent of grapefruit, but sweet instead of sour edible flesh. Pulp is colored white, yellow or pink - depending on cultivar. Juicy pulp eaten raw, in fruit salads or juiced. The skinned segments are broken apart and used in salads, desserts or preserves. The rind is rich in pectin for making jelly. The peel is often candied. Generally harvested when just beginning to turn yellow. Keeps for long periods & ships well because of thick peel. After 3 months, the peel will be deeply wrinkled but the pulp will be juicier and more appealing in flavor than in the fresh fruit. Turns bitter after 4 or more months of storage.

Flowers

Used for scenting tea. Among the largest citrus flowers.

CAUTIONS & CONSIDERATIONS

Health

One quarter of pomelo provides 130% of daily requirements of vitamin C. CAUTION: Peels, like that of other citrus fruits, contain skin irritants.

Pests

Citrus diseases; scale, spider mites, mealybugs, leaf-miners, stinging red ant (Pheidologeton sp.) and aphids.

Landscape design

Principal ancestor of grapefruit. Shelter from wind. Espaliered. Common varieties include: Chandler, Ichang, Red Shaddock, Reinking, & Webber.

Porterweed

Stachytarpheta jamaicensis

HARDINESS ZONES: 9A TO 11

A low-growing and sprawling wildflower. This evergreen just might bloom all year. Native to the southern coastal regions of Florida, as well as throughout the Caribbean. The foaming property of brewed leaves is linked to the common name, "porterweed:" The tea resembles porter-style beer. Great for xeriscaping. Planted as an ornamental in butterfly gardens. Considered by herbalists to be anti-inflammatory and calming! In the Verbenaceae family.

SIZE h*w	SUN	SOIL	WATER	EDIBLE
1.5ft*3ft	full to partial	well-draining; poor, acidic - OK	drought tolerant	leaves, stems, flowers

PROPAGATION METHODS

- SEEDS: Germinates at 75-80F. Hybridizes. Self-sows readily.
- CUTTINGS: Stem and tip cuttings root in water or soil.

RECIPE

PORTERWEED TEA: Steep 1 tbs of dried, washed leaves in 1 cup of steaming hot water (not boiling). Allow to steep covered, 5 minutes.

Strain and add sweetener of choice to taste. Drink with caution as a medicinal tea.

CULTURAL SIGNIFICANCE

- Larval host for tropical buckeye butterfly (Junonia genoveva) & provides nectar for many other species as well as hummingbirds
- Used in folk healing (e.g., for antibacterial, anti-inflammatory, & antifungal properties; for cold & flu. Decoction used as bath detox remedy - for headache; tea for reflux)
- Found naturally occurring in coconut plantations in the Caribbean
- Flowers are used to make earrings

CULINARY USE

Leaves

A foaming, porter-like brew, much like beer, is made from at least one species in the Bahamas. Green leaves are chopped and cooked alone or mixed with other vegetables. Often blended with coconut milk and groundnuts. Astringent, bitter flavor. Added to beer brewing like hops.

Flowers

Flowers may be eaten raw and have a delicate, mushroom-like flavor. A beautiful addition to salads! Flower blooms last about a day.

Stems

Flower spikes can be used the same way as a bay leaf to season soups or stews. Tips of the twigs are used as a pot herb and condiment. Become woody as the plant ages.

CAUTIONS & CONSIDERATIONS

Health
CAUTION: Consume in moderation. Medicinal. Not recommended in pregnancy or cases of low-blood pressure. May be confused with Verbena officinalis.

Pests
Resilient. Root rot in wet areas.

Landscape design
Used as a pollinator-friendly groundcover. Lives up to 5 years. Compare with Category II invasive Stachytarpheta cayennensis (3ft) or Stachytarpheta urticifolia (5ft); also "porterweed" but grow erect. Coral flower varieties also exist.

Prickly Pear Cactus

Opuntia ficus-indica

HARDINESS ZONES: 8 TO 11

"Nopale cactus" is a fast-growing succulent and ideal crop for dry areas. Minimal maintenance. Highly nutritious. As economically important as maize & blue agave in Mexico - often eaten daily! Outstanding landscape value as a screen, or fence. Economically significant. Cultivated since pre-Columbian times. In the Cactaceae family.

SIZE h*w	SUN	SOIL	WATER	EDIBLE
16ft*16ft	full to partial	sandy - OK	drought tolerant	fruit, seeds, leaves, flowers, gum

PROPAGATION METHODS

- CUTTINGS: Cuttings of leaf pads; remove from the plant, leave to thoroughly dry and callous. Pot up into a sandy compost. Very easy to root quickly. NOTE: Hybridizes easily.

RECIPE

GRILLED NOPALE: While wearing gloves, use a flat, paring or filet knife and scrape along the surface at each bump to remove spines (even if "spineless"). Cut all edges off to remove edge spines as well. Rinse. Lightly oil & season with salt, & pepper. Grill on open fire to burn off any missed spines (10 min each side). Slice and serve.

CULTURAL SIGNIFICANCE

- Provides water for cattle during drought
- Erosion-control hedge
- Cochineal insect in fruit yields magenta dye
- Juice of boiled stem segments is very sticky – added to plaster as an adhesive
- Mucilage from prickly pear may serve as bioremediation such as with oil spills
- Growing near the front door believed to bring good luck/ protection
- Pads used as poultices

CULINARY USE

Fruit/ Seeds
Also called "tuna." Edible raw, cooked or dried for later use; watermelon flavor. One of the highest concentrations of vitamin C of any fruit! Fermented into alcohol. Seeds edible and swallowed by most. Seeds also ground into meal - contains beneficial linoleic acid.

Flowers
Edible raw; colorful garnish.

Leaves
Often BBQ'd as a French beans substitute. Sliced into strips & fried with eggs and jalapeños as a breakfast treat. Slices infused in water as a tea for stomach issues. Nutritive value decreases with age of cladodes. Eat young.

Gum
Edible gum is obtained from the stem.

CAUTIONS & CONSIDERATIONS

Health
Rich in bioactive (phytochemicals) compounds. CAUTION: often confused with other species (any white sapped cactus is poisonous). Barbed glochids(hairs) - Cook on open flame to burn off. Good source of vitamin A, calcium and magnesium.

Pests
Fungal & bacterial diseases; cottony cochineal, cactus moth.

Landscape design
Spineless varities include: Opuntia ficus-indica, O. robusta, O. streptacantha. May behave invasively. Shelter from wind.

Purple Collard

Brassica oleracea v. acephala

HARDINESS ZONES: 9 TO 12

A perennial cousin of kale and collard greens. This tree collard can grow up to 10 feet tall. Fairly rare. Purple collard trees are not only a conversation piece but a staple food source in permaculture landscape. In the Cruciferae (Brassicaceae) family. Plants in this family are historically considered the "drug of the poor" given nutrients & anti-inflammatory properties.

SIZE h*w	SUN	SOIL	WATER	EDIBLE
10ft*2ft	full to partial	prefers slightly acidic	moist	leaves, stems

PROPAGATION METHODS

- SEEDS: Germinates at 45-85F. High germination rate but flowers & seed pods rarely appear.
- CUTTINGS: Roots readily in soil; very easy to propagate.

RECIPE

STEWED COLLARDS: 12 cups leaves, 1/3 cup oil, 2 tsp minced ginger, ¼ tsp ground dried red/hot pepper, 1 tsp salt.

Remove ribs. Combine oil, ginger, pepper in pan; cook 1 min over medium. Add collards, salt, 1 ½ cups water. Cover & boil over medium-high for 8-10 min. Then uncover to evaporate water.

CULTURAL SIGNIFICANCE

- Collard cooking traditions owe a heavy debt to African culinary culture
- In 2010, purple tree collard became 'official green' of Richmond, California; considered a metaphor for what the city aspired to be: tough, healthy and productive
- Collards have been cultivated in Europe for thousands of years; cultivation dates back to Greeks and Romans in 1st Century

CULINARY USE

Leaves & Stems

Can be used raw or cooked in any recipes that call for kale, collards or cabbage. May be tough when raw but when steamed or cooked, purple collard soften nicely and may be sweeter tasting than the standard collards. Especially delicious after a cold-spell. Frost sweetens them up. Pick the youngest, freshest looking leaves throughout the year. They are usually enjoyed blanched, boiled or steamed until just tender and served alone as a green vegetable or added to stews etc. Traditionally, in the West, collards are used as a New Year's Day dish along with black-eyed peas along with cornbread; said to ensure wealth in the coming year.

CAUTIONS & CONSIDERATIONS

Health

No known hazards. NOTE: Brassica family has thyroid suppressing goitrogens. Blanch. Strain.

Pests

Vulnerable to any pest or disease that attacks garden cabbage: slug, snail, aphid and sparrow.

Landscape design

Plants can last up to 20 years! Highly productive perennial Brassica. Compare with Lacinato/ Dinosaur Kale (Brassica oleracea Lacinato).

Quinoa

Chenopodium quinoa

HARDINESS ZONES: 8 TO 10

Called the "mother of all grains" and has been called a "vegetable caviar." First cultivated over 7,000 years ago. A perennial in the Amaranthaceae family with a high-protein content. Includes all essential amino acids! More nutritious than wheat! Can be used in all the same ways as rice for savory or sweet dishes. Gluten-free! Can grow almost anywhere — salty soils, dry soils - even high altitudes. Easily digested.

SIZE h*w	SUN	SOIL	WATER	EDIBLE
6ft*1ft	full	well-draining; acidic, poor - OK	drought tolerant	grains, leaves

PROPAGATION METHODS

- SEEDS: Germinates at 65-75F. Rapid germination. Sow in situ. The seed can either be sown broadcast or in rows. Usually self-pollinates, but cross pollination occurs.

RECIPE

QUINOA PORRIDGE: Cut stalks of mature seed. Hang until dried out. Thresh to remove chaff. Winnow to remove husk. Soak 2 hours then rinse until foam disappears/ water runs clear to remove the pericarp & eliminate the bitter layer containing saponins. Dry at 115F. Toast on medium heat. Boil 1 c quinoa with 2 c nut milk, 1 tbs maple syrup & 1/8 tsp sea salt for 15 min or until liquid is absorbed.

CULTURAL SIGNIFICANCE

- Removed saponins have potential in pharmaceuticals or integrated pest management
- Chosen crop for NASA's Controlled Ecological Life Support System for long-duration human occupied space flights
- Used in the Jewish community as a flour substitute in place of leavened grains
- Can replace whole wheat as a flour in recipes at a 1:1 ratio

CULINARY USE

Seeds

Seeds are typically a pale-yellow color, but the color can vary from shades of orange, pink, red, purple, and black. Harvest continuously as seeds mature at different rates. White & yellow varieties have mildest, nutty flavor. Red & black varieties have slightly stronger, earthier flavors & hold their shape better after boiling - better for cold salads. Also, ground into flour, boiled like rice, used in soup, etc. Also made into an alcoholic beverage. Higher unsaturated fats than most grains; a rich source of iron. Officially classified as a seed but thought as a whole grain. Pre-rinsed, dried and then usually toasted before boiling as a rice substitute.

Leaves

Leaves are eaten as a leaf vegetable, much like amaranth. Cooked like spinach. Blanch then stirfy.

CAUTIONS & CONSIDERATIONS

Health

CAUTION: Wash, sook, and/or toast before consuming seed. Contains saponins. Leaves contain oxalic acid. Blanch.

Pests

Resilient: aphids, flea beetles, leaf miners affect leaves.

Landscape design

Not all varieties behave as perennials. Compare with Lezpedeza (Lespedeza bicolor), perennial buckwheat (Fagopyrum esculentum), Good King Henry (Chenopodium bonus-henricus), crabgrass (digitaria sanguinalis) or crowfoot grass (dactyloctenium aegyptium).

Red Maple

Acer rubrum

HARDINESS ZONES: 3 TO 10

A Florida native & long-lived perennial. Offers a delightful sweetener! Also called Swamp Maple. Tapped trees yield maple syrup! A deciduous, fast-growing tree in the Sapindaceae (Soapberry) family. Beautiful fall color and showy late winter & early spring flowers. Easy to grow as a handsome shade tree. Gorgeous, rounded crown.

SIZE h*w	SUN	SOIL	WATER	EDIBLE
50ft*40ft	full to partial	poor draining - OK	seasonal flooding - OK	sap, leaves, seed, inner bark

PROPAGATION METHODS

- SEEDS: Germinates at 60-75F. Ripen May - June. Self-seeds readily. Often grown from bare root seedlings & transplants.

RECIPE

MAPLE SYRUP: Use a half-inch, drill-bit pointed slightly upward to drill a 3" hole on the sunny side of the tree, 3 feet above the ground. Gently hammer a spile/ sap spigot into place with the notch facing up to hang your pail. Once you've collected a quantity in the pail, boil down to desired consistency. Adjust heat to avoid scorch.

CULINARY USE

Sap
Sweet. Used as a drink or concentrated into a syrup by boiling off the water. A good quality maple syrup. Modest yield. Harvested in late winter after leaves have dropped on a warm day, ideally following a frost. Two taps per tree.

Seeds
Present in spring. Eaten cooked. Wings are removed & the seeds boiled. About 1/5 inch long; produced in clusters. Two-winged samara. May bear fruit in as little as 5 years. Vary in bitterness. If bitter, soak in water overnight. Boiled & then roasted seeds; described as delicious.

Inner Bark
Inner bark consumed cooked - dried, ground into a powder and then used as a thickening in soups or mixed with cereals when making bread.

CULTURAL SIGNIFICANCE

- Great wildlife value! Birds eat the seeds and butterflies enjoy nectar from flowers. Larval host for numerous moths
- Wood strips used to make baskets
- The widest-ranging (north-to-south) tree species in eastern North America
- Brown & black dyes from bark
- Sap serves as drinking water when other water sources are contaminated

CAUTIONS & CONSIDERATIONS

Health
No known adverse health effects. CAUTION: Some cultivars are highly allergenic. Leaves are toxic to horses.

Pests
Aphids, leafhoppers, borers, scale & caterpillars; verticillium wilt, canker, fungal leaf spot and root rots.

Landscape design
Shelter from wind. Shallow, spreading root system. Used as a bonsai. Avoid pruning in spring when sap is running. Yields half the syrup obtained from sugar maple (A. saccharum). Compare with Easten Redbud (cercis canadensis).

Red Mombin

Spondias purpurea

HARDINESS ZONES: 10 TO 12

One of the most popular small fruits of the American tropics! A unique tree in the mango & cashew family, Anacardiaceae. Considered one of the best living fence posts and hedges for a food forest! Very easily propagated. Cultivated by Mesoamerican Indigenous populations for food & medicine over thousands of years. An ancient crop of the Mayas in Yucatán. Flowers & fruits nearly all year in ideal conditions.

SIZE h*w	SUN	SOIL	WATER	EDIBLE
32ft*32ft	full	well-draining; acidic - OK	drought tolerant; seasonal flooding - OK	fruit

PROPAGATION METHODS

- SEEDS: Germinates at 77-82F. Yields in 5 years.
- CUTTINGS: Preferred method. Even large limbs root quickly. Fruit in 2-3 years. Cuttings should be 4+ ft long & 2+ inches thick.

RECIPE

WINE: Press very ripe fruit to expel juice. Transfer to a wide mouth vessel. Stir one direction to create a funnel. Then, stir other direction to create opposing funnel & introduce oxygen. Allow to ferment 2-5 days, until bubbly. Strain. Transfer to a narrow-necked jug or container. Cover (may bubble over). Once any foaming subsides, drink or airlock.

CULTURAL SIGNIFICANCE

- Used for forest restoration affected by mining
- Light wood used in paper production
- Leaves serve as forage for livestock
- Used in folk healing (e.g., Various parts are used to treat gastric disorders - as an antidiarrheal & diuretic. Believed to have anti-inflammatory, antidiarrheal, antibacterial properties)
- Some report that seed is a viable flour source once roasted in oven at 130 °C for 30 min

CULINARY USE

Fruit

Fruit flavor and color differ by variety & cultivar. Eaten green, half mature or ripe. Ripe fruits eaten raw (skin and all) or cooked in desserts. Thin-skinned; carefully pick or cut of at the stem. Pulp is yellowish, very juicy. Flavor resembles a plum. Can be de-seeded and dried like raisins. Unripe fruits are pickled, made into a sauce or eaten with salt & vinegar as a relish-like snack. High in vitamin A. Good levels of potassium, iron and calcium. An Easter dessert/ syrup in Nicaragua is prepared by boiling red mombin with papaya, and cinnamon. Drizzled on ice cream. Strained juice of cooked fruits yields an excellent jelly, wine or vinegar.

Leaves

Young shoots and leaves are washed to remove any sap and then boiled and strained. 5.5% protein. See health notes.

CAUTIONS & CONSIDERATIONS

Health

CAUTION: In poison ivy family. Consume in moderation. Do not eat seed unless processed. Sap can cause dermatitis.

Pests

Fruit flies, mites, root rot, spot anthracnose.

Landscape design

Spreading, low-branching habit. Brittle wood, superficial rooting - shelter from wind. Drops leaves in drought. Many different varieties. Prune up to 3x per year for ideal size/shape but only take off 25% or less. Pruning enlarges fruit. Compare with Jaboticaba (Myrciaria cauliflora).

Red Roselle
Hibiscus sabdariffa

HARDINESS ZONES: 9 TO 10

Also called, "Florida Cranberry." Produces cranberry-flavored, bright calyxes used to create red beverages, jellies, pies, & teas. Adds color & value to botanical and cooking ventures. Aromatic & so easy to grow! A major cash crop in China & Sudan. The highly nutritious seeds are being researched as a protein staple. Matures in just 6 months, fruiting in November/December. Perfect timing for holidays! A flavorful relative of hibiscus & okra. In the Malvaceae family.

SIZE h*w	SUN	SOIL	WATER	EDIBLE
7ft*5ft	full to partial	well-draining	moist; flood tolerant	roots, seeds, leaves, fruits

PROPAGATION METHODS

- SEEDS: Germinate at 80-86F. Seeds ripen from October to November.
- CUTTINGS: Such plants remain smaller and are harvestable earlier.

RECIPE

"FLORIDA CRANBERRY" SAUCE: 2 c fresh, shucked roselle calyxes, 1/2 c water, 1/2 cup agave, 1/2 tsp salt, 1 tsp cinnamon.

Wash roselle & simmer in water covered until soft. Strain. Save liquid as a tea. Puree calyxes with sweetener, salt & cinnamon.

CULTURAL SIGNIFICANCE

- Decorative stalks with ripe, red fruits exported to Europe for flower arrangements
- Used in folk healing (e.g., calyx tea: relief of sore throat, to lower fever. Leaves: as a poultice to heal wounds; as a calming tea)
- Stems are a substitute for jute in weaving - called rosella hemp. Dried calyces used as red food colorant. Seed oil used in soap & cosmetics. Yellow dye from the petals

CULINARY USE

Flowers
Flowers from Aug-Oct. Harvest every 2-3 days. Flowers only last a day on the plant. Citrus-like flavor. Dehydrate to store. In Thailand tea is made from the dried flower.

Seeds
High in protein (28%). Roasted and brewed like coffee or ground for meal as a flour or added to soups and salads.

Calyxes (outer whorl of flower)
Makes a delicious tea called, "agua de Jamaica" Popular in Mexico. A substitute for cranberries! Use fresh, dried or frozen. Also, used in cordials, pies, chutney, or jams (rich in pectin). Cut off before turn browning; separate from seeds. Used to make wine. High in calcium, iron, niacin and riboflavin.

Leaves
Young leaves and tender stems used as cooked greens or added raw for a nice "zing" to a salad, drinks, or soups.

CAUTIONS & CONSIDERATIONS

Health
No known adverse health effects. Calyxes are high in antioxidants, anthocyanins.

Pests
Nematodes, mealybugs, leaf beetles, aphids, fungus.

Landscape design
Early pruning will increase branching/ more flowering shoots. One plant yields up to 12 pounds of fruits. Cut to the ground after flowering to promote perennial behavior. Compare with Lipstick Plant/ Annatto (Bixa orellana) and Vegetable Hummingbird (Sesbania grandiflora).

Root Beer Plant

Piper auritum

HARDINESS ZONES: 8 TO 11

Native to the Americas & called hoja santa/ "sacred leaf." An aromatic herb with a velvety leaf. This plant will likely show up without being planted as it spreads aggressively. Pot it up as a perfect houseplant to help curb its enthusiastic growth. Commonly used as a medicinal in Mesoamerica. In the Piperaceae family.

SIZE h*w	SUN	SOIL	WATER	EDIBLE
6ft*6ft	partial to full shade	acidic	constantly moist soil	leaves and stems

PROPAGATION METHODS

NOT RECOMMENDED
- SEEDS: Germinates 77–86F.
- CUTTINGS: Rhizomes grow readily. Grows from cuttings with nodes.

RECIPE

CURLY CRISPIES: Cut leaves into strips and fry until crisp in hot oil for about two minutes or until they turn dark green and curl up. Drain on a towel or rack. Add a pinch of salt.

Use as a garnish for any entree, especially fish or pumpkin.

CULTURAL SIGNIFICANCE

- Used in folk healing (e.g., for antifungal, antibacterial, anti-inflammatory, antidiabetic, and antiulcer properties. Used to relieve symptoms for fever & sore throat)
- Employed as bait to catch fish. Allowing fish to feed on leaves for 2 weeks seasons their flesh
- An alternative to sassafras oil; raw material for Heliotropin (fragrance) and Piperonyl Butoxide (Pyrethum synergist)

CULINARY USE

Leaves and Stems
Used fresh. Loses flavor when dried. Young leaves occasionally cooked and eaten as greens. Taste compared to licorice, mint, tarragon, and black pepper. Used in Mexican cuisine for tamales; an essential ingredient in mole verde. Used to flavor eggs and soups. In Mexico, a green liquor called verdín is made from hoja santa. In some regions of Mexico, goat cheese is wrapped in hoja santa leaves and imbued with its flavor. In Guatemala, snail soup is seasoned with its leaves & is considered a delicacy. Leaves and stems are also eaten raw in salads. A famous recipe from the Veracruz province is Pescado en Hoja Santa (fish wrapped in pepper leaves), which is baked and served with a spicy tomato sauce. Leaves used for tea & flavoring for chocolate drinks. Once a source of sassafras flavoring for root beer.

CAUTIONS & CONSIDERATIONS

Health
CAUTION: Consume in moderation. Contain safroles which give its leaves and roots a strong anise aroma - considered medicinal.

Pests
Resistant and hardy.

Landscape design
An invasive species in Florida. Plant indoors in pots; repot every 2 to 3 years. Some call for eradication. Compare with Blue Spur Flower (Coleus/ Plectranthus barbatus) which also should be grown in a pot within an enclosed area.

Rose
Rosa 'Knock Out'

HARDINESS ZONES: 4 TO 10

A deciduous perennial. Named an 'All-America Rose Selections' winner in 2000. This showy, fragrant bloomer attracts many pollinators. Queen of flowers! Roses are used in many dishes and drinks around the world. A delicious, nutritious and beautiful addition to the food forest! Symbol of love & beauty. Rose petal tea believed to help heal heartache. In the Rosaceae family and related to cherries, peaches.

SIZE h*w	SUN	SOIL	WATER	EDIBLE
5ft+*5ft+	full to partial	well-draining; slightly acidic - OK	average	petals, rose hips

PROPAGATION METHODS

- SEEDS: Germinates at 68-75F within 2 years.
- CUTTINGS: Mature wood of the current season's growth. A high percentage succeeds.
- DIVISION: Divide suckers in dormant season.

RECIPE

ROSE PETAL WATER: 1 cup washed rose petals (about 2 roses); 2 cups water.

Chop and place rose hips/petals in a stove pot on low. Cover. Do not let the water boil. After 20 minutes, the petals will be pale and the water will be colored. Store in fridge up to 3 months. Use as a tea or to flavor cookies, cakes, and more.

CULTURAL SIGNIFICANCE

- Fossil evidence shows roses are 35 million years old
- Used as confetti at celebrations
- 17th century royalty used roses as legal tender, barter & payment
- Roses live a long time - the wall of roses on the German Cathedral of Hildesheim is over 1000 years old
- Roses are mentioned in the Bible
- 54% of Ecuador & 80% of Zambia land is roses

CULINARY USE

Petals

Remove white part - bitter. Used to make rose water, baklava, ice cream, jelly and jam. Added to salads, pickled, and used make rose water or tea. Simply pull petals from the flower head so you still get rose hips. Often infused in honey. Rose buds (the unopened flowers) used tea, cocktails, desserts, or chutney.

Rose hips
Best cooked. Technically, a "false fruit" with more Vitamin C than oranges - one of the richest plant sources known. Tastes like a tangy apricot. Harvest when all green fades to red or orange. Store in the freezer until you've collected enough for jam, pudding, sauce, etc.

Leaves
Pick young for best flavor. Used as tea. Polyphenol source.

CAUTIONS & CONSIDERATIONS

Health
No known adverse health effects. Thorns. Avoid seeds/fine hairs which may cause itchiness.

Pests
Resilient. Good air circulation helps control foliar diseases.

Landscape design
Excellent hedge. May form thickets. Mulch in summer. Prune in early spring; cut just above a dormant bud. Darker-colored roses have a stronger taste. Other FL-Friendly roses: 'Louis Philippe', 'Mutabilis', and 'Mrs. B.R. Cant.' NOTE: Rosa multiflora is considered highly invasive.

Rosemary
Rosmarinus officinalis

HARDINESS ZONES: 6 TO 10

An aromatic evergreen, perennial shrub with leaves similar to Christmas tree needles. Attractive and drought tolerant. Perfect ornamental plant for xeriscape landscaping. A good indoor plant for a sunny window location. Sacred to ancient Egyptians, Romans, Greeks. Prominent in Christian mythology. Oil used in perfumes, soaps, shampoos, and cosmetics like anti-wrinkle cream. Dried sprigs burnt as incense. A symbol for remembrance. In the Lamiaceae family.

SIZE h*w	SUN	SOIL	WATER	EDIBLE
4ft*3ft	full to partial	loam; alkaline	drought tolerant	leaves, flowers

PROPAGATION METHODS

- SEEDS: Germinates at 60-64F. Seeds ripen from August to October.
- CUTTINGS: Soft new growth 4–6 in long, strip leaves from bottom, planting directly into soil.

RECIPE

ROSEMARY DAILY TONIC: 2 tbs rosemary, 1 tbs cardamon, 1 tbs coriander, 1tbs ginger, 2 c vinegar.

Dehydrate herbs. Crush with a mortar & pestle. Place in a jar. Cover with vinegar. Use a plastic lid or separate metal lid from jar with wax paper to prevent rust. Infuse 4-6 weeks. Shake often. Strain. Mix with water and honey to taste as a tonic/ tea.

CULTURAL SIGNIFICANCE

- Used in Egyptians burial rituals. Ancient Greeks created head garlands to enhance mood & concentration; believed to be a brain tonic
- Used in folk healing (e.g., As a pick-me-up when depressed, tired, nervous, or with headache. Flowers & leaves macerated in olive oil used for joint pain & to heal wounds)
- Repels insects; sachets placed in cupboards
- In Shakespeare's Winter's Tale: Act 4 Scene 4. In Don Quixote: Part I, Ch XVII

CULINARY USE

Leaves

Herbal tea made from the leaves. When roasted with meat or fish, the leaves impart a mustard-like aroma. Offers an additional fragrance of charred wood that goes well with barbecued foods. Enhances stews, breads, stuffing, herbal butters or vinegars. Pairs well with peas and spinach, and sweet biscuits, cakes, jams and jellies. Can be used fresh or dried. Chop leaves finely or include as sprigs which can be removed after cooking. A natural antioxidant & improves the shelf-life of perishable foods.

Flowers

Milder version of the leaves. An infusion of the flowering stems is used in folk healing to alleviate headaches, colic, colds and nervousness.

CAUTIONS & CONSIDERATIONS

Health
CAUTION: Consume in moderation (2 tbs dried = daily max). Side effects if over-consumed.

Pests
Susceptible to powdery mildew in humid, wet conditions.

Landscape design
Numerous cultivars with varied flower & leaf color. Trim after flowering. The cultivar 'Miss Jessopp's Upright' or 'Fastigiatus' suitable for hedging. Good companion for plants except potatoes. FL native alternative: False Rosemary (Conradina brevifolia) - a federally listed endangered species.

Saba Nut
Pachira glabra

HARDINESS ZONES: 9B TO 12

Often called "French Peanut" and regularly mistaken as 'Money Tree.' This ornamental, evergreen is fast-growing, reaching 10 feet within 2 years from seed. A protein-oil staple crop! Considered among the more notable yet under-appreciated tropical, staple crops. A relatively maintenance free, understory tree. Withstands hurricane winds with little damage. Stabilizes the soil. In the Malvaceae family.

SIZE h*w	SUN	SOIL	WATER	EDIBLE
50ft*50ft	full to partial	well-draining	drought tolerant; seasonal flooding - OK	seed/ nut; oil

PROPAGATION METHODS

- SEEDS: Germinates at 80-90F. Fruits after 4-5 years, producing 50-80 fruits per year with numerous seeds inside.
- CUTTINGS: Roots readily.

RECIPE

SABA NUT IN TOMATO SAUCE: 10 seeds; 1/2 pureed, roasted tomato; 1 tsp ground cinnamon, 1 tbs coriander seeds, 1 c coconut milk, 1 tbs coconut oil.

Boil seeds 20 minutes in water. Strain. Allow to dry on a rack. Peel off husk. Sauté tomato & coriander in oil until fragrant. Add coconut milk, cinnamon & seeds. Simmer, covered 10 min.

CULTURAL SIGNIFICANCE

- Used in folk healing (e.g., Leaves believed to be antimicrobial, antifungal, nematocidal and anti-inflammatory)
- Rich in lipids, carbohydrates and proteins
- and believed to be a solution to protein-calorie malnutrition
- According to feng shui, bringing a five-leaved plant (like this one) into the home ensures financial prosperity

CULINARY USE

Seeds/ Nut

Smooth green fruit split open naturally, revealing 10-25 brown, 1-inch-long seeds. Wait for the pod to open on its own. Unripe seeds are bitter and not palatable.

Seed is most commonly cooked, sauteed, boiled, fried or roasted like chestnuts. Soak in water overnight then peel outer layer off - the husk. Rich in oil. Tastes like peanut or cashew. Seeds are rich in oil and contain 16% protein and approximately 40–50% fat. Roasted seeds are also ground, roasted, and brewed to make a hot drink similar to hot chocolate. When ground as a flour, it serves as a nutrient-dense functional food for biscuits, bread, and cakes. Good source of calcium & phosphorus.

CAUTIONS & CONSIDERATIONS

Health
No known adverse health effects.

Pests
Highly resilient.

Landscape design
Well-suited for planting in narrow areas. Compare with P. aquatica & P. insignis. Many ornamentals sold as P. aquatica are actually P. glabra. P. aquatica has larger seeds. Leaf drop enriches soil. Suitable in containers or as a houseplant. Do not plant against the house as it may attract pests.

Sage
Salvia officinalis

HARDINESS ZONES: 5 TO 10

A perennial in the Lamiaceae, mint family. Named after the Latin word "salveo" meaning to "save" or "heal" given the long history of folk-healing use. Called a panacea! Very attractive to hummingbirds, bees and butterflies! Used since ancient times for warding off evil, increasing women's fertility, and more. Good for xeriscaping. Cross-culturally significant. Considered the herb of immortality & wisdom.

SIZE h*w	SUN	SOIL	WATER	EDIBLE
2ft*2ft	full	well-draining	drought tolerant	leaves, flowers

PROPAGATION METHODS

- SEEDS: Germinates at 68-77F in 2 weeks.
- Cuttings: Root readily in soil.
- LAYERING: Mound soil onto stem branches so they root; remove and plant out 8 months later.

RECIPE

SAGE TEA: Wash 5 medium leaves under cool running water. Cover with steaming hot (but not boiling) water. Allow to steep, covered for 10 minutes. Strain. Dilute and sweeten to taste.

Touted in some cultures as an herbal remedies to stave off illness.

CULINARY USE

Leaves & Flowers
75 days to harvest. Fragrant, furry leaves. Leaves and flowers eaten raw or cooked, serving as an aromatic flavoring in cooked foods. An herb tea is made from the fresh or dried leaves and is believed to improve digestion. Added to fatty dishes for this reason. Adds a unique, slightly peppery flavor. Traditionally, included in stuffing for Christmas, Thanksgiving, and classic Sunday roast dinners. Pairs well with egg dishes. The flavor of sage is considered to be little bit sausage-like. High in antioxidants. Rich in volatile oils, flavonoids and phenolic acid. High in vitamins and minerals.

Blooms in the early summer.

CULTURAL SIGNIFICANCE

- Folk healing uses (e.g., for antimicrobial, antifungal & antioxidant effects; tea gargled for sore throats, cold & flu; leaves rubbed on teeth to clean)
- Composted to increase bacterial activity. A good companion plant; said to repel pests
- Used in religious ceremonies (e.g., burning dried leaves to cleanse a space or person)
- Mentioned in the folk song "Scarborough Fair"
- Aztecs used seed in drink: 'chianzotzolatolid'

CAUTIONS & CONSIDERATIONS

Health
CAUTION: Consume in moderation. Medicinal. Herbalists consider purple-leafed forms more potent.
Pests
Root rot, slugs, spider mites, spittle bugs, and wilt.
Landscape design
Trim in spring. A good groundcover. Needs mulching or gravel at base to reflect heat and prevent fungus. Cannot compete with weeds. Ornamental cultivars (e.g., tricolor). Compare with White Sage (Salvia apiana) & Pineapple sage (S. elegans).

Sapodilla
Manilkara zapota

HARDINESS ZONES: 9 TO 10

Exceptionally sweet, malty flavor! A textural mix of a pear and crunchy brown sugar. Delicious and highly desirable. Highly ornamental leaves. Serves as a productive and attractive addition to the food forest. However, this tree is listed as a FL Category 1 Invasive. Even if you don't plant it, birds may bring you a tree. Eat the fruit to prevent spread. In the Sapotaceae family.

SIZE h*w	SUN	SOIL	WATER	EDIBLE
36ft*26ft	full	poor - OK	drought tolerant	fruit, leaves

PROPAGATION METHODS

- SEEDS: Germinates at 75-78F. May self-seed readily. Takes 5-8 years to bear fruit. Collect fruit carefully to prevent spread.

RECIPE

DEHYDRATED SAPODILLA: Cut fully ripe fruit from stem and allow to soften on the counter. Once firm-soft, transfer to the fridge. Once there is a batch of fruit ready, cut in half, de-seed, and cut into wedges; spoon flesh out of the skin.

Line wedges on a tray. Dehydrate at 115F until dry. Tastes like brown sugar!

CULINARY USE

Fruit

Scratch the fruit to make sure the skin is not green beneath. If the skin is brown and the fruit separates from the stem easily without leaking latex, it is fully mature. Cut from stem and keep at room temperature for a few days to soften. It should be eaten when slightly soft, but not mushy. Firm-ripe sapodillas may be kept for several days in good condition in a refrigerator. Sapodilla pie is popular in Florida. Used as a date substitute in energy bars/ balls. Made into a fruit juice with citrus to prolong shelf-life. Dehydrating enriches flavor and accentuates texture.

Leaves

Young leafy shoots (washed of sap) eaten raw or steamed with rice in Indonesia.

CULTURAL SIGNIFICANCE

- In 1999, the Rainforest Alliance certified sapodilla "chicle"/ chewing gum in Yucatán as 1st non-timber forest product. Sap latex also serves as an adhesive or modeling clay
- Red heartwood valued for archer's bows; timbers in Mayan temple ruins found intact.
- Aztecs & Mayans tapped the tree for the sap
- Folk healing uses (e.g., leaf tea for colds; fruit as laxative)

CAUTIONS & CONSIDERATIONS

Health

Many health benefits. Believed to protect against degenerative disease. CAUTION: Ingestion of more than 6 seeds causes abdominal pain and vomiting.

Pests

Insect and disease resistant. Wooly White Fly.

Landscape design

Wood is strong - able to withstand winds. Sapodilla trees yield fruit twice a year, though flowering may continue year-round. Requires very little pruning.

Saw Palmetto
Serenoa repens

HARDINESS ZONES: 8 TO 11

A low-maintenance, evergreen shrub in the Arecaceae/ Palmae family. Flowers are showy and fragrant. A perfect ornamental edible for xeriscaping designs. Slow growing but very long lived - some plants reportedly 500–700 years old! Attracts butterflies. A major nectar source for over 300 insect species! NOTE: As of July 17, 2018, a permit is required for any landowner/ contractor to commercially harvest.

SIZE h*w	SUN	SOIL	WATER	EDIBLE
9ft*6ft	full to partial	well-draining; saline - OK	drought tolerant	fruit, seed, heart, leaf

PROPAGATION METHODS

- SEEDS: Germinates at 72-82F. Low & slow germination rates. Plants fully establish after three to six years.
- DIVISION: Horizontal stems and rhizomes.

RECIPE

SAW PALMETTO HEART SALAD: Choose a saw palmetto with vigorous new growth in the spring. With a hand saw, remove top 5" of trunk just below the newest frond. Make a vertical slit in the 5" removed portion with saw. Peel off outer husks to reveal white innermost cylinder - the heart. Chop it. Eat it raw as a salad with a splash of citrus juice, sea salt and honey.

CULTURAL SIGNIFICANCE

- Used in folk healing (e.g., to improve digestion, help increase strength, to treat coughs & for sex drive - called "spring of life")
- Serenoa/ Permixon drug is made from fruits to treat prostrate & bladder & urinary issues
- Seminole Indians make dolls & rope with fiber, cork out of stems & scrub brushes out of root
- Florida panther & endangered FL grasshopper sparrow use as a habitat

CULINARY USE

Fruit
The olive-shaped fleshy fruits are green, yellow and orange when unripe and bluish-black when ripe. Fruit eaten raw or cooked. Has a strong vanilla, peppery, blue cheese flavor. Seminoles gathered and ate the berries in late summer or fall. Often dried & boiled into juice/tea. Rich in oil.

Seeds
Eaten raw or cooked.

Heart
Terminal buds of trunks have edible heart like cabbage palm but smaller. Eaten raw or cooked. Leave 1-2 green fronds & center core so plant lives. Harvest up to 2x per year.

Leaf/ Stems
Crown end of growing leaf eaten raw or cooked.

CAUTIONS & CONSIDERATIONS

Health
CAUTION: Fine, sharp spines along the edges. Avoid eating fruit/seed if taking medications impacting hormones. Consume no more than 5 berries at a time - medicinal. Beware of snakes which like to curl up into palmettos.

Pests
Resilient.

Landscape design
Endangered Plant Advisory Council added saw palmetto to exploited plant list. Taproot. Foliage is highly flammable. Place 20ft+ from home. Common understory in coastal strands & in oak-pine communities.

Scallion

Allium fistulosum

HARDINESS ZONES: 6 TO 10

So easy to grow!!! Harvested year-round in Florida. Cultivated for more than 2000 years as a culinary herb. In the Amaryllidaceae family. Important in Chinese medicine; believed to improve metabolism, prevent cardiovascular disorders, and prolong life. Showy flowers typically bloom from late May to August. One of the most important crops grown worldwide in terms of economic value. Particularly important in Chinese, Japanese, and Korean cuisine. Very hardy.

SIZE h*w	SUN	SOIL	WATER	EDIBLE
2ft*1ft	full	well-draining	average	bulb, leaves, flower

PROPAGATION METHODS

- SEEDS: Germinates at 60-65F. Cross-pollinates & hybridizes.
- DIVISION: Growth habit is clumping. Divide any time but spring is most recommended.

RECIPE

SCALLION-GINGER SLEEPYTIME TEA: Sautee 1/4 c scallion leaves (chopped) with 1/2 inch of diced ginger root in 1 tsp oil until fragrant. Add 2 cups of water and simmer 10 minutes. Add a pinch of sea salt and 3 tsp sweetener of choice. Stir until well incorporated. Strain and serve. Alternatively, purée all ingredients after simmering and drink as a warm smoothie.

CULTURAL SIGNIFICANCE

- Rich in sulphur compounds. Folk healing use (e.g., bulb used for antibacterial, antiseptic, diuretic, vermifuge properties. Used to treat colds, insomnia in children; impedes parasites)
- High antioxidant activity: Allicin
- Used as a companion plant to repel garden pests. Juiced or pulverized with water and sprayed over garden plants

CULINARY USE

Bulb
Very similar in taste and odor to common onions. Bulb eaten raw or cooked. Offers a strong flavor. Used in salads, as a cooked vegetable or as a spice. Rather small, usually less than an inch in diameter. 5 months from seeding to harvesting bulb. Good substitute for spring onion or shallot.

Leaves
Hollow leaves eaten raw or cooked. A mild onion flavor. Added to salads or cooked as a vegetable. Often used as a garnish in soups. Serves as a chive/leek substitute. Leaf portions are snipped off as needed and regrow quickly. Leaves tend to bend over. Cut at fold.

Flowers
Young inflorescence is sometimes deep-fried and eaten as a snack.

CAUTIONS & CONSIDERATIONS

Health
No known adverse health effect for humans. Poisonous to dogs in large quantities.

Pests
Resilent. Bulb rot in wet soils. Slugs, mildew, rust & thrips.

Landscape design
Plant 1/2" apart, 1/2" deep. Two cultivar-groups: Japanese Bunching & Welsh Onion. Mulch heavily - cannot compete with weeds. Red bulb variety (Red Beard). Compare with Walking Onion (Allium cepa proliferum) or Chives (Allium schoenoprasum).

Sea Grape
Coccoloba uvifera

HARDINESS ZONES: 9B TO 11

A protected, low-maintenance Florida native offering fall color and belonging to the buckwheat family (Polygonaceae). A perennial evergreen but leaves frequently turn completely red in winter. A picturesque specimen with a contorted, twisting trunk! A great, fast-growing, ornamental, shade-tree & windbreak. The flowers contain abundant nectar & the resulting Sea Grape honey is pale-colored and spicy.

SIZE h*w	SUN	SOIL	WATER	EDIBLE
25ft*20ft	full to partial	salty - OK	flood & drought tolerant	fruit

PROPAGATION METHODS

- SEEDS: Germinates at 77-86F. <u>Dioecious</u>. Short viability.
- CUTTINGS: Preferred. Needs male & female cross-pollination. One male for 5-7 females.

RECIPE

SEAGRAPE WINE: Wash fruit and press through a sieve to de-seed. Juice. Pour juice into a glass container and cover with cloth or a fermentation lid. Allow to ferment for 3-5 days. Stir daily. Look for active bubbling. If bubbling does not occur within 2 days, add a bit of agave nectar to speed fermentation.

CULINARY USE

Fruit
Compared to muscadine grapes. Clusters of marble-sized fruit set in mid-summer. The clusters deepen to a red or purple color as they ripen in the fall around October. Can be made into jelly, eaten raw, or juiced and fermented into sea grape wine or vinegar. Fruits range from tart to sweet in flavor. Remove seed which may account for up to 2/3 of fruit volume. Mash through a sieve to separate seed from pulp. Also made into ice cream and syrup. Phytochemicals in fruit (e.g. anthocyanins, ascorbic acid, phenolic compounds, & flavonoids)

A large female tree generally produces several thousand fruit per season - enough for individual, family use.

CULTURAL SIGNIFICANCE

- Enriches soil & suppresses weeds. Large, slowly decomposing leaves
- Dune stabilizer & protective habitat. Tall sea grape plants help shield sea turtles from lights
- Bark oozes astringent, tannin-rich, red sap used as dye, for tanning & as a medicinal
- Unripe, green fruits made into leis
- Leaves used as plates and paper
- Roots made into baskets, wood for furniture or firewood

CAUTIONS & CONSIDERATIONS

Health
No known adverse health effects. Seed is hard. Remove before eating.
Pests
Resilent. Seagrape borer, nipple gall.

Landscape design
Male & female plants distinguished by flowers: Males show dead flower stalks. Grown as a shrub or tree. Pruned into a hedge, screen, or windbreak or even a bonsai. Variegated cultivar available. Compare with related Pigeon Plum (Coccoloba diversifolia).

Sea Salt
Sodium chloride

HARDINESS ZONES: 1 TO 13

The only rock humans eat! Once worth as much as gold! Ingrained within human history! An essential ingredient in nearly every recipe from savory to sweet. One of the five basic categories of taste. Most common world-wide food seasoning. Harvested for food preservation going back thousands of years (6,000BC). Local sea salt is rich in minerals, free of anti-caking agents & man-made additives. The ecosystem & extraction technique affect flavor of the salt - similar to wine-making.

SIZE h*w	SUN	SOIL	WATER	EDIBLE
pond/pan size: 6in deep	full	dense sand/ clay	saline	salt cystals

PROPAGATION METHODS

- ONGOING HARVEST: Dig canals from seawater to marshland. Pipe to shallow, clay ponds in full sun. Evaporate water. Rake & skim salt. Fill every 15 days on high tide (full/ new moon).

RECIPE

SEA SALT: Select a low-pollution site safe for swimming & fishing. Collect a gallon of salt water. Strain through a cotton cloth 3x to remove impurities. Boil in a stainless-steel pot until 90% of water is gone. Pour into a glass dish & place in dehydrator at 158F until all water is gone & salt crystals are dry. Yields about 3oz of salt.

CULTURAL SIGNIFICANCE

- "Merroir": Salt's flavor due to environment
- Many governments have imposed salt taxes
- Gandhi's Salt March - an act of nonviolent civil disobedience, saying: "Next to air and water, salt is perhaps the greatest necessity of life."
- Wars fought <u>over</u> & <u>with</u> salt; "salting the earth" = killing plants to starve enemy
- Egyptians, Greeks & Romans invoked gods with salt & water offerings. Hebrew Bible refers to salt in 35 verses

CULINARY USE

Crystalized Salt

Harvested in the dry season. Ocean water has nearly 1.2 oz of solids per liter - 3.5% salinity. Lakes and rivers may have sea water in quantity as well. Once the water is filtered to remove impurities, salt is harvested by either solar evaporation ponds or pans (shallow basins).

As the water dries, the salt crystals are raked into piles. "Sel gris" are cube-like, course, salt crystals which fall to the bottom of the pond. "Fleur de sel" is collected from the top of salt ponds when wind and humidity are lacking; magnesium-rich, white, crispy, and flaky. 'Fleur de sel' fetches 20 times the price of coarse salt.

CAUTIONS & CONSIDERATIONS

Health
CAUTION: Ocean used as a dump. Research site history. Deep sea harvest may have fewer contaminants. Excessive consumption may increase risk of cardiovascular diseases.

Pests
N/A - Bacteria/ microorganisms die in dehydration process. Microplastics may be present in food-grade salt.

Landscape design
Compare with halophyte/ salty-tasting plants: Sea asparagus (Salicornia bigelovii), Sea purslane (Sesuvium portulacastrum) and Saltwort (Batis maritima).

Seashore Palm
Allagoptera arenaria

HARDINESS ZONES: 9 TO 11

Cultivated in South America as "guriri" for edible fruits eaten fresh or made into a drink or jam. Easily maintained. A slow-growing plant. Able to adapt to many types of soils. The fruit is described as tasting similar to coconut. Requires almost no care, only a bit of patience. Beautiful feathery foliage. Blue-green, silvery hues. An interesting novelty, ornamental and child/pet-friendly windbreak. In the Arecaceae family.

SIZE h*w	SUN	SOIL	WATER	EDIBLE
6ft*6ft	full	poor, sandy - OK; well-draining	salt spray - OK	fruit

PROPAGATION METHODS

- SEEDS: Germinates at 90-95F.
- DIVISION: Separate tufts - underground stools.

RECIPE

SEASHORE PALM JUICE: Soak fruits in water to loosen from seed. Strain out seeds. Puree pulp and soaking water into a frothy drink.

OPTIONAL: Add sweetener of choice to taste.

CULTURAL SIGNIFICANCE

- As a palm, represents the 3rd most important plant family for human use; palms often thought of as symbols of the tropics
- Considered a pioneer species of important ecological importance on sandy dunes
- Regarded as one of the more ancient of palms, a predecessor
- Can resist fire and re-sprout after
- Leaves are used to make baskets and other woven objects

CULINARY USE

Fruit
Fully ripe when it turns from green to yellow. The ripe yellow pulp has a very strong sweet odor and thinly covers a large seed.

Produces fruits and seeds consistently. Fruits have a pleasant flavor with citric notes and a sweet taste.

Can be eaten raw or used to prepare juices, creams, desserts, moquecas (fish stew) and sauces, among others. It is a nutritious food with a high fiber content.

The unusual inflorescence emerges from within the leaf-crown. The single-seeded fruit is yellow to brown, growing in crowded clusters.

CAUTIONS & CONSIDERATIONS

Health
No known adverse health effects. Typically has soft, leathery leaves - however one report of spines. Compare with Allagoptera brevicalyx to ensure correct identification.

Pests
Resilient. Virtually impervious to insect and disease attack.

Landscape design
Rare in South Florida landscape. May form thickets. May bloom all year. Very old plants can grow 9' to 15' wide. Excellent in containers. Seeds highly sought after - ensure ethical source. Watershed protection & erosion control.

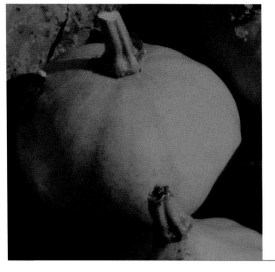

Seminole Pumpkin

Cucurbita moschata

HARDINESS ZONES: 4 TO 11

Native to South Florida! One of the tastiest and most reliable pumpkins for home gardens. Can survive relentless summer heat. Mature fruits often weigh 6- 12 pounds. Thrive on neglect. Worth planting in spring & fall! A staple food! Grow on a trellis or let ramble for enhanced vigor! Prefers dappled light & leaf litter found under oaks, pines, or elms. In the Cucurbitaceae family.

SIZE h*w	SUN	SOIL	WATER	EDIBLE
25ft*2ft	full to dappled	well-draining	average	fruit, seeds, flowers, leaves

PROPAGATION METHODS

- SEEDS: Germinates at 70-85F. Direct sow. <u>Cross pollinates</u>. Avoid planting more than one pumpkin variety on property to maintain type. Seeds can be stored for up to a year.

RECIPE

PUMPKIN SOUP: 2 medium pumpkins, 1 tbs coconut oil, 1 c minced onion, 2 minced garlic cloves, 1 tsp minced turmeric, 3 c coconut milk.

Cut pumpkin in half, scoop out seeds and inner fiber. Roast pumpkin for 1 hr face down at 350F. On stovetop, sauté spices in oil until fragrant. Purée roasted pumpkin meat, spices, and milk until soupy. OPTIONAL: Add salt & maple syrup to taste.

CULTURAL SIGNIFICANCE

- Traditionally grown by the Calusa, Creek, and Miccosukee peoples. Pumpkin "fry-bread" is still featured during tribal ceremonies, usually under a cooking chickee
- Hollowed-out rind can be dried and used for crafting to make bowls, cups, woven mats or even instruments
- Pumpkin is used in cosmetics and as a healthy skin supplement
- Used in salsas, chutneys, and relishes

CULINARY USE

Fruit
Inner flesh is orange, similar to butternut squash, but sweeter. Pumpkin can be eaten raw, boiled, fried, baked, mashed, steamed, stuffed, dried, or used in pies, soups, beverages, puddings, or breads. Save pumpkin fruits by cutting them into strips and drying. Later grind into a meal for baking bread. Young green fruits, from which the flowers have just fallen, may be cooked, mashed, seasoned, and eaten as a vegetable without peeling.

Seeds
Seeds are eaten raw or roasted. Yields seed oil. High in zinc.

Flowers & Leaves
Beautiful yellow flowers are edible raw, stuffed, or even fried. Leaves, and young stems are eaten as a cooked green vegetable such as when added to soups.

CAUTIONS & CONSIDERATIONS

Health
No known adverse health effects. Good source of nutrients; may cross pollinate and result in bitter fruits containing Cucurbitacin - avoid eating bitter fruit. Stem hairs may irritate skin.

Pests
Gummy stem blight, squash borer beetle.

Landscape design
Gourd shapes & sizes vary. Interplanted as understory. Related, Florida-friendly varieties include calabaza: 'La Primera' or 'La Segunda' cultivars especially.

Simpson's Stopper

Myrcianthes fragrans

HARDINESS ZONES: 8B TO 11

Also called "Twinberry." This evergreen, Florida native is a member of the Eucalyptus family. Dark green, densely growing leaves contain aromatic oils and smell like nutmeg! A warm nostalgic fall-like aroma! Fragrant flowers appear periodically throughout the year. Blooms have a delightful scent reminiscent of gardenia. Great for attracting wildlife darlings like butterflies, bees, & birds.

SIZE h*w	SUN	SOIL	WATER	EDIBLE
20ft*15ft	full to partial	wet - OK	seasonal flooding - OK; drought tolerant	berries

PROPAGATION METHODS

- SEEDS: Germinates best at 80-90F. Short viability. Plant fresh. Most fruit in Aug-Sept. Easily germinates.
- DIVISIONS: Both suckers and seedlings appear.
- CUTTINGS: Half-ripe wood in spring.

RECIPE

SIMPSON'S "LEMONADE": Purée 1 c of de-seeded, washed stoppers with, 3 cups water. Strain if desired. Add sweetener to taste.

ALTERNATIVE: Warm the sweetened purée on the stove top with cinnamon and ginger. Drink warm.

CULINARY USE

Fruit

Yields clusters of two to four edible berries about 1/2-inch wide. The small, orange-red, edible berry-fruit have a mild, citrus-like flavor. An initial sweetness, followed by a grapefruit-like aftertaste. Made into jellies and jams. Similar to kumquat. The sweet, mealy flesh of the fruit is edible raw, but eating the bitter seeds is not recommended. Soak fruit and press through a strainer to remove in bulk quantity. Some stoppers have one or two seeds, others have many seeds.

Leave some fruit on the bush at all times so that birds can eat and disseminate seed. By aiding threatened or endangered species, we can help increase their numbers & ensure their long-term survival.

CULTURAL SIGNIFICANCE

- Reportedly called "stopper" because bark & leaves were used to stop flu-like symptoms & diarrhea (CAUTION: anecdotal accounts only)
- Named in 1788 but has had 27 genus & species name changes since (e.g., Eugenia simpsonii)
- Name after Charles Torrey Simpson, a self-taught naturalist, botanist, author, & conservationist
- Listed by FL Dept of Agriculture & Consumer Services as threatened

CAUTIONS & CONSIDERATIONS

Health

CAUTION: Limited information on edibility. Ethnobotanical accounts only. Issues with taxonomy accounts/ renaming.

Pests

Resilient. No real pest or disease issues.

Landscape design

Hurrican wind resistant. Tap-rooted. Planted as a xeriscaping hedge. Easily trained. Tolerates severe pruning to stay low (e.g. 3ft). Good bonsai, topiary, or container plant. Flourishes in Florida's high-alkaline soils & tolerates salt well.

Society Garlic
Tulbaghia violacea

HARDINESS ZONES: 7 TO 11

Also known as Wild Garlic. A fast-growing, evergreen perennial in the Alliaceae/ Amaryllidaceae family. Features very ornamental, star-shaped, lilac-colored flowers which are very fragrant at night. Often used as a groundcover along paths - perfect for xeriscaping. A good substitute for chives and garlic. Can be grown as a container or houseplant. Naturally grows along forest margins and stream banks. Attracts hummingbirds! Can live up to 10 years!

SIZE h*w	SUN	SOIL	WATER	EDIBLE
1.5ft*1ft	full	any; well-draining	average	flowers, leaves

PROPAGATION METHODS

- SEEDS: Germinates at 68-75F. Hybridizes. Self-sows. Sprouts within 2 weeks. 1-2 years until bloom.
- DIVISIONS: When dormant, separate corms.

RECIPE

STIR-FRIED SOCIETY GARLIC: Finely chop 2 cups of society garlic leaves and stems. Sautee briefly in 1 tbs oil. Add 1/4 cup of coconut milk. Simmer 5 min covered. Use as a gravy on starch vegetables (e.g., cassava mash). Garnish with society garlic flowers.

CULINARY USE

Leaves & Stems

Sword-like leaves and stems eaten raw or cooked - chopped fine. Mild garlic flavor. Used to flavor soups, salads, breads, and more. Resembles garlic chives (Allium tuberosum). A nice peppery seasoning for starches - much milder than normal garlic.

Harvest in bulk as a means to cut back in late fall in preparation for winter. Can be used fresh or dried. Used as a spinach substitute in some cultures.

Flowers

Flowers June - September. Eaten raw or cooked. Added to salads, used as a garnish or as a flavoring in stir-fries, stews, soups, etc. A sweet, onion-like heat. Usually harvested from early summer to early fall.

CULTURAL SIGNIFICANCE

- Believed to have antibacterial, antifungal, antioxidant, androgenic & anthelmintic properties. Tubers used medicinally by Zulu people in Africa to treat many ailments
- Name "society garlic" may have come from an old rumor that this plant tastes like garlic without causing bad breath
- More than 20 species of society garlic - all found in South Africa
- Planted around homes to keep snakes out

CAUTIONS & CONSIDERATIONS

Health

No known adverse health effects. Consume in moderation.

Pests

Resilient. Slugs and snails, aphids, whiteflies, root rot.

Landscape design

Appears grass-like when not flowering. Goes dormant in areas with cold or dry seasons. Species & several cultivars (e.g., 'Purple Eye,' 'Silver Lace') received the Royal Horticultural Society's Award of Garden Merit. Be sure of identification of seed grown plants. Several seed exchanges list the Nothoscordum gracile as Tulbaghia violacea.

Sorghum
Sorghum hybrids

HARDINESS ZONES: 7 TO 12

Perennial sorghum grows fast and offers a balanced carbohydrate. The ideal staple in the Poaceae family. High in protein and carbohydrates - more nutritious than corn. Grown for grain, forage, syrup and sugar, and industrial uses of stems and fibers. A heat-loving plant, growing best in climates with long summers. Sweet sorghum was once the predominate table sweetener in the U.S. A true permaculture plant ideal for any homesteader property.

SIZE h*w	SUN	SOIL	WATER	EDIBLE
9ft*3ft	full	well-draining	drought tolerant	seed, stem

PROPAGATION METHODS

- SEEDS: Germinates at 72-80F within 2 weeks. To maintain a variety for generations, save seeds from 10-25 plants. Viable 10 years.
- DIVISION: Divide in spring and keep in shade until new growth shows.

RECIPE

SORGHUM BEER: Soak 2lbs sorghum in water overnight. Drain. Dry. Crush. Cover with water. Boil 15 minutes. Drain. Add 4 quarts of hot water. Let sit 1 hour. Transfer liquid portion to a pot. Add 8 quarts of hot water. Let cool. Add 1 cup of the crushed sorghum ("malt" from the germinated grains). Stir vigorously. Ferment for 2-5 days. Stir 2x daily. Strain. Serve. Typically up to 8% alcohol.

CULTURAL SIGNIFICANCE

- Essential to world's human diet - over 300 million people dependent on it
- Stalks used as animal feed/ fodder
- First introduced to the U.S. in 1852 by Isaac Hedges who called it the "Northern Sugar Plant" due to the stalk's high sugar content
- Some varieties of sorghum (e.g., broom corn, are used for crafts)
- Biomass sorghum has the largest stature - bred for bioenergy

CULINARY USE

Seeds

The threshed grain is ground into a wholesome flour & used in brewing "kiffir beer." Some cultures make porridge and muffins from sorghum meal. Dried seed used as a coffee substitute. Consumed as flat breads/ tortillas, porridges, and a couscous substitute. Used in place of brown rice or barley. Can be popped like popcorn. Seeds are easily threshed by rubbing seed heads by hand or by stripping the stalks. Seeds can then be screened and winnowed to remove casings, or glumes.

Stem

Large juicy stems containing as much as 10% sucrose, used in manufacture of syrup. Upon harvest, sugars rapidly degrade. Juice and boil down soon after harvest. Used as a healthy alternative sweetener & to produce whiskey & rum.

CAUTIONS & CONSIDERATIONS

Health
CAUTION: Pollen can induce hay fever. Some species of sorghum can contain levels of hydrogen cyanide, hordenine, and nitrates.

Pests
Wire & root worms, grubs/ beetle larvae, aphids, midge.

Landscape design
Spreads by rhizomes/ stolons. "Rattoons" for several years when cut back in winter. Hybrids can produce strong plants, disease resistance & mammoth yields. Plant far from home - may attract pests. Compare with Sorghum halepense.

Spanish Thyme
Lippia micromera

HARDINESS ZONES: 9 TO 11

Popular in the Caribbean and Hawaii for its edible leaves. An aromatic herb with a scent and flavor very similar to traditional thyme. A more robust, slightly spicy flavor. Butterflies love the tiny but abundant white or pink flowers!! Easy to grow and a well-behaved container plant. In the Verbenaceae family.

SIZE h*w	SUN	SOIL	WATER	EDIBLE
4ft+*4ft+	full to partial	well-draining	drought tolerant	leaves, flowers

PROPAGATION METHODS

- CUTTINGS: Semi-ripe and basal/ nodal softwood cuttings.

RECIPE

SOOTHING, SPANISH THYME TEA: Take 1 tsp washed leaves and steep in 1 cup of steaming hot water (not boiling). Cover for 5 minutes to allow to infuse.

Add sweetener of choice. Drink as an after-dinner tea.

CULINARY USE

Leaves & Flowers

Thin, woody stems bear opposite pairs of small oval leaves and tiny, white or pink, tubular flowers. Small leaves and young stems smell like a cross between oregano and thyme. Used as a flavoring in soups, salads and other foods like curries, pizzas, stuffing, frying fish, & cooking stews. Often dried. Some prefer the flavor of the dried leaves over the fresh.

As a tea, it is described as calming and is believed by herbalists to warm the blood. Leaf oil is high in cavacrol and it offers an essential oil rich in thymol.

CULTURAL SIGNIFICANCE

- Used in folk healing (e.g., leaves are used for treating coughs and colds; also used to treat "fright" an illness/ ethnomedical syndrome, causing on-going distress & an overload of stressful emotions like fear, anguish or worry)
- European use of thyme is similar to Caribbean uses of Spanish thyme. For example, in England, the most important reason for drinking thyme tea has been to calm the nerves before sleep & prevent bad dreams

CAUTIONS & CONSIDERATIONS

Health
No known adverse health effects. Potent antimicrobial activity.

Pests
Resilient.

Landscape design
Plant genus Lippia, numbers over 200 species, most of which bear edible leaves and have culinary as well as medicinal uses. Compare with Thyme (Thymus vulgaris), Mexican Oregano (lippia graveolens), Lemon Verbena (Lippia citriodora).

Spicebush

Lindera benzoin

HARDINESS ZONES: 4 TO 10

A rare but hardy Florida native & host plant. Attracts birds and butterflies! A deciduous shrub in the Lauraceae/ Lindera family that creates clouds of yellow flowers in spring and fall. Native Americans, including the Cherokee, Creek, and Iroquois used the plant medicinally. Lovely and graceful in growth habit. A versatile restoration understory shrub with incredible flavor and aroma.

SIZE h*w	SUN	SOIL	WATER	EDIBLE
9ft*9ft	partial	acidic - OK	seasonal flooding - OK	fruit, leaves, twigs

PROPAGATION METHODS

- SEEDS: Germinates at 77-90F. <u>Dioecious</u>. Short viability. May produce perfect flowers.
- CUTTINGS: Cuttings of half-ripe wood. Preferred method - easy gender identification.

RECIPE

SPICEBUSH TEA: Soak 1 cup of berries in water to soften. Remove pit. Boil in 3 cups of water. Puree, strain and sweeten to taste.

OPTIONAL: Dehydrate the strained berry pulp and add to stews and soups to extract any remaining aromatics.

CULINARY USE

Fruit
Grows in clusters along the stem. The fruit drupes are about 1-inch long and 1/4 inch wide with a pit in the center. Deep red color when mature. Olive-sized fruit are often used as a substitute for the seasoning 'allspice'. Rich in essential oils. Gently simmered to extract the fragrant oils in decoctions or teas. Dehydrate and freeze them for future use. Brightens both sweet & savory dishes.

Leaves & Twigs
Young leaves, twigs contain an aromatic essential oil and make a very fragrant tea with a mild, chai flavor tea. Pleasant hot or iced. Best gathered when in flower; the nectar adds considerably to the flavor. Spicy, citrusy-lemony smell. Young shoots are harvested during the spring and used fresh or dried.

CULTURAL SIGNIFICANCE

- Leaves contain small quantities of camphor - used to repel insects
- Used in folk healing (e.g., for fevers, colds & intestinal parasites. A steam bath with the twigs used to ease aches & pains in the body)
- Hosts several species including spicebush swallowtail butterfly; songbirds eat fruits
- Dried fruits have been used in fragrant sachets
- Extracted essential oil described as "woody-floral", "grassy-eucalyptus" and "citrus-spicy"

CAUTIONS & CONSIDERATIONS

Health
No known adverse health effects. Consume in moderation. Medicinal.

Pests
Resilient but susceptible to laurel wilt.

Landscape design
Grows frequently in a clonal colony to form thickets. Only the females have edible berries. Also compare with FL native, Sassafrass (Sassafras albidum), Ginberry (Glycosmis pentaphylla) or Allspice (Pimenta dioica).

Spiderwort

Tradescantia ohiensis

HARDINESS ZONES: 3 TO 9

A Florida native and host plant in the Commelinaceae family. Attracts pollinators as a long-blooming perennial - especially butterflies, bumblebees and dragonflies! Charming and low maintenance. Can bloom year-round in many parts of Florida. Useful as ground cover, creating a meadow-like appearance. Cucumber-flavored blooms, leaves and stems!

SIZE h*w	SUN	SOIL	WATER	EDIBLE
2.5ft*2ft	full to partial	well-draining acidic, poor - OK	drought tolerant; seasonal flooding - OK	leaves, stems, flowers

PROPAGATION METHODS

- SEEDS: Germinates at 65F. Ripen August to October. Self-sows. Hybridizes. Space 1ft.
- DIVISION: Clump forming - divide in spring
- CUTTINGS: Young shoots root quickly.

RECIPE

SPIDERWORT FLOWER GARNISHES: Cut off flower stalks with open blooms in early morning and put stem in a glass of water. The open flowers stay firm until mid-afternoon. New flowers open daily. Pick blossoms as they open and put them in a glass dish in the refrigerator or freezer. Collect and use as a garnish on soup, salad, or cake; cold-brew into a tea or freeze in ice cubes.

CULTURAL SIGNIFICANCE

- Used in folk healing (e.g., poultice of leaves applied to stings, insect bites; roots used as a laxative or for digestive complaints)
- Stamens said to reveal radiation. Exposure turns bluish filament hairs on stamen pink
- Some report seeds can be roasted & ground into flour, but nutritional information lacking
- Brought to 17th-century Europe as ornamentals

CULINARY USE

Leaves & Stems

Grassy appearance. Leaves eaten raw or cooked. Added to salads or blanched and eaten much like spinach. Mucilaginous texture; frying removes but eliminates benefit. Adding citrus juice cuts through the texture without impacting nutrition. Used to thicken soup and stews. Stems braised like asparagus - tender if cut prior to flowering.

Flowers

Flowers June to October with blooms 1 to 1½ inches across. Colored blue, rose or white with 3 egg shaped petals. Each flower blooms for a single day, opening in morning and shriveling into a jelly in heat. Petals are often candied as a garnish for salads, cakes, and soups. Each flower has six dark bluish-purple stamens with filaments covered in sticky hairs - remove these prior to eating.

CAUTIONS & CONSIDERATIONS

Health

CAUTION: Stems ooze a jelly-like sap - may cause skin irritation; used medicinally like aloe vera. May be confused with inedible look-alikes. Not all varieties are edible. May hybridize which can impact edibility.

Pests

Very hardy. Snails and rabbits occasionally eat foliage.

Landscape design

Cut back in mid-summer to encourage fall blooms. May spread aggressively. Four species are native to Florida.

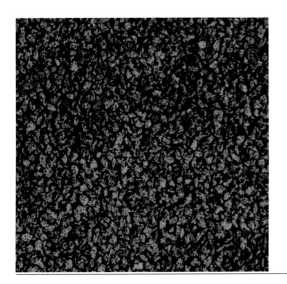

Spiralina
Spirulina platensis

HARDINESS ZONES: 10 TO 12

An edible, blue-green algae in the Cyanophyceae family. Used as a health food around the world for centuries. Considered the oldest food on earth! Highly nutritious & safe when produced in controlled culture. 60-70% protein - recognized as one of the best plant sources of protein & a proven source of B12! A historical staple for the Aztecs & used for antioxidant, anti-inflammatory, & immune system boosting properties. Easily grown indoors by a southern window.

SIZE h*w	SUN	SOIL	WATER	EDIBLE
7.5mm*4mm	partial/ dappled	N/A	very alkaline, shallow; uncontaminated	algae

PROPAGATION METHODS

- CULTURE: Live spirulina as a starter. Ensure seller is certified to avoid contamination. Usually sold as a bottle containing spirulina algae in water. Keep culture between 95-100F. pH around 10.

RECIPE

SPIRULINA GUACAMOLE: Mash 1 tsp spirulina with 2 avocados, 1 tbs citrus juice, 2 minced cloves of garlic, salt to taste.

The spirulina makes the guacamole a beautiful hue. Serve with crackers or tortillas/ chips.

CULTURAL SIGNIFICANCE

- Often found wild in subtropical/ tropical warm alkaline lakes (e.g., Great Rift Valley of Africa)
- Gets its name from microscopic shape of the plant which looks like little spirals
- NASA has selected it as among the most important plants for future space stations
- Considered original producer of earth's oxygen
- Nutritional yield is equivalent to 10x soybeans, 20x corn and 200x beef cattle
- By far the most-studied nutritional algae

CULINARY USE

Algae
Can be harvested daily (under the optimal conditions). Consumed dried and fresh. Fresh spirulina is often preferred and is superior in taste and nutrients - odorless and has a mild flavor. Highly digestible. Among Aztecs, spirulina was made into breadcakes mixed with grains & a sauce made from tomatoes and spices. The African, Kanembu people eat spirulina in nearly 70% of their meals, using 3 ounces per person per day. Contains a total of 18 amino acids. To harvest, scoop spirulina out with water. Strain through a fine cloth or mesh.

Often added to juice or made into smoothies when combined with fruit. Also put into pesto, dips, and sauces or sprinkled onto popcorn or salads.

CAUTIONS & CONSIDERATIONS

Health
No known adverse health effects. Algae absorbs toxins in environment. Harvest from uncontaminated water.
Consume in moderation: Max of 3oz per adult per day.

Pests
High pH prevents parasites, germs, viruses.

Landscape design
Each square meter pool provides up to 1 tbs of harvested & pressed Spirulina a day. The Spirulina Society offers open source/ free tools & resources. Compare with Duckweed (Lemna gibba).

Sprawling Asiatic Dayflower

Commelina communis

HARDINESS ZONES: 6 TO 10B

This plant will likely show up without being planted! Cultivated as a vegetable in China and used for generations in traditional Chinese medicine. Attracts pollinators. Behaves invasively in Florida. The best way to control spread is to prevent it going to seed by eating or using it. In the Commelinaceae family.

SIZE h*w	SUN	SOIL	WATER	EDIBLE
2ft*5in	partial	well-draining	average; seasonal flooding - OK	leaves, flowers

PROPAGATION METHODS

NOT RECOMMENDED
- SEEDS: Germinates at 68F within 5 weeks.
- CUTTINGS: Stems sprawl along the ground, rooting as they go. Cut and pull segments.

RECIPE

CREAMED DAYFLOWER: 1/2 pound of tender tops of dayflower leaves and stems; 2 tbs water; 1 tbs oil, 2 tbs coconut cream, 2 tsp coriander seeds; pinch of sea salt; Dayflower blooms for garnish.

Heat oil at medium with coriander until fragrant. Add water & dayflower leaves & stems, stirring until wilted. Add cream. Salt to taste. Garnish.

CULINARY USE

Leaves & Flowers
Harvest in bulk prior to seed setting. Seeds ripen from August to October. Blooms last for only one day. In flower from July to September (possibly year-round in South Florida). Shoots are most tender during late spring and early fall, when new growth is sprouting. Break off top 4 inches.

Leaves and young stems best chopped, cooked in soups, stews, or stir-fries. Sweet taste. Mucilaginous. Green-bean flavor. Flowers used as a decorative accent to cupcakes. The two upper petals are blue to purplish-blue, and the third lower petal is white. In other species all three petals are blue.

NOTE: Carefully identify. One of 20+ dayflower varieties. This variety is never bitter and has pea-like sweetness.

CULTURAL SIGNIFICANCE

- Used in folk healing (e.g., as a throat gargle to relieve sore throats; as a diuretic; as a poultice for inflammation or for antibacterial activity)
- Bright blue dye from petals. Used in Japanese Ukiyo-e woodcuts in 18th & 19th centuries
- Bioaccumulates metals in soils. Used to clean spoiled copper mines
- Compared in appearance to a little mouse
- Many landscape varieties have been bred
- Reports that seeds are edible & resemble peas

CAUTIONS & CONSIDERATIONS

Health
CAUTION: Contains oxalates. Avoid consuming if soil is contaminated with heavy metals. May be confused with Tropical Spiderwort (C. diffusa - equal blue petals; or C. benghalensis - has edible starchy roots; listed as a noxious weed by U.S. Dept of Ag).

Pests
Highly resilient.

Landscape design
Ground cover in moist, woody areas. Compare with edible FL native C. erecta for upright habit and drought tolerance.

Star Apple
Chrysophyllum cainito

HARDINESS ZONES: 10 TO 12

Also called "Caimito." An evergreen in the Sapotaceae family that can serve as a windbreak and ornamental shade tree. Canopy forms an umbrella shape with underside of leaves exuding a golden color contrasting the top emerald color. Can bear fruit year-round in ideal conditions. High antioxidant & anti-inflammation properties. Nobel Prize-winning poet, Derek Walcott immortalized the fruit as a symbol of the Caribbean in his 1979 work, "The Star-Apple Kingdom."

SIZE h*w	SUN	SOIL	WATER	EDIBLE
60ft+*45ft+	full	well-draining; clay - OK	drought tolerant	fruit

PROPAGATION METHODS

- SEEDS: Germinates at 80-85F within six weeks. 70% success. Bears within 10 years.
- CUTTINGS: Greenwood or mature stems.
- GRAFTING: May bear first year.

RECIPE

JAMAICAN SHAVED-ICE, FRUIT-SALAD: Spoon out and dice star apple flesh. Purée 5 coconut water ice cubes. Serve fruit in dessert bowls topped with coconut ice.

Garnish with edible flowers or mint leaves. Add agave syrup & sea salt to taste.

CULINARY USE

Fruit
Oval shaped fruit, 2-4" in diameter when ripe. Feb. to May season. Color varies by cultivar. Trees bear fruits with light green skin and white flesh, or dark purple skin and purple flesh. Smooth skinned but when fully ripe, the skin is dull, a bit wrinkled, and the fruit is slightly soft to the touch. Sweet and eaten raw or processed into preserves. Fruit do not fall from tree when ripe so clip from the stem - pulling the fruit off may damage the peel and release latex into the pulp. Remove skin and rind prior to eating. Cut in half and spoon out flesh, leaving seed cells and core. A drink called "matrimony" is prepared by scooping out the inside pulp of a star apple and adding it to a glass of citrus juice. The pulp makes an excellent jelly. Can bear 150lbs of fruit when fully mature!

CULTURAL SIGNIFICANCE

- Branches used as a medium for growing orchids; wood pulp is made into high quality paper; bark yields tannin
- Seed kernels reportedly used to make imitation milk-of-almonds but must be boiled/ processed to remove toxin (see health notes)
- Folk healing uses (e.g., leaves used in bath infusions for rheumatism & wound healing; stem bark/ leaf tea believed to lessen diabetes symptoms)

CAUTIONS & CONSIDERATIONS

Health
CAUTION: Do not consume seeds; they contain a cyanogenic glucoside. Immature fruit is astringent and oozes a sticky, white latex. Eat only when ripe.

Pests
Resilient: Rust, fungal diseases.

Landscape design
Some seedlings require cross pollination to set fruit. Prune to form 3-5 main scaffold limbs and maintain at 8 to 12 ft height to aid harvesting. Leaf drop occurs in severe drought.

Star Fruit

Averrhoa carambola

HARDINESS ZONES: 10 TO 12

A beautiful and abundantly producing fruit tree known for its edible fruit and folk-healing uses. The fruits go great with salads and for juicing or wine (tangy and not too sweet). Grown as ornamentals for brightly colored fruits, attractive dark green leaves and lavender to pink flowers. However, caution is needed: Listed on the top 10 most dangerous fruits in the world for those with kidney problems. In Oxalidaceae family.

SIZE h*w	SUN	SOIL	WATER	EDIBLE
12ft*25ft	full to partial	well-draining	average	fruits, flowers, leaves

PROPAGATION METHODS

- SEEDS: Germinates at 70-80F. Short viability. Planted out when 1 ft tall.
- BUDDING/GRAFTING: Can produce fruiting plants within 10 months.

RECIPE

SPAGHETTI SAUCE: 5 ripe, yellow star fruit (winged tips removed, chopped, de-seeded, blanched), 6 garlic cloves minced, 1 c chopped onion, 4 sprigs of chopped basil, 1 tbs oil, salt to taste.

Sauté garlic and onion in oil until golden and fragrant. Add chopped, blanched startfruit. Simmer until soft. Remove from heat. Add oil, basil and salt.

CULTURAL SIGNIFICANCE

- Used in folk healing (e.g., fruit as a laxative and against fever, cough, sore throat; leaves for rheumatism)
- Introduced into Florida over 100 years ago from Southeast Asia as specimen trees
- Juice used to clean rusty, tarnished metal, or bleach rust stains from cloth
- Unripe fruits contain potassium oxalate, which is used in dyeing (mordant). Wood used for construction and furniture

CULINARY USE

Fruit
Very juicy! High antioxidant property said to efficiently scavenge free radicals. Entire fruit is edible, including the slightly waxy skin best consumed when skin is bright yellow or even with a light shade of green. Taste varies from very sour to mildly sweetish. Unripe star fruits are firmer and sour - like green apples and are often mixed with other chopped spices to make relishes, dipped in rock salt or cooked with shrimp. Peeling off the green 'wing' edges removes most of the oxalic acid. Blanching often aids further removal. Fruits are star-shaped when cut horizontally.

Leaves
Eaten either raw or cooked for an acid flavoring.

Flowers
Eaten raw or cooked and usually added to salads.

CAUTIONS & CONSIDERATIONS

Health
Fruit is a good source of potassium & vital nutrients.
CAUTION: Fruits contain caramboxin and oxalic acid, harmful for those with kidney problems. May interfere with medication. NOTE: Adding calcium chloride to starfruit juice can reduce the soluble oxalate.

Pests
Scale insects.

Landscape design
Very wind sensitive - shelter. Compare with Tree Tomato (Cyphomandra betacea) and Cucumber-tree (Averrhoa bilimbi).

Strangler Fig

Ficus aurea

HARDINESS ZONES: 9B TO 11

A long-lived, Florida native that starts out as an epiphyte and later strangles its host, becoming a self-supporting, shade tree. An excellent windbreak. Can withstand hurricane winds. Young trees are highly ornamental. One of the best trees for birds to feed from! Provides significant food and cover for wildlife. In the Moraceae family.

SIZE h*w	SUN	SOIL	WATER	EDIBLE
60ft*50ft	full to partial	any	seasonal flooding - OK; drought tolerant	fruit

PROPAGATION METHODS

- SEEDS: Germinates at 75-82F. Brush dried seeds onto soil. Do not cover seeds with soil.
- CUTTINGS: Half-ripe wood roots in soil.

RECIPE

STRANGLER FIG CURRY: Soak 2 c of thoroughly washed fruit in warm water until swollen and very soft (about 8-12 hours). Strain. Mash. Add 2 tsp of cinnamon and 1 cup of nut milk to fig mash in a pot. Simmer on medium heat stirring continuously to incorporate. Add salt and sweetener to taste. Ladle over vegetables, grains, or use as a dip for bread.

CULTURAL SIGNIFICANCE

- Larval host for daggerwing butterflies
- Pollinated by the wasp, Pegascapus jimenezi
- Latex was used for chewing gum, to treat wounds & to curdle milk for cheese making
- Aerial roots used to make arrows, bowstrings, fishing rods/lines, and more; fruit makes rose-colored dye
- Considered a keystone species
- In India, people have used strangler fig for centuries as living bridges over rivers

CULINARY USE

Fruit
Produces large amounts small fig fruits (which are actually edible flowers!) Used for food by the Native Americans and early Florida settlers. Fruits start out golden yellow, turning red to purple when ripe. Fruits nearly year-round.

Each fruit is about 1/2 inches wide - pea sized. Soft when ripe. Raw fruit can be eaten out of hand. Can also be made into jam, relish, jellies, or baked into breads such as with blueberries. Cooked with spices as a curry or chutney.

Wash fruits thoroughly as birds often feed in the tree and may deposit droppings.

CAUTIONS & CONSIDERATIONS

Health
CAUTION: Latex may cause allergic reations in some.

Pests
Aphids, scales, sooty mold.

Landscape design
Tends to invade built structures and foundations. Can lift sidewalks. Plant 40ft or further from roads and homes. Never plant near septic drainage system, wells, or pool. Prune for strong structure. Compare with other FL native species: Paradise tree (Simarouba glauca), Mastic (Sideroxylon foetidissimum), or Pigeon Plum (Coccoloba diversifolia).

Strawberry
Fragaria spp

HARDINESS ZONES: 4 TO 10

Often the first fruit a gardener tries because they can produce abundantly with little care. Florida is the winter strawberry capital of the world. Typically, the mother plant is productive for four or five years but creates runners which can continue indefinitely. Goes dormant in severe weather - grown as an annual but actually a perennial! Fertilize just before dormancy to promote perennial behavior. Finicky but worth the effort! Good for containers if in partial sun! In the rose family, Rosaceae.

SIZE h*w	SUN	SOIL	WATER	EDIBLE
1ft*1ft	full to partial	well-draining; acidic - OK	average	fruit, leaves/ tops

PROPAGATION METHODS

- SEEDS: Germinates at 65-75F in 4+ weeks.
- DIVISION: Preferred method. Dormant bare-roots. Must be thinned annually. Plant in fall or winter. Harvests 90-110 days after planting.

RECIPE

STRAWBERRY SORBET: 2 c frozen strawberries, 2 c cold coconut milk, ½ c maple syrup.

Puree all ingredients. Pour into a frozen container. Stir every 20-30 minutes for the first hour to prevent ice from forming. Thaw 10 min prior to serving.

CULINARY USE

Fruit
Pick berries when at least three-fourths red or ripened color. Strawberries can come in numerous colors: non-runner types are available in red, white and yellow. Once picked, berries will not sweeten further. Harvest every two to four days. Bruise easily - cut from stem. Only keep a few days. Freeze to preserve longer. 1 to 2 pints of fruit per plant over the season. Made into jam, preserves, used fresh on salads and used as a base for balsamic glaze.

Leaves & Tops
Leaves and tops of some varieties are edible. Young leaves eaten raw or cooked like spinach. Rich in antioxidants. Consume in moderation - contain tannins. Brewed into a tea. NOTE: Do not eat stems - toxic.

CULTURAL SIGNIFICANCE

- National Strawberry Day is Feb. 27
- Strawberries are a $300 million-a-year industry in Florida - most grown in central FL; Plant City-Dover area considered mecca
- In 1982, the Florida Strawberry Growers Association (FSGA) formed along with Florida Strawberry Patent Service Corporation (FSPS)- license required to propagate some cultivars
- Commercial strawberries listed as among most contaminated produce

CAUTIONS & CONSIDERATIONS

Health
No known adverse health effects but a potential allergen.

Pests
Powdery mildew, aphids, thrips, spider mites.

Landscape design
Grown on mounds to prevent rot. Grow in dappled shade in South Florida. Florida-Friendly cultivars include, 'Florida Brilliance'; 'Florida127'. Compare with wilder or Asian varieties tolerant of heat/humidity like Mock Strawberry (Duchesnea indica), Beach Strawberry (Fragaria chiloensis), Wild Strawberry (Fragaria virginiana).

Strawberry Tree

Muntingia calabura

HARDINESS ZONES: 10 TO 12

Also called "Jamaican cherry." A fast-growing, evergreen, pioneer species! Thrives with little to no care! Blooms all year. Profusely fruits. Attracts pollinators- Visited by bees, butterflies, diurnal moths and hummingbirds! Bats consume the fruits. In the Elaeocarpaceae/ Muntingiaceae family. Often grown as an ornamental. A wonderful fruit tree for pots.

SIZE h*w	SUN	SOIL	WATER	EDIBLE
30ft*40ft	full	well-draining; poor- OK	drought tolerant	leaves, flowers, fruit

PROPAGATION METHODS

- SEEDS: Germinates at 85-95F. Fruits contain hundreds of tiny seeds. Requires light to germinate. Flowers in 2 years.
- CUTTING: Half-ripe wood.
- SUCKERS: Preferred method. Dig in spring.

RECIPE

COTTON CANDY COBBLER: Wash 5 cups of berries. Fill a pie dish. Cover with 2 cups coconut meal mixed with maple syrup (1 tbs), cinnamon (1 tsp) and sea salt (1/2 tsp).

Bake at 350F for 30 minutes until the berries are bubbling and the crust is browned.

CULINARY USE

Fruit
Fruits are produced abundantly and are round shaped. Sweet, and juicy. Cotton-candy or fig-like flavor. Very good to eat out of hand and can also be used in jams, tarts, pies. Tiny, 1/2-inch diameter or smaller. The green, immature fruit ripens quickly, changing to a red (or sometimes yellow) within a day. Harvest daily and refrigerate to accumulate in quantity. Ripe fruits can be shaken from branches and caught on cloth on ground. Wash well before eating as the tree attracts birds which may leave droppings.

Leaves & Flowers
Medicinal tea can be made from the leaves & flowers. Flowers resemble strawberry bloom, hence the common name, "Strawberry Tree." Rich in antioxidants.

CULTURAL SIGNIFICANCE

- Wood used to carve small boxes, casks, & for general carpentry; also a source of paper pulp & fuel for cooking - burns with intense heat but gives off very little smoke
- Bark used for lashing together supports of rural houses - yields a very strong, soft fiber for twine & rope
- Used in folk healing (e.g., flowers believed to be antiseptic. An infusion/tea of flowers & leaves used to relieve headache & colds)

CAUTIONS & CONSIDERATIONS

Health
No known adverse health effects.

Pests
Fruit flies.

Landscape design
Thicket forming. May behave invasively. Both red and yellow fruited varieties. Said to grow better than any other tree in polluted air areas. Planted on riverbanks as falling flowers & fruits serve as bait, attracting fish. Compare with Miracle Berry (Synsepalum dulcificum) & Peanut butter fruit tree (Bunchosia grandulifera).

Sugar Cane

Saccharum officinarum

HARDINESS ZONES: 8 TO 12

One of the most widely cultivated crops worldwide! This is a cash crop which adds landscaping flair. As its name (officinarum, "of dispensaries") implies, sugar cane is used in folk-healing world-wide. Thanks to its calorie-dense sugar content, this plant is considered a staple. Larval butterfly host plant! In the Poaceae family – Actually a perennial grass! 500 million-dollar industry in Florida!

SIZE h*w	SUN	SOIL	WATER	EDIBLE
16ft*3ft	full	acidic – OK	well-draining; moderate flood tolerance	flower head, cane juice

PROPAGATION METHODS

- CUTTING: Must contain at least one bud from mature cane called "setts." Sugarcane setts should be planted horizontally or at a 45° angle in furrows 6–12 inches deep.

RECIPE

MOLASSES: Peel sugarcane stalks, cut inner core into wedges, extract liquid using a masticating juicer.

Pour the sugarcane juice into a pot and boil on low 6 hrs. Stir often. A green layer may form - skim off. Light molasses is obtained in the first boil. For darker molasses, keep boiling. Fermentable!

CULINARY USE

Flower head
Unexpanded flower head of Saccharum edule (duruka) is eaten raw, steamed, or toasted. Flowers when grown as a perennial.

Cane
Harvest in fall. Contains sweet sap - main source of sucrose. Raw sugarcane core of fresh stems is chewed as a sweet refreshment. Rapadura is a sweet flour from refining sugarcane juice, common in Latin American countries (called papelón). Often burned prior to harvesting to remove unwanted leaves and evaporate water in the stems, concentrating the sugar. Products include molasse & rum. Fermented alcoholic beverages are made using the juice. An average sugar cane stalk weighing 3 lbs contains about 1/3 lb of sugar.

CULTURAL SIGNIFICANCE

- Florida produces 52% of the total U.S. sugar cane - 70% being in Palm Beach County. Over 401,000 documented acres in 2016 in Florida
- Used in folk healing (e.g., juice for sore throat)
- Produces the highest number of calories per sq. ft. of growing area of any plant
- Brought to the Americas in 1493 by Columbus
- Reeds made into pens, mats, screens, thatch,
- Livestock fodder, fiber for papermaking

CAUTIONS & CONSIDERATIONS

Health
CAUTION: Some varieties have siliceous hairs, spines or sharp edges; use extreme caution when handling.

Pests
Cane beetle reduces crop yield by eating roots; Vulnerable to pathogens.

Landscape design
Some sugarcane varieties are nitrogen fixing. Other varieties can exhaust soil. Intercrop with leguminous plants. Compare with Stevia (Stevia rebaudiana) & Aztec sweet herb (Lippia dulcis).

Sun Artichoke ⭐

Helianthus tuberosus

HARDINESS ZONES: 4 TO 10

Originally, named after "girasole," the Italian word for sunflower, this robust perennial was cultivated by the Native Americans and became popular in French cuisine. The swollen potato-like roots are sweet, with a nutty flavor and can be appreciated raw, steamed or boiled. Excellent wildlife value! Grows up to 12 ft tall! Used for many centuries as a staple crop. Rich in inulin, potassium, iron, phosphorous. Encourages healthy gut flora! In the Asteraceae family.

SIZE h*w	SUN	SOIL	WATER	EDIBLE
7ft*2ft	full, dappled	poor - OK	drought tolerant	tuber

PROPAGATION METHODS

- SEEDS: Germinates at 75F. Ripen in November. Direct sow outdoors in autumn. Self-sows freely.
- DIVISION: Plant tubers; space 2ft.
- CUTTINGS: Herbaceous stem cuttings.

RECIPE

ROASTED SUNCHOKES: 1 lb sunchokes rinsed, peeled, and cut into ½-inch thick slices, 1½ tbsp oil, salt & pepper to taste, 1-2 sprigs fresh rosemary finely chopped.

Toss together all ingredients until sunchokes are well coated. Spread on a thin layer on a pan. Roast for 20 minutes, flipping halfway.

CULTURAL SIGNIFICANCE

- Has potential in ethanol-fuel production
- Folk healing use (e.g., for aphrodisiac, diuretic, stomachic, and tonic properties; used for diabetes & rheumatism)
- Grows well with corn
- July-Oct flowers attract birds; 58 species of butterflies & moths use as a host plant
- Weed eradicator/ makes dense shade; alleopathic leaves and stems
- Livestock fodder: pigs-tubers; horses-foliage

CULINARY USE

Tuber
Harvest mid to late fall. Dig with shovel. Used for cooking and baking in the same ways as potatoes but can be eaten raw. Roasted tubers are a coffee substitute. Grated raw into salads, boiled and/or mashed somewhat like potatoes, roasted or added to soups. Fewer calories per gram than the 'Irish Potato.' Fermenting (pickling) & cooking helps convert the inulin to fructose, aiding digestion. Keep in a paper bag in fridge crisper drawer for up to a week or two. The peel is edible and adds an earthy flavor; peel with a spoon to remove. Cutting them up prior to cooking aids cleaning and dirt removal. Cut them into slices like water chestnuts. Boil in lemon juice mixed with water to aid digestibility. Bruise easily and lose moisture rapidly. Harvest as needed.

CAUTIONS & CONSIDERATIONS

Health
No known adverse health effects. NOTE: The prebiotic, inulin can cause excess flatulence with over consumption.

Pests
Slugs; Rust, leaf fungal spots and powdery mildew; caterpillars and beetles chew foliage.

Landscape design
Tubers persist in ground for years. Each plant produces 2-5 pounds of tubers per year. May behave invasively. Helianthus maximiliani is similar with lower yield. Compare with Yacon (Polymnia edulis).

Sunflower
Helianthus annus

HARDINESS ZONES: 2 TO 11

An easy to grow plant with an many benefits and uses. As much an ornamental as a commercial crop. Tolerates poor soils and is drought tolerant! Dwarf and mammoth varieties available. Given the high protein and oil content of the seeds, this annual is worth planting and serves as a staple crop! World's second most important source of edible oil! Cleans soils through phytoremediation and rhizofiltration! In the Asteraceae family.

SIZE h*w	SUN	SOIL	WATER	EDIBLE
4ft*6in variety-specific	full	acidic - OK	drought tolerant	seeds, flower bud, stalk

PROPAGATION METHODS

- SEEDS: Seeds ripen from September to October. After the seeds have been dispersed, the dried stalk and leaves may be chopped up for mulch.

RECIPE

SUNFLOWER SEED BUTTER/ FLOUR: Use mortar/ pestle to crush hulls; lightly blow hulls off kernels. Soak kernels overnight. Strain. Sauté briefly & then press seed through a juicer. Use ground meal as flour. Collect the sunflower butter inside juicer receptacle. To extend flour shelf-life, boil meal in water to separate from the oil which floats to the top. Strain. Dehydrate meal at 115F until crisp.

CULTURAL SIGNIFICANCE

- Seeds form golden angle, 137.5°, Fermat's spiral/ Fibonacci mathematical numbers
- Remediates soil: Used to remove toxins after Chernobyl/ Fukushima Daiichi nuclear disaster
- Wild bird food, livestock forage; 58 species of butterflies & moths use as a host plant
- "Fourth sister" crop to corn, beans, squash
- Oil used for margarine, soap, candles, paint;
- Stem for paper and cloth; petals for dye

CULINARY USE

Seed
Raw or cooked; nut-like flavor. Rich in fats - between 44 - 72% linoleic acid. Can be ground into a powder, made into a peanut butter alternative or seed yogurt (germinated seed is blended with water and left to ferment). Roasted seed is a coffee substitute. Meal can replace flour in baking such as with German Sonnenblumenkernbrot bread. Also used to thicken soups.

Flower Bud
Young flower buds - steamed and served like globe artichokes. Flower tea is used in folk medicine as an astringent, diuretic and expectorant. Petals of open flowers have a bitter-sweet flower; yield a food dye.

Stalk
Leaf stalks can be boiled and then stir-fried.

CAUTIONS & CONSIDERATIONS

Health
CAUTION: Can accumulate nitrates when fed artificial fertilizers.

Pests
Filamentous fungus, downy mildew, broomrape.

Landscape design
Drooping head varieties reduce bird damage/ diseases. Allelopathic properties. 38 perennial sunflower varieties. Plant is considered "greedy" for nutrients - rotate locations; may behave invasively. Compare with medicinal, FL native: H. angustifolius.

Surinam Cherry

Eugenia uniflora

HARDINESS ZONES: 9 TO 11

Also called "Pitanga." This fast-growing, evergreen shrub in the Myrtaceae family will likely show up without you planting it. A past favorite for Florida hedges, the plant is now considered invasive. Harvesting will help curb the spread. Two crops or more per year! One untrimmed tree can produce nearly 3,000 fruit annually, close to 25 pounds! A pioneer species with wildlife value.

SIZE h*w	SUN	SOIL	WATER	EDIBLE
25ft*18ft	full to partial	well-draining	drought tolerant	fruit

PROPAGATION METHODS

NOT RECOMMENDED
- SEEDS: Germinates at 80-95F. Seed production year-round when rainfall is abundant.
- GRAFTING: Typical where the fruit is commercially cultivated (e.g., Brazil and India).

RECIPE

SURINAM CURRY: 4 c Surinam cherry purée, 4 chili peppers, honey to taste, 1/2 c vinegar, 2 cloves crushed garlic, 1 inch of peeled ginger, 1 tbs oil.

Purée all ingredients. Simmer for 30 minutes on medium heat covered. Serve over vegetables, grains, or as a dip for bread.

CULINARY USE

Fruit

Aromatic, subacid flavor. Eaten raw or cooked. Flesh is orange-red when ripe and juicy. Pick when fruits fall off the stem at the lightest touch; shake the bush to release. Otherwise resinous. Gather daily or twice a day. When grown from seed, flavor varies from tartness like a green bell pepper to as sweet as a mango. Rich in antioxidants and vitamins A and C. If chilled within an hour of harvest fruit remain fresh 14 days in the refrigerator.

For table use, slit vertically on one side, spread open to release the seed, chill 2-3 hours to dispel any resinous aroma. Can be made into jam, jelly, relish, pickles, wine, vinegar, pie or sauce or preserved whole in syrup. An excellent addition to fruit cups, salads, pudding, ice cream.

CULTURAL SIGNIFICANCE

- Leaves contain polyterpenes, sequiterpenes & citronella; spread over floors to repel insects
- Flowers rich in pollen for honeybees
- Bark rich in tannin for treating leather
- Chefs chose Surinam cherry as part of a "12 Trees Project" due to its culinary versatility, attractive color, and unique flavor
- Used in folk healing (e.g., for phytonutrients, & antimicrobial, antiviral, antifungal and antioxidant properties)

CAUTIONS & CONSIDERATIONS

Health
CAUTION: Seeds are reportedly toxic. Avoid ingesting.

Pests
Fruit flies, scale insects. Known to host recognized pests & pathogens.

Landscape design
Tolerates high winds. Most productive if unpruned. Prune only in 6th or 7th year. Used for bonsai, as an ornamental, and as hedgerows. Forms dense thickets. Two distinct cultivars, a wilder, red-colored fruit and a sweeter, dark purple, Florida cultivar, named 'Zill.'

Sweet Acacia
Acacia farnesiana

HARDINESS ZONES: 8B TO 11

A fast-growing & occasionally deciduous Florida native! A long-lived wildlife attractor and true multipurpose species. All parts of the plants have use! Low maintenance yet provides a feast for the senses. Exquisite smelling flowers - famous worldwide as perfume! Showy, yellow, puff-ball blooms provide a year-round delightful contrast in the food forest. Its flowering branches are sold as cut flowers. In the Fabaceae family.

SIZE h*w	SUN	SOIL	WATER	EDIBLE
15ft*10ft	full	well-draining; poor - OK	drought tolerant	gum, flowers

PROPAGATION METHODS

- SEEDS: Germinates at 77-95F in 4 weeks. Scarify & pre-soak 12 hours in warm water.
- CUTTINGS: Half-ripe wood, stolons, runners, suckers.

RECIPE

SWEET ACACIA TEA: Collect 2 flowers after the morning dew has dried. Wash & dry. Cover with steaming hot (not boiling) water (1 cup). Steep for 5 minutes. Strain.

Add sweetener to taste.

Consume in moderation - medicinal.

CULTURAL SIGNIFICANCE

- An essential oil (i.e. Cassie) distilled from the flowers- used in European perfumery
- Flowers added to ointment & rubbed on the forehead to treat headaches
- Bark & fruit rich in tannin for dyes & inks; gum used as glue in arts
- Woody branches used in India as toothbrushes
- Pods and leaves are forage for livestock
- Some believe Jesus' Crown of Thorns was an Acacia species

CULINARY USE

Gum
Gum obtained from the plant is used to prepare sweets. Considered superior to gum arabic & used as a natural stabilizer & thickening agent in foods like syrups, gumdrops and marshmallows.

Flowers
Flowers 3rd year from seed. Used in folk healing tea as a stomachic, aphrodisiac & food flavoring. In Malaysia, flower tea is mixed with turmeric as post-partum aid.

Seeds/ Pods & Young Leaves
NOTE: Conflicting data on ediblity. Caution! Seed pods (tender fruit) - roasted and eaten by Australian Aborigines; however, anti-nutrients present. Astringent. Seeds also pressed for oil or sprouted. Young leaves eaten after boiling by some. Used as a tamarind flavoring for chutneys.

CAUTIONS & CONSIDERATIONS

Health
CAUTION: Thorny. Anecdotal reports that uncooked seeds used to kill dogs in Brazil. HCN in leaves - boil 30 min & dump water. Occasionally confused with other species.

Pests
Resilient. No real pest or disease issues: borers, root rot.

Landscape design
Nitrogen fixer. Great hedge, windbreak & erosion control. May form thickets. Compare with Pink Mimosa (Albizia julibrissin) or FL native, Sweetgum (Liquidambar styraciflua) & Pineland Acacia (Vachellia farnesiana var. pinetorum - rare).

Sweet Laurel

Laurus nobilis

HARDINESS ZONES: 8 TO 10

An aromatic evergreen in the Lauraceae family with showy spring flowers- also called, "Bay Laurel." Long history of folk healing use to aid to digestion and relieve flu symptoms. Highly esteemed since ancient times - dedicated to Apollo & used as a symbol of peace and victory. Used to make wreaths to crown the victors of various contests like emperors, generals and poets. May be grown in containers as a houseplant. Widely cultivated as an ornamental. A great companion plant!

SIZE h*w	SUN	SOIL	WATER	EDIBLE
40ft*30ft	full to partial	well-draining	average	leaves, fruit

PROPAGATION METHODS

- SEEDS: <u>Dioecious.</u> Germinates at 70F. Short viability. Erratic germination.
- CUTTINGS: Half-ripe or mature side shoots. Slow to root (6-18 months). High success rate.
- AIR-LAYERING: Preferred.

RECIPE

BAY LEAF TEA: Wash 6 bay leaves and cover with 3 cups of boiling water. Cover and allow to steep 10 minutes. Sweeten to taste.

Flavor notes of cinnamon, clove, nutmeg and allspice. Can be made with fresh or dried leaves.

CULINARY USE

Fruit
Dried fruit used as a flavoring much like the leaves.

Leaves
Leaves used fresh or dried for a spicy, aromatic flavoring in casseroles, soups & stews. Considered an essential ingredient of the herb mix 'Bouquet Garni'. Leaves typically harvested in the summer and dried. Flavor and scent intensify with drying. Oils are more concentrated. Dried leaves lose flavor after a year. Dried leaves brewed into a herbal tea. Often added whole to Italian pasta sauces. Ground bay leaves can be also added to smoothies and Bloody Mary drinks. Whole leaves are used as an aromatic garnish to dishes.

CULTURAL SIGNIFICANCE

- Yields an essential oil used in soap making; insect repellent to protect stored grain, beans & used in massage therapy/ aromatherapy
- Sweet-smelling wood used for marqueterie work, walking sticks & fire-starter friction sticks
- Folk remedy/ poultice for rashes from poison ivy, poison oak, and stinging nettle
- In ancient Greece, plant was called "Daphne" after the priestess of Gaia (Mother Earth)
- Dried leaves used in potpourri

CAUTIONS & CONSIDERATIONS

Health
No known adverse health effects. Remove whole leaves after cooking - choking hazard or may create cuts inside digestive tract/ mouth (leaves are sharp).

Pests
Resilient. Scale, mealybugs, spider mites, anthracnose and powdery mildew.

Landscape design
A good windbreak hedge. Size & shape easily controlled by pruning. Often pruned to 8' tall or less. A good topiary - slow growing.

Sweet Potato ⭐

Ipomoea batatas

HARDINESS ZONES: 10 TO 12

The prized, large, starchy, sweet-tasting tubers are reason enough to grow this perennial vine. However, the pretty ornamental heart-shaped leaves and the note-worthy flowers add delightful color to the garden. Member of the morning glory (Convolvulaceae) family. Grown as an annual throughout the U.S. but a perennial in South Florida. Purple sweet potatoes are a main food in the traditional diet of Okinawa, a region known for its high concentration of centenarians.

SIZE h*w	SUN	SOIL	WATER	EDIBLE
10ft*1ft	full to partial	acidic sandy, loamy	flood tolerant	tuber, leaves, shoots

PROPAGATION METHODS

- CUTTINGS: Roots readily in water. Once tuber sprouts, place half-way in water using toothpicks to elevate from base. NOTE: Propagation from seed possible but usually reserved for breeding.

RECIPE

SWEET POTATO NOODLES: Thoroughly wash and peel 3 sweet potatoes. Slice off ends and cut in half through the middle so they are not so long. Spiralize. Place them on an oiled baking sheet. Drizzle with the olive oil and sprinkle with sea salt. Roast them in the oven at 450F until tender, about 10-15 minutes. Serve with sauce of choice.

CULINARY USE

Tuber
Consumed boiled, baked or fried. Candied sweet potatoes are a side dish for Thanksgiving in Western U.S. In some countries, sweet potato is often served with a peanut or tamarind sauce. Another popular method is to bake it and then drench with honey. Used in soup, served as "fries" with rock sugar and ginger. Bread and noodles are also made from tubers. The tubers yield everything from flour, dried chips, juice, bread, candy, and pectin. After digging but before cooking, sweet potatoes are traditionally cured to improve storage, flavor, and nutrition. In Japan, the tubers are fermented into a liquor/ spirit called: imo-jōchū.

Leaves & Shoots
Most often eaten blanched or sautéed and served with a garlic and soy sauce mixture.

CULTURAL SIGNIFICANCE

- Considered 5th most important crop world-wide
- A naturally transgenic food
- Most efficient staple food to grow
- Juice of red sweet potatoes is combined with lime juice for pink to black cloth dye
- Purple sweet potato is a popular food coloring
- "Slips" are ideal in aquaponics to clean water and provide hiding for aquatic life
- Fibers yield a biodegradable plastic

CAUTIONS & CONSIDERATIONS

Health
No known adverse health effects. Significant nutrients. Center for Science in the Public Interest ranked nutritional value of sweet potatoes among the highest known.

Pests
Fungal leaf diseases.

Landscape design
Some cultivars of Ipomoea batatas are grown as ornamental plants under the name "tuberous morning glory," and have edible tubers but are less tasty. Other varieties have red or purple flesh - purple variety is famous for being 70% of the Okinawan "longevity"/ Blue Zone diet.

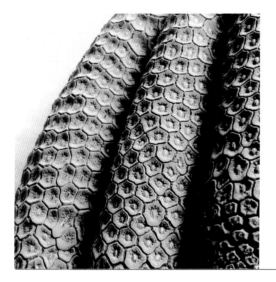

Swiss Cheese Plant

Monstera deliciosa

HARDINESS ZONES: 9 TO 12

A fast-growing and low maintenance vine in the Araceae/ the arum lily family. One of the world's most common houseplants! A perfect understory! Plants can flower and produce delicious fruit year-round! Starts life as a terrestrial, turning epiphytic when in contact with a tree. Bears beautiful, white flowers resembling calla lilies.

SIZE h*w	SUN	SOIL	WATER	EDIBLE
65ft*19ft	partial sun; full shade	acidic - OK; well-draining	seasonal flooding - OK	fruit

PROPAGATION METHODS

- CUTTINGS: Suckers fruit in 2 to 4 years; cuttings in 4 to 6 years. Plant cuttings in soil with at least one leaf. Vines with established aerial roots can be buried within 2-3" of the first leaf node.

RECIPE

MONSTERA PRESERVES: Rinse 2 cups of "berry" segments and stew for 10 minutes in a little water. Then add a cup of agave and a tablespoon of citrus juice. Simmer for 20 minutes and preserve in sterilized jars. Store in the refrigerator for up to 2 months.

CULINARY USE

Fruit
The juicy, subacid fruits look like a green corn on the cob. Fruits are an aggregate of creamy-white berries covered by green hexagonal "scales." The fruit is ripe once the green scale covering falls off. The fruit can take 12-14 months to ripen. There are often immature & mature fruits together on the plant. The fruit tastes like a combination of bananas, mangos & pineapples. Made into jellies, jams, ice creams, sherbets, & soft drinks. To harvest, cut fruit with at least an inch of stem when the tile-like sections of rind separate and appear slightly bulged. Keep at room temperature to further ripen over 5 or 6 days. Evenly wrap the entire fruit in paper. Once ripened, pulp will fall from the inedible core. Keep in the refrigerator for up to a week.

CULTURAL SIGNIFICANCE

- Aerial roots used as furniture embellishments, ropes & for basket-making
- Seedlings in the wild grow towards darker areas & towards larger trees for climbing (an unusual "negative phototropism" behavior)
- Leaf holes & slits permit wind to pass through without damaging the foliage
- Epithet "deliciosa" means "delicious", referring to the edible fruit. "Monstera" - Latin for "monstrous" for "abnormal"

CAUTIONS & CONSIDERATIONS

Health
CAUTION: Potential allergen/ not pet friendly. All parts of the plant contain calcium oxalate crystals and/or oxalic acid. While many consume the ripe fruit raw, cooking may be safest. Sap may cause skin irritation.

Pests
Resilient. Aphids, mealybugs, thrips, scale or spider mites.

Landscape design
Can be kept to 6-8' for ease of harvest; trim the terminal new growth. Varieties with variegated leaves may not have edible fruits. May behave invasively.

Sword Fern

Nephrolepis cordifolia

HARDINESS ZONES: 8 TO 10

This perennial evergreen is likely already on your property. It may have even formed a dense ground cover colony in some areas. Considered a Category I Invasive. Distinguished from similar ferns by the edible tuber - high nutritional value according to FAO/WHO nutrient standards! In the Polypodiaceae/ Nephrolepidaceae family. Widely cultivated for its ornamental foliage. Suitable as a houseplant.

SIZE h*w	SUN	SOIL	WATER	EDIBLE
30in*4in	full sun to full shade	well-draining	drought tolerant	tuber

PROPAGATION METHODS

NOT RECOMMENDED
- SEEDS: Germinates at 77-85. Spores on the underside of leaves are dispersed by the wind.
- DIVISION: Spreads by underground runners.

RECIPE

ROASTED SWORD FERN: Rinse tubers and bath in a solution of 1:1 vinegar to water for 15 min. Rinse. Dry and rub surfaces with oil. Sprinkle with sea salt, ground pepper, and ground garlic to taste. Roast at 350 until soft (10-30 min depending on size). Remove from oven when soft and golden in color.

CULTURAL SIGNIFICANCE

- Indigenous to Hawaiian Islands. Fashioned as lei for wrists, ankles & head
- Used since ancient times as traditional medicine (e.g., diuretic, for liver ailments; believed to be antibacterial, antifungal & hepatoprotective)
- Cited as a potential commercial crop
- Leaflets described in research as having an enormous nutritional potential and significant contribution to food supplementation

CULINARY USE

Tubers
Produces round, fleshy tubers about 1/2 inch (marble-size) in diameter year-round. Tubers are found along the prostrate stolons. Rich source of carbohydrates and calcium. Roasted tubers eaten in Nepal. Consumed in the form of vegetables, salad, soup and pickles in the Garhwal area of the Himalayas. Several phytochemical compounds naturally present. Flavor like Jerusalem Artichokes; potato aroma. Texture of a water chestnut. Consume young tubers only. Avoid consuming tubers with any bluish coloration.

Leaves
Some reports of edibility but see health cautions.

CAUTIONS & CONSIDERATIONS

Health
No known adverse health effects but caution advised with ferns since some contain carcinogens and/or thiaminase. Some plants are difficult to pull; the rachis can cut skin - wear heavy gloves.

Pests
Resilient; mealy bugs, scale, slugs.

Landscape design
An epiphytic and epilithic plant. Compare with FL native sword fern (N. exaltata).

Tamarind
Tamarindus indica

HARDINESS ZONES: 10 TO 12

A low maintenance, evergreen in the legume/ Fabaceae family with showy flowers. Often grown as ornamental, shade tree and cultivated since ancient times. Long-lived and productive! Adult trees may still be productive after 200 years. Can yield 400lbs of fruit per year. One of the richest natural sources of tartaric acid (8-10%) - immune boosting benefits! The seeds are a staple crop; they offer a balanced carbohydrate for flour. Countless culinary uses!

SIZE h*w	SUN	SOIL	WATER	EDIBLE
50ft+*40ft+	full	well-draining; poor, saline, acidic - OK	drought tolerant	pulp, seed/pod, leaves & flowers

PROPAGATION METHODS

- SEEDS: Germinates at 75-83. Viable for years. Soak 24 hours. Bears fruit after 7 - 10 years.
- CUTTINGS: Greenwood.

RECIPE

TAMARIND PASTE: Break & peel the shells off pulp. Remove "strings" from pulp. Pull apart the seeds and place in a bowl with steaming hot water. Soak 15 minutes. Once cooled, massage pulp off seeds. Strain. Boil the liquid down to form a paste. Add a pinch of salt. Use in chutney, sauce, drinks, ice cream & more!

CULTURAL SIGNIFICANCE

- All parts of tree have utility - Seed oil used for paints and varnishes; fruit pulp mixed with sea salt to polish metal; leaves yield a red dye (rich in tannin); wood used for carpentry; ideal fuel & charcoal; fruit pulp used as a fixative with turmeric or annatto in dyeing
- Many folk-healing uses (e.g. A tea of leaves is used to relieve throat infection, cough, fever; fruit used for laxative effects)
- In Asian countries, it is grown as a bonsai

CULINARY USE

Fruit
Fruit ripens mainly in June-September. Brown pods are filled with a sweet/ sour pulp eaten raw or cooked. Mixed with water to make a lemonade-like drink. An important ingredient in chutneys, curries and sauces. Popular in ice cream. Rich in calcium, phosphorus, iron, & thiamine.

Seeds & Seedpod
Rich source of carbohydrates & protein, but must be boiled to remove tannins & the testa. Mature seeds are soaked, dried, then toasted or boiled & de-shelled. Ground into flour or roasted as a coffee substitute. Immature seedpods pickled or added to soups, stews & sauces.

Leaves & Flowers
Young leaves and flowers edible raw or cooked such as in salad. Seedlings are cooked like a vegetable.

CAUTIONS & CONSIDERATIONS

Health
No known adverse health effects. High in antioxidants.

Pests
Resilient: Scale, mealybug, borers, caterpillars, aphids, thrips, leaf spots & rot.

Landscape design
Taproot. Responds well to coppicing & pollarding. Allelopathic. Can behave invasively. Cross-pollination often results in better fruiting. Two types: sour (most common) and sweet (mostly comes from Thailand). Compare with FL native, Wild Tamarind (Lysiloma latisiliquum).

Tea
Camelia sinensis

HARDINESS ZONES: 7 TO 10

An evergreen shrub loved the world over for providing a tea which lends feelings of comfort and exhilaration. Used in Chinese herbalism as one of 50 fundamental, medicinal herbs. Showy blooms have a delightful scent! An ideal understory! Fragrant flowers attract pollinators. Often pruned to a low height of 3-5ft to produce a profusely branching and spreading bush ready for constant harvesting. Limbs are carved for walking sticks! In the Theaceae family.

SIZE h*w	SUN	SOIL	WATER	EDIBLE
13ft*8ft	partial; dappled	acidic - OK; well-draining	average	leaves, stems, flowers

PROPAGATION METHODS

- SEEDS: Germinates at 70-75F. Produces few seeds with low viability.
- CUTTINGS: Any time if using hardwood; high percentage root but slowly.

RECIPE

TEA-SOAKED MANGO: Soak 1 cup of sliced, dehydrated mango in 2 cups of very, freshly brewed, hot green tea. Cover and allow to infuse for 10 minutes. Drain.

Use as a spread on crackers, yogurt, or ice cream.

CULTURAL SIGNIFICANCE

- Edible seed oil - refine before consuming (not be confused with "tea tree oil"); also used in textile, soap, hair oil, lubricants, inks & paint
- Essential oil distilled from fermented dried leaves used for food flavoring (e.g., beverages, desserts, candy, baked goods & puddings)
- Infused leaves yield varieties of food coloring
- Leaves used as a poultice for cuts, sore eyes, headaches, burns, bruises, bites, swellings
- Believed to aid dental health - fluoride in leaf

CULINARY USE

Leaves, Stems & Flowers
Bush leaves are picked on rotation every 7-15 days to allow renewal of tender, desirable shoots. Leaves infused in hot water produce "white," "green," "Oolong," or "black tea," depending on preparation. Green tea is made from the steamed, dried leaves, while black tea is made from leaves that have been fermented and then dried. Contains protective polyphenol & catechins antioxidants. Cold tea used as a soaking liquid to flavor dried fruit. Kukicha tea uses twigs and stems rather than leaves. Occasionally used as a boiled vegetable. Boiling water is consumed separate due to caffeine.

Flowers are made into 'tempura' using the edible oil that is obtained from the seed.

CAUTIONS & CONSIDERATIONS

Health
CAUTION: Consume in moderation. Contains caffeine & tannins. May cause adverse reaction in those with heart disease or thyroid conditions. Children should not consume - risk of anemia.

Pests
Resilient. Fungal diseases, scale insects, aphids, planthoppers and spider mites.

Landscape design
Excellent shade hedge. October to December blooms. Compare with Moujean tea (Cereus robinii).

Tindora
Coccinia grandis

HARDINESS ZONES: 8 TO 11

Also called "Ivy Gourd." A perennial cucumber of sorts. This plant is full of nutrients and develops very fast. That said, this hardy plant is best grown indoors, in a screened enclosure or a greenhouse given its enthusiastic dominance - can smother a tree! Grows up to four inches per day. Purchase the sterile variety/ root stock for planting to prevent self-seeding. A good source of several micronutrients!

SIZE h*w	SUN	SOIL	WATER	EDIBLE
9ft*1ft	full to partial	well-draining	constant moist	leaves, fruit

PROPAGATION METHODS

- TUBER: Hermaphrodite & sterile. NOTE: Can be grown from seed but unlikely to reliably produce fruit. <u>Dioecious.</u>

RECIPE

TANGY IVY GOURD PICKLE: Wash 3 c of tindora gourds and dry. Trim ends. Slice thinly. Add 1 tbs salt & 3 tbs vinegar. Toss. Cover overnight. Heat 3/4 c oil on medium & add 1 tsp turmeric, & 1 tbsp fennel seeds. Stir until fragrant. Remove from heat and toss with tindora. Add all content to a glass jar. Keep covered for 3 days. Stir daily.

CULTURAL SIGNIFICANCE

- Introduced as a food crop in several countries in Asia, Australia, Pacific Islands, Africa, the Caribbean, and southern U.S.
- Valued in folk healing (e.g., for saponin, alkaloids, steroids, flavonoids and glycosides; Considered anti-inflammatory, antimicrobial, antidiabetic, antioxidant, hypoglycemic, antitussive)
- Introduced to Hawaii as a backyard food crop. Now on the Hawaii State Noxious Weed List

CULINARY USE

Fruit
Young and tender green fruits - raw in salads or cooked and added to curries. Considered best cooked. Ripe scarlet fruit - raw. Fleshy and sweet. Commonly eaten in Indian cuisine. Eaten as a curry, by deep-frying it along with spices, stuffing it with masala and sauteing it, or boiling, then frying it. Used in sambar, a vegetable and lentil-based soup. Immature fruit used to make a quick fresh pickle. One of the ingredients of the very popular Thai clear soup dish called, kaeng jued tum lueng and curries called, kaeng khae curry and kaeng lieng curry.

Leaves
Young leaves and long slender stem tops eaten cooked as a potherb or added to soups. Leaves are also blanched, boiled or stir-fried. Dried and used as a medicinal tea.

CAUTIONS & CONSIDERATIONS

Health
No known health hazards. Rich in beta-carotene.

Pests
Aphids, whiteflies, mites and thrips; acts as a host for melon fly and is a reservoir for other crop pests possibly including ring spot virus.

Landscape design
Likely to behave invasively. Can produce fruit year-round. Compare with FL native: Creeping Cucumber (Melothria pendula), Cucumber tree/ Bilimbi (Averrhoa bilimbi) or Bitter Melon/ Cerasee (Momordica Charantia).

Toona Tree

Toona sinensis

HARDINESS ZONES: 6 TO 11

An interesting, fast-growing deciduous tree & vegetable protein in the Meliaceae family. Flowers have a powerful, rich scent. Valued as a long-lived ornamental. Leaves change from pinkish red to bronze, then to green. Leaves, fruits & bark used in traditional Chinese medicine for over a thousand years to fight diabetes, male infertility & liver disease. Fragrant, small branches are burned in Buddhist temples during ceremonies.

SIZE h*w	SUN	SOIL	WATER	EDIBLE
65ft*30ft	full	well-drained; alkaline - OK	average; drought tolerant	leaves, shoots

PROPAGATION METHODS

- SEEDS: Germinates at 77F. Soak 24 hrs. Short viability.
- DIVISION: Plants form suckers from underground runners. Take in winter.

RECIPE

FRIED EGG WITH TOONA: 1 c young toona leaves (stems removed, washed, dried, & chopped), 3 eggs - beaten, pinch of salt, diced chili/pepper to taste.

Mix all ingredients. In an oiled pan on medium heat, add mixture. Fry 3 min. Flip. Fry another 3 min. Middle should be solid. Serve warm.

CULINARY USE

Leaves & Shoots

Young shoots and leaves eaten cooked - usually blanched and then prepared. Taste resembles onions with floral notes. Reddish leaves are said to taste best. Cut new growth for several months in spring and early summer. The pinker or redder the new growth, the greater the bioactive properties. Smells like garlic and pepper when cut. Often stir-fried with egg, pickled, or roasted and dried as tea. Leaves contain about 6-10% protein and are ground into a seasoning paste. Rich in carotene and vitamins A, B and C.

Older larger leaves get tough. May be used like a Bay Leaf to flavor soups, stews, and more but removed before eating.

CULTURAL SIGNIFICANCE

- Timber is hard; valued for furniture & guitars
- In China, used metaphorically - A common phrase is: "wishing your Toona sinensis and daylily are strong and happy" (椿萱并茂). Toona sinensis represents the father & daylily, the mother
- Fruit is a star-shaped capsule resembling a wooden rose - can be used in crafts
- Used in folk healing (e.g., tender leaves for anti-inflammatory, detoxifying effects)

CAUTIONS & CONSIDERATIONS

Health

No known adverse health effects. Consume in moderation - history of medicinal uses.

Pests

Resilient.

Landscape design

Cut to the ground every few years to maintain size. Dig or cut runners to prevent spread. Pungent smell in close quarters. Flamingo variety is said to be most vibrant. Shelter young seedlings from direct sun. Compare with native Winged Sumac (Rhus copallinum).

Tropical Almond

Terminalia catappa

HARDINESS ZONES: 10 TO 12

Considered a staple due to high protein and oil content. You are likely to find this tree growing in the wild given that the seeds readily germinate. Rich source of zinc! A good nutcracker (or hammer) is needed to break the shell but worth the effort! A handsome tree with autumn color. In the Combretaceae family.

SIZE h*w	SUN	SOIL	WATER	EDIBLE
90ft*70ft	full	acidic, alkaline - OK	drought tolerant	fruit. oil, nut/seed

PROPAGATION METHODS

- SEEDS: Germinates at 77-86F - high success rate. Pre-soak 24 hours. Viable years. Produces within a few years.

RECIPE

ALMOND MACAROONS: ¾ cup almond flour, 2 egg whites. Optional: Sandwich 2 with jam.

After shelling, soaking (overnight) & dehydrating almonds, grind into a flour. Mix in egg whites. Spoon 2 tbs onto a greased baking sheet 1 ½" apart. Bake 20 min at 325 center rack; until light brown. Cool on wire rack.

CULTURAL SIGNIFICANCE

- Environmental benefits (e.g., Host plant for brown awl butterfly; in aquaculture, leaves reduce fungal infections)
- Pharmacological research confirm antimicrobial, anti-inflammatory, antioxidant & hepatoprotective properties
- Shell is rich in tannin for leather preparation
- Black dye from the bark and fruit; wood used for furniture, buildings, boats, bridges
- Heavy leaf fall is a good provider of mulch

CULINARY USE

Fruit
The fruits have a tender skin and a thin layer of subacid juicy flesh. As it matures and ripens, it turns from green to orange.

Nut/ Oil
Seed can be eaten raw but is best cooked. The almond-flavored seeds are typically roasted, chopped and added to cookies, bread mixes, dessert fillings, sweets, soups and stews. Can be processed for candied almonds and as flour for making cakes. Contains about 50% semi-drying oil used in cooking. Rather similar to standard almond oil, but less prone to become rancid. A single tree can yield around 11lbs of kernels per year! Contains up to 25% protein and 15% carbohydrates. A good source of calcium, iron & lipid acids.

CAUTIONS & CONSIDERATIONS

Health
Rich in macro and micronutrients! Ants may inhabit hollow twigs. May be confused with Fagraea crenulata.

Pests
No serious insect or disease problems. Leaf spot may occur. Thrips; grasshoppers and beetles.

Landscape design
Vast root system binds together sandy soils. Fruit could stain cars, pavement and sidewalks. Compare with Java Almond (Canarium vulgare) & Sweet Almond (Prunus dulcis).

Turks Cap

Malvaviscus arboreus var. drummondii

HARDINESS ZONES: 7 TO 10

A favorite in "old Florida" landscapes. The brilliant flower adds a cheerful pop of color when many summer-flowering plants have fizzled out. This marvelously resilient plant is beloved for the sweet nectar at the base of the flowers. So delicious! A solid Florida native & great subcanopy plant! Blooms in shade! In the Malvaceae family.

SIZE h*w	SUN	SOIL	WATER	EDIBLE
10ft*10ft	partial	acidic sandy, loamy	flood tolerant	flowers, fruit, leaves

PROPAGATION METHODS

- SEEDS: Germinates at 78-86F. Plant immediately upon germination; roots are fragile.
- CUTTINGS: Softwood roots readily in water when not flowering. Abundant suckers from the base.

RECIPE

TURKS CAP TEA: Collect 1 cup of tightly wrapped flowers (these have more nectar) in the morning after dew has dried. Wash and pat dry. Pour 2 cups nearly boiling water over the flowers. Allow to steep 2 minutes covered. Strain.

OPTIONAL: Add sweetener of choice to taste.

CULTURAL SIGNIFICANCE

- Understory shrub offering an important food source for juvenile Ruby-throated Hummingbirds (Archilochus colubri) and Black-chinned Hummingbirds
- Blooms May-Nov; may bloom in winter in So FL
- Primary host plant for the caterpillars of the Turk's-cap White-Skipper

CULINARY USE

Flower
Pluck off the flower and eat raw or in salad or simply sip the nectar from the plucked end. If you've ever had a tasty hibiscus tea, you'll appreciate Turk's Cap tea.

Fruit
M. arboreus var. drummondii yields marble-size red fruit and while the berries are edible fresh, the seeds dominate, so you get more flavor and food from making something out of the berries like jam or tea.

Leaves
The young leaves are touted as great fresh in salads but also stand up well to steaming, cooking into quiches, frittatas and dressing up familiar dishes such as pastas and pizzas. Harvest the majority of leaves in spring when tender.

CAUTIONS & CONSIDERATIONS

Health
CAUTION: Literature provides few nutritional details. Numerous taxonomic problems in the naming. Some sources list Malvaviscus drummondii as a separate species. Edibility is mostly anecdotal.

Pests
Few pest problems; whiteflies.

Landscape design
Often confused with Malvaviscus penduliflorus which does not fruit. Unique cultivars include pink 'Pam Puryear', aka 'Pam's Pink', white Turk's cap and the Mexican variety, 'Big Momma', whose red flowers are larger and showier.

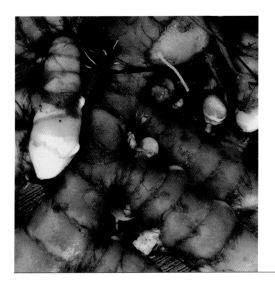

Tumeric
Curcuma longa

HARDINESS ZONES: 8 TO 11

Called "the world's healthiest spice!" A perennial member of the Zingiberaceae family. Cultivated for thousands of years for cuisine, medicine, and cultural practices. Traditionally, women rubbed turmeric into cheeks or added to bath water to improve skin tone & counteract aging. Associated with fertility, prosperity, & good luck! Provides a bountiful harvest! A great companion to ginger & katuk and a good house plant!

SIZE h*w	SUN	SOIL	WATER	EDIBLE
2ft*1ft	partial	well-draining	seasonal flooding - OK	rhizome, flowers

PROPAGATION METHODS

- RHIZOMES: Division in spring or summer; cut 1 to 1½ inches long with one "eye" if possible. Allow to dry 1-2 days. Plant up to 4" deep. Grows in summer/ rainy season. Dormant in winter. NOTE: Flowers are sterile; no viable seeds.

RECIPE

TURMERIC TEA: Heat a pot on medium. Melt 1 tsp coconut oil. Stir in 1 tsp cracked peppercorn & 1/2 inch of washed, peeled, diced turmeric until fragrant. Add 3c coconut milk. Puree in blender with 1 tbs sweetener of choice. Return to pot. Boil 5 min. Fill cup. Refrigerate up to 3 days.

OPTIONAL: Top with frothed nut milk to taste.

CULTURAL SIGNIFICANCE

- Rhizome used for pH sensitive dye (e.g., yellow turns dark red with alkalinity/ baking powder)
- Mustard or saffron substitute. Leaves used for wrapping & cooking food
- Folk healing use (e.g., to aid digestion, lower blood pressure, treat liver ailments, manage Alzheimer's disease, prevent gallstones. Believed to have anti-bacterial, anti-fungal, antioxidant & anti-inflammatory properties)

CULINARY USE

Tuber/ Rhizome
Harvested in the fall when the foliage begins to wilt and dry out. Main ingredient in curry powder for taste and distinctive yellow-orange color. Great addition to juices, smoothies, curries, and salads. Turmeric has a warm, flavor and an earthy, mustard-like aroma. 1 inch of fresh turmeric is equivalent to 1 tablespoon of freshly grated turmeric, or 1 teaspoon of ground turmeric. Keeps well frozen: wash, peel, and freeze. Adding pepper to a recipe with turmeric may boost the absorption of curcumin (the active ingredient in turmeric) and amplify reported benefits. Added to nut milk with ginger, pepper, & cardamom in "Golden Milk" recipes.

Flowers
Plant flowers eaten as a vegetable.

CAUTIONS & CONSIDERATIONS

Health
No known adverse health effects. NOTE: Will stain hands & clothing. Some develop an allergic reaction to the dye. Deliberate contamination of bulk turmeric powder in some commercial products.

Pests
Red spider mites if soil is too dry; slugs and snails.

Landscape design
Multicolored varieties (blue, yellow, orange). Compare with mango ginger (C. amada), narrow-leaved turmeric (C. angustifolia), and wild turmeric (C. aromatica).

Ulluco

Ullucus tuberosus

HARDINESS ZONES: 8 TO 10

A staple crop in the Basellaceae family. Used in South America just like potatoes. Pretty! Tubers are colored yellow, orange, red/purple, green, or white - sometimes with spots! Stems range green to red. All parts of the plant are edible at all stages of growth! Grows well with garlic or onions! Grown much like related New Zealand & Malabar spinach.

SIZE h*w	SUN	SOIL	WATER	EDIBLE
3ft*1/2ft	full to partial	poor - OK	drought tolerant	tubers, leaves

PROPAGATION METHODS

- DIVISION: Divide tubers once foliage dies back. Tubers produced in short days of fall. Stored tubers sprout at room temperature in spring.
- CUTTINGS: Root very easily.

RECIPE

ULLUCO FLOUR: Dehydrate sliced ulluco at 125F until crisp. Grind into a flour in a food processor. Add to a sourdough starter. Use in any bread, cookie, or cake recipe.

OPTIONAL: Slice & dry ulluco in a freeze dryer to preserve color. Eat as a "potato chip."

CULTURAL SIGNIFICANCE

- Called, "Earth Gems" in New Zealand
- Dehydrated ulluco leaves studied as a breakfast cereal replacement
- Most widely grown, economically important root crop in Andean region, 2nd only to potato
- A popular cash crop sold in markets of multiple South American cities
- In markets, red is the preferred skin and tissue color and cooked was the most popular preparation method

CULINARY USE

Tuber
Harvest once the top growth has died back. Tubers grow up to 3 inches in diameter but average 1-2 inches. Shape varies from round to oblong, curved or twisted. Typically eaten cooked. Starchy. Tastes like nutty/ sweet corn raw. Added to salads. Julienned as a slaw. When boiled or fried they taste like a beet/ potato combination. Commonly prepared in soups and stews. Loses color when cooked. Minimize color loss by acidifying cooking water & minimizing cooking time. Does not require peeling. Dried and powdered to bake bread, cakes, & cookies. Lasts up to 12 months in cool conditions. Rich in antioxidants.

Leaves
Leaves eaten raw or cooked. Rich in protein, calcium, and carotene. Mucilaginous. Used like spinach.

CAUTIONS & CONSIDERATIONS

Health
No known adverse health effects.

Pests
Slugs, volves/ mice. Varieties susceptible to viruses.

Landscape design
Plant in part shade/ dappled light in areas where temperatures exceed 75 degrees. Varieties available for purchase from: https://www.cultivariable.com. Compare with Oca (Oxalis tuberosa), Mashua (Tropaeolum tuberosum).

Vanilla
Vanilla planifolia

HARDINESS ZONES: 10 TO 12

A fast-growing, evergreen, and perennial climber, in the Orchidaceae family. Showy flowers! Economically productive for up to 15 years. Can be grown as a house plant or ornamental. Each flower opens for only one day, so hand-pollinating is a labor of love. One of the most important ingredients in perfumery. Historically, indigenous people valued vanilla as a sacred plant.

SIZE h*w	SUN	SOIL	WATER	EDIBLE
60ft*5ft	partial	well-drained; poor - OK	drought tolerant	seedpod/seeds

PROPAGATION METHODS

- SEEDS: Germinates at 68-77F. Scatter on soil/ mulch. Do not cover.
- CUTTINGS: 1-8 weeks to root. 40in cuttings fruit within 2 years. Shorter cuttings take up to 5 years. Leave at least three leaf nodes.

RECIPE

VANILLA INFUSED MAPLE SYRUP: 8 oz maple syrup, 2 vanilla pods - slit lengthwise & cut into quarters.

Bring syrup to a near boil. Gently stir in pods. Allow to cool. Pour into jars. Infuse 2 weeks in the refrigerator.

CULINARY USE

Seedpod/ Seeds
Skinny fruit pods (6-10" long) are picked when beans are fully formed and firm. Beans are then cured. Pods are harvested before ripe and immersed in hot steam, then allowed to ferment for up to four weeks. During fermentation, the pods to turn black from oxidization & form a glaze of glucose and vanillin crystals on the surface, giving the spice its aroma and flavor. Seedpod used as a flavoring in a wide range of foods like cakes, ice creams, confectionery, puddings etc. Seedpods contain about 3.5% vanillin.

Pod can be placed in sugar, oil, or alcohol and left to diffuse flavor into the sugar. First used by the Aztecs - combined with chocolate to make a fragrant drink called tlilxochitl.

CULTURAL SIGNIFICANCE

- Most expensive spice after saffron; most stores sell synthetic versions. Less than 1% of vanilla in stores comes from the orchid
- The only orchid which produces an edible fruit
- Used in folk healing (e.g., to reduce fevers, as an aphrodisiac, carminative, emmenagogue, for antimicrobial properties)
- Grows wild in tropical forests of Mexico and Central and northern South America but is now rare due to habitat loss & exploitation

CAUTIONS & CONSIDERATIONS

Health
CAUTION: Calcium oxalate crystals in plant - may cause dermatitis. Wear gloves.

Pests
Fungus rot, spider mites and mealybugs.

Landscape design
Hand-pollinate in early morning, daily (lift rostellum so anther can be pressed onto the stigma). Shelter from wind. Often intercropped with sugarcane. "Semi-epiphytic" - plant in the ground or as an air plant. UF/ IFAS Tropical Research and Education Center (TREC) is trialing species.

Vegetable Hummingbird

Sesbania grandiflora

HARDINESS ZONES: 9 TO 12

A fast-growing, low maintenance, deciduous tree in the Fabaceae family and important agroforestry species. Blooms all year! Flowers are the most widely used part in recipes. A perfect companion plant. Provides protection and enriches nutrients to neighboring crops. Pollinated by birds.

SIZE h*w	SUN	SOIL	WATER	EDIBLE
40ft*25ft	full	acidic- OK	drought tolerant; seasonal flooding - OK	flowers, seedpods, young leaves & shoots

PROPAGATION METHODS

- SEEDS: Germinates at 75-86F. Some varieties require scarification. Pour hot water on the seeds. Soak 24 hours. 80% germination. Plant during rainy season.
- CUTTINGS: Half-ripe wood.

RECIPE

SESBANIA OMELETTE: 1 ½ c flowers (rinsed with center removed), 2 tbs oil, 2 eggs, 4 garlic cloves peeled and chopped), 1 tsp sea salt.

Heat an oiled pan over medium-high. Beat eggs in a bowl with garlic, sesbania flowers, & salt. Pour mixture into pan. Fry 2 minutes. Flip. Fry 2 minutes. Remove from heat. Serve.

CULTURAL SIGNIFICANCE

- Used in folk healing (e.g., Leaves are considered aperient & diuretic; applied as a poultice to sprains, bruises, swellings, rheumatism, stings)
- Wood is a source of pulp for paper making
- Used as a windbreak for citrus, banana & coffee, as a living fence, as shelterbelt, or as a live support for vanilla and pepper
- A clear gum from the bark is used in foods
- Seed oil rich in fatty acid: oleic, linoleic, stearic

CULINARY USE

Flowers

Eaten raw or cooked. Added to salads, boiled as a potherb, fried or used in curries. Rich in iron; tastes like mushrooms. Often lightly steamed after removing calyx and pistil which are bitter. White flowers preferred in flavor over red ones. Astringent but sweet taste.

Seedpods

Ripe pods harvested 9 months after planting. Long, narrow pods are boiled and eaten like string beans. Often prepared in coconut milk "gravy." The protein rich seeds are also fermented into tempeh.

Leaves & Shoots

Young leaves and shoots are cooked in curries, stews, and soups, lightly fried, steamed or boiled. Mildly tart in taste. Consumed as a staple food around the world.

CAUTIONS & CONSIDERATIONS

Health

No known adverse health effects. Can be mistaken for other species (e.g., for Sesbania formosa).

Pests

Leaf webbers/ feeders, stem borers, root-knot nematode.

Landscape design

Nitrogen fixing. Great green manure. Extensive root system offers erosion control. A life span of about 20 years. Brittle and weak limbs - shelter from strong wind. Some named varieties. Naturalizes - may behave invasively.

Violets
Viola sororia

HARDINESS ZONES: 8A TO 10B

A dainty, ground-cover, & perennial. Host plant for many different Fritillary butterfly species and attracts native bees! High in vitamins A and C. Ten native species occur in Florida and this variety is very common throughout the state. Great for rock gardens! Can live & propagate for 10 or more years. Historically used for both food & medicine. In the Violaceae family.

SIZE h*w	SUN	SOIL	WATER	EDIBLE
5in*5in	full to partial	poor - OK; well-draining	average	leaves, flowers

PROPAGATION METHODS

- SEEDS: Germinates at 65-75F. Self-seeds.
- DIVISION: Rhizomes form and spread. Grows in clumps forming a thick ground cover.
- CUTTINGS: Stem or root.

RECIPE

VIOLET "MOOD" TEA: Infuse 2 c washed, violet flowers in 2 c steaming hot (not boiling water). Steep, covered overnight/ 12 hours. Strain. The water will be blue. Add citrus juice and the water will turn pink. Add as much citrus juice as suits your taste, yielding a mood-based color!

CULTURAL SIGNIFICANCE

- Offers important wildlife value: Eaten by rabbits, deer, wild turkeys, birds, and more
- Folk healing uses (e.g., an infusion of the leaves and flowers used for coughs, colds, & congestion; poultice of the leaves to relieve headache)
- Known as a poetic symbol of love & modesty (e.g., Sappho, Shakespeare, Christina Rossetti)
- First cultivated in Greece around 400 BC - Athens was known as the "violet-crowned city"

CULINARY USE

Flowers

Flower color varies but blue varieties have highest edibility. Blooms from spring through the summer months. Can bloom year-round in South Florida. Adds color to any salad and can also be candied. Bland, nutty flavor. Used to make syrups. Flowers produce a pH-sensitive dye much like Butterfly Pea flowers.

NOTE: Violets have many look-alikes; some are inedible or poisonous. Harvest only when in flower for positive ID.

Leaves

Dark-green, heart-shaped leaves are hairy & eaten raw, dried (as a tea), or cooked like spinach. Often mixed with stronger tasting leaves. Added to soup to thicken, similar to Okra - mucilaginous. Puréed into a pesto or hummus.

CAUTIONS & CONSIDERATIONS

Health

CAUTION: Consume in moderation. Eating violet leaves in excess can cause nausea and vomiting. Many look alikes.

Pests

Slugs, snails, aphids, spider mite, violet gall midge, powdery mildew & leaf spot.

Landscape design

May behave invasively. Compare with 'Threatened' FL native, Bog Violet (Viola lanceolata). Also compare with Wood Sorrel (Oxalis florida/ O. corniculata; O. intermedia/ O. debilis var. corymbosa).

Walnut
Juglans neotropica

HARDINESS ZONES: 10 TO 12

Also called, "Andean Walnut" since it is native to the Andes of Columbia, Ecuador, and Peru. An endangered, slow-growing, deciduous tree in the Juglandaceae family. Attracts wildlife. Larger than the common walnut (Juglans regia). Easy to grow in warm climates even where no other walnut will! Yet, rare in the U.S. Red-colored inner wood is high-prized timber.

SIZE h*w	SUN	SOIL	WATER	EDIBLE
80ft*60ft	full	alkaline - OK	seasonal flooding - OK	nut/ seed

PROPAGATION METHODS

- SEEDS: Germinates at 60-70F. Seedlings used as rootstock for J. regia. Possible hybridization. Scarify with sandpaper. 50% or fewer typically germinate.

RECIPE

WALNUT COOKIES: 1 c walnuts (soaked 12 hours/ drained); 1/4 c coconut flour, 8 tbsp oil, 1/2 c maple syrup, 1 tsp ground cinnamon, 1 tsp vanilla extract.

Purée all ingredients until smooth. Refrigerate 2 hours until firm. Spoon onto cookie sheet. Bake 15 min at 325. Allow to cool 20 min.

CULINARY USE

Seeds

Rich and pleasant flavor. Often sold in Ecuador farmer's markets. Harvest fruits from the ground or the crown when yellowish. Gloves must be worn to prevent staining hands. Soak fruits in water 24–48 hours, but don't ferment. Simply soak to loosen the husk and enable manual removal to reveal the walnut inside. Roasted, candied & added to salads. Marinated in savory sauces and then used as a ground beef substitute. Ground into a meal and used as a flour substitute. Seed is rich in oil and fatty acids!

Varies greatly in size depending on conditions. Can be as large as a tennis ball!

CULTURAL SIGNIFICANCE

- Exploited for timber: Wood is ideal for veneer, cabinetry, interior carpentry, decors, guitars, fuel and charcoal
- Brown dye from leaves. Fruit dye requires no mordant (unripe fruit husks - yellow; ripe fruits - red to brown or if cooked in iron - black)
- Listed as 'Endangered' in the IUCN Red List of Threatened Species in 1998. Loss of habitat through human activities & logging for prized wood

CAUTIONS & CONSIDERATIONS

Health
No known adverse health effects. CAUTION: Potential allergen - as with most nuts.

Pests
Fruit fly.

Landscape design
Shelter from winds. A tropical plant adapted to higher elevations. Succeeds along streams, rivers. Fosters reservoirs of biodiversity. Allelopathic. Seeds sold by rarepalmseeds.com. Compare with English walnut (Juglans regia) & Hazelnut (Corylus avellana).

Water Lotus
Nelumbo nucifera

HARDINESS ZONES: 5 TO 11

One of the most well-known, ornamental plants and dietary staples throughout Asia. Seeds are a balanced carbohydrate - similar to wheat! Used as a medicinal herb for well over 1,500 years. Showy and fragrant! An exotic beauty, exuding a sweet perfume. A fast-growing perennial in the Nymphaeaceae family. Good for container gardening! Many named varieties!

SIZE h*w	SUN	SOIL	WATER	EDIBLE
3ft*3ft	full	loamy; acidic - OK	calm margins; up to 8ft deep	root, seed, leaves, stem, flowers

PROPAGATION METHODS

- SEEDS: Germinates at 75 to 85°F. Viable for many years. File across center, soak in warm water, change the water 2x a day until germination which occurs within 4 weeks.

RECIPE

LOTUS ROOT CHIPS: Wash, peel and slice 1 lotus root ⅛ inch thick. Paint both sides with a bit of oil and sprinkle with sea salt. Bake on a cookie sheet 10 min at 400F. Flip after 5 min and rotate pan. Remove when golden brown in color.

CULTURAL SIGNIFICANCE

- Used in folk healing (e.g. Root starch to treat diarrhea; seed for lowering cholesterol)
- Exhibits thermoregulation - flowers heat when surrounded by air cool
- The sacred Lotus of India is used in religious symbolism for Hinduism & Buddhism: Purity of mind and body, detachment from desire, unsullied by surrounding influences
- Seed receptacle used in flower arrangements; yields lotus silk woven into Buddhist robes

CULINARY USE

Root
Cooked as a starchy vegetable. Relished in Chinese cooking. Mild, sweet-tangy flavor; crisp texture. Deep-fried, stir-fried, stuffed with meats or preserved fruits, soaked in syrup or pickled in vinegar. Eat fresh. Poor shelf-life.

Seeds
Seed can be popped like popcorn or ground into a flour for bread, moon cakes, and noodles. Bitter-tasting embryo is removed. High in protein and 70% carbohydrates! Made into nut milk or roasted as a coffee substitute.

Leaves, Stems, Flowers
Young leaves cooked as a vegetable or used to wrap small food such as during steaming. Also used as disposable plates. Stems peeled & eaten cooked. Tastes like a beet. Flower petals used as a garnish. Stamens used to flavor tea.

CAUTIONS & CONSIDERATIONS

Health
No known adverse health effects. Water crop - risk of parasites. Safest cooked. Don't harvest from polluted water.

Pests
Resilent. Aphids, red spider mites.

Landscape design
May behave invasively. Pink form preferred for seeds; white- for roots. Used in bioremediation. Quickly removes heavy metals – including arsenic, copper & cadmium. Compare with N. Lutea.

Wax Myrtle

Myrica cerifera

HARDINESS ZONES: 7 TO 11

A fast-growing, nitrogen-fixing, evergreen shrub & Florida native. Also called "Candle Berry" since candles are made from melting the wax off of the berries for old-fashioned Christmas decorations. In the Myricaceae family. Attracts birds and hosts butterflies. Foliage and berries are pleasantly aromatic. Planted widely in 18th-20th centuries for medicinal & industrial purposes.

SIZE h*w	SUN	SOIL	WATER	EDIBLE
30ft*10ft	full to partial	well-draining	average; drought tolerant; seasonal flooding - OK	leaves

PROPAGATION METHODS

- SEEDS: Dioecious. Germinates at 68-77F. Sow in autumn.
- CUTTINGS: Half-ripe wood, 6 inches long with a heel in spring. Preferred method.

RECIPE

WAX MYRTLE TEA: Wash 3 leaves and steep in steaming - not boiling - water. Cover. Allow to steep 2 minutes. Strain.

Sweeten to taste.

NOTE: Medicinal. See Health notes.

CULTURAL SIGNIFICANCE

- Blue dye from fruit
- Grayish-white, 1/8 inch wide fruits are heavily coated with wax. Massed in clusters on previous season's stems. Can hang on plant several years. Wax extracted by immersing fruit in boiling water - the wax floats. Skim off and strain to make soap, candles, sealant, & shaving lather. The wax is brittle but does not smoke or get greasy in heat. 4 lbs of berries yields 1 lb of wax

CULINARY USE

Leaves

Leaves used as a food flavoring. Adds an aromatic, attractive and agreeable seasoning. Used in flavoring soups, stews etc. The dried leaves are brewed into a tea. In grilling, leaves have been used to smoke fish, meat and vegetables. Comparable with Bay Leaf (Laurus nobilis) and Bay Rum (Pimenta racemosa)

NOTE: Used in folk healing primarily. Tea from leaves used to treat fevers or as a wash for itchy skin. Also historically employed to increase circulation, stimulate perspiration and treat bacterial infections.

Fermented leaves used in folk healing for fever, stomach aches, and headaches.

CAUTIONS & CONSIDERATIONS

Health

CAUTION: Medicinal. Consume in moderation. Do not consume wax off berries - believed carcinogenic. Avoid using plant if pregnant.

Pests

Resilient. Leaf anthracnose and leaf mosaic.

Landscape design

Numerous cultivars. Informal hedge plant especially around ponds. Leaves, stems and branches contain flammable aromatic compounds - plant 20ft+ from home.

Wedelia

Sphagneticola trilobata

HARDINESS ZONES: 9 TO 12

Also called "Singapore Daisy" & "Creeping Oxeye." This plant is a member of the Asteraceae family and has a long history as traditional medicine. A long-lived perennial widely cultivated as an ornamental groundcover. Profuse, nearly year-round blooming. Remediates polluted soils. You will likely find this on your property without planting. IUCN has listed it in the reported, "Top 100 Most Invasive Species."

SIZE h*w	SUN	SOIL	WATER	EDIBLE
2ft*6in	full to partial	well-draining	drought tolerant; seasonal flooding - OK	leaves, flowers - medicinal

PROPAGATION METHODS

NOT RECOMMENDED
- CUTTINGS: Runners & stems root readily. NOTE: Rarely produces seed.

RECIPE

WEDELIA TEA: Boil 3 tender, young leaves in 3 cups of water with 5 Red Roselle calyxes for 5 min covered. Allow to cool, sweeten to taste.

CAUTION: Medicinal. See health notes.

CULINARY USE

Leaves & Flowers
The 1-inch diameter, yellow-orange flowers and tender young, leaves, are steeped into a medicinal tea in numerous countries including: South America, China, Japan, & India. In the Caribbean, the leaves and flowers are used in folk healing treatments for bronchitis, colds, abdominal pains, dysmenorrhea and as a fertility enhancer.

Sold commercially as a dried Jamaican herb with listed applications such as: reproductive problems, amenorrhea, dysmenorrhea, symptoms of colds and flu; fevers and inflammations.

CULTURAL SIGNIFICANCE

- Used in folk healing (e.g., to treat flu/ chest colds & liver/ reproductive issues; poultice, ointment & bath infusion for aches, stings; to dye grey hair. Believed to have antioxidant, anti-inflammatory, antimicrobial properties)
- Important nectar source for pollinators
- Allelopathic compounds inhibit growth & germination of other plants
- Known to result in aborted fetuses in farm animals

CAUTIONS & CONSIDERATIONS

Health
CAUTION: Medicinal. Toxic if ingested in quantity. Avoid if pregnant. Do not collect in polluted areas.

Pests
Highly resilient. No known biological controls.

Landscape design
Used as an ornamental for improved soil retention, fertility, phyto-remediation & erosion control. Forms a dense ground cover. Fast-growing. Aggressive. Climbs up shrubs inhibiting growth. Mowing or slashing should be avoided - promotes new plants. Tolerates foot traffic.

West India Bay

Pimenta racemosa

HARDINESS ZONES: 10 TO 12

An evergreen also called "Bay Rum" in the myrtle family (Myrtaceae). Crushed leaves are put into hot baths to refresh and relax. The aroma is popular for men's personal care products. Highly attractive peeling trunk. Peeled bark is aromatic along with the leaves. Historically, a type of cologne named, "Bay Rum" was made by distilling the oil using rum and water - hence the name! Small white flowers resemble tiny bouquets of shimmering cotton!

SIZE h*w	SUN	SOIL	WATER	EDIBLE
30ft*15ft	full to part	well-draining	moist	leaves

PROPAGATION METHODS

- SEEDS: Germinates at 65-70 within 6 weeks.
- Sow as soon as it is ripe.
- BUDDING: In spring.

RECIPE

BAY RUM TEA: Boil 6 washed leaves for 15 to 20 minutes in 3 cups of water. Allow to steep, covered 10 minutes. Strain.

Sweeten to taste with honey, agave, or maple syrup.

CULINARY USE

Leaves

Crushed leaves smell like a combination of clove and cinnamon. Used as a spice in cooking. Used fresh or dried and stored indefinitely. Prized when cooked in an oat porridge or with plantains. The secret ingredient in many Caribbean dishes from stews, and sweets to the popular Christmas drink, sorrel (red roselle).

Also, popular when brewed into a tea with lemongrass. Young light green leaves yield a menthol-like taste so mature leaves are preferred. Darker green leaves have the most cinnamon-like flavor.

NOTE: Unlike allspice, the fruits are not edible.

CULTURAL SIGNIFICANCE

- Fruit, bark, & leaves yield essential oil with many medical uses; leaves are up to 5% essential oil used in perfume & soaps
- Used in folk healing (e.g., for treating sore muscles, strains, and sprains. Considered an analgesic in aromatherapy)
- Leaves serve as air fresheners and insect repellents. Placed with fruits, in pantries and cupboards to keep bugs away

CAUTIONS & CONSIDERATIONS

Health
No known adverse health effects. May be mistaken for allspice (Pimenta dioica).

Pests
Eucalyptus rust/ fungus, canker, caterpillars, whiteflies, thrips, weevils, and scale

Landscape design
Taprooted. Trees shed leaves every 2-3 years. Can be topped & coppiced for increased leaf production. Useful for high traffic, small spaces. Pimenta racemosa var. citrfolia "Lemon Scent" is rarer but more resilient to fungus.

Wild Bitter Melon

Momordica charantia

HARDINESS ZONES: 9 TO 11

Also called, "Cerasee." A fast-growing plant which will likely show up on its own. Highly invasive. Harvest to control spread! A versatile vegetable & valued traditional medicine. Related to larger, cultivated bitter melons, culturally attritbuted to health & longevity. Showy flowers last up to 6 months, producing tiny gourds. In the cucumber, (Cucurbitaceae) family.

SIZE h*w	SUN	SOIL	WATER	EDIBLE
6ft+*1ft	full to partial	well-draining	average	gourds

PROPAGATION METHODS

NOT RECOMMENDED

- SEEDS: Germinates at 75-82F. Self-seeds readily.

RECIPE

BITTER MELON STIR FRY: Cut 1 lb green melons in half lengthwise. Remove & discard seeds. Slice into 1/4" widths. Degorge by sprinkling salt over slices & draining in a colander for 15 minutes (or blanch 2 min in boiling water). Rinse gourds. Heat 2 tbs oil with 1 tbs minced garlic & 1/2 tsp chili pepper until aromatic. Add sliced melon. Stir fry 5 min. Add 2 tbs wine. Cook 2 more min. Add salt to taste.

CULTURAL SIGNIFICANCE

- Used in folk healing (e.g., for inflammation-associated diseases; leaf baths used for rheumatism, to treat insect bites & skin problems; leaf tea for liver detoxification - drank up to 2x per month with breaks in between use)
- Host reservoir for Papaya ringspot virus type P in Jamaica
- Many varieties. Each variety differs greatly in shape & flavor/ bitterness of the fruit

CULINARY USE

Fruit
Green fruits harvested starting 2 weeks after flowering. Gourds should be green with a little white at the bottom and then boiled at least once and strained. Continuous harvesting of fruits prolongs production. Similar to cucumber, chayote or green bell pepper. Bitter unless blanched or steeped in salty water. Also fried, pickled or used in curries. The skin is tender and edible. Flat seeds are removed. Mini gourds used in stir-fry, soups, stews, dim sum, in herbal teas and as hops replacement in Chinese & Okinawan beers. Yield of 9-13 fruits per plant.

Leaves
Used as pot-herbs. Made into medicinal tea. Leafy shoot tips are often used as salad greens.

CAUTIONS & CONSIDERATIONS

Health
CAUTION: Ripe fruits, fruit coats, and seeds can cause ill health effects (e.g., seeds are abortifacient & anti-spermatogenic).

Pests
Root knot nematodes, thrips, beetles.

Landscape design
Considered a problem in sugarcane fields as the melon vines may smother new growth. Compare with cultivated bitter melons like "Jyunpaku" - the Okinawan White Bitter Melon credited with prolonging health.

Wild Lime

Zanthoxylum fagara

HARDINESS ZONES: 9B TO 11

Also called, "Colima." A long-lived perennial, semi-deciduous shrub, and Florida native in the Rutaceae family. Hosts the federally endangered Schaus' swallowtail butterfly (Heraclides aristodemus ponceanus)! Fruit is enjoyed by birds! Used as a culinary spice & a traditional Chinese medicine. Not a true citrus plant, but closely related to true limes. Wild populations in Florida are endangered. A great hedge or privacy screen! Can also be trained for bonsai.

SIZE h*w	SUN	SOIL	WATER	EDIBLE
10ft*10ft	full to partial	well-draining	drought tolerant; seasonal flooding - OK	leaves

PROPAGATION METHODS	CULINARY USE

PROPAGATION METHODS

- SEEDS: <u>Dioecious.</u> Germinates at 68-77F. Sow in autumn.
- DIVISION: Divide root ball when in dormancy.
- CUTTINGS: In early spring before new growth.

RECIPE

WILD LIME TEA: Wash 5 leaves and boil in 1 cup of water for 5 minutes - uncovered. Strain.

Sweeten to taste.

NOTE: Used culturally as a sudorific and nerve tonic. See health notes.

CULINARY USE

Leaves
Crushed foliage smells like limes. Ground up and used as a spice - similar to zest. Crushed or chopped to make a tart condiment. Fried in oil to imbue a citrusy flavor. Described as similar to Kaffir lime leaves which are used in curries, marinades, soups, & stir-fries.

In the Bahamas, wild lime leaves are boiled and used as a folk-healing, strengthening tea & tonic. Considered a time-honored custom.

NOTE: Use sparingly. Medicinal. Be sure to cook the leaves by boiling or frying: saponin-rich.

CULTURAL SIGNIFICANCE

- Wood used for yellow dye, general construction, poles, stakes, cart bodies
- Seminoles used wild-lime for bows & arrows
- Zanthoxylum species believed to have bactericidal, insecticidal, fungicidal properties
- Reports that fruit is edible. Taste reminiscent of lime zest: Tingly, then numbing effect. May have anti-parasitic properties
- One of the safest places for local birds to nest due to thorns

CAUTIONS & CONSIDERATIONS

Health
CAUTION: Sharp thorns. Consume with caution: Medicinal use. Syn: Zanthoxylum affine. May cause skin irritation.

Pests
Resilient: no serious pests or diseases; caterpillar damage.

Landscape design
Compare with related but more popular, Chinese Pepper (Zanthoxylum simulans); Toothache Plant (Acmella oleracea) along with Florida native (Zanthoxylum clava-herculis) for numbing effect; Florida native lime, Ogeechee Lime (Nyssa ogeche) or Caviar lime (Citrus australasica).

Winged Bean
Psophocarpus tetragonolobus

HARDINESS ZONES: 8 TO 12

Also known as, "Asparagus Pea," due to similar taste. This perennial is resilient and fun to grow! Root to flower edible. How efficient! In the Fabaceae/ Leguminosae family. Extremely high yielding! A vigorous vine; use a trellis! The protein content (dried seeds-30%, dried roots-25%) make this a delicious and pretty staple crop. Seed protein digestibility rivals soybean and is rich in the antioxidant, tocopherol, copper, iron, & manganese.

SIZE h*w	SUN	SOIL	WATER	EDIBLE
10ft*12ft	full to partial	any, well-drained	average; maritime - OK	leaves, flowers, seed/pod, root

PROPAGATION METHODS

- SEEDS: Germinates at 77-89°F within a week. Pre-soak 12-24 hours in warm water. Sow early spring or year-round in subtropics. Bears pods after 45 days! Manure & ash improves yields.

RECIPE

WINGED SOUP: 3 cups trimmed & blanched beans, 1 tbs oil, 1/2 c onion of choice, minced; 1 garlic clove; 1 inch peeled, minced ginger; 1 sprig rosemary - chopped, 4 cups coconut milk.

Sauté beans, onion, garlic, ginger, & rosemary until fragrant. Purée all ingredients. Simmer for 10 min.

CULTURAL SIGNIFICANCE

- Blue flowers used as a food coloring
- Used for soil improvement and restoration; green manure with nitrogen-fixing properties. Symbiotic relationship with certain soil bacteria
- Intensively cultivated in Burma and India
- Stems and leaves are used as cattle forage
- Nick-named: Four-Cornered Bean, Princess Bean, and Dragon Bean
- Hunan variety grows well in USA

CULINARY USE

Seeds & Pods
Harvest and blanch pods under 5 inches long. Tastes like French beans (Phaseolus vulgaris). Store fresh up to 21 days in an air-tight container in the fridge. Half-ripe seeds/pods used in soups. Mature, dry seeds are eaten after soaking/ boiling and are rich in oil (nearly 20%!), protein, vitamin E and calcium. Cooked mature seed is pureed with water and sweetener to make "milk," roasted and eaten like peanuts, dried/ ground into flour or fermented as tempeh or tofu.

Leaves & Flowers
Top three tender leaflets most desired - cooked like spinach. Mushroom-tasting flowers/ buds often cooked.

Root
Root is cooked like potatoes and tastes nutty/ sweet. 20% or more protein (12 times potatoes). Air-dry to peel easier.

CAUTIONS & CONSIDERATIONS

Health
No known adverse health effects. All parts edible raw but most nutritious cooked. Excess consumption of raw leaves reported to cause nausea & flatulence. As with most beans/ seeds: Mature seeds require cooking to destroy trypsin inhibitors & hemagglutinins that inhibit digestion.

Pests
Resilient: nematodes. fungi: leaf spot and powdery mildew.

Landscape design
Aggressive growth. Many named varieties - one with purple pods! Intercropped with bananas, sugarcane, & achira.

Xanthosoma

Xanthosoma violaceum

HARDINESS ZONES: 8 TO 11

A perennial, low-maintenance plant also called "Malanga "or "Cocoyam." In the Araceae family. Often grown as an ornamental for its tropical foliage, but this tuber is a staple root vegetable in Africa, Oceana & Asian tropical regions. A good container plant. Cultivated and consumed since the pre-Columbian era. Increasing economic potential! Demand has been gradually increasing in Europe and United States over the past decade.

SIZE h*w	SUN	SOIL	WATER	EDIBLE
4ft*4ft	part to full shade	well-draining	average	leaves, tubers

PROPAGATION METHODS

- DIVISION: Plant out smaller corms/ bulbs on sides of main corm. NOTE: Seeds are rarely produced. Corms may be found at international grocers.

RECIPE

MASHED MALANGA: Chop & boil tuber 25 minutes. Strain and rinse. Mash and mix with oil and salt to taste.

For additional flavor, add 1/2 cup coconut milk and top with 2 tbs of chopped chives.

CULTURAL SIGNIFICANCE

- An important crop - provides carbohydrates, proteins, fat and vitamins
- National Academy of Sciences classified as a neglected food crop with economic potential, - underexploited & insufficiently studied
- Rare and hard-to-find, Xanthosoma albomarginata has variegated foliage: white with hues of green
- Cyanide present in the leaves are 1-5% of that found in cassava leaves and tubers

CULINARY USE

Root

Growing cycle of 9 to 11 months. Rich in starch. Peeled, boiled & eaten like potatoes. Used in stews, custards and pancakes. Boiled then fried for chips. Ground into a hypoallergenic flour. Popular in Cuba, Dominican Republic & Puerto Rico for alcapurrias/ stuffed fritters. Replacement for yams. Earthy and nutty flavor. Corms generally weigh 1/2 to 2 pounds. Natural thickener for stews.

NOTE: Often confused with Alocasia and Colocasia plants. Identify carefully.

Leaves

Young leaves and petioles are chopped, boiled 20 min, strained, & eaten as a spinach substitute. Grown in Trinidad & Jamaica for callaloo/ a sautéed greens dish.

CAUTIONS & CONSIDERATIONS

Health

CAUTION: May be confused with inedible elephant ears. Must be cooked. All parts of the plant contain calcium oxalate crystals. Those with rheumatism, arthritis, gout, or kidney stones - avoid eating. May cause skin irritation.

Pests

Dasheen mosaic virus (DMV).

Landscape design

Multiple varieties of malanga. Rhizomes may be planted directly in the ground (18" apart). Grow under the forest canopy. Compare with eddo or taro (Colocasia esculenta).

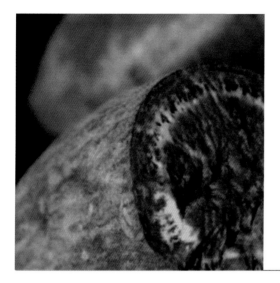

Yam

Dioscorea alata

HARDINESS ZONES: 9 TO 12

A starchy staple crop also called "Ube." A fast-growing perennial climber cultivated since ancient times. In the Dioscoreaceae family. A vivid, violet-purple color! Will likely show up without planting. Listed as a noxious weed & Category I Invasive. Considered an ornamental edible and grown on pergolas & trellises. A vigorous, high yielding plant. Harvest often to control spread! Crushed leaves smell of cinnamon. High in B6!

SIZE h*w	SUN	SOIL	WATER	EDIBLE
30ft*3ft	partial	well-drained; poor - OK	average	tuber

PROPAGATION METHODS

NOT RECOMMENDED - PROHIBITED
- SEEDS: Germinates at 65-70F. Dioecious.
- DIVISION: Small tubers are detached from larger tubers for planting.

RECIPE

UBE LATTE: Puree an 8oz piece of ube (boiled 25 min or until soft and peeled) with 1/2 cup honey; 1/2 cup coconut milk. Top with 1 cup frothed coconut milk.

OPTIONAL: Freeze in ice cube trays and blend just prior to serving as an ice cream.

CULINARY USE

Tuber
Greyish-brown skins & purple flesh. 10 months to harvest. Root is eaten cooked: Boiled, fried, or baked as a vegetable. Ground into flour. Also made into sauces. A mildly sweet, earthy and nutty taste. An average of 3 roots are produced by each plant, weighing around 15lbs but can be up 100lbs. Occasionally produces 4" aerial tubers and these can be eaten in the same way as the tubers.

Popular Philippine desserts because of the attractive color. Made into ice cream, milk, donuts, tarts, jam and other types of pastries. Moister and more anthocyanin than sweet potatoes.

CULTURAL SIGNIFICANCE

- One of the most important staple crops in South-East Asia cultures; most expensive & important root crop in the Philippines
- Distinct dormancy period enabling efficient storage, shipping & export
- Edible Dioscorea have opposite leaves; poisonous species have alternate leaves (e.g., Dioscorea bulbifera)
- Used in folk healing (e.g., relieve depression, high blood pressure)

CAUTIONS & CONSIDERATIONS

Health
CAUTION: Uncooked tuber is toxic (due to saponins). Cook. Carefully identify - poisonous look alike plants.
Pests
Anthracnose, aphids, scale, mealybugs, nematodes.
Landscape design
Forms blankets of leaves over native vegetation & mature trees. Compare with Okinawa sweet potato (Ipomoea batatas var. Ayamurasaki), CushCush/Name (Dioscorea trifida). NOTE: Medicinal yams consist of about 50 species with high sapogenin content/ steroidal components.

Yerba Mate

Ilex paraguariensis

HARDINESS ZONES: 9 TO 11

This slow-growing, evergreen is often touted as a health food due to its rich concentration of phenolic compounds. Some research supports the belief in its benefits on decreasing inflammation and increasing metabolism. A member of the Holly family (Aquifoliaceae). Used as a stimulating, caffeinated drink for hundreds of years. Found worldwide in various energy drinks as well as in bottled or canned iced tea. Can be grown indoors.

SIZE h*w	SUN	SOIL	WATER	EDIBLE
40ft*30ft	full to partial	well-draining	average	leaves

PROPAGATION METHODS

- SEEDS: Dioecious. Germinates at 70-75F very slowly within 3 years
- CUTTINGS: Challenging. Semi-wood in summer dipped in rooting hormone. Also, air-layering.

RECIPE

YERBA MATE TEA: Cover 2 teaspoons dried Yerba Mate with 1 c of hot (but not boiling) water. Allow to sit overnight in the refrigerator.

Dilute with additional water and sweeten to taste. Consume immediately or refrigerate the tea up to a week.

CULTURAL SIGNIFICANCE

- Friends gather & drink mate (matear) in Paraguay, Argentina, southern Brazil, & Uruguay rather than for coffee
- Used in folk healing: (e.g., to improve allergy symptoms, act as an appetite suppressant, improve mental energy, focus, & mood)
- Traditional utensils for drinking maté are cuia (a gourd) and bombilla (a spoon-like straw)
- First consumed by indigenous Guaraní people in Paraguay - likely taught Spanish to use it

CULINARY USE

Leaves

The leaves of the plant are steeped in hot water to make a beverage known as, "mate." Brewed cold, it is used to make tereré. Contains caffeine. A characteristic earthy taste with a surprising depth of flavors. Adding warm frothed milk helps to bring out a more complex taste. Generally bitter if boiled. Often sweetened and blended with other herbs (such as peppermint) or citrus rind. Indigenous South Americans occasionally chew fresh leaves for an energy boost.

Packs a punch with 24 vitamins and minerals, 15 amino acids, and an abundance of antioxidants. Type of soil, levels of moisture, and temperatures all impact flavor and nutrients.

CAUTIONS & CONSIDERATIONS

Health

CAUTION: Consume in moderation. Contains caffeine. Active compounds include polyphenols, xanthines, saponins, & caffeic acid derivatives, believed to have antimicrobial, antioxidant, antidiabetic, cardioprotective properties.

Pests

Blight, cucurbit beetle; basal rot.

Landscape design

Compare with Florida native, Yaupon Holly (Ilex vomitoria).

Zinnia

Zinnia elegans

HARDINESS ZONES: 3 TO 10

In the "daisy" family (Asteraceae). Attracts beneficial insects to the food forest. An annual worth your time which will keep the pollinators delighted! May even behave like a perennial in zones 9 & 10! Supplies both pollen & nectar to smaller bees. Great low-maintenance companion plant! Giant blooms that tower above many weeds! One of the quickest flowers to bloom from seed! Excellent for inexpensive, edible landscape color. Starts blooming in spring and continues until the fall.

SIZE h*w	SUN	SOIL	WATER	EDIBLE
36in+*12in+	full to partial	well-draining	average	petals

PROPAGATION METHODS

- SEEDS: Germinates at 80-85F. Reseed readily. Viable for years. Sow seed directly after last frost (or fall in South Florida) and at 2-week intervals through the end of June.

RECIPE

ZINNIA CONFETTI ICE CUBES: Pick flowers in the morning after dew has dried. Remove the pistils and stamen. Wash zinnia petals in 1:1 bath of vinegar and water. Rinse and place into an ice cube tray. Fill with water and freeze.

CULINARY USE

Petals
One of the more common edible flowers. Dark, pointed seeds are attached to bases of outer petals, with more in the center. Remove seeds from petals prior to eating. Neutral, faintly bitter flavor. Used as a garnish for the rainbow of colors. Used as an accent on tacos. Adds interest to a pitcher of herb tea. Petals can also be used in syrups, jellies, perfumed butters and sweet spreads. Make sure there are no insects stuck inside your flowers before plating.

NOTE: Petals present with a single row with a visible center (single-flowered) or with numerous rows of petals with an invisible center (double-flowered).

CULTURAL SIGNIFICANCE

- Great cut flowers - can last a week or more
- Second plant to be tested in the space station's hydroponic VEGGIE lab
- Symbolic of reunion among friends but meaning varies by color - like roses. During Victorian times, red and magenta Zinnia flowers conveyed desire & romantic intention
- For Zinnia-themed artwork, see Vincent Van Gogh and Clementine Hunter

CAUTIONS & CONSIDERATIONS

Health
No known adverse health effects. Consuming pollen can irritate those with seasonal allergies. Do not to eat flowers sprayed with chemicals.

Pests
Powdery mildew, leaf spots, root rots, blight, whiteflies, aphids, thrips, Japanese beetles & caterpillars.

Landscape design
NOTE: variety "California Giant" used for this profile sheet. Deadhead to prolong blooms. Color options & height vary by cultivar. For a perennial version, see Zinnia acerosa.

Appendix A
DESIGN REFERENCE TABLE
What Goes Where?

KEY: In "Level" column, "*" indicates the plant is a staple crop.

SUN/WATER	LAYER	GERMINATION	NAME	LEVEL	HARVEST
Full, dry	Ground cover	Fall, 60°F–74°F	New Zealand Spinach	1	All
Full, dry	Ground cover	Spring, 64°F–75°F	Pineapple	2	Summer
Full, dry	Ground cover	Spring, 68°F–70°F	Goldenrod	2	Summer
Full, dry	Ground cover	Spring, 68°F–75°F	Echinacea	3	Summer
Full, dry	Ground cover	Spring, 70°F–80°F	Cowpea	*1	Summer–Fall
Full, dry	Ground cover	Spring, 75°F–78°F	Aloe	2	Spring and Fall
Full, dry	Ground cover	Spring, 75°F–80°F	Porterweed	2	Summer
Full, dry	Ground cover	Spring, 77°F–85°F	Florida Sea Oats	*1	Fall
Full, dry	Ground cover	Spring, 77°F+	Agave	*2	Spring
Full, dry	Ground cover	Summer, 82°F–90°F	Adam's Needle	1	Summer
Full, dry	Herbaceous	Fall, 60°F–70°F	Cilantro	2	Spring–Summer
Full, dry	Herbaceous	Fall, 65°F–75°F	Eggplant Pea	3	All
Full, dry	Herbaceous	Fall, 68°F–77°F	Sage	2	All
Full, dry	Herbaceous	Fall, 75°F	Sunchoke	*1	Fall
Full, dry	Herbaceous	Spring, 65°F–75°F	Quinoa	*2	Fall
Full, dry	Herbaceous	Spring, 65°F–80°F	Phenomenal Lavender	1	All
Full, dry	Herbaceous	Spring, 68°F–77°F	Lemongrass	1	All
Full, dry	Herbaceous	Spring, 68°F–70°F	Amaranth	*2	Fall
Full, dry	Herbaceous	Spring, 70°F–75°F	African Marigold	2	Summer and Winter
Full, dry	Herbaceous	Spring, 72°F–80°F	Sorghum	*2	Fall
Full, dry	Herbaceous	Spring, 77°F–86°F	Chia	*1	Fall
Full, dry	Herbaceous	Spring, 85°F–95°F	Jing Okra	*1	Summer–Fall
Full, dry	Herbaceous	Winter, 70°F–78°F	Sunflower	*2	Fall and Spring
Full, dry	Herbaceous	Winter, 75°F–85°F	Bidens Alba	2	All
Full, dry	Low tree	Fall, 75°F–78°F	Sapodilla	3	Spring–Summer
Full, dry	Low tree	Spring, 78°F–90°F	Gumbo Limbo	1	Spring

SUN/WATER	LAYER	GERMINATION	NAME	LEVEL	HARVEST
Full, dry	Low tree	Spring, 80°F–85°F	Jujube	2	Fall
Full, dry	Low tree	Summer, 70°F–85°F	Guava	3	Fall
Full, dry	Low tree	Summer, 86°F–95°F	Cabbage Palmetto	1	Fall
Full, dry	Low tree, pruned	Fall, 75°F–80°F	Akee	*3	Winter–Spring
Full, dry	Low tree, pruned	Spring, 75°F–83°F	Tamarind	*2	Summer–Fall
Full, dry	Low tree, pruned	Spring, 75°F–85°F	Pistachio	3	Summer
Full, dry	Low tree, pruned	Spring, 77°F–82°F	Golden Apple	2	Summer
Full, dry	Low tree, pruned	Spring, 80°F–85°F	Star Apple	2	Summer
Full, dry	Low tree, pruned	Spring, 80°F–90°F	Marula	*2	Spring
Full, dry	Low tree, pruned	Summer, 75°F–90°F	Moringa	*1	Spring–Fall
Full, dry	Low tree, pruned	Summer, 86°F–98°F	Honeypod Mesquite	*2	Fall
Full, dry	Low tree, pruned	Summer, 90°F–95°F	Cashew	*3	Summer
Full, dry	Low tree, pruned	Winter, 77°F	Toona	2	Spring
Full, dry	Low tree/shrub	Spring, 68°F–75°F	Loquat	1	Winter
Full, dry	Low tree/shrub	Spring, 85°F–95°F	Strawberry Tree	2	Spring–Fall
Full, dry	Low tree/shrub	Spring, 75°F–80°F	Frangipani	3	Summer–Fall
Full, dry	Low tree/shrub	Winter, 70°F–81°F	Fig	2	Summer and Fall
Full, dry	Shrub	Fall, 72°F–82°F	Saw Palmetto	*2	Summer–Fall
Full, dry	Shrub	Fall, 80°F–85°F	Firebush	1	Summer
Full, dry	Shrub	Spring, 65°F–70°F	Mulberry	*1	Spring–Summer
Full, dry	Shrub	Spring, 70°F–80°F	Spanish Thyme	1	All
Full, dry	Shrub	Spring, 70°F–80°F	Jamaican Mint	2	All
Full, dry	Shrub	Spring, 75°F–86°F	Pigeon Pea	*1	Spring–Fall
Full, dry	Shrub	Spring, 80°F–90°F	Chaya	*3	All
Full, dry	Shrub	Summer, 77°F–86°F	Lipstick Tree	2	Summer
Full, dry	Shrub	Summer, 77°F–95°F	Sweet Acacia	2	Winter–Spring
Full, dry	Shrub	Summer, 80°F–95°F	Surinam Cherry	3	Fall and Spring

SUN/WATER	LAYER	GERMINATION	NAME	LEVEL	HARVEST
Full, dry	Shrub	Summer, 80°F–100°F	Prickly Pear Cactus	2	All
Full, dry	Shrub	Summer, 90°F–95°F	Seashore Palm	2	Summer
Full, dry	Shrub	Winter, 60°F–64°F	Rosemary	2	All
Full, dry	Tall tree	Spring, 85°F–95°F	Magnolia	1	Spring
Full, dry	Tall tree	Spring, 86°F–95°F	Hickory/Pecan	*1	Fall
Full, dry	Tall tree	Summer, 77°F–86°F	Tropical Almond	*2	Summer
Full, dry	Tuber	Fall, 60°F–75°F	Creole Garlic	2	Summer
Full, dry	Tuber/ground cover	Fall, 65°F–75°F	Chicory	2	Fall–Winter
Full, dry	Tuber/ground cover	Winter, 65°F–85°F	Daikon Radish	2	Spring
Full, dry	Tuber/shrub	Spring, 80°F	Cassava	*3	Spring and Fall
Full, dry	Vine	Fall, 80°F–90°F	Kudzu	*3	Fall
Full, dry	Vine	Spring, 77°F–86°F	Lab-Lab	*2	Fall
Full, dry	Vine	Spring, 77°F–89°F	Winged Bean	*1	Spring–Fall
Full, dry	Vine	Summer, 70°F–85°F	Passionflower	2	Summer–Winter
Full, moist	Ground cover	Fall, 65°F–75°F	Strawberry	2	Summer
Full, moist	Herbaceous	Fall, 60°F–65°F	Scallion	1	All
Full, moist	Herbaceous	Fall, 68°F–75°F	Agastache	1	Summer
Full, moist	Herbaceous	Fall, 68°F–75°F	Society Garlic	1	All
Full, moist	Herbaceous	Spring, 68°F–86°F	Kimchi Pepper	2	Summer
Full, moist	Herbaceous	Spring, 78°F–82°F	Hemp	3	Fall
Full, moist	Herbaceous	Spring, 78°F–85°F	Achira	*1	Fall
Full, moist	Herbaceous	Spring, 80°F–85°F	Zinnia	1	Summer–Fall
Full, moist	Herbaceous	Spring, 80°F+	African Basil	2	Fall and Spring
Full, moist	Herbaceous	Winter, 58°F–60°F	Hollyhock	1	Spring
Full, moist	Herbaceous	Winter, 60°F–70°F	Calendula	2	Spring
Full, moist	Low "tree"/ herbaceous	Spring, 60°F–85°F	Clumping Bamboo	2	Winter
Full, moist	Low "tree"/ herbaceous	Spring, 75°F–85°F	Papaya	2	Fall and Summer
Full, moist	Low "tree"/ herbaceous	Spring, 78°F–86°F	Banana	*1	Spring and Summer
Full, moist	Low "tree"/ herbaceous	Summer, 75°F–95°F	Ensete	*1	Fall
Full, moist	Low tree	Spring, 77°F–86°F	Guanabana	2	Summer
Full, moist	Low tree, pruned	Fall, 68°F–80°F	Olive	*2	Winter

SUN/WATER	LAYER	GERMINATION	NAME	LEVEL	HARVEST
Full, moist	Low tree, pruned	Fall, 70°F–80°F	Starfruit	2	Summer and Winter
Full, moist	Low tree, pruned	Fall, 70°F–80°F	Avocado	*2	Summer–Winter
Full, moist	Low tree, pruned	Fall, 79°F–85°F	Jackfruit	*1	Summer–Fall
Full, moist	Shrub	Spring, 68°F–75°F	Rose	1	Spring–Fall
Full, moist	Shrub/ herbaceous	Spring, 75°F–80°F	Gooseberry	2	Summer–Fall
Full, moist	Shrub/low tree	Spring, 68°F–86°F	Grumichama	1	Spring
Full, moist	Tall tree, pruned	Spring, 80°F–95°F	Mango	3	Summer
Full, moist	Tuber/ground cover	Fall, 65°F–75°F	Chufa	*1	Fall–Spring
Full, moist	Vine	Spring, 68°F–87°F	Loofah	*1	Summer–Fall
Full, moist	Vine	Spring, 75°F–82°F	Wild Bitter Melon	3	Summer–Fall
Full, moist	Vine	Spring, 77°F–86°F	Inca Peanut	*2	All
Full, moist	Vine	Spring, 80°F–85°F	Butterfly Pea	2	Spring–Fall
Full, moist	Vine	Spring, 80°F–90°F	Muscadine Grape	1	Summer–Fall
Full, moist	Vine	Summer, 70°F–90°F	Tindora	2	All
Full, seasonally wet	Aquatic	Spring, 77°F–85°F	Pickerelweed	*1	Spring–Fall
Full, seasonally wet	Aquatic	Summer, 90°F–100°F	Sea Salt	2	Summer–Fall
Full, seasonally wet	Ground cover	Spring, 77°F–85°F	Gotu Kola	2	All
Full, seasonally wet	Herbaceous	Spring, 70°F–80°F	Sugarcane	*2	Fall
Full, seasonally wet	Low tree	Spring, 60°F–75°F	Red Maple	*1	Winter–Spring
Full, seasonally wet	Low tree, pruned	Spring, 80°F–95°F	Lychee	2	Summer
Full, seasonally wet	Shrub	Spring, 80°F–90°F	Elderberry	3	Summer–Fall
Full, seasonally wet	Tall tree	Spring, 60°F–70°F	Walnut	*1	Summer–Fall
Full, seasonally wet	Tall tree	Spring, 68°F–86°F	Elm	*1	Summer
Full, seasonally wet	Tall tree	Spring, 80°F–90°F	Pine	*2	Fall–Winter
Full, seasonally wet	Tall tree	Summer, 70°F–80°F	Live Oak	*2	Fall

SUN/WATER	LAYER	GERMINATION	NAME	LEVEL	HARVEST
Full, seasonally wet/dry	Low tree	Spring, 75°F–86°F	Vegetable Hummingbird	*1	Fall–Summer
Full, seasonally wet/dry	Low tree	Spring, 77°F–82°F	Red Mombin	2	All
Full, seasonally wet/dry	Low tree	Spring, 80°F–90°F	Saba Nut	*1	Spring
Full, seasonally wet/dry	Low tree, pruned	Spring, 77°F–86°F	Macadamia Nut	*1	Fall–Spring
Full, seasonally wet/dry	Shrub	Fall, 68°F–77°F	Wild Lime	2	Summer–Fall
Full, seasonally wet/dry	Shrub	Spring, 80°F–86°F	Red Roselle	*1	Fall
Full, seasonally wet/dry	Shrub	Spring, 80°F–90°F	Simpson's Stopper	2	Summer–Fall
Full, seasonally wet/dry	Shrub	Spring, 85°F–95°F	Cocoplum	*1	Summer
Full, seasonally wet/dry	Shrub/low tree	Summer, 77°F–86°F	Sea Grape	1	Summer
Full, seasonally wet/dry	Tall tree	Spring, 80°F–85°F	Coconut	*2	All
Full, wet	Aquatic	Spring, 75°F–80°F	Water Lotus	*1	Spring–Fall
Full, wet	Aquatic/tuber	Fall, 70°F–86°F	Duck Potato	*2	Fall
Full, wet	Aquatic/tuber	Summer, 85°F–90°F	Cattails	*1	Spring–Summer
Part, dry	Tuber/ground cover	Spring, 64°F–75°F	Ulluco	*1	Fall
Part, moist	Ground cover	Fall, 65°F–75°F	Violet	2	Winter
Part, moist	Ground cover	Fall, 68°F–75°F	Nasturtium	2	Spring–Summer
Part, moist	Ground cover	Fall, 70°F–75°F	Longevity Spinach	1	All
Part, moist	Ground cover	Spring, 70°F–75°F	Okinawa Spinach	1	All
Part, moist	Herbaceous	Winter, 45°F–85°F	Purple Collard Tree	*1	All
Part, moist	Low tree	Winter, 65°F–70°F	West India Bay	2	All
Part, moist	Low tree	Winter, 70°F	Sweet Laurel	1	Spring
Part, moist	Low tree, pruned	Spring, 80°F–90°F	Neem	2	All
Part, moist	Low tree, pruned	Summer, 77°F–86°F	Longan	2	Summer
Part, moist	Shrub	Spring, 65°F–77°F	Pomelo	2	Winter
Part, moist	Shrub	Spring, 70°F–75°F	Tea	2	Spring
Part, moist	Shrub/low tree	Spring, 70°F–75°F	Yerba Mate	2	All
Part, moist	Vine	Fall, 68°F–77°F	Vanilla	2	Spring

SUN/WATER	LAYER	GERMINATION	NAME	LEVEL	HARVEST
Part, moist	Vine	Fall, 70°F–85°F	Seminole Pumpkin	*1	Winter and Summer
Part, moist	Vine	Spring, 80°F–90°F	Pepper	1	Fall–Winter
Part, moist	Vine/tuber	Fall, 65°F–70°F	Yam	*3	Fall–Winter
Part, seasonally wet	Aquatic	Summer, 95°F–100°F	Spirulina	*1	Summer
Part, seasonally wet	Ground cover	Spring, 68°F	Sprawling Day Flower	3	Summer–Fall
Part, seasonally wet	Mushroom	Summer, 75°F–90°F	Oyster Mushroom	2	Fall and Summer
Part, seasonally wet	Shrub	Spring, 77°F–90°F	Spicebush	1	Fall
Part, seasonally wet	Shrub	Spring, 78°F–86°F	Turks Cap	2	Spring–Fall
Part, seasonally wet	Tuber	Summer, 70°F–95°F	Turmeric	2	Fall and Winter
Part, seasonally wet	Tuber/vine	Summer, 85°F–95°F	Sweet Potato	*1	Fall and Winter
Part, seasonally wet	Vine	Spring, 70°F–80°F	Malabar Spinach	1	Spring–Fall
Part, seasonally wet/dry	Ground cover	Fall, 77°F–85°F	Sword Fern	3	Fall
Part, seasonally wet/dry	Ground cover	Winter, 68°F–95°F	Wedelia	3	Spring–Fall
Part, seasonally wet/dry	Herbaceous	Spring, 65°F	Spiderwort	2	Summer–Fall
Part, seasonally wet/dry	Low "tree"	Spring, 75°F–82°F	Strangler Fig	2	Fall
Part, seasonally wet/dry	Shrub/low tree	Fall, 68°F–77°F	Wax Myrtle	2	All
Part, seasonally wet/dry	Tall tree, pruned	Spring, 80°F–90°F	Maya Nut	*1	Spring
Partial, dry	Ground cover	Fall, 65°F–70°F	Flax	*2	Summer
Partial, dry	Ground cover	Fall, 65°F–75°F	Cuban Oregano	2	All
Partial, dry	Ground cover	Fall, 65°F–85°F	Geranium	3	Summer
Partial, dry	Ground cover	Winter, 64°F–70°F	Fennel	2	Spring–Summer
Partial, dry	Herbaceous	Spring, 80°F–90°F	Egyptian Spinach	*2	Summer–Fall
Partial, dry	Low tree	Spring, 85°F	Atemoya	2	Fall

SUN/WATER	LAYER	GERMINATION	NAME	LEVEL	HARVEST
Partial, dry	Shrub	Fall, 70°F–75°F	Chestnut	*1	Fall
Partial, dry	Shrub	Fall, 70°F–85°F	Barbados Cherry	2	Spring–Fall
Partial, dry	Shrub	Spring, 60°F–70°F	Calamondin	1	All
Partial, dry	Shrub	Spring, 65°F	Beautyberry	1	Fall
Partial, dry	Shrub	Winter, 60°F–70°F	Goji Berry	2	Summer
Partial, dry	Shrub/low tree	Fall, 70°F–75°F	Curry Tree	1	All
Partial, dry	Tuber/ground cover	Fall, 60°F–70°F	Daylily	2	Fall
Partial, dry	Vine	Fall, 64°F–82°F	Dragon Fruit	2	Summer
Partial, moist	Ground cover	Winter, 64°F–71°F	Gai Lon Broccoli	1	Spring
Partial, moist	Ground cover	Winter, 68°F–77°F	Everglades Tomato	2	Fall–Spring
Partial, moist	Herbaceous	Spring, 70°F–75°F	Cranberry Hibiscus	2	Fall
Partial, moist	Herbaceous	Spring, 70°F–80°F	Asparagus	2	Spring
Partial, moist	Herbaceous	Spring, 75°F–85°F	Juanilama	1	All
Partial, moist	Low tree, pruned	Spring, 65°F–70°F	Cinnamon	2	Winter
Partial, moist	Low tree/shrub	Spring, 60°F–75°F	Florida Prince Peach	2	Summer
Partial, moist	Shrub	Spring, 65°F–70°F	Chickasaw Plum	2	Spring
Partial, moist	Shrub	Spring, 80°F–86°F	Aibika	*1	All
Partial, moist	Shrub	Winter, 70°F	Blueberry	1	Spring–Summer
Partial, moist	Shrub/herbaceous	Spring, 68°F–80°F	Cordyline	*2	Fall
Partial, moist	Shrub/vine	Spring, 77°F–85°F	Blackberry	2	Spring
Partial, moist	Tuber	Fall, 70°F	Apio	*1	Spring
Partial, moist	Vine	Spring, 80°F–85°F	Chayote	*1	Summer
Partial, seasonally wet	Herbaceous	Spring, 70°F	Bee Balm	1	Summer
Partial, seasonally wet	Low tree, pruned	Spring, 77°F–85°F	Chocolate Pudding Tree	2	Winter
Partial, seasonally wet	Low tree, pruned	Spring, 80°F–85°F	Breadfruit	*1	Spring and Fall
Partial, seasonally wet	Shrub	Spring, 80°F+	Basket Vine	3	Spring
Partial, seasonally wet	Tuber/ground cover	Fall, 70°F	Betony	2	Spring
Partial, seasonally wet/dry	Herbaceous	Spring, 68°F–77°F	Katuk	*1	All

SUN/WATER	LAYER	GERMINATION	NAME	LEVEL	HARVEST
Partial, seasonally wet/dry	Tall tree	Spring, 85°F–90°F	Ice Cream Bean	*1	Winter
Partial, seasonally wet/dry	Tuber	Spring, 70°F–85	Ginger	2	Fall
Partial, wet	Aquatic/tuber	Spring, 70°F–90°F	Arrowroot	*1	Fall
Shade, dry	Ground cover	Spring, 75°F	African Potato Mint	*2	Fall
Shade, moist	Shrub	Spring, 80°F–85°F	Coffee	2	Summer
Shade, moist	Mushroom	Fall, 77°F–90°F	Indigo Milk Cap	2	Fall
Shade, moist	Tuber/herbaceous	Spring, 68°F–75°F	Xanthosoma	*2	Fall–Winter
Shade, seasonally wet	Ground cover	Summer, 77°F–95°F	La Lot	1	All
Shade, seasonally wet	Herbaceous	Spring, 70°F–85°F	Cardamom	1	Fall
Shade, seasonally wet	Shrub	Fall, 77°F–86°F	Root Beer Plant	3	All
Shade, seasonally wet	Shrub/low tree	Spring, 80°F–85°F	Cocoa	*2	Summer
Shade, seasonally wet	Vine	Spring, 70°F–75°F	Swiss Cheese Plant	2	Fall and Winter
Shade, seasonally wet/dry	Shrub	Summer, 95°F–100°F	Noni	2	All

Appendix B

EXAMPLE FOOD-FOREST HARVEST SCHEDULE AND WEEKLY MENU

FOOD FOREST PLANTS

Fennel, mint, garlic, muscadine grapes/ **mulberry**/ elderberry (for wine), tomato, calendula (saffron substitute), **green banana/ jackfruit nuts (for pasta)**, eggs, olives/ oil, African potato mint/cordyline/ (culurgiones filling), bay leaf/ wax myrtle, walnuts, capers, onion, basil, honey, almonds, cardamom, asparagus, calamondin, hollyhock, zinnia, rose, lavendar, magnolia, pomelo, bay rum, **moringa**

Papaya, chia seeds, culantro/ cilantro, banana, plaintain, **cassava, juanilama**, peppers & chiles, pineapple, agave, mango, avocado, cocoa, coconut, chaya, red roselle, honey, chayote, chufa, **jackfruit ("pulled pork")**, garlic, onion, tomatos, sugarcane, lime, passion fruit, lemongrass, eggs, palms (hearts), cuban oregano, nasturtiums, **pigeon pea**, yacon, ice cream bean, prickly pear cactus, purslane, breadfruit, hoja santa, yerba mate

Turmeric, mushrooms, leaf tea, sea grapes, day lily, luffa, daikon, lotus root, longan, **pumpkin**, starfruit, burdock root, **chives**, achira, aibika, garlic, onion, bitter melon, sesame seed/ oil, boniato, black pepper, eggs, leek, sweet potato, beans/ peas, katuk, coconut, peach leaves, Inca peanut, sugarcane, calamondin, moringa, acerola, winged bean, chaya, curry tree, cow pea, bamboo, duck potato, gotu kola, la lot, toona, ginger, okinawa spinach, butterfly pea tea,

Turmeric, mushrooms, day lily, luffa, daikon, lotus root, longan, pumpkin, starfruit, burdock root, chives, achira, aibika, garlic, onion, bitter melon, black pepper, eggs, leek, **sweet potato**, beans/ peas, katuk, **butterfly pea** tea, coconut, peach leaves, Inca peanut, sugarcane, calamondin, moringa, acerola, **green pigeon pea "edamame,"** winged bean, chaya, curry tree, cow pea, bamboo, duck potato, gotu kola, la lot, toona, **ginger,** yam

Aibika, hemp & sunflower seeds, cashew, inca peanut, **coconut**, beauty berry, african basil, raspberry, gai lon broccoli, purple collard tree, quinoa, amaranth, oats, chia seeds, flax seeds, cocoplum, **pumpkin seeds**, chicory root and leaves, bee balm, bidens alba, echinacea, goji berry, pecan, vanilla, lavender, chestnut, lamb's quarters, maya nut, maple syrup, spiderwort, pine nut, violets, guava, **longevity spinach**

Banana, blueberry, blackberry, pineapple, **aibika**, katuk, **avocado**, citrus fruits, tomato, tindora, jujube, fig, cranberry hibiscus, agastache, cattails, bidens alba, dragon fruit, goldenrod, gooseberry, gramichama, **papaya (green as salad)**, turks cap, strawberry tree, red mombin, malabar spinach, loquat, red roselle leaves, **mango**, kudzu, mostera deliciousa, pickerelweed, simpson's stopper, spicebush, cashews, sea grapes (for jam)

Golden apple (wine), fish, eggplant, tomato, coffee, firebush (wine), honey pod mesquite, okra, sunchokes, oregano, rosemary, sage, mint, **pigeon pea (for flour)**, grape leaves, chicory, **chaya** moringa, purslane, long beans, lab lab, acorn, sweet potato, pumpkin, honey, maple syrup, sorghum, moringa, New Zealand spinach, olives/oil, sisso spinach, pistachio, purple collard, scarlet runner bean, toona, ulluco, onion, garlic, betony, quinoa, cinnamon

MACARONI MONDAY: SARDINIA, ITALY

LESSON: Involve the grandparents
TOOLS: Pasta press, drying rack, coffee/ flour grinder
TECHNIQUES: Pasta (e.g., fregola-balls), bread sculptures, Zuppa gallurese (sourdough bread "lasagna"), minestrone, wine, candied peel, cookies, flower water (*Phytonutrient color priority: tan & red*)

TACO TUESDAY: NICOYA, COSTA RICA

LESSON: Big breakfast, medium lunch, tiny dinner & "¡pura vida!"
TOOLS: Cast iron skillet, tortilla press
TECHNIQUES: Salsa, slaw, chia tea, fermented hot sauce, fruit syrups, tortillas, fried veggie hash/ cakes, pre-soak beans, veggie ceviche, horchata/ nut milk, (*Phytonutrient color priority: brown*)

ONE-POT WEDNESDAY: OKINAWA, JAPAN

LESSON: "Hora hachi bu" - only 80% full
TOOLS: coconut opener, veggie shredder/ noodle maker
TECHNIQUES: Clear broth soup, fermented/sprouted beans (tofu, tempeh), stir fry/ "champuru", steamed "cakes"/"breads", herbed/flower salts & teas, eggs in soup, 70% of diet is sweet potato, (*Phytonutrient color priority: orange*)

THANKFUL THURSDAY: OKINAWA, JAPAN

LESSON: "Moai," - friends; "ikigai " - purpose; forest bathe
TOOLS: Steamer, grill set, basket
TECHNIQUES: Clear broth soup, fermented/sprouted beans (tofu, tempeh), stir fry/ "champuru", steamed "cakes"/"breads", herbed/flower salts & teas, eggs in soup, 70% of diet is sweet potato (*Phytonutrient color priority: blue & purple*)

FRESH FRIDAY: LOMA LIMA, CA

LESSON: No wine, technology, or TV after sunset
TOOLS: Vitamix blender, Omega/ masticating juicer, dehydrators
TECHNIQUES: Pesto, juicing greens, nut "milk," smoothies, bean & nut dips, nut butters & yogurts, crackers, jams, dried fruits/ veggies, herbed oils & vinegars - vinaigrettes (*Phytonutrient color priority: white & green*)

7TH DAY SATURDAY: LOMA LIMA, CA

LESSON: Forage / hike. Nap. No sugar, salt, caffeine, or alcohol
TOOLS: No technology, TV, phone
TECHNIQUES: Fresh fruit salads with herbs, sandwiches, salads, cereal "coffee", energy bars/ balls, frozen fruit "ice cream," cold & hot brew tea (*Phytonutrient color priority: yellow & orange*)

SLOW SUNDAY: IKARIA, GREECE

LESSON: Slow cook, sleep-in, fast (intermittent), socialize
TOOLS: Dutch oven, dehydrator
TECHNIQUES: Greek coffee (boiled), fermented foods, slow cooked vegetable stews and casseroles, sun-dried vegetables, herb teas, forage wild greens (*Phytonutrient color priority: brown & green*)

Appendix C
SAFETY CHECKLIST

SAFETY CONCERN	PRECAUTION ACTION CHECKLIST
Identification	▪ Use the Latin botanical name and multiple indicators to identify plants. ▪ Start with 20 Level 1 plants to supply bulk nutrition. ▪ Distinguish edibles from lookalikes one by one.
Consumption	▪ Research how to remove antinutrients and toxins for each plant. ▪ Research which parts of the plant are edible in which ways. ▪ Wash and soak in a 1:1 ratio of water to vinegar for 15 minutes. ▪ Cook thoroughly; boil and discard water if leaching toxins. ▪ Taste small amounts of new foods, and wait 24 hours. ▪ Adhere strictly to safety guidelines when preserving foods.
Toxins	▪ Test the soil for toxins, like lead and arsenic. ▪ Amend soil with truckloads of compost, muck, or mulch. ▪ Leave no bare soil patches to prevent air-soil contamination. ▪ Plant large trees to help remove toxins. ▪ Avoid harvesting or planting near old buildings (e.g., lead risk). ▪ Use beds or Hügelkultur for tubers and herbs within 10 feet of buildings. ▪ Establish a hedge to reduce windblown road contamination. ▪ Stay aware if neighbors spray pesticides. ▪ Wash pesticide-sprayed plants (15 minutes, 1:1 water to baking soda bath). ▪ Interplant soil-remediating chop-drop crops (e.g., sunflowers).
Outdoor Hazards	▪ Plant native trees as windbreaks. ▪ Locate dermatitis and allergy-causing plants away from paths. ▪ Keep paths free of trip hazards and stray limbs. ▪ Remove plants that cause toxic reactions (e.g., poison ivy). ▪ Time activity by season and potential exposure to pollen and toxins. ▪ Plant trees with large, hard fruits (e.g., coconut) away from buildings.
Physical Health	▪ Don't track dirt indoors; remove shoes and spray clean. ▪ Keep ears dry in rainy weather to avoid fungal infections. ▪ Avoid walking through the garden when plants are wet. ▪ Shower before preparing meals. ▪ Exercise and stretch outside of gardening to avoid injury. ▪ Wear protective clothing and equipment (e.g., long sleeves, gloves). ▪ Wear respiratory protection when necessary (e.g., moving mulch or soil). ▪ Stock epinephrine in the case of an allergic reaction. ▪ Maintain checkups (e.g., blood tests for heavy metals and micronutrients).

GLOSSARY

30–20–10 biodiversity rule: a process of maximizing protection against pest and disease outbreaks by planting in the following ratios: 30% or fewer from the same family; 20% or fewer from the same genus; 10% or fewer from the same species

air layering: removing leaves, twigs, and bark on a stem; wrapping with moss or soil; and securing it with aluminum foil or plastic until roots form; ideal for nut trees

annual crops: plants that die after just one season, so the work of maintaining a traditional garden is never-ending; require fertilizer and constant irrigation

antinutrients: toxins and food components that may limit the absorption of vitamins and minerals, including lectins, tannins, protease inhibitors, and oxalic acid

biochar: a biologically active charcoal that is extremely porous and therefore has a high capacity to store water and nutrients; an excellent habitat for soil microorganisms

blue zones: clusters of healthy, long-lived people who regularly live to over 100 and often care for a permaculture garden in their backyards; notable locations include Okinawa, Japan; Nicoya, Costa Rica; Sardina, Italy; Loma Lima, California; and Ikaria, Greece

carbon sequestration: a process by which carbon dioxide is removed from the atmosphere, such as when large trees uptake carbon during their growth process

Category 1 invasive: plant deemed to cause ecological damage by altering native plant communities, displacing and hybridizing with natives

chemical scarification: placing seeds in a shot glass of water mixed with a cap of hydrogen peroxide to promote germination

chop and drop: a process of cutting plants and stems and dropping the content onto the ground at the base of a neighboring plant to fertilize it; also called green manure because it adds nitrogen and amends the soil

community-supported agriculture (CSA): a community-building process of purchasing food directly from a farmer

community-supported kitchens (CSK): a community-building process of purchasing food from a farmer; going inside a farm kitchen; and learning about the foods, the farmers, and how to make nutritious, wholesome meals from raw goods

companion planting: designing mutually beneficial planting arrangements to promote growth and disease resilience

coppicing: cutting a plant almost to the ground to stimulate new growth (e.g., moringa)

cover crops: plants that grow quickly and prevent erosion while creating healthy soil

Dust Bowl: a period of the Great Depression when farms turned into deserts, many people starved, and the soil blew away due to drought followed by plowing and planting shallow-rooted annuals

fall: Florida temperatures averaging 75°F–85°F

Florida ecotypes: Distinct ecosystems found throughout Florida that create microclimates and habitats; examples include beaches/dunes and maritime forests, pine flatwoods, rocklands, hardwood forests, scrub forests, sandhills, swamp forests, saltwater and fresh-water marshes, cabbage palm forests, and prairies

Florida USDA hardiness zones: 8–11 marked by mild winters and nearly year-round gardening conditions

food forests: an approach to edible landscaping designed to be both beautiful and to pro-duce abundant food in as little as 3,000 square feet, with seven to nine layers: (1) tall trees, (2) short trees, (3) shrubs, (4) herbaceous plants, (5) ground covers, (6) tubers, (7) vines, (8) aquatic/wetland crops, and (9) mushrooms

grafting: splicing one plant onto another to have new growth take on new taste or growth characteristics; usually done while both scion and rootstock are still dormant; ideal for fruit trees, like avocado and mango

guilds: a cluster of plants serving as mutual support for pest and disease resilience within a regenerative design to reduce labor, time, and cost

Hügelkultur: a process of planting that involves burying and backfilling clippings and yard waste, then growing crops in the mound; keeps materials on the land while slowly break-ing down over time, producing a rich soil

hunger-obesity paradox: lacking access to nutritious food, resulting in obesity and higher incidents of disease; a trend of being overweight while also being grossly deficient in vitamins and minerals due to modern food-production and -processing methods

hydroponic: a means of rooting/propagating plants quickly; can be as simple as putting stems in a glass of water (the Kratky method); a more formal system can be a $20 fish tank bubbler/aerator placed in a Tupperware container with drilled holes for plants to fit down into aerated water

invasive: A term for plants that display rapid growth without natural controls (e.g., some-thing to eat it); can negatively affect surrounding vegetation, such as by increasing fire risks or clogging water channels

JADAM: a process of inoculating beneficial bacteria and microbes into soil system through compost teas

keystone natives: plants that host a large number of beneficial insects and foster a healthy ecosystem; term coined by Doug Tallamy in his work on pollinator-friendly yards

lasagna composting: layering food scraps, cardboard, and manure or mulch on top of weeds to amend soil and prepare it for planting

lifestyle diseases: illness resulting from habits and choices, such as diet and physical activity; often marked by obesity

macronutrient: calories from starch, carbohydrates, protein, and oils

micronutrients: vitamins and minerals, such as from dark leafy green vegetables, crucifer-ous vegetables, colorful fruits, vegetables, and tubers

mulch: wood chips, preferably from native oak or pine trees, which breaks down quickly, leaving the food forest with a moisture-retentive, rich, organic, dark soil; usually added to locations in quantities of three inches or more

mycorrhizal fungi: an interconnecting network of fungus that improves plant health and growth

natives: plants growing in Florida prior to colonization by Spaniards

noxious: a legal designation used for specific plants subject by law to certain restrictions; generally prohibited

nurse plants: crops, like bananas, used as living irrigation systems because these plants sop up excess water and then release it to other plants in times of drought

Oktoberfest: a popular holiday started in 1811 to promote agriculture and the Bavarian economy; now the holiday associated with fermentation processes

organic food: crops grown without pesticides, herbicides, chemical fertilizers, or other hazardous additives; has been found to have substantially more minerals, as much as 90% more compared with nonorganic foods

perennial crops: plants that live multiple years and can become self-sustaining and regenerative, eliminating the need for extensive effort; can flourish even in poor soils and drought; improves the soil's organic matter, structure, and porosity, resulting in better water-holding capacity through the slow and steady decomposition of roots and leaves; often more nutritious in both macro- and micronutrients than annuals

permaculture: a historically rich approach to farming; intercrops perennials, resulting in a biodiverse ecosystem

phytochemicals: medicinal components found in plants, such as spices and herbs

pioneer species: plants that tolerate poor soil, drought, direct sun, and a total lack of care

plant genders: three categories of presentations, including monoecious (male/female flowers on the same plant), hermaphrodite (self-fertile flowers), and dioecious (male/female flowers on separate plants)

pollarding: cutting off the top of a plant to promote ideal growth patterns (e.g., mango)

positive identification: a process of matching plant characteristics (e.g., plant size, form, leaf shape, flower color, odor) with a Latin scientific botanical name to correctly understand plant attributes, including toxicity

riparian plants: those plants that protect floodplains and shorelines from erosion during floods; includes bananas, achira, raspberries, chufa, cattails, and more

Sisyphus: a character in Greek mythology who was punished by being forced to roll an immense boulder uphill, only for it to roll down every time it neared the top; he was doomed to repeat this action for eternity

soil amendment: adding mulch, compost, and other materials to improve nutrients available to plants and therefore make the food more nutritious

sourdough: a natural leavening and a process that has been a part of human history for thousands of years; considered more nutritious and less-allergy-provoking because the fermentation process can remove antinutrients, reduce allergenic qualities, and promote better digestion

spring: Florida temperatures averaging 77°F–84°F

staple foods: crops people consume almost daily because they provide a bulk of nutrients; in permaculture gardens, staple crops are often around 20 plants

summer: Florida temperatures averaging 81°F+

sustainability: a system of values upon which to build a life and routine

tip layering: placing the tip of a current season's growth in soil; the tip grows roots and resprouts upward; tip can then be separated from the parent plant and transplanted; great for plants like blackberries

Tu Bishvat: historically considered a "tree birthday" documentation process, where the age of trees are used to know when to allow them to fruit in order to optimize root and stem health

windbreaks: multilevel rows of trees and shrubs that protect the home, structures, and landscapes from prevailing winds

winter: Florida temperatures averaging 50°F–82°F

winter solstice: originally included celebrations related to oaks; now associated with such holidays as Christmas

NOTES

PREFACE

1. Althubaiti, H., (2022), The role of healthy diet (HD) on COVID-19 pandemic during and after, *Health*, *14*(1), 96–103.

CHAPTER 1

1. Flachs, A., (2010), Food for thought: The social impact of community gardens in the greater Cleveland area, *Electronic Green Journal*, *1*(30).

2. Park, H., Turner, N., & Higgs, E., (2018), Exploring the potential of food forestry to assist in ecological restoration in North America and beyond, *Restoration Ecology*, *26*(2), 284–293.

3. Castro, J., Krajter Ostoic, S., Cariñanos, P., Fini, A., & Sitzia, A., (2018), Edible urban forests as part of inclusive, sustainable cities, *Unasylva*, *69*(250), 59–65; Goodman, D., (2015), *Create your own food forest*, Florida Food Forests.

4. Wright, L., Gupta, P., & Yoshihara, K., (2019), Accessibility and affordability of healthy foods in food deserts in Florida: Policy and practice implications, *Florida Public Health Review*, *15*(1), 11.

5. Razali, N., El Sheikha, A. F., Mustafa, S., Azmi, A. F. M. N., Amid, M., & Abd Manap, M.Y., (2012), Chemical and nutritional composition of *Coleus tuberosus* (Ubi Kemili) tubers from Malaysia: Preliminary studies, *Food*, *6*(1), 100–104.

6. Lal, R., (2020, June 23), Home gardening and urban agriculture for advancing food and nutritional security in response to the COVID-19 pandemic, *Food Security*, *12*, 871–876.

7. Diep, F., (2011, July 3), *Lawns vs. crops in the continental US: Your grassy lawn comes at the cost of high water use*, Scienceline, https://scienceline.org/2011/07/lawns-vs-crops-in-the-continental-u-s/

8. Goodman (2015).

9. Tallamy, D. W., (2020), *Nature's best hope: A new approach to conservation that starts in your yard*, Timber Press.

10. Leni-Konig, K., (2020), *Beyond school gardens: Permaculture food forests enhance ecosystem services while achieving education for sustainable development goals* [Master's thesis, Harvard Extension School], Digital Access to Scholarship at Harvard, https://nrs.harvard.edu/URN-3:HUL.INSTREPOS:37365007

11. Frey, D., & Czolba, M., (2017), *The food forest handbook: Design and manage a home-scale perennial polyculture garden*, New Society.

12. Fonk, S. G., Lenderink, R., & Sendar, N., (2018), Effective managing, initiate and monitoring food forests, in N. Ferreiro-Domínguez & M. R. Mosquera-Losada (Eds.), *Proceedings of the 4th European Agroforestry Conference: Agroforestry as sustainable land use: 28–30 May 2018, Nijmegen, the Netherlands* (pp. 406–410), European Agroforestry Federation; University of Santiago de Compostela in Lugo, https://www.researchgate.net/publication/325871425_Proceedings_of_the_4th_European _Agroforestry_Conference_Agroforestry_as_Sustainable_Land_Use

13. Park, Turner, & Higgs (2018); Toensmeier, E., (2007), *Perennial vegetables: From artichokes to zuiki taro, a gardener's guide to over 100 delicious and easy to grow edibles*, Chelsea Green.

14. Castro et al. (2018).

15. Kaminski, J., (2014), Cultivating nurturing learning e-scapes: A food forest analogy, *Canadian Journal of Nursing Informatics*, *9*(3–4).

16. Weiseman, W., Halsey, D., & Ruddock, B., (2014), *Integrated forest gardening: The complete guide to polycultures and plant guilds in permaculture systems*, Chelsea Green.

17. Saroinsong, F. B., Ismail, Y., Gravitiani, E., & Sumantra, K., (2021, September 25–26), Utilization of home gardens as a community empowerment-based edible landscape to combat stunting, in *2nd international symposium of earth, energy, environmental science and sustainable development (JEESD 2021)* [Symposium], IOP Conference Series: Earth and Environmental Science, Jakarta, Indonesia, https://iopscience.iop.org/issue/1755-1315/940/1

18. Leni-Konig (2020).

19. Frey & Czolba (2017).

20. Leni-Konig (2020).

21. Toensmeier (2007).

22. Chenyang, L., Currie, A., Darrin, H., & Rosenberg, N., (2021), Farming with trees: Reforming US farm policy to expand agroforestry and mitigate climate change, *Ecology Law Quarterly*, *48*(1), https://www.ecologylawquarterly.org/print/farming-with-trees-reforming-u-s-farm-policy-to-expand-agroforestry-and-mitigate-climate-change/

23. Toensmeier (2007).

24. Lorenz, K., & Lal, R., (2018), *Carbon sequestration in agricultural ecosystems*, Springer.

25. Kreitzman, M., Toensmeier, E., Chan, K., Smukler, S., & Ramankutty, N., (2020), Perennial staple crops: Yields, distribution, and nutrition in the global food system, *Frontiers in Sustainable Food Systems*, *4*, https://doi.org/10.3389/fsufs.2020.588988

26. Park, Turner, & Higgs (2018).

27. Centers for Disease Control (CDC), (2022), *Obesity and overweight*, Centers for Disease Control and Prevention, https://www.cdc.gov/nchs/fastats/obesity-overweight.htm; Wright, Gupta, & Yoshihara (2019).

28. Caudill, S. B., Costello, M., Mixon, F. G., Jr., & Affuso, E., (2021), Food deserts and residential real estate prices, *Journal of Housing Research*, *30*(1), 98–106.

29. Sunderland, T., Powell, B., Ickowitz, A., Foli, S., Pinedo-Vasquez, M., Nasi, R., & Padoch, C., (2013), *Food security and nutrition: The role of forests* [Discussion paper], Center for International Forestry Research (CIFOR), https://www.cifor.org/knowledge/publication/4103/

30. US Department of Health and Human Services & US Department of Agriculture, (2015, December), *2015–2020 dietary guidelines for Americans* (8th ed.), US Department of Health and Human Services; US Department of Agriculture, https://health.gov/our-work/nutrition-physical-activity/dietary-guidelines/previous-dietary-guidelines/2015

31. Sunderland et al. (2013).

32. Lal (2020).

33. Caudill et al. (2021).

34. Caudill et al. (2021).

35. Pithford, P., (2002), *Healing with whole foods: Asian traditions and modern nutrition*, North Atlantic Books.

36. Althubaiti, H., (2022), The role of healthy diet (HD) on COVID-19 pandemic during and after, *Health*, *14*(1), 96–103.

37. Poe, M. R., McLain, R. J., Emery, M., & Hurley, P. T., (2013), Urban forest justice and the rights to wild foods, medicines, and materials in the city, *Human Ecology*, *41*(3), 409–422; Soga, M., Gaston, K. J., & Yamaura, Y., (2017), Gardening is beneficial for health: A meta-analysis, *Preventive Medicine Reports*, *5*, 92–99.

38. Thompson, R., (2018), Gardening for health: A regular dose of gardening, *Clinical Medicine*, *18*(3), 201.

39. Thompson (2018).

40. Keniger, L. E., Gaston, K. J., Irvine, K. N., & Fuller, R. A., (2013), What are the benefits of interacting with nature? *International Journal of Environmental Research and Public Health, 10*(3), 913–935; Stoltz, J., & Schaffer, C., (2018), Salutogenic affordances and sustainability: Multiple benefits with edible forest gardens in urban green spaces, *Frontiers in Psychology, 9*, 23–44.

41. Chenyang et al. (2021).

42. Rhodes, D., (2019), Nutritional genomics: Connecting crop improvement to human health, *Cereal Foods World, 64*(1).

43. Kennedy, G., Ballard, T., & Dop, M. C., (2011), *Guidelines for measuring household and individual dietary diversity*, Food and Agriculture Organization of the United Nations; Kreitzman et al. (2020).

44. Buettner, D., (2015), *The blue zones solution: Eating and living like the world's healthiest people*, National Geographic Books.

45. Buettner (2015).

46. Native Wildlife Federation, (2021), *Find native plants: Search by zip code to find plants that host the highest numbers of butterflies and moths to feed birds and other wildlife where you live*, https://www.nwf.org/NativePlantFinder; Tallamy, D. W., (2021), *The nature of oaks: The rich ecology of our most essential native trees*, Timber Press.

47. Goodman (2015).

48. Frey & Czolba (2017).

49. Frey & Czolba (2017).

50. Goodman (2015).

51. Crawford, D. E., (2019), *A subtropical family food forest in southeast Texas* [Doctoral dissertation, Prescott College].

52. Crawford (2019).

53. Crawford (2019).

54. Snow, L., (personal communication, November 9, 2021).

CHAPTER 2

1. Saroinsong, F. B., Ismail, Y., Gravitiani, E., & Sumantra, K., (2021, September 25–26), Utilization of home gardens as a community empowerment-based edible landscape to combat stunting, in *2nd international symposium of earth, energy, environmental science and sustainable development (JEESD 2021)* [Symposium], IOP Conference Series: Earth and Environmental Science, Jakarta, Indonesia, https://iopscience.iop.org/issue/1755-1315/940/1

2. Saroinsong et al. (2021); Scholar, A., (2020), Exploring the effect of landscaping on property value in meeting the contemporary sub-Sahara environment, *African Scholar Journal of Environmental Design and Construction Management, 18*(4), 79–110.

3. Soga, M., Gaston, K. J., & Yamaura, Y., (2017), Gardening is beneficial for health: A meta-analysis, *Preventive Medicine Reports, 5*, 92–99.

4. Li, Z., Bradley, L., Sherk, J., & Spafford, A., (2020, November 17), *Growing edibles in the landscape*, NC State Extension Publications, https://content.ces.ncsu.edu/growing-edibles-in-the-landscape

5. Lawton, G. (Presenter), (2008), *Establishing a food forest the permaculture way* [Documentary], EcoFilms Australia.

6. Frey, D., & Czolba, M., (2017), *The food forest handbook: Design and manage a home-scale perennial polyculture garden*, New Society.

7. Haley, K., (personal communication, November 9, 2021).

8. Nicodemou, C., (personal communication, November 9, 2021).

9. Buettner, D., (2015), *The blue zones solution: Eating and living like the world's healthiest people*, National Geographic Books.

10. Goldstein, B., (personal communication, November 9, 2021).

11. Hassan, M., (personal communication, November 9, 2021).

12. Hassan (2021).

13. Nicodemou (2021).

14. Gershuny, G., & Martin, D. L. (Eds.), (2018), *The Rodale book of composting, newly revised and updated: Simple methods to improve your soil, recycle waste, grow healthier plants, and create an earth-friendly garden*, Rodale Books.

15. Frey & Czolba (2017).

16. Goodman, D., (2021), *Florida survival gardening*, Good Books.

17. Hassan (2021).

18. Cowan, S., (personal communication, November 9, 2021).

19. Katz, S. E., (2012), *The art of fermentation: An in-depth exploration of essential concepts and processes from around the world*, Chelsea Green.

20. Jay, J., (personal communication, November 9, 2021).

21. Poe, M. R., McLain, R. J., Emery, M., & Hurley, P. T., (2013), Urban forest justice and the rights to wild foods, medicines, and materials in the city, *Human Ecology*, *41*(3), 409–422; Scholar (2020).

22. Frey & Czolba (2017).

23. Scholar (2020); Setyabudi, I., Alfian, R., & Hastutiningtyas, W. R., (2018), Green technology concept on sensory garden for mental disability at Sumber Dharma Extraordinary School, in A. Citraningrum, W. Iyati, & Y. A. Yusaran (Eds.), *Nusantara as the basic of smart culture for prospering built environment: Proceedings of International Conference on Sustainable Architecture in Nusantara* (pp. 22–28), Department of Architecture, Faculty of Engineering, Universitas Brawijaya; Institut für vergleichende Architekturforschung—Institute for Comparative Research in Architecture; Yakimova, S., Maintenant, C., & Taillandier-Schmitt, A., (2020), How positive and negative emotions influence cognitive performance in secondary schools, *Psychological Applications and Trends*, 79.

24. Pithford, P., (2002), *Healing with whole foods: Asian traditions and modern nutrition*, North Atlantic Books.

25. Thomas, M., (2017), *Homegarden cuisine toolkit: Ideas for making food in the humid subtropics*, CreateSpace.

26. Escobedo, F., Northrop, R., Orfanedes, M., & Iaconna, A., (2010), Comparison of community leader perceptions on urban forests in south Florida, *EDIS*, *2010*(2).

27. Hackel, A., (personal communication, November 9, 2021).

28. Goodman, D., (2015), *Create your own food forest*, Florida Food Forests.

29. Corazon, S. S., Stigsdotter, U. K., Jensen, A. G. C., & Nilsson, K., (2010), Development of the nature-based therapy concept for patients with stress-related illness at the Danish healing forest garden Nacadia, *Journal of Therapeutic Horticulture*, *20*, 33–51; Yakimova, Maintenant, & Taillandier-Schmitt (2020).

30. Crawford, D. E., (2019), *A subtropical family food forest in southeast Texas* [Doctoral dissertation, Prescott College]; Li et al. (2020).

31. Fonk, S. G., Lenderink, R., & Sendar, N., (2018), Effective managing, initiate and monitoring food forests, in N. Ferreiro-Domínguez & M. R. Mosquera-Losada (Eds.), *Proceedings of the 4th European Agroforestry Conference: Agroforestry as sustainable land use: 28–30 May 2018, Nijmegen, the Netherlands* (pp. 406–410), European Agroforestry Federation and the University of Santiago de Compostela in Lugo, https://www.researchgate.net/publication/325871425_Proceedings_of_the_4th_European_Agroforestry_Conference_Agroforestry_as_Sustainable_Land_Use

32. Elson, M., (personal communication, November 9, 2021).

33. Elson (2021).

34. Saroinsong et al. (2021).

35. Demers, C., Long, A., & Williams, R., (2012), Controlling invasive exotic plants in north Florida forests, *EDIS*, *2012*(4).

36. Burnett, F. H., (2011), *The secret garden*, Oxford University Press.

37. Andren, C., (personal communication, November 9, 2021).

38. Demers, Long, & Williams (2012).

39. Fern, K., (1997), *Plants for a future: Edible and useful plants for a healthier world*, Permanent Publications, https://pfaf.org/user/default.aspx

40. Fern (1997).

41. Quoted in Guth, J. H., (2007), Law for the ecological age, *Vermont Journal of Environmental Law*, *9*, 431.

42. Katz (2012).

43. Krieger, E., (2008), *The food you crave: Luscious recipes for a healthy life*, Taunton Press.

44. Damerow, G., (2010), *Guide to raising chickens*, Storey.

45. Damerow (2010).

46. Goodman (2021).

47. Cowan (2021).

48. Reynolds, J., (personal communication, November 9, 2021).

49. Reynolds (2021).

50. Reynolds (2021).

51. Simson, S., & Straus, M., (1997), *Horticulture as therapy: Principles and practice*, CRC Press.

52. Goodman (2021).

53. Gulko, J., (personal communication, November 9, 2021).

54. Stoltz, J., & Schaffer, C., (2018), Salutogenic affordances and sustainability: Multiple benefits with edible forest gardens in urban green spaces, *Frontiers in Psychology*, *9*, 23–44.

55. Nicodemou, (2021).

56. Ellis, A., (personal communication, November 9, 2021).

57. Nicodemou (2021).

58. Castro, J., Krajter Ostoic, S., Cariñanos, P., Fini, A., & Sitzia, A., (2018), Edible urban forests as part of inclusive, sustainable cities, *Unasylva*, *69*(250), 59–65.

59. ECHO, (2021), *Hope against hunger*, https://echonet.org/

60. Weiseman, W., Halsey, D., & Ruddock, B., (2014), *Integrated forest gardening: The complete guide to polycultures and plant guilds in permaculture systems*, Chelsea Green.

61. Weiseman, Halsey, & Ruddock (2014).

62. Easley, T., & Horne, S., (2016), *The modern herbal dispensatory: A medicine-making guide*, North Atlantic Books.

63. Simson & Straus (1997).

64. Weiseman, Halsey, & Ruddock (2014).

65. Toensmeier, E., (2007), *Perennial vegetables: From artichokes to zuiki taro, a gardener's guide to over 100 delicious and easy to grow edibles*, Chelsea Green.

66. Cowan (2021).

67. Goodman (2015).

CHAPTER 3

1. Althubaiti, H., (2022), The role of healthy diet (HD) on COVID-19 pandemic during and after, *Health*, *14*(1), 96–103.

2. Krieger, E., (2008), *The food you crave: Luscious recipes for a healthy life*, Taunton Press.

3. Lairon, D., (2010), Nutritional quality and safety of organic food: A review, *Agronomy for sustainable development*, *30*(1), 33–41.

4. Krieger (2008).

5. Manheim, J., (2012), *The healthy green drink diet: Advice and recipes for happy juicing*, Skyhorse.

6. Layton, P., (2012), *Emergency food storage and survival handbook: Everything you need to know to keep your family safe in a crisis*, Clarkson Potter.

7. Boudreau, D., & Hawke, M., (2020), *Foraging for survival: Edible wild plants of North America*, Skyhorse.

8. Boudreau & Hawke (2020).

9. Bolarinwa, I. F., Oke, M. O., Olaniyan, S. A., & Ajala, A. S., (2016), A review of cyanogenic glycosides in edible plants, in M. L. Larramendy & S. Soloneski (Eds.), *Toxicology: New aspects to this scientific conundrum* (pp. 179–192), IntechOpen.

10. Boudreau & Hawke (2020).

11. Pithford, P., (2002), *Healing with whole foods: Asian traditions and modern nutrition*, North Atlantic Books.

12. Mombo, S., Foucault, Y., Deola, F., Gaillard, I., Goix, S., Shahid, M., Schreck, E., Pierart, A., & Dumat, C., (2016), Management of human health risk in the context of kitchen gardens polluted by lead and cadmium near a lead recycling company, *Journal of Soils and Sediments*, *16*(4), 1214–1224.

13. Neimes, M., (personal communication, November 9, 2021).

14. Reid, L., (personal communication, November 9, 2021).

15. Reid (2021).

16. Toensmeier, E., (2007), *Perennial vegetables: From artichokes to zuiki taro, a gardener's guide to over 100 delicious and easy to grow edibles*, Chelsea Green.

17. Toensmeier (2007).

18. Gershuny, G., & Martin, D. L. (Eds.), (2018), *The Rodale book of composting, newly revised and updated: Simple methods to improve your soil, recycle waste, grow healthier plants, and create an earth-friendly garden*, Rodale Books.

19. Simson, S., & Straus, M., (1997), *Horticulture as therapy: Principles and practice*, CRC Press.

20. Gershuny & Martin (2018).

21. Layton (2012).

22. Gershuny & Martin (2018).

23. Elson, M., (personal communication, November 9, 2021).

24. Gershuny & Martin (2018).

25. Thompson, R., (2018), Gardening for health: A regular dose of gardening, *Clinical Medicine*, *18*(3), 201.

26. Toensmeier (2007).

27. Gershuny & Martin (2018).

28. Gershuny & Martin (2018).

29. Toensmeier (2007).

30. Saroinsong, F. B., Ismail, Y., Gravitiani, E., & Sumantra, K., (2021, September 25–26), Utilization of home gardens as a community empowerment-based edible landscape to combat stunting, in *2nd international symposium of earth, energy, environmental science and sustainable development (JEESD 2021)* [Symposium], IOP Conference Series: Earth and Environmental Science, Jakarta, Indonesia, https://iopscience.iop.org/issue/1755-1315/940/1

31. Li, Z., Bradley, L., Sherk, J., & Spafford, A., (2020, November 17), *Growing edibles in the landscape*, NC State Extension Publications, https://content.ces.ncsu.edu/growing-edibles-in-the-landscape;

Nelson, G., (2003), *Florida's best native landscape plants*, University Press of Florida; Thomas, M., (2017), *Homegarden cuisine toolkit: Ideas for making food in the humid subtropics*, CreateSpace; Toensmeier (2007).

CHAPTER 4

1. Layton, P., (2012), *Emergency food storage and survival handbook: Everything you need to know to keep your family safe in a crisis*, Clarkson Potter.

2. Pithford, P., (2002), *Healing with whole foods: Asian traditions and modern nutrition*, North Atlantic Books.

3. Kushi, M., Blauer, S., & Esko, W., (2004), *The macrobiotic way: The definitive guide to macrobiotic living*, Penguin.

4. Pithford (2002).

5. Buettner, D., (2015), *The blue zones solution: Eating and living like the world's healthiest people*, National Geographic Books.

INDEX

economy, 3, 15, 19, 20

erosion, 8, 12, 20; riparian plants, 41, 43, 99, 130, 156, 163, 171, 227, 232; prevention, 58, 72, 79, 82, 91, 96, 97, 105, 129, 133, 140, 161, 162, 172, 178, 194, 213

fast-growing, 23, 42, 51, 55, 59, 60, 72, 82, 94, 98, 103, 104, 118, 127, 128, 129, 130, 131, 133, 137, 142, 144, 146, 157, 161, 162, 168, 169, 172, 174, 178, 181, 197, 208, 212, 213, 216, 221, 226, 227, 230, 231, 232, 234, 238

fats. *See* oil

fertilizer, 3–4, 7, 12, 19, 22, 31, 35

fire, fuel for, 77, 124, 129, 130, 144, 173, 192, 214

fragrant, 49, 61, 68, 69, 72, 79, 89, 95, 98, 125, 137, 142, 149, 152, 168, 170, 173, 185, 188, 190, 196, 197, 219, 221, 230

fungus. *See* mushroom

garden: of Eden, 3, 14, 137; beds, 3–4, 7, 13, 16, 36

gender, plant, 29, 33; dioecious, 81, 126, 141, 155, 156, 158, 159, 167, 175, 192, 200, 214, 220, 231, 235, 238, 239

Great Depression, 3

guild, 8, 12, 28

hedge, 13, 29, 41, 58, 69, 75, 79, 88, 90, 95, 98, 103, 109, 122, 137, 138, 144, 149, 150, 161, 163, 178, 182, 185, 192, 196, 213, 214, 219, 231, 235

Hippocrates, 6, 93

Homesteading, 19, 72, 198

hummingbird: attracts, 41, 42, 46, 61, 79, 100, 109, 128, 130, 142, 171, 177, 188, 197, 208, 223; pollinated by, 174

hurricane, 8, 15: liability, 87; resilient, 49, 60, 68, 88, 111, 125, 187, 206

hydroponic, 34–35, 153, 164, 240

identification, positive, 25, 96, 101, 132, 194, 197

immunity, 4–5; used to boost: 50, 61, 63, 100, 117, 137, 143, 163, 202, 218

insects, beneficial, 7, 19

invasive roots, 12–13

irrigation, 2–3, 6–7, 14, 36, 57

Jackfruit, 5, 9, 34, 133

JADAM, 14

kudzu, 20, 39, 140

license: nursery 19; hemp 19, 126; hunting 23; propagation, 207

macronutrient, 5, 17, 24

maintenance, 3–4, 11–12, 17, 21; low, 42, 44, 47, 59, 72, 78, 97, 99, 100, 107, 119, 123, 151, 152, 164, 178, 187, 190, 192, 201, 213, 216, 218, 227, 237, 240

micronutrient, 4–6, 17, 24, 36

good source, 48, 131, 136, 220, 222

Monet, Claude, 160

money: income, 10, 19, 45, 52, 131

mortality: infant and maternal, 4

moth, host, 42, 60, 61, 70, 71, 77, 79, 91, 92, 109, 115, 119, 127, 134, 145, 151, 155, 159, 181, 208, 210, 211; as pest, 106, 114, 139, 159, 178

mulch, 3, 8, 13–15, 19, 23–24, 27–29, 35–37

National Gardening Association, 8

National Wildlife Federation, 7, 19

Native Plant Society, 7

native: keystones, 7, 65, 77, 79, 104, 110, 127, 145, 158, 159, 173, 181, 206; species, 42, 53, 59, 60, 61, 62, 64, 65, 68, 74, 77, 79, 88, 99, 100, 103, 104, 106, 109, 111, 115, 119, 125, 127, 129, 132, 136, 152, 159, 168, 171, 173, 177, 181, 192, 195, 196, 200, 201, 206, 213, 223, 228, 231, 235, 238

nitrogen: high in, 41, 130; fixing, 67, 91, 172, 209, 213, 227, 231, 236

nutrition, 2, 4–5, 10–11, 33, 35

obesity: hunger-obesity paradox, 4–5

oil, 6, 49, 51, 56, 64, 71, 72, 78, 82, 83, 87, 88, 97, 108, 110, 112, 113, 123, 124, 126, 127, 128, 131, 135, 144, 148, 151, 155, 157, 159, 160, 161, 165, 175, 183, 184, 187, 190, 195, 211, 218, 219, 222, 227, 231, 236; essential, 43, 46,

ACKNOWLEDGMENTS

A special thanks to the Florida food foresters who provided support, interviews, growing substrates, and plant materials that contributed to the making of this book: Carl Andren, Chad Angelocci, Gabriella Balatovis-McNally, Carolyn Bellamy, Jerry Berkowitz, Scott Bitterly, John Cannon, Jeff Cara, Dorlah Carson, Sarah Christoph, Will Christophersen, Brooke Wood Connaughton, Sue-Ann Pinney Cowan, Lauren Cripe, Jennifer Cunningham, J-C and Haden de Boer, Annie Ellis, Mike Elson, Patrizia Galantucci, Kristi Gaza, Bree Goldstein, Judith Gulko, Anna Hackel, Katie Haley, Chris Halfpap, "Jungle Jay" Hartman, Muaaz Hassan, Rob Hofmann, Ashley Prang Huffman, Kari Juul, Snow Lam, Michelle Lee, Audie Eve Longson, Ana and Chris Lozada, Suji Martens, Sara Henick Montage, Michael Neimes, Christina Nicodimou, Robert Pike, Lonny Reid, Jay Reynolds, Eric Ross, Winnie Said, Kimberly Nieves Santos, Ally and Andy Sauber, Larry Shatzer; Shelby Sheene, Jillian Simensky, Ken and Gia Salardi Stevens, and Ken Wilson.

I am immensely grateful to the businesses and community leaders who have helped make food forestry easier and more attainable for me: American Meadows; Baker Creek; Danny Barnett at Landscape Solutions, LLC; David the Good; Echo Farm; Food Town; Greene Deane; Grower Jim; Incredible Edible Landscapes; Integrity Tree Service; Johnny's Selected Seeds; Let It Rot; Outside Pride; Rare Palm Seeds; Rosetta's Produce; and Tucka Bee, LLC.

I sincerely extend appreciation to the online Facebook communities that help food forestry thrive through networking and international collaborations: Backyard Fruit Growers, Florida Food Forest, the Florida Homestead, Florida Tropical Fruit Growers, Food Foresters, Foraging Florida, Local Food Movement—Garden Group, Organic Gardening, Regenerative Agriculture Group, and South Florida Edible Gardening and Sustainable Living.

Without local and international organizations and sites and the wisdom and knowledge they offer, this book would not be possible. I am so thankful for Eat the Weeds, Florida Native Plant Society, National Gardening Association, National Wildlife Federation, Plant Real Florida, and Plants for a Future.

This book was very much improved by community feedback; special thanks to the Food Forest Rangers—Jupiter Farms 4-H group, Carolyn Cameron, Patrizia Galantucci, James Pike, and Irene Pratka.

ABOUT THE AUTHOR

Amanda Pike, PhD, ATR-BC is a board-certified art therapist, professional educator, certified educational leader, local 4-H program facilitator, and past president of the Florida Art Therapy Association. Dr. Pike grew up spending summers exploring her grandparents' forest and farmland and also lived in Cuernavaca, Mexico, for multiple years, working for a holistic wellness company. During this time, she learned to grow and use plants to create health and beauty products. Throughout her master's and bachelor's degrees, she lived and worked on farms and brings to her writing firsthand experience. She owns a two-acre permaculture farm in Jupiter, Florida, where she manages her food forest, complete with free-roaming chickens and 26 beehives. Dr. Pike also serves as education chair and chapter representative for the Palm Beach County chapter of the Native Plant Society and provides ongoing consultations for educational and community-based programs. Her last book, *Eco-Art Therapy in Practice*, which published internationally, highlights the importance of growing and using plants in educational and therapeutic settings. Dr. Pike aims to help make food forestry an accessible and practical landscaping option.